Lecture Notes in Computer Science 6169

Commenced Publication in 1973
Founding and Former Series Editors:
Gerhard Goos, Juris Hartmanis, and Ja

Francisco J. Perales   Robert B. Fisher (Eds.)

Articulated Motion and Deformable Objects

6th International Conference, AMDO 2010
Port d'Andratx, Mallorca, Spain, July 7-9, 2010
Proceedings

 Springer

Volume Editors

Francisco J. Perales
UIB, Department of Computer Science and Mathematics
Computer Graphics and Vision and Artificial Intelligence Group
C/Valldemossa Km.7.5, PC 07122 Palma de Mallorca, Baleares, Spain
E-mail: paco.perales@uib.es

Robert B. Fisher
University of Edinburgh, School of Informatics, 1.26 Informatics Forum
10 Crichton St, Edinburgh EH8 9AB, UK
E-mail: rbf@inf.ed.ac.uk

Library of Congress Control Number: Applied for

CR Subject Classification (1998): I.4, I.5, I.2.10, H.5, I.3, I.2

LNCS Sublibrary: SL 6 – Image Processing, Computer Vision, Pattern Recognition, and Graphics

ISSN   0302-9743
ISBN-10   3-642-14060-2 Springer Berlin Heidelberg New York
ISBN-13   978-3-642-14060-0 Springer Berlin Heidelberg New York

springer.com

© Springer-Verlag Berlin Heidelberg 2010
Printed in Germany

Typesetting: Camera-ready by author, data conversion by Scientific Publishing Services, Chennai, India
Printed on acid-free paper   06/3180

Preface

The AMDO 2010 conference took place at the Hotel Mon Port, Port d'Andratx (Mallorca), during July 7–9, 2010, institutionally sponsored by MICINN (Ministerio de Ciencia e Innovación, Spanish Government), the Conselleria d'Economia, Hisenda i Innovació (Balearic Islands Government), the Consell de Mallorca, the AERFAI (Spanish Association in Pattern Recognition and Artificial Intelligence), the EG (Eurographics Association) and the Mathematics and Computer Science Department of the UIB. In addition important commercial sponsors collaborated with practical demonstrations, and the main contributors were: VICOM Tech, ANDROME Iberica, Robot S.A, DAT S.L, Aquateknica S.L.

The subject of the conference is the ongoing research in articulated motion on a sequence of images and sophisticated models for deformable objects. The goals of these areas are the understanding and interpretation of the motion of complex objects that can be found in sequences of images in the real world. The main topics considered as priority are: geometric and physical deformable models, motion analysis, articulated models and animation, modelling and visualization of deformable models, deformable model applications, motion analysis applications, single or multiple human motion analysis and synthesis, face modelling, tracking, recovering and recognition models, virtual and augmented reality, haptics devices, and biometrics techniques. The conference topics were grouped into these tracks: **Track 1**: Computer Graphics (Human Modelling and Animation), **Track 2**: Human Motion (Analysis, Tracking, 3D Reconstruction and Recognition), **Track 3**: Multimodal User Interaction (VR and AR, Speech, Biometrics) and **Track 4**: Affective Interfaces (recognition and interpretation of emotions, ECAs - Embodied Conversational Agents in HCI).

The AMDO 2010 conference was the natural evolution of previous editions and has been consolided as an European reference for symposiums in the topics mentioned above. The new goal of this conference was to promote interaction and collaboration among researchers working directly in the areas covered by the main tracks. New perceptual user interfaces and the emerging technologies increase the relation between areas involved with human–computer interaction. The new perspective of the AMDO 2010 conference was the strengthening of the relationship between the areas that share as key point the study of the human body using computer technologies as the main tool. The response to the Call for Papers for this conference was very satisfactory. From 45 full papers submitted, 29 were accepted for oral presentation. The review process was carried out by the Program Committee, each paper being assessed by at least two reviewers. The conference included several sessions of orally presented papers and two tutorials. Also, the conference benefited from the collaboration of the invited speakers treating various aspects of the main topics.

These invited speakers were:

Elisabeth André, Lehrstuhl für Multimedia-Konzepte und Anwendungen, Institut für Informatik Universität Augsburg, Germany.

Taku Komura, Institute for Perception, Action and Behaviour School of Informatics University of Edinburgh, UK.

Enrique Vidal, Multimodal Interaction: Approaches and Applications PRHLT/ITIUPV, Spain.

July 2010   F.J. Perales
                                                             R. Fisher

Organization

AMDO 2010 was organized by the Computer Graphics, Vision and Artificial Intelligence team of the Department of Mathematics and Computer Science, Universitat de les Illes Balears (UIB) in cooperation with AERFAI (Spanish Association for Pattern Recognition and Image Analysis) and EG (Eurograhics Association).

Executive Committee

General Conference Co-chairs   F.J. Perales, Mathematics and Computer
Science Department, UIB (Spain)
R. Fisher, University of Edinburgh (UK)
Organizing Chairs   M.J. Abásolo, D. Arellano, J.M. Buades,
A. Delgado, G. Fiol, M. González, A. Jaume,
A. Igelmo, C. Manresa, R. Mas, M. Mascaró P.,
M. Miró, G. Nicolau, P. Palmer, X. Varona
Dep. Math. and Computer Science
(UIB, Spain)
Tutorial Chairs: M. González, J. Varona, F.J. Perales
UIB (Spain)

Program Committee

Abásolo, M.J.	DMI-UIB, Spain
Aloimonos, Y.	University of Maryland, USA
Bagdanov, A.D.	CVC-UAB, Spain
Baldasarri, S.	University of Zaragoza, Spain
Bartoli, A.	CNRS - LASMEA, France
Baumela, L.	Technical University of Madrid, Spain
Boulic, R.	EPFL, Switzerland
Bowden, R.	University of Surrey, UK
Brunet, P.	UPC, Spain
Campilho, A.	University of Porto, Portugal
Cerezo, E.	University of Zaragoza, Spain
Coll, T.	DMI-UIB, Spain
Courty, N.	Université de Bretagne-Sud, France
Davis, L. S.	University of Maryland, USA
Del Bimbo, A.	University of Florence, Italy
Dogan, S.	I-Lab/centre CCSR, University of Surrey, UK

Dugelay, J.L.   EURECOM, France
Fernandez-Caballero, A.   University of Castilla La Mancha, Spain
Fiol-Roig, G.   DMI-UIB, Spain
Flerackers, E.   Hasselt University, Belgium
Flores, J.   Mar-USC, Spain
Göbel, M.   FleXilution, Germany
Gonzàlez, J.   CVC-UAB, Spain
González-Hidalgo, M.   DMI-UIB, Spain
Hilton, A.   University of Surrey, UK
Igelmo, A.   DMI-UIB, Spain
Iñesta, J.M.   University of Alicante, Spain
Kakadiaris, I.A.   University of Houston, USA
Komura, T.   IPAB, University of Edinburgh, UK
Marcialis, G.L.   University of Cagliary, Italy
Mas, R.   DMI-UIB, Spain
Matey, L.   CEIT, Spain
Medioni, G.   University of Southern California, USA
Pérez de la Blanca, N.   University of Granada, Spain
Pla, F.   University Jaume I, Spain
Qin, H.   Stony Brook University, New York, USA
Radeva, P.   CVC-UAB, Spain
Roca, X.   CVC-UAB, Spain
Sanfeliu, A.   IRI, CSIC-UPC, Spain
Serón, F.   University of Zaragoza, Spain
Skala, V.   University of West Bohemia, Czech Republic
Susin, A.   University Polytechnic Catalunya, Spain
Tavares, J.M.   University of Porto, Portugal
Terzopoulos, D.   New York University, USA
Thalmann, D.   EPFL, Switzerland
Torrensen, J.   University of Oslo, Norway
Van Reeth, F.   LUC/EDM, Belgium

Sponsoring Institutions

AERFAI (Spanish Association for Pattern Recognition and Image Analysis)
EG (Eurograhics Association)
IEEE Spain Section Board
MICINN (Ministerio de Ciencia e Innovación, Spanish Government)
Conselleria d'Economia, Hisenda i Innovació (Balearic Islands Government)
Consell de Mallorca
Maths. and Computer Science Department, Universitat de les Illes Balears (UIB)
Ajuntament d'Andratx. Sol de Ponent
Ajuntament de Palma
Sa Nostra. Caixa de Balears

Commercial Sponsoring Enterprises

VICOM-Tech S.A., www.vicomtech.es
ANDROME Iberica S.A, www.androme.es
Robot, www.robotmallorca.com
Aquateknica, http://www.aquateknica.com
DAT (Development Advanced Technology), www.dat-inf.com/home.html

Table of Contents

Articulated Motion and Deformable Objects AMDO 2010

Compatible Particles for Part-Based Tracking

Brais Martinez[1], Marc Vivet[2], and Xavier Binefa[1]

[1] Information and Communication Technologies Department
Universitat Pompeu Fabra, Barcelona
brais.martinez@upf.edu
[2] Computer Science Department
Universitat Autonoma de Barcelona

Abstract. Particle Filter methods are one of the dominant tracking paradigms due to its ability to handle non-gaussian processes, multi-modality and temporal consistency. Traditionally, the exponential growth on the number of particles required (and therefore in the computational cost) with respect to the increase of the state space dimensionality means one of the major drawbacks for these methods. The problem of part based tracking, central nowadays, is hardly tractable within this framework. Several efforts have been made in order to solve this problem, as the appearance of hierarchical models or the extension of graph theory by means of the Nonparametric Belief Propagation. Our approach relies instead on the use of Auxiliary Particle Filters, models the relations between parts dynamically (without training) and introduces a compatibility factor to efficiently reduce the growth of the computational cost. We did run the experiments presented without using a priori information.

Keywords: Particle Filters, Part-based Tracking, Spatial Relations, Density Estimation, Auxiliary Particle Filter.

1 Introduction

The problem of part-based tracking is of great importance as a first step for higher level processes (e.g. facial expression recognition) and is complementary to classification algorithms based on object parts (bag of words, constellation model,...). The problem of part-based tracking is naturally posed in a high dimensional space. Each part requires parameters controlling variables such as its aspect, angle of rotation or scale. The challenge is to estimate these parameters efficiently preserving a consistent spatial arrangement of the different parts of the object, given the previous spatial arrangements and the nature of the tracked object. The presence of rotations out of the image plane and flexible movements hinders the applicability of spatial relations, by changing them almost arbitrarily. Furthermore, the computational cost of a probabilistic search in high dimensional spaces becomes intractable since the cost of sampling grows exponentially respect to the dimensionality of the state space. Our paper refers to this two problems, modeling the spatial relations and how to introduce them, while keeping the method computationally efficient.

F.J. Perales and R.B. Fisher (Eds.): AMDO 2010, LNCS 6169, pp. 1–10, 2010.

Some of the problems, like facial component or facial feature tracking, enable the introduction of the spatial priors extracted from a training set, coding for example the anthropomorphic structure of the face [6]. In this last work, the joint probability is factorized (the part trackings are performed independently) and a reweighting scheme for compensating the difference between the joint probability and the factorized probability is introduced. In [8] the tracking of facial features is, as well, divided into the tracking of several subsets. The spatial coherence between the parts is set in a second step by using a Belief Propagation algorithm. A training of the possible relative positions of the parts is needed. [1] analyzes the high dimensional feature space in terms of its covariance and partitions the feature space so the difference between the factorized probability and the joint probability are minimum. [4] defines a hierarchy which lowers the dimensionality of the search space and therefore the computational cost.

One of the most important articles regarding the problem of coding the spatial relations is the Nonparametric Belief Propagation, presented in [9]. In here, the different parts are considered as nodes of a graph. The relations between the nodes are modeled accordingly to a dataset used for training purposes. Each part is described using a set of variables coding its position and its aspect (using PCA coefficients for coding the aspect of each part). Each of the variables of the description vector is coupled with the same variables of the description vector of a part joined by an edge, and modeled using a Gaussian Mixture Model (GMM). The Belief Propagation framework, used for minimizing a Network with discrete states, is extended in here to Networks with continuous states, as those modeled as GMMs. The drawbacks of such a method are important. First, the computational cost is huge since each step requires a costly sampling and a refitting step for each state using GMMs. The reported computing time required for each frame in a 5 part model is of several minutes. Some works, as [5], alleviate this problem by formulating more efficient algorithms. Another problem comes from the modeling of the relations between parts. The modeling using GMM produce an important bias towards the mean values, and perfectly plausible but less frequent situations are heavily penalized. It is also important to note that the training stage requires strong a priori knowledge, in general only applicable to face and body tracking.

We use a graph representation of the tracked parts since it guarantees a good approximation of the underlying relations and it still provides a tractable probabilistic framework. We merge it with the Particle Filter framework, due to its probabilistic nature and its ability to model dynamics. The main contributions of our work are, first, to model the spatial relations using the dynamics during the sequence. In this way, the need of a priori knowledge is prevented and the applicability of the algorithm is guaranteed. This constitutes a more consistent approach with respect to the tracking problem philosophy, which consists in modeling the possible states of a target provided the previous states, in contrast to the problem of object classification, which models the whole set of possibilities for a certain class. In second place, the relations between the different parts are described using a non-parametric modeling, based on kernel density estimation

[2]. Lastly, instead of performing an individual sampling for each part and applying the spatial relations in a second separate step, we use the Auxiliary Particle Filter framework [7] for sampling proportionally to the a posteriori distribution, which already includes the spatial relations in the sampling process.

2 Particle Filters and Auxiliary Particle Filter

Particle filters (PF) are a class of Bayesian filters for approximating, for each time step t, the a posteriori distribution of the state of the target, $\hat{x}_t$. The state is a vector that may include the position, scale or any variable related to the target aspect. For the case of part-based tracking, these variables are required for each of the parts, leading to high dimensional spaces. In the PF framework, the a posteriori probability distribution of the target state is computed as the product of what can be expected at time $t - 1$ provided the previous target states (the a priori distribution), and the observation evidences obtained at time t (the likelihood probability distribution). Both distributions are computed over a discrete set of points (called particles) that represent them efficiently, but the selection of these points differs between different PF methods.

Provided the particles (hypothesis) $\{x_t^i\}$ and weights (likelihood of the hypothesis) $\{\pi_t^i\}$, the a priori distribution can be approximated as:

$$p(x_{t+1}|x_t) = \sum_{i=1}^{N} p(x_{t+1}|x_t^i)\pi_t^i \tag{1}$$

In here, $p(x_{t+1}|x_t^i)$ is defined by the transition model, which is in general composed by a deterministic part containing the position dynamics and a random gaussian noise factor, leading to an equation such as $x_{t+1} = f(x_t) + N(0, \Sigma)$.

The likelihood distribution, $p(y_{t+1}|x_{t+1})$, requires that it can be evaluated at any given point, while its computation is only required at the discrete point set given by the sampling of the a priori distribution.

By using Bayes' theorem, the posterior distribution is (proportional to) the result of multiplying the a priori distribution and the likelihood distribution. Taking the approximation of the a priori given by eq. 1, the a posteriori approximation in its continuous form comes to:

$$p(x_{t+1}|y_{t+1}) \propto p(y_{t+1}|x_{t+1}) \sum_{j=1}^{M} p(x_{t+1}|x_t^j)\pi_t^j \tag{2}$$

Therefore, the estimation of the a posteriori is summarized as sampling from the a priori distribution (eq. 1) and then evaluating the likelihood over these samples. The empirical estimation of the a posteriori is given by:

$$p(x_{t+1}|y_{t+1}) = \sum_{i} \pi_{t+1}^i \delta(x_{t+1} - x_{t+1}^i) \tag{3}$$

where δ is the Kronecker delta function and the set x_{t+1}^i is a particular realization (a sampling) of the a priori distribution. The update of the weights π_{t+1}^i and the sampling strategy vary between different particle filter methods.

For each time step t, the final estimation of the target state $\hat{\mathbf{x}}_t$ is calculated from the particles and their weights, for example as the weighted mean of all the particles.

One of the problems of this method is that the particles ideally should be sampled with a probability proportional to the a posteriori distribution, although they are in general extracted according to the a priori distribution. In cases of disparity between the a priori and the a posteriori distribution, the sampling is not efficient. The Auxiliary Particle Filter (APF) [7,10] tackles this problem. In the first step of the APF, the particles are sampled from the a priori distribution and propagated to $\mu_t^k = f(x_t^k)^1$ and its likelihood λ_{t+1}^k is computed. This likelihood is used as a measure of how good the a posteriori will be if a certain particle k is propagated. In the second step, the sampling is done accordingly to the weights λ_{t+1}^k, constituting a sampling where the likelihood of a particle is proportional to its a posteriori probability. The pseudocode of the APF is summarized in table 1.

Table 1. The Auxiliary Particle Filter pseudocode

For $n = 1 \ldots N$
Compute μ_{t+1}^k
Compute $\lambda_{t+1}^k = \pi_t^n p(z_{t+1}|\mu_{t+1}^k)$
For each particle k
Choose index i with probability λ_{t+1}^i
Draw a sample x_{t+1}^k from $p(x_{t+1}|x_t^i)$
Assign weight $\pi_{t+1}^k = \frac{p(z_{t+1}|x_{t+1}^k)}{p(z_{t+1}|\mu_{t+1}^k)}$
Normalize weights, $\sum_k \pi_{t+1}^k = 1$

3   Compatible Particle Filter

The ideal sampling procedure should take into account the spatial relations in order to achieve an optimal efficiency. However, some articles modify the weighting process of particle filter algorithms to add, in a second step, the information of the spatial relations. In here we derive a particle filtering with a sampling strategy taking into account the spatial relations. The only assumption is the graph structure of the parts and the Markov assumption.

3.1   Spatial Coherence Using Auxiliary Particle Filters

Our approach can be considered as a factorization where each part corresponds to a factor. Each of the parts interact actively with the others during both the sampling and weighting process. We add a superindex noting the part we are referring to. To prevent confusions, from now on we note as $\mathbf{x}_t^n$ the state variable

---

[1] In fact, μ_t^k just need to be a meaningful value of the propagated distribution generated by particle k, but the mean is the most simple and effective election

of part n whereas $x_t^{i,n}$ is a particular realization (the ith) of the variable $\mathbf{x}_t^n$. A set of state variables will be noted with capital letter, $X_t^S = \{x_t^m/m \in S\}$. We assume a network structure on the variables. We therefore also note $N(n)$ to the neighbors of (or parts related to) part n.

An important modification of the APF algorithm comes from the introduction of a new dependency on the a posteriori probability formula, modifying therefore equation 2. The derivation produces a new factor, called the compatibility factor, coding the information coming from the rest of the parts:

$$p(\mathbf{x}_{t+1}^n|y_{t+1}^n, X_{t+1}^{N(n)}) \propto p(y_{t+1}^n|\mathbf{x}_{t+1}^n) \cdot$$

$$p(\mathbf{x}_{t+1}^n|X_{t+1}^{N(n)}) \sum_{j=1}^{M} p(\mathbf{x}_{t+1}^n|x_t^{n,j})\pi_t^{n,j} \qquad (4)$$

In here, $p(y_{t+1}^n|\mathbf{x}_{t+1}^n, X_{t+1}^{N(n)}) = p(y_{t+1}^n|\mathbf{x}_{t+1}^n)$ and the equation is derived by using Bayes' rule.

By assuming a graph structure, the compatibility factor, $p(\mathbf{x}_{t+1}^n|X_{t+1}^{N(n)})$, is decomposed in factors depending on its parts:

$$p(\mathbf{x}_{t+1}^n|X_{t+1}^{N(n)}) = \prod_{m \in N(n)} p(\mathbf{x}_{t+1}^n|\mathbf{x}_{t+1}^m) \qquad (5)$$

At this point it is possible to make use of the discretization of the state of each part provided by the particles, computing it as:

$$p(\mathbf{x}_{t+1}^n|\mathbf{x}_{t+1}^m) = \sum_i p(\mathbf{x}_{t+1}^n|x_{t+1}^{i,m})\pi_{t+1}^{i,m} \qquad (6)$$

In here, the compatibility model, $p(\mathbf{x}_{t+1}^n|x_{t+1}^{i,m})$, must be previously defined, as in the case of the transition model or the observation model. We will define an adequate compatibility model in the next section.

The a posteriori is now computed as in eq. 3, but modifying the weights:

$$\pi_{t+1}^{k,n} = \frac{p(y_{t+1}|x_{t+1}^{k,n})p(x_{t+1}^{k,n}|X_{t+1}^{N(n)})}{p(y_{t+1}|\mu_{t+1}^{k,n})p(\mu_{t+1}^{k,n}|X_{t+1}^{N(n)})} \qquad (7)$$

because the sampling of the a priori was made proportional to $p(y_{t+1}|\mu_{t+1}^{k,n})p(\mu_{t+1}^{k,n}|X_{t+1}^{N(n)})$. The denominator is the probability used for extracting the samples and is a term required when the sampling is not proportional to the a priori distribution [7].

The pseudocode is summarized in table 2.

3.2   Compatibility Computation Using Density Estimation

In this section we describe how we define $p(\mathbf{x}_{t+1}^n|\mathbf{x}_{t+1}^m)$. The spatial relation between part n and part m at time $t-1$ is defined as $D_{t-1}^{n,m} = \hat{\mathbf{x}}_{t-1}^m - \hat{\mathbf{x}}_{t-1}^n$. Since

Table 2. The Compatibility Particle Filter pseudocode

For each part n and each particle k
Compute $\mu_{t+1}^{k,n}$
Compute $\lambda_{t+1}^{k,n} = \pi_t^{k,n} p(y_{t+1}|\mu_{t+1}^{k,n})$
For each part n and each particle k
Compute $c_{t+1}^{k,n}$
Compute the posterior as $\lambda_{t+1}^{k,n} = \pi_{t+1}^{k,n} c_{t+1}^{k,n}$
For each part n and each particle k
Choose index i with probability proportional to $\lambda_{t+1}^{i,n}$
Draw a sample $x_{t+1}^{k,n}$ from $p(\mathbf{x}_{t+1}^n|x_t^{i,n})$
Assign weight $\pi_{t+1}^{k,n} = \dfrac{p(y_{t+1}|x_{t+1}^{k,n})p(x_{t+1}^{k,n}|X_{t+1}^{N(n)})}{p(y_{t+1}|\mu_{t+1}^{k,n})p(\mu_{t+1}^{k,n}|X_{t+1}^{N(n)})}$
Normalize weights, $\sum_{k=1}^{N} \pi_{t+1}^{k,n} = 1$

there is no a priori information of the spatial relations between parts, the spatial relations at time t can be considered a dynamic system and be estimated (ideally we should model $p(D_t^{n,m}|D_{t-1:t}^{n,m})$). The simplest election is $\hat{D}_t^{n,m} = D_{t-1}^{n,m}$. A common definition would be to set $\hat{D}_t^{n,m}$ as a weighted mean of the last spatial relations.

We define the compatibility of $\mathbf{x}_{t+1}^n$ respect to $\mathbf{x}_{t+1}^m$ as the evaluation over the a posteriori distribution of part m on the points $x_{t+1}^{i,n} + \hat{D}_t^{n,m}$. Since it is only necessary to evaluate each factor in equation 5 in $x_{t+1}^{i,n}$, we define:

$$p(x_{t+1}^{i,n}|\mathbf{x}_{t+1}^m) = p(\{x_{t+1}^{i,n} + D_{t+1}^{m,n}|\mathbf{x}_{t+1}^m)\} \tag{8}$$

The problem is that the likelihood at part m is computed at the discrete set of points $\{x_{t+1}^{i,m}\}$ and it is needed to compute it over $\{x_{t+1}^{i,n} + D_{t+1}^{m,n}\}$, which are not the same points. Instead of performing an exponential number of evaluations of the a posteriori, we use a kernel density estimation [2] to calculate these values.

In order to get some flexibility we use a modification of a Normal distribution with mean 0 and variance σ.

$$p(x_{t+1}^n, x_{t+1}^m) = N_{0,\sigma}\left(max(0, \|x_{t+1}^n + \hat{D}_{t+1}^{m,n} - x_{t+1}^m\| - r)\right) \tag{9}$$

where r is a parameter that controls the tightness of the spatial restrictions. σ can be computed depending as the weighted variance of $\{D_{t:t-\Delta t}^{n,m}\}$ and r depending on it. In the experiments shown in this article, r was set to 1 for both simplicity and for preventing complex parametrizations. In equation 9, if the relation between the two variables $\mathbf{x}_{t+1}^n$ and $\mathbf{x}_{t+1}^m$ varies respect to the estimated value $\hat{D}_t^{n,m}$ less than r, there is no penalization. For a bigger displacement the penalization grows at a speed controlled by σ. The final estimation, joining eq. 8 and 9 comes to:

$$p(x_{t+1}^n|\mathbf{x}_{t+1}^m) = \sum_j N_{0,\sigma}\left(max(0, \|x_{t+1}^n + \hat{D}_{t+1}^{m,n} - x_{t+1}^{j,m}\| - r)\right) \pi_{t+1}^{j,m} \tag{10}$$

This is therefore a nonparametric method for the estimation of the spatial coherence and it is important to note that no a priori knowledge is required.

4 Experimental Results

The experiments shown in this section are focused on showing both the effective maintenance of the geometric coherence along a tracked sequence and the good performance achieved respect to flexible movements. It is important to note that no a priori knowledge has been used. In the case of facial component tracking, the vast amount of information available would certainly provide important benefits, since it is possible to train the aspect of each component in a robust way. The performance of our tracking algorithm for the case of a rigid object quickly rotating out of image plane is also shown.

The sequence shown in figure 1 illustrates how the spatial relations are kept throughout a sequence in case of a partial occlusion. The tracking overcomes two partial occlusions (from frame 312 to 334 and from 421 to 439). This tracking has been performed using 60 particles per part. In contrast, the sequence presented in figure 2 shows the failure of particle filter trackings for the case of considering the full joint probability with 300 particles and the case of dividing the tracking into independent trackings of the parts, which does not contain spatial relationships. For the first case, the higher dimensionality of the state space causes that even sampling with much more particles (300 against 60) does not provide a reliable insight of the a posteriori distribution. As expected, for the case of the individual trackings the tracking get lost when one part is occluded. In figure 3 an insight on a frame iteration is shown. In this case, since the eye is occluded, the likelihood misleads the tracker. The spatial restrictions keep the tracker well placed while the a posteriori distribution is still correct and the final state is correctly found. This figure also shows the pdf of the spatial restrictions imposed by the left eye onto the right eye. The probability $p(\mathbf{x}_{t+1}^{reye}|\mathbf{x}_{t+1}^{leye})$ is shown for two different values of r (see eq. 9) and it shows also how the tightness of the restriction can be modulated through this variable.   In figure 4, the performance over flexible movements is shown. The process of the smile is fully tracked without a priori information. The movement is very fast (from neutral to apex in 5 frames)

Fig. 1. Frames 68, 315, 340 and 389 of a video sequence. 60 particles are used per part.

Fig. 2. Upper row: On the left, initialization of both trackers. The central and right image shows frames 78 and 234 for the case of the joint state space (12 dimensions). Lower row: Each part is tracked individually. The green stars show the estimated position. The left image shows how the right eye tracking is totally lost (draught by the hand) after the partial occlusion.

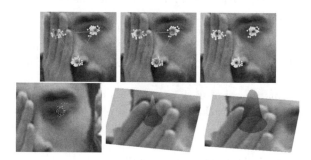

Fig. 3. The upper row, left to right: The likelihood, the compatibility and the a posteriori. Blue spots for the final state and green triangles for the spatial relations. The lower row, left to right: the particles and weights of the distribution over the left eye, the density imposed over the right eye with $r = 1$ and with $r = 6$. The tightness of the spatial relations is increased as r decreases.

Fig. 4. Frames 1, 14 and 37 showing a fast flexible movement over a sequence. The estimated position is not shown with squares for providing a better visualization.

Fig. 5. Sequence showing frames 1, 89 and 123 where a rotation out of the image plane is present

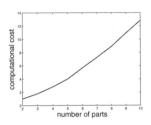

Fig. 6. The y-axis show the time cost respect to tracking with 2 parts

and therefore challenging to track while keeping the spatial restrictions. Figure 5 shows the robustness of the method to out of plane rotations. These kind of rotations can only be modeled parametrically by a projective transformation, which is complex to be estimated. Therefore, the case is similar to that of the flexible movements, where a parametrization of the movement is unfeasible. Again, the displacement is fast and the aspect change is large. The sequence is composed by 125 frames. Regarding the computational cost, the number of particles required for a precise estimation of the a posteriori distribution is stable and, therefore, the cost grows linearly in the number of parts. On the other hand, the inclusion of the compatibility is quadratic in the number of parts, while it constitutes a minor factor for not very high number of parts. Since many times the spatial information is redundant, for further lowering the computational costs, some options are possible, as to define a hierarchy or apply an algorithm to automatically eliminate relations (edges in the graph), as the one presented in [3]. The increase of the computational cost depending on the number of parts is shown in figure 6.

5   Conclusions

We have presented a modification of the APF algorithm capable of performing part-based tracking with a low increase of the computational cost. It is both capable of maintaining the spatial coherence and dealing with flexible movements without the need of a priori information. Furthermore, the spatial coherence is considered as another dynamic system as the position estimation. The relations between the different parts are defined using a nonparametric method.

Acknowledgments

The work of the authors was partially funded by the Spanish MITC under the Avanza Project Ontomedia (TSI-020501-2008-131). The work of Marc Vivet has also been partially funded by a UAB predoctoral grant.

References

1. Deutscher, J., Davison, A., Reid, I.: Automatic partitioning of high dimensional search spaces associated with articulated body motion capture. In: IEEE Conference on Computer Vision and Pattern Recognition, vol. 2, pp. 669–676 (2001)
2. Duda, R.O., Hart, P.E., Stork, D.G.: Pattern Classification, 2nd edn. Wiley-Interscience, Hoboken (2000)
3. Gu, L., Xing, E.P., Kanade, T.: Learning gmrf structures for spatial priors. In: Conference on Computer Vision and Pattern Recognition, pp. 1–6 (2007)
4. McCall, J.C., Trivedi, M.M.: Facial action coding using multiple visual cues and a hierarchy of particle filters. In: Proceedings of the 2006 Conference on Computer Vision and Pattern Recognition Workshop, p. 150 (2006)
5. Park, M., Liu, Y., Collins, R.: Efficient Mean Shift Belief Propagation for Vision Tracking. In: Conference on Computer Vision and Pattern Recognition (2008)
6. Patras, I., Pantic, M.: Particle filtering with factorized likelihoods for tracking facial features. In: International Conference on Automatic Face and Gesture Recognition, pp. 97–102 (2004)
7. Pitt, M.K., Shephard, N.: Filtering via simulation: Auxiliary particle filters. Journal of the American Statistical Association 94(446), 590–599 (1999)
8. Su, C., Zhuang, Y., Huang, L., Wu, F.: A two-step approach to multiple facial feature tracking: temporal particle filter and spatial belief propagation. In: International Conference on Automatic Face and Gesture Recognition, pp. 433–438 (2004)
9. Sudderth, E.B., Ihler, A.T., Freeman, W.T., Willsky, A.S.: Nonparametric Belief Propagation. In: Conference on Computer Vision and Pattern Recognition, vol. 1, pp. I-605–I-612 (2003)
10. Vlassis, N., Terwijn, B., Krse, B.: Auxiliary particle filter robot localization from high-dimensional sensor observations. In: International Conference on Robotics and Automation, pp. 7–12 (2002)

Combining Edge Detection and Region Segmentation for Lip Contour Extraction

Usman Saeed and Jean-Luc Dugelay

Eurecom
2229 Routes des Cretes,
06560 Sophia Antipolis, France
{Usman.Saeed,Jean-Luc.Dugelay}@Eurecom.fr

Abstract. The automatic detection of the lip contour is relatively a difficult problem in computer vision due to the variation amongst humans and environmental conditions. In this paper we improve upon the classical methods by introducing fusion. Two separate methods are first applied, one based on edge detection and the other on region segmentation to detect the outer lip contour, the results from them are then combined. Empirical evaluation of the detection process is also presented on an image subset of the Valid database, which contains lighting, pose and speech variation with promising results.

Keywords: Image Processing, Lip Detection.

1 Introduction

Lip detection is still an active topic of research; the significant interest in this topic originates from the numerous applications where lip detection either serves as a preprocessing step or directly provides visual information to improve performance. It has been applied successfully to Audio-Video Speech and Speaker recognition, where it has considerably improved recognition results, especially in the presence of noise. Another domain of application is gesture recognition for closely related fields of human computer interaction, affective computing. It has also been used in the analysis and synthesis of lips for talking head in video conferencing applications.

In this paper we propose a lip contour detection algorithm based on fusion of two independent methods, edge based and region based. The basic idea is that both techniques have different characteristics and thus exhibit distinct strengths and weaknesses. We also present empirical results on a dataset of considerable size with illumination and speech variation. The rest of the paper is divided as follows. In Section 2 we give the state of the art and in Section 3 we elaborate the proposed method, after that we report and comment our results in section 4 and finally we conclude this paper with remarks and future works in section 5.

2 State of the Art

Lip detection literature can be loosely classified in three categories. The first category of techniques directly uses image information, the second tries to build models and

F.J. Perales and R.B. Fisher (Eds.): AMDO 2010, LNCS 6169, pp. 11–20, 2010.

the third is a hybrid approach that combines the image and model based techniques to increase robustness.

2.1 Image Based Techniques

Image based techniques use the pixel information directly, the advantage is that they are computationally less expensive but are adversely affected by variation such as illumination.

Color Based Techniques. Several algorithms base the detection of lips directly on color difference between the lip and skin, but lack of contrast and illumination variation adversely affects these techniques. Some have also suggested color transforms that increase the contrast between skin and lip regions. [1] have reported that difference between red and green is greater for lips than skin and proposed a pseudo hue as a ratio of RGB values. [2] have also proposed a RGB value ratio based on the observation that blue color plays a subordinate role so suppressing it improves segmentation.

Color clustering has also been suggested by some, based on the assumption that there are only two classes i.e. skin and lips, this may not be completely true if facial hair or teeth are visible. Fuzzy clustering was applied for lip detection in [3] by combining color information and spatial distance between pixels in an elliptical shape function. [4] have used expectation maximization algorithm for unsupervised clustering of chromatic features for lip detection in normalized RGB color space. Markov random fields also been proposed to add spatial continuity to segmentation based on color, thus making segmentation more robust in [5].

Subspace Based Techniques. [6] have proposed a lip detector based on PCA, firstly outer lip contours are manually labelled on training data, PCA is then applied to extract the principal modes of contour shape variation, called eigencontour, finally linear regression was applied for detection. LDA has been employed in [7] to separate lip and skin pixels. [8] have proposed a method in which a Discrete Hartley Transform (DHT) is first applied to enhance contrast between lip and skin, then a multi scale wavelet edge detection is applied on the C3 component of DHT.

2.2 Model Based Techniques

Model based techniques are based on prior knowledge of the lip shape and can be quite robust. They are however computationally expensive as compared to image based techniques as they usually involve minimization of a cost function.

[9] have proposed a real time tracker that models the dynamic contours of lips using quadratic B-Splines learned from training data using maximum likelihood estimation algorithm. Tracking is then carried out using Kalman filtering for both frontal and profile view of the lips. [10] have proposed a model consisting of two parabolas for the upper lip and one for lower lip.

Snakes have been commonly used for lip segmentation [11] and achieve reasonable results but need to be properly initialized. Another problem faced by snakes is there inability to detect lip corners as they are located in low gradient regions. [12] have proposed a jumping snake that removes the limitations present in classical snake.

It can be initialized far from the lip edge and the parameter adjustment is easy and intuitive.

[13] have proposed Active Shape Models (ASM) and Active Appearance Models (AAM), which learn the shape and appearance of lips from training data that has been manually annotated. Next PCA is applied to reduce the dimensionality and using cost functions, models are iteratively fitted to test images for lip detection. Deformable templates initially proposed by [14] has been extended and modified by several others. [15] have proposed a lip detection method based on Point Distribution Model (PDM) of the face.

2.3 Hybrid Techniques

These methods combine image based and model based techniques for lip detection. Image based techniques are considered computationally less expensive but not so robust to illumination and other types of variation. Model based techniques on the other hand are robust and accurate but are much more computationally complex. Thus majority of the hybrid techniques proposed in the literature use color based techniques for a quick and rough estimation of the candidate lip regions and then apply a model based approach to extract accurate lip contours.

[16] have proposed a hybrid technique that first applies a color transform to reduce the effect of lighting. Then horizontal and vertical projections of the lip are analyzed to detect the corner points and finally a geometric lip model is applied. [17] have combined a fuzzy clustering algorithm in CIELAB color space for rough estimation and then an ASM for accurate detection of lip contours. [18] have proposed a hybrid system that models the lip area by expectation maximization algorithm after a color transform in RGB space has been applied. Then a snake is initialized, which is fitted on the upper and lower contours of the mouth by a multi level gradient flow maximization. [19] have proposed a lip tracking by combining lip shape, color and motion information. The shape has been modeled using two parabolas, lip and skin color is modeled by Gaussian distribution and motion by modified Lucas-Kanade tracking.

3 Proposed Lip Detection

In this section we present a lip detection method to extract the outer lip contour that combines edge based and region based algorithms. The results from the two methods are then combined by AND/OR fusion. The novelty lies in the fusion of two methods, which have different characteristics and thus exhibit different type of strengths and weaknesses. The other significance of this study lies in the extensive testing and evaluation of the detection algorithm on a realistic database. Most previous studies either never carried out empirical comparisons to the ground truth at all or suffced by using a limited dataset. Even if empirical testing was done by some studies [24], [8] they were limited to high resolution images with constant lighting conditions.

Figure 1 gives an overview of the lip detection algorithm. Given an image, it is assumed that a human face is present and already detected; the first step is to select the mouth Region of Interest (ROI) using the lower one third of the detected face. The next step involves the outer lip contour detection where the same mouth ROI is provided to the edge and region based methods. Finally the results from the two methods are fused to obtain the final outer lip contour.

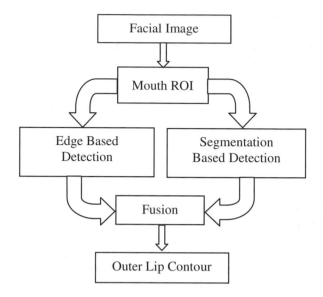

Fig. 1. Overview of the proposed lip detection method

3.1 Edge Based Detection

The first algorithm is based on a well accepted edge detection method. It consists of two steps, the first one is a lip enhancing color transform and the second one is edge detection based on active contours. Several color transforms have already been proposed for either enhancing the lip region independently or with respect to the skin. Here, after evaluating several transforms we have selected the color transform proposed by [2]. It is based on the principle that blue component has reduced role in lip / skin color discrimination and is defined in eq. 1.

$$I = \frac{2G - R - 0.5B}{4}.$$

(1)

Where R,G,B are the Red, Green and Blue components of the mouth ROI. The next step is the extraction of the outer lip contour, for this we have used active contours [20]. Active contours are an edge detection method based on the minimization of an energy associated to the contour. This energy is the sum of internal and external energies; the aim of the internal energy is to maintain the shape as regular and smooth as possible. The most straightforward approach grants high energy to elongated contours (elastic force) and to high curvature contours (rigid force). The external energy models the edge of the object and is supposed to be minimal when the active contours (snake) is at the object boundary. The simplest approach consists in using regularized gradient as the external energy. In our study the contour was initialized as an oval half the size of the ROI with node separation of four pixels.

Since we are have applied active contours which have the possibility of detecting multiple objects, on a ROI which may include other features such as the nose tip, an additional cleanup step needs to be carried out. This consists of selecting the largest detected object approximately in the middle of the image as the lip and discarding the rest of the detected objects.

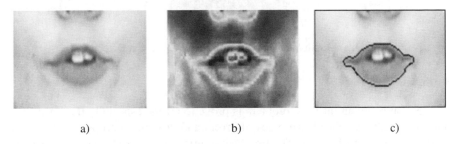

a)　　　　　　　　　　　　　　b)　　　　　　　　　　　　　　c)

Fig. 2. a) Mouth *ROI,* b) Color Transform, c) Edge Detection

3.2 Region Based Detection

In contrast to the edge based technique the second approach is region based after a color transform in the YIQ domain. As in the first approach we experimented with several color transform presented in the literature to find the one that is most appropriate for lip segmentation. [21] have presented that skin/lip discrimination can be achieved successfully in the YIQ domain, which firstly de-couples the luminance and chrominance information. They have also suggested that the I channel is most discriminant for skin detection and the Q channel for lip enhancement. Thus we transformed the mouth ROI form RGB to YIQ color space using the equation 2 and retained the Q channel for further processing.

$$
\begin{bmatrix} Y \\ I \\ Q \end{bmatrix} = \begin{bmatrix} 0.299 & 0.587 & 0.114 \\ 0.595716 & -0.274453 & -0.321263 \\ 0.211456 & -0.522591 & 0.31135 \end{bmatrix} \begin{bmatrix} R \\ G \\ B \end{bmatrix}. \tag{2}
$$

In classical active contours the external energy is modeled as an edge detector using the gradient of the image, to stop the evolution of the curve on the boundary of the desired object while maintaining smoothness in the curve. This is a major limitation of the active contours as they can only detect objects with reasonably defined edges. Thus for the second method we selected a technique called "active contours without edges" [25], which models the intensities in different region of the image and uses it as the stopping term in active contours. More precisely this model [25] is based on Mumford–Shah functional and level sets. In the level set formulation, the problem becomes a mean-curvature flow evolving the active contour, which will stop on the desired boundary. However, the stopping term does not depend on the gradient of the image, as in the classical active contour models, but is instead based on Mumford–Shah functional for segmentation.

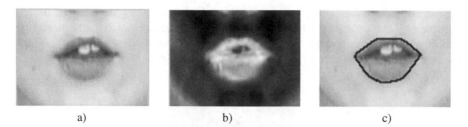

a)   b)   c)

Fig. 3. a) Mouth *ROI,* b) Color Transform, c) Region Detection

3.3 Fusion

Lip detection being an intricate problem is prone to errors, especially the lower lip as reported by [22]. We faced two types of errors and propose appropriate error detection and correction techniques. The first type of error, which was commonly observed in the edge based method, was caused when the lip was missed altogether and some other feature was selected. This error can easily be detected by applying feature value and locality constraints such as the lip cannot be connected to the ROI's boundary and cannot have an area value less than one-third of the average area value in the entire video sequence. If this error was observed, the detection results were discarded.

The second type occurs when the lip is not detected in its entirety, e.g. missing the lower lip, such errors are difficult to detect thus we proposed to use fusion as a corrective measure, under the assumption that both the detection techniques will not fail simultaneously.

The detected outer lip contours from the above described methods are then used to create binary masks which describe the interior and the exterior of the outer lip contour. These masks are then fused using AND and OR logical operators.

4   Experiments and Results

In this section we elaborate the experimental setup and discuss the results obtained. Tests were carried out on a subset of the Valid Database [23], which consists of 106 subjects. The database contains five sessions for each subject where one session has been recorded in studio conditions while the others are in uncontrolled environments such as the office or corridors. In each session the subjects repeat the same sentence, "Joe took father's green shoe bench out". One image was extracted from each of the five videos to create a database of 530 facial images. The reason for selecting one image per video was that the database did not contain any ground truth for lip detection, so ground truth had to be created manually, which is a time consuming task. The images contained both illumination and shape variation; illumination from the fact that they were extracted from all five videos, and shape as they were extracted from random frames of speaker videos.

As already described above the database did not contain any ground truth with respect to the outer lip contour. Thus the ground truth was established manually by a single operator using Adobe Photoshop. The outer lip contour was marked using the magnetic lasso tool which separated the interior and exterior of the outer lip contour by setting the exterior to zero and the interior to one.

To evaluate the lip detection algorithm we used the following two measures proposed by [8], the first measure determines the percentage of overlap (OL) between the segmented lip region A and the ground truth A_G. It is defined by eq. 3.

$$OL = \frac{2(A \mathbf{I} A_G)}{A + A_G} * 100.$$
(3)

Using this measure, total agreement will have an overlap of 100%. The second measure is the segmentation error (SE) defined by eq. 4.

$$SE = \frac{OLE + ILE}{2 * TL} * 100.$$
(4)

OLE (outer lip error) is the number of non-lip pixels being classified as lip pixels and ILE (inner lip error) is the number of lip-pixels classified as non-lip ones. TL denotes the number of lip-pixels in the ground truth. Total agreement will have an SE of 0%.

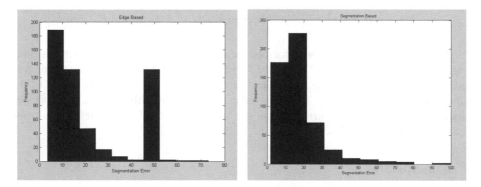

Fig. 4. Histograms for Segmentation Errors

Initially we calculated the overlap and segmentation errors for edge and region based methods individually, and it was visually observed that edges based method was more accurate but not robust and on several occasions missed almost half of the lip. This can also be observed in the histogram of segmentation errors; although the majority of lips are detected with 10% or less error but a large number of lip images exhibit approximately 50% of segmentation error. On the other hand region based method was less accurate as majority of lips detected are with 20% error but was quite robust and always succeeded in detecting the lip.

Table 1. Lip detection Results

Lip Detection Method	Mean Segmentation Error (SE) %	Mean Overlap (OL) %
Segmentation Based	17.8225	83.6419
Edge Based	22.3665	65.6430
OR Fusion	**15.6524**	83.9321
AND Fusion	18.4067	84.2452
OR Fusion on 1st Video	13.9964	87.1492

Table 1 describes the results obtained, the best results were observed for OR fusion with 15.65% mean segmentation error. "OR Fusion on 1st Video" are the results that were obtained when OR fusion was applied to only the images from the first video, which are recorded in studio conditions.

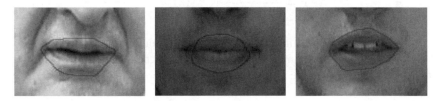

Fig. 5. Example of Images with approximately 15 % Segmentation Error

The minimum segmentation error obtained was 15.65%, which might seem quite large, but on visual inspection of Figure 5, it is evident that missing the lip corners or including a bit of the skin region can lead to this level of error. Another aspect of the experiment that must be kept in mind is the ground truth, although every effort was made to establish an ideal ground truth but due to limited time and resources some compromises had to be made.

5   Conclusions

In this paper we have presented a novel lip detection method based on the fusion of edge based and region based methods, along with empirical results on a dataset of considerable size with illumination and speech variation. We observed that the edge based technique is comparatively more accurate, but is not so robust and fails if lighting conditions are not favorable, thus it ends up selecting some other facial feature. On the other hand the region based method is robust to lighting but is not as accurate as the edge based method. Thus by fusing the results from the two techniques we achieve comparatively better results than using only one method. The proposed methods were tested on a real world database with adequate results.

Although the results achieved are quite promising, there is still some room for improvements. Currently we compensate for errors by fusion, we would like to automatically evaluate the results from the independent methods and detect failure, then propose an appropriate fusion approach. We have only tested two fusion approaches; it would be interesting to study others such as a post-classifier.

References

1. Hulbert, A., Poggio, T.: Synthesizing a Color Algorithm from Examples. Science 239, 482–485 (1998)
2. Canzlerm, U., Dziurzyk, T.: Extraction of Non Manual Features for Video based Sign Language Recognition. In: Proceedings of IAPR Workshop, pp. 318–321 (2002)
3. Leung, S.-H., Wang, S.-L., Lau, W.-H.: Lip image segmentation using fuzzy clustering incorporating an elliptic shape function. IEEE Transactions on Image Processing 13(1), 51–62 (2004)
4. Lucey, S., Sridharan, S., Chandran, V.: Adaptive mouth segmentation using chromatic features. Pattern Recogn. Lett. 23, 1293–1302 (2002)
5. Zhang, X., Mersereau, R.M.: Lip feature extraction toward an automatic speechreading system. In: Proc. IEEE Int. Conf. Image Processing, vol. 3, pp. 226–229 (2000)
6. Lucey, S., Sridharan, S., Chandran, V.: Initialised eigenlip estimator for fast lip tracking using linear regression. In: Proceedings of 15th International Conference on Pattern Recognition, vol. 3, pp. 178–181 (2000)
7. Nefian, A., Liang, L., Pi, X., Xiaoxiang, L., Mao, C., Murphy, K.: A couple HMM for audio-visual speech recognition. In: Proc. ICASSP, pp. 2013–2016 (2002)
8. Guan, Y.-P.: Automatic extraction of lips based on multi-scale wavelet edge detection. IET Computer Vision 2(1), 23–33 (2008)
9. Kaucic, R., Dalton, B., Blake, A.: Real-Time Lip Tracking for Audio-Visual Speech Recognition Applications. In: Buxton, B.F., Cipolla, R. (eds.) ECCV 1996. LNCS, vol. 1065. Springer, Heidelberg (1996)
10. Coianiz, T., Torresani, L., Caprile, B.: 2D deformable models for visual speech analysis. In: NATO Advanced Study Institute: Speech reading by Man and Machine, pp. 391–398 (1995)
11. Aleksic, P.S., Williams, J.J., Wu, Z., Katsaggelos, A.K.: Audiovisual speech recognition using MPEG-4 compliant visual features. EURASIP J. Appl. Signal Processing, 1213–1227 (2002)
12. Eveno, N., Caplier, A., Coulon, P.: Accurate and quasi-automatic lip tracking. IEEE Transactions on Circuits and Systems for Video Technology 14, 706–715 (2004)
13. Cootes, T.F.: Statistical Models of Appearance for Computer Vision. Technical report, University of Manchester (2004)
14. Yuille, A.L., Hallinan, P.W., Cohen, D.S.: Feature extraction from faces using deformable templates. Int. J. Comput. Vision 8, 99–111 (1992)
15. Huang, C.L., Huang, Y.M.: Facial Expression Recognition Using Model-Based Feature Extraction and Action Parameters Classification. Journal of Visual Communication and Image Representation 8, 278–290 (1997)
16. Werda, S., Mahdi, W., Ben-Hamadou, A.: Colour and Geometric based Model for Lip Localisation: Application for Lip-reading System. In: 14th International Conference on Image Analysis and Processing, pp. 9–14 (2007)
17. Mok, L.L., Lau, W.H., Leung, S.H., Wang, S.L., Yan, H.: Person authentication using ASM based lip shape and intensity information. In: International Conference on Image Processing, vol. 1, pp. 561–564 (2004)
18. Bouvier, C., Coulon, P.-Y., Maldague, X.: Unsupervised Lips Segmentation Based on ROI Optimisation and Parametric Model. In: IEEE International Conference on Image Processing, vol. 4, pp. 301–304 (2007)
19. Tian, Y., Kanade, T., Cohn, J.: Robust lip tracking by combining shape, color and motion. In: Proc. ACCV, pp. 1040–1045 (2000)

20. Michael, K., Andrew, W., Demetri, T.: Snakes: active Contour models. International Journal of Computer Vision 1, 259–268 (1987)
21. Thejaswi, N.S., Sengupta, S.: Lip Localization and Viseme Recognition from Video Sequences. In: Fourteenth National Conference on Communications (2008)
22. Bourel, F., Chibelushi, C.C., Low, A.A.: Robust Facial Feature Tracking. In: Proceedings of the 11th British Machine Vision Conference, UK, vol. 1, pp. 232–241 (2000)
23. Fox, N.A., O'Mullane, B., Reilly, R.B.: The realistic multi-modal VALID database and visual speaker identification comparison experiments. In: Kanade, T., Jain, A., Ratha, N.K. (eds.) AVBPA 2005. LNCS, vol. 3546, Springer, Heidelberg (2005)
24. Liew, A.W.-C., Shu Hung, L., Wing Hong, L.: Segmentation of color lip images by spatial fuzzy clustering. IEEE Transactions on Fuzzy Systems 11(4), 542–549 (2003)
25. Chan, T.F., Vese, L.A.: Active contours without edges. IEEE Transactions on Image Processing 10(2), 266–277 (2001)

Retrieving Articulated 3D Objects Using Normalized Distance Function

Waleed Mohamed and A. Ben Hamza

Concordia Institute for Information Systems Engineering
Concordia University, Montréal, QC, Canada

Abstract. In this paper we propose a skeletonization approach that encodes a 3D object into a skeletal Reeb graph using a normalized mixture distance function. Then, we introduce a novel graph matching algorithm by comparing the relative shortest paths between the skeleton endpoints. Experimental results demonstrate the feasibility of the proposed topological Reeb graph as a shape signature for 3D object retrieval using a benchmark of articulated shapes.

Keywords: 3D retrieval, articulated objects, skeletal graph.

1 Introduction

With the increasing use of scanners to create 3D models, shape recognition of 3D objects has become an active research field with the recent developments in solid modeling and visualization [1]. Nowadays, vast amounts of 3D models are being developed and are distributed freely or commercially on the Internet. 3D objects consist of geometric and topological information, and their compact representation is an important step towards a variety of computer vision applications, particularly matching and retrieval in a database of 3D models. The first step in 3D object matching usually involves finding a reliable shape descriptor or skeletal graph which will encode efficiently the 3D shape information. Most 3D shape representation techniques proposed in the literature of computer graphics and computer vision are based on geometric and topological representations which represent the features of an object [4,2,3,5]. An alternative to feature-based representations is global methods, which represent a 3D object by a global measure or shape distribution defined on the surface of the object [6,7,8,9].

In this paper, we propose an invariant skeletal graph for 3D object representation using a normalized mixture distance function. The key idea is to identify and encode regions of topological interest of a 3D object in the Morse-theoretic framework [10]. The main motivation behind using the distance function is it rotational invariance, which makes it more adapted to object recognition than the Morse height function. Using this skeletal graph as a shape signature, we also introduce a novel 3D graph matching and retrieval approach by comparing the relative shortest paths between the skeleton endpoints.

The rest of this paper is organized as follows. Section 2 briefly describes the basic concepts of Morse theory for 3D topological modeling. In Section 3, we

F.J. Perales and R.B. Fisher (Eds.): AMDO 2010, LNCS 6169, pp. 21–30, 2010.

propose a normalized mixture distance function-based approach to construct invariant skeletal graphs of 3D objects. Section 4 introduces a new graph matching algorithm. In Section 5, we demonstrate the feasibility of the proposed skeletal graph as a shape signature for robust retrieval of articulated 3D objects. And finally we conclude in Section 6.

2   Morse Theory for Topological Modeling

In computer graphics and geometric-aided design, 3D objects are usually represented as polygonal or triangle meshes. A triangle mesh $\mathbb{M}$ is usually denoted by $\mathbb{M} = (\mathcal{V}, \mathcal{T})$, where $\mathcal{V} = \{\boldsymbol{p}_1, \ldots, \boldsymbol{p}_m\}$ is the set of vertices and $\mathcal{T} = \{\boldsymbol{t}_1, \ldots, \boldsymbol{t}_n\}$ is the set of triangles.

Morse theory explains the presence and the stability of singular points in terms of the topology of the underlying smooth manifold. The basic principle is that the topology of a manifold is very closely related to the singular points of a smooth function defined on that manifold [10]. A smooth function $f : \mathbb{M} \rightarrow \mathbb{R}$ on a smooth manifold $\mathbb{M}$ is a *Morse function* if all its singular points are nondegenerate, i.e. the Hessian matrix is nonsingular at every singular point.

An interesting concept related to Morse theory and very useful to analyze a surface topology is the Reeb graph. The latter is defined as a quotient space $\mathbb{M}/\sim$ with the equivalence relation given by $\boldsymbol{p} \sim \boldsymbol{q}$ if and only if $f(\boldsymbol{p}) = f(\boldsymbol{q})$ and $\boldsymbol{p}, \boldsymbol{q}$ belong to the same connected component of $f^{-1}(f(\boldsymbol{p}))$. An equivalence class is defined as $[\boldsymbol{p}] = \{\boldsymbol{q} \in \mathbb{M} : \boldsymbol{p} \sim \boldsymbol{q}\}$.

3   Proposed Reeb Graph Approach

Denote by $\boldsymbol{V} = (\boldsymbol{p}_1 \ \boldsymbol{p}_2 \ \ldots \boldsymbol{p}_m)^T$ the $m \times 3$ mesh vertex matrix having as rows the coordinates of the mesh vertices, where $\boldsymbol{p}_i = (x_i, y_i, z_i)^T \in \mathcal{V}$.

Let $\boldsymbol{c} = (\bar{x}, \bar{y}, \bar{z})^T$ be the centroid of the triangle mesh, that is $\boldsymbol{c}$ is the center of the minimal enclosing sphere of the mesh vertices $\mathcal{V}$. We define the $m \times 3$ centered vertex matrix as

$$V_{\boldsymbol{c}} = (\boldsymbol{p}_1 - \boldsymbol{c} \ \boldsymbol{p}_2 - \boldsymbol{c} \ \ldots \ \boldsymbol{p}_m - \boldsymbol{c})^T = \begin{pmatrix} x_1 - \bar{x} & y_1 - \bar{y} & z_1 - \bar{z} \\ x_2 - \bar{x} & y_2 - \bar{y} & z_2 - \bar{z} \\ \vdots & \vdots & \vdots \\ x_m - \bar{x} & y_m - \bar{y} & z_m - \bar{z} \end{pmatrix}. \quad (1)$$

The Euclidean distance function of $\mathbb{M}$ to $\boldsymbol{c}$ is defined as

$$d_{\boldsymbol{c}}^{euc} : \mathbb{M} \rightarrow \mathbb{R} \quad \text{such that} \quad d_{\boldsymbol{c}}^{euc}(\boldsymbol{p}) = \|\boldsymbol{p} - \boldsymbol{c}\|^2, \quad (2)$$

and it can be easily shown that it is rotation and translation invariant.

Let $A = m(V_{\boldsymbol{c}}^T V_{\boldsymbol{c}})^{-1}$, we define the affine distance function as follows

$$d_{\boldsymbol{c}}^{aff} : \mathbb{M} \rightarrow \mathbb{R} \quad \text{such that} \quad d_{\boldsymbol{c}}^{aff}(\boldsymbol{p}) = \|\boldsymbol{p} - \boldsymbol{c}\|_A^2 = (\boldsymbol{p} - \boldsymbol{c})^T A (\boldsymbol{p} - \boldsymbol{c}), \quad (3)$$

and it can be shown that it is invariant to affine transformations [11].

3.1   Mixture Distance Function

We define the mixture distance function as a convex combination of the Euclidean and the affine distance functions:

$$d_{\boldsymbol{c}} : \mathbb{M} \to \mathbb{R} \text{ such that } \quad d_{\boldsymbol{c}}(\boldsymbol{p}) = \lambda\|\boldsymbol{p} - \boldsymbol{c}\|^2 + (1 - \lambda)\|\boldsymbol{p} - \boldsymbol{c}\|_A^2, \qquad (4)$$

where $\lambda \in (0, 1)$ is a mixture parameter that needs to be estimated or chosen *a priori*. From the invariance properties of the Euclidean and affine distance functions, it is easy to verify that the mixture distance function is invariant to orthogonal and translation transformations. To make $d_{\boldsymbol{c}}$ scale invariant, we define the normalized mixture distance function as

$$\widetilde{d}_{\boldsymbol{c}}(\boldsymbol{p}) = \frac{d_{\boldsymbol{c}}(\boldsymbol{p}) - d_{\min}}{d_{\max} - d_{\min}}, \quad \forall \boldsymbol{p} \in \mathcal{V}, \qquad (5)$$

where $d_{\min} = \min d_{\boldsymbol{c}}(\boldsymbol{p})$ and $d_{\max} = \max d_{\boldsymbol{c}}(\boldsymbol{p})$.

3.2   Proposed Skeletonization Algorithm

The main algorithmic steps of the mixture distance-based Reeb graph are described in Algorithm 1. Fig. 1 shows the skeletal Reeb graph of a 3D cow model.

Algorithm 1. Proposed skeletonization approach

1: Find the centroid of $\boldsymbol{c}$ of the 3D mesh $\mathbb{M} = (\mathcal{V}, \mathcal{T})$
2: Find the maximum distance $d_{\max} = \max d_{\boldsymbol{c}}(\boldsymbol{p})$, $\forall \boldsymbol{p} \in \mathcal{V}$
3: **for** $(k = 1 \text{ to } R)$
4:     $d(k) = k * d_{\max}/R$; $\Leftarrow R$ is the resolution parameter
5: VerticesSet$_p$[0,1] = setIntersect($\mathbb{M}$,1); $\Leftarrow$ Find vertices subset of $\mathbb{M}$ from $\boldsymbol{c}$ to $d(1)$
6: NodeSet$_p$ = centroid(VerticesSet$_p$[0,1](n)); $\Leftarrow$ Assign a node to each connected component at its centroid.
7: Connect $\boldsymbol{c}$ and NodeSet$_p$
8: **for** $k = 2$ to R **do**
9:     VerticesSet$_c$[$k - 1, k$] = setIntersect($\mathbb{M}, k - 1, k$);$\Leftarrow$ Find intersection of $\mathbb{M}$ from distance $d(k - 1)$ to $d(k)$
10:     **for** each component VerticesSet$_c$ [$k - 1, k$](n) **do**
11:         NodeSet$_c$ = centroid(VerticesSet$_c$ [$k - 1, k$](n))
12:         **for** each connected portion **do**
13:             Connect NodeSet$_c$ and NodeSet$_p$
14:         **end for**
15:     **end for**
16:     NodeSet$_p$ = NodeSet$_c$
17:     VerticesSet$_p$ = VerticesSet$_c$
18: **end for**

---

4   Reeb Graph Matching

In this section, we introduce a novel method for 3D shape matching. The proposed skeleton graph matching is based on the dissimilarity of the shortest paths between the endpoints of the skeletal Reeb graph. A skeleton endpoint refers to the skeleton node that is connected by only one edge as shown in Fig. 1. It is worth pointing out that endpoints are the salient points of the skeleton and can be seen as visual parts of the original 3D shape [12]. Considering only the shortest skeletal paths between endpoints would help avoid the instability problem of the skeleton junction points (i.e. points having three or more adjacent points) and also to make our proposed method more robust to shape deformation. The shortest path between each endpoint and all other endpoints of the skeleton provides an important endpoint feature that will be incorporated into our matching dissimilarity measure.

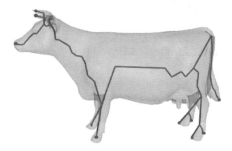

Fig. 1. The cow's Reeb graph and its skeleton endpoints

After generating the 3D shape skeleton, our next step is to develop a robust approach for skeletal graph matching. To this end, we match any two Reeb graphs by establishing a correspondence of their endpoints. Then, we apply a pruning algorithm [13] to remove non-salient nodes from the skeleton graph. The proposed matching method consists of two main steps. The first step, which we refer to as indexing, reduces the number of skeletons to be compared with. In the second step, we match the Reeb graphs by applying a dissimilarity measure to retrieve the closest 3D model. These two steps are explained in more details in the following subsections.

4.1   Indexing

A linear search through a database of 3D models is inefficient for large databases, as it requires comparing the query object to each model in the database and selecting the closest one [5]. Using our skeletonization algorithm, we may formulate the indexing problem as finding skeletons whose topological structures are similar to the query skeleton. It is important to note that similar shapes will have the same skeleton even if they are subject to some deformation or transformation. Moreover, these skeletons will have the same number of endpoints. Thus, in our indexing mechanism we use the number of skeleton endpoints as the base for indexing, with an error rate of 2 or 3 nodes, meaning that for two skeletons to be in the same index group they should have the same number of endpoints. However, due to noise there might be a difference of 1 or 2 nodes at most, as a result of the pruning process.

4.2   Endpoints Correspondence

We assign to each endpoint in the Reeb graph (query or model) some features that may help identify the closet endpoint in the other skeletal graph. Thus, our skeleton graph matching problem may be reduced to finding the best correspondence between the endpoints in the query and the endpoints in the model. This can be achieved by minimum weight matching of the two sets of endpoints. A dissimilarity measure between the set of endpoints in both query and model skeletons is used. Therefore, the matching problem aims at finding the best correspondence between the query skeleton endpoints and the database skeletons endpoints. Two endpoints are said to be in close correspondence if the dissimilarity measure between their endpoints has a smaller value. In other words, the matching problem is now reduced to finding the maximum correspondence, minimum weight matching of the two sets of endpoints. The endpoints correspondence process is shown in Algorithm 2.

Algorithm 2. Endpoints correspondence

Let $E = (\boldsymbol{v}_i)_{i=1,..,n_1}$ and $\widetilde{E} = (\tilde{\boldsymbol{v}}_j)_{j=1,..,n_2}$ be two sets of endpoints.
For each endpoint $\boldsymbol{v}_i \in E$:

1: Compute a dissimilarity measure between $\boldsymbol{v}_i$ and all the nodes in $\widetilde{E}$
2: Find the node $\tilde{\boldsymbol{v}}_j$ with the minimum dissimilarity and assign its correspondence to $\boldsymbol{v}_i$
3: Delete $\boldsymbol{v}_i$ and $\tilde{\boldsymbol{v}}_j$ from the list of nodes in E and $\widetilde{E}$, respectively

Repeat steps 1-3 for all nodes in E until one of the node sets E or $\widetilde{E}$ is empty

---

4.3   Matching Endpoints Using Skeleton Paths

Endpoint Features. When generating the skeletal Reeb graph of a 3D shape we assign three features to each endpoint of the skeleton. The first feature is the relative node area, which is equal to the area of the neighboring triangles of the endpoint divided by the total area of the 3D model. This feature provides important information about the endpoint as sometimes the skeletons of two models may look similar, albeit their shapes are completely different. Thus, adding this feature to an endpoint will help discriminate between endpoints based on the original 3D shape and not just its skeleton. The reason behind using the relative area is due to its invariance to scaling. The second feature assigned to an endpoint is the relative node path, which is equal to the sum of

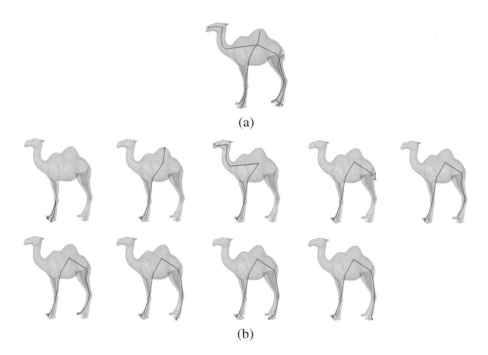

(a)

(b)

Fig. 2. (a) Camel's Reeb graph. (b) Shortest paths between pairs of endpoints on the skeleton.

shortest path distances from each endpoint to all other endpoints of the skeleton (see Fig. 2(b)) divided by the sum of the shorted paths from the mesh centroid (root node) to each endpoint. And the third feature is the relative centroid path, which is the shortest path distance from the mesh centroid to each endpoint (see Fig. 3), divided by the sum of the shortest paths from the mesh centroid to all endpoints.

Endpoints dissimilarity. Let $\mathbb{M}$ and $\widetilde{\mathbb{M}}$ be two 3D objects with skeletal Reeb graphs G and $\widetilde{G}$, respectively. And denote by $E = (\boldsymbol{v}_i)_{i=1,..,n_1}$ and $\widetilde{E} = (\tilde{\boldsymbol{v}}_j)_{j=1,..,n_2}$ the skeleton endpoints sets of G and $\widetilde{G}$, respectively. We define the dissimilarity measure between two endpoints $\boldsymbol{v}_i$ and $\tilde{\boldsymbol{v}}_j$ as follows:

$$\Phi(\boldsymbol{v}_i, \tilde{\boldsymbol{v}}_j) = [(a_i - \tilde{a}_j)^2 + (d\boldsymbol{v}_i - d\tilde{\boldsymbol{v}}_j)^2 + (dc_i - d\tilde{c}_j)^2]^{1/2}, \tag{6}$$

where

- a_i and $\tilde{a}_j$ are the relative node areas of $\boldsymbol{v}_i$ and $\tilde{\boldsymbol{v}}_j$
- $d\boldsymbol{v}_i = \sum_{k=1}^{n_1} dist(\boldsymbol{v}_i, \boldsymbol{v}_k)/\sum_{k=1}^{n_1} dist(\boldsymbol{c}, \boldsymbol{v}_k)$ and
  $d\tilde{\boldsymbol{v}}_j = \sum_{k=1}^{n_2} dist(\tilde{\boldsymbol{v}}_j, \tilde{\boldsymbol{v}}_k)/\sum_{k=1}^{n_2} dist(\tilde{\boldsymbol{c}}, \tilde{\boldsymbol{v}}_k)$ are the relative node paths of $\boldsymbol{v}_i$ and $\tilde{\boldsymbol{v}}_j$
- $dc_i = dist(\boldsymbol{c}, \boldsymbol{v}_i)/\sum_{k=1}^{n_1} dist(\boldsymbol{c}, \boldsymbol{v}_k)$ and $d\tilde{c}_j = dist(\tilde{\boldsymbol{c}}, \tilde{\boldsymbol{v}}_j)/\sum_{k=1}^{n_2} dist(\tilde{\boldsymbol{c}}, \tilde{\boldsymbol{v}}_k)$ are the relative centroid paths of $\boldsymbol{v}_i$ and $\tilde{\boldsymbol{v}}_j$

Fig. 3. Shortest paths between the mesh centroid and an endpoint on the skeleton

- c and $\tilde{c}$ are the centroids of $\mathbb{M}$ and $\widetilde{\mathbb{M}}$, respectively
- $dist(\cdot, \cdot)$ denotes the Dijkstra's shortest path distance.

Thus, the dissimilarity between two skeletal Reeb graphs may be defined as:

$$\mathcal{D}(G, \widetilde{G}) = \sum_{i=1}^{n_1} \sum_{j=1}^{n_2} \Phi(\boldsymbol{v}_i, \tilde{\boldsymbol{v}}_j). \tag{7}$$

The main algorithmic steps of the proposed graph matching approach are described in more details in Algorithm 3.

Algorithm 3. Proposed graph matching approach

Given two 3D objects $\mathbb{M}$ and $\widetilde{\mathbb{M}}$

1: Generate the skeletal Reeb graphs G and $\widetilde{G}$ of $\mathbb{M}$ and $\widetilde{\mathbb{M}}$, respectively
2: Apply graph pruning to remove non-salient nodes
3: Find the skeleton endpoints sets $E = (\boldsymbol{v}_i)_{i=1,..,n_1}$ and $\widetilde{E} = (\tilde{\boldsymbol{v}}_j)_{j=1,..,n_2}$ of G and $\widetilde{G}$, respectively
4: **for** all endpoints $(\boldsymbol{v}_i)$ and $(\tilde{\boldsymbol{v}}_j)$ **do**
5:    Compute the relative node areas a_i and $\tilde{a}_j$ of $\boldsymbol{v}_i$ and $\tilde{\boldsymbol{v}}_j$, respectively
6:    Compute the relative node paths $d\boldsymbol{v}_i$ and $d\tilde{\boldsymbol{v}}_j$
7:    Compute the relative centroid paths $d\boldsymbol{c}_i$ and $d\tilde{\boldsymbol{c}}_j$
8: **end for**
9: Apply Algorithm 2 to find the correspondence between G and $\widetilde{G}$
10: Compute the dissimilarity $\mathcal{D}(G, \widetilde{G})$ given by Eq. (7).

---

5   Experimental Results

We tested the performance of the proposed retrieval algorithm using the McGill Shape Benchmark [14]. This publicly available benchmark database provides a

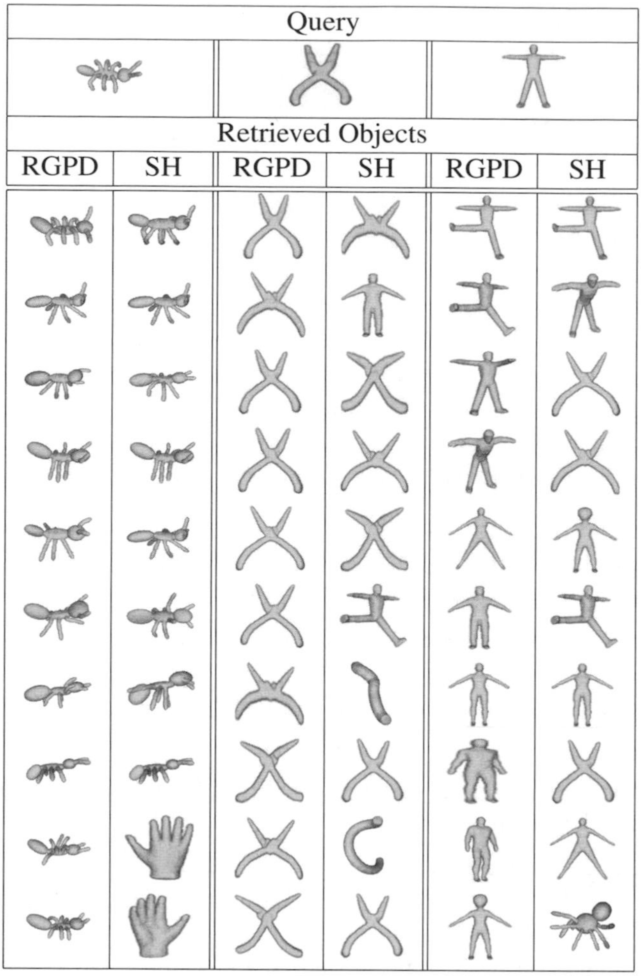

Fig. 4. Retrieval results using the McGill Shape Benchmark. The query shapes are shown in the second row. The top ten retrieved objects (top-to-bottom) using spherical harmonics (SH) and our proposed Reeb graph path dissimilarity (RGPD) are shown in rows 5 to 14.

3D shape repository, which includes a considerable number of articulated objects. The database objects are represented by voxel grids as well as by triangle meshes. In all the experimental results, we used a data-dependent mixture distance parameter λ given by:

$$\lambda = \max(\|\boldsymbol{p}_i\|^2 / (\|\boldsymbol{p}_i\|^2 + \|\boldsymbol{p}_i\|_A^2)).$$

In other words, the value of λ is computed automatically from all the vertices of the 3D shape. Also, The resolution parameter R was set to $R = 22$.

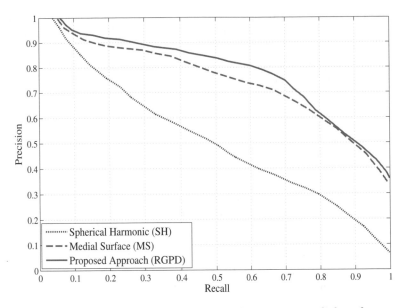

Fig. 5. Precision vs. Recall curves for spherical harmonics, medial surfaces and proposed approach using the McGill Shape Benchmark [14]

We compared our approach with spherical harmonics (SH) [9] and medial surfaces (MS) [5]. The results show that our method achieve better retrieval results than the spherical harmonic approach as shown in Fig. 4, where the top ten retrieved 3D objects are displayed (top-to-bottom). As can be seen in Fig. 4, the proposed approach returns correct results whereas the spherical harmonics method yields poor retrieval results (columns 2, 4, and 6).

To carry out comparison experiments on the entire benchmark of articulated 3D objects, we evaluated the retrieval performance of the proposed approach using the standard information retrieval evaluation measure of precision *versus* recall curve. A precision-recall curve that is shifted upwards and to the right indicates superior performance. It is evident from Fig. 5 that our method significantly outperforms spherical harmonics and medial surfaces.

The complexity of the proposed skeletonization algorithm can be determined as follows. Computing the centroid and the normalized mixture distance function for a 3D triangle mesh with m vertices takes $\mathcal{O}(m)$ time. Constructing the nodes and edges of the skeletal graph requires calculating the connected component of triangles and hence also takes $\mathcal{O}(m)$ time. The overall complexity is, therefore, $\mathcal{O}(m)$, which shows an improvement over geodesic function based Reeb graphs with complexity $\mathcal{O}(m \log m)$ [3].

6   Conclusions

In this paper, we introduced a normalized mixture distance function-based approach to topological modeling of 3D objects in the Morse-theoretic framework.

The proposed algorithm preserves well the topology of 3D shapes, and it is robust, accurate, and has a low computational complexity. The experimental results on McGill articulated shape benchmark database indicate the feasibility of the proposed approach and a much better performance compared to spherical harmonics and medial surfaces.

References

1. Fomenko, A.T., Kunii, T.L.: Topological modeling for visualization. Springer, Tokyo (1997)
2. Siddiqi, K., Shokoufandeh, A., Dickinson, S.J., Zucker, S.W.: Shock graphs and shape matching. Int. Jour. Computer Vision 35(1), 13–32 (1999)
3. Hilaga, H., Shinagawa, Y., Kohmura, T., Kunii, T.L.: Topology matching for fully automatic similarity estimation of 3D shapes. In: SIGGRAPH, pp. 203–212 (2001)
4. Shinagawa, Y., Kunii, T.L., Kergosien, Y.L.: Surface coding based on Morse theory. IEEE Computer Graphics and Applications 11(5), 66–78 (1991)
5. Siddiqi, K., Zhang, J., Macrini, D., Shokoufandeh, A., Bouix, S., Dickinson, S.: Retrieving articulated 3-D models using medial surfaces. Machine Vision and Applications 19(4), 261–275 (2008)
6. Ankerst, M., Kastenmüller, G., Kriegel, H., Seidl, T.: 3D shape histograms for similarity search and classification in spatial databases. In: Güting, R.H., Papadias, D., Lochovsky, F.H. (eds.) SSD 1999. LNCS, vol. 1651, pp. 207–226. Springer, Heidelberg (1999)
7. Osada, R., Funkhouser, T., Chazelle, B., Dobkin, D.: Shape distributions. ACM Trans. Graphics 21(4), 807–832 (2002)
8. Ben Hamza, A., Krim, H.: Geodesic matching of triangulated surfaces. IEEE Trans. Image Processing 15(8), 2249–2258 (2006)
9. Kazhdan, M., Funkhouser, T., Rusinkiewicz, S.: Rotation invariant spherical harmonic representation of 3D shape descriptors. In: Proc. ACM Sympo. Geometry Processing, pp. 156–164 (2003)
10. Milnor, J.: Morse theory. Princeton University Press, New Jersey (1963)
11. Nielson, G.M., Foley, T.A.: A survey of applications of an affine invariant norm. Mathematical Methods in Computer Aided Geometric Design, pp. 445–467. Academic Press, Boston (1989)
12. Bai, X., Latecki, L.J.: Path similarity skeleton graph matching. IEEE Trans. Pattern Analysis and Machine Intelligence 30(7), 1282–1292 (2008)
13. Bai, X., Latecki, L.J., Liu, W.Y.: Skeleton pruning by contour partitioning with discrete curve evolution. IEEE Trans. Pattern Analysis and Machine Intelligence 29(3), 449–462 (2007)
14. http://www.cim.McGill.ca/shape/benchmark

Finding Optimal Parameter Configuration for a Dynamic Triangle Mesh Compressor

Oldřich Petřík and Libor Váša

University of West Bohemia, Univerzitní 22, Plzeň, CZ 30614, Czech Republic
opetrik@kiv.zcu.cz, lvasa@kiv.zcu.cz

Abstract. This paper proposes a method of rate-distortion optimisation of an algorithm for compressing dynamic 3D triangle meshes. Although many articles regarding compression methods for this kind of data have been published in the last decade, the problem of rate-distortion optimisation has only been addressed by a very few of them. An exhaustive search method, where a grid of parameter configurations is used in the compressor and only the configurations producing good results are selected, is still widely used even though it requires a number of tries exponential to the number of parameters. Our proposed method can find better solutions (i.e. closer to an optimum) in expected linear to quadratic time.

Keywords: Rate-Distortion Optimisation; Dynamic Mesh; Compression; Principle of Equal Slopes.

1 Introduction

3D graphics has gained much popularity in the recent decades and became a crucial part of many disciplines such as medicine, entertainment or advertising. With the increasing precision of 3D data acquisition and growing hardware capabilities, the complexity of the datasets and, consequently, the amount of information stored are growing fast. Thus, efficient compression techniques are required to store the sets in a reasonable storage space, transmit them over a network or broadcast them in a 3DTV system.

In this article, we will be dealing with compression of a dynamic 3D triangle meshes sharing the same topology. These can be viewed as animations consisting of frames with each frame being a triangle mesh. All the frame meshes in an animation have the same number of vertices and contain edges between the same vertices.

There are many algorithms for compressing such data. Most of them started out with a small number of compression parameters. Though, as the algorithms evolve to offer higher compression ratios, the number of parameters usually grows along to allow better adaptation to different input and output conditions. Finding the optimal parameter configuration for a certain case using brute-force search may then become very difficult or almost impossible, as the number of tries needed increases exponentially with the number of parameters. Moreover,

F.J. Perales and R.B. Fisher (Eds.): AMDO 2010, LNCS 6169, pp. 31–42, 2010.

brute-force approaches strongly trade off accuracy for computation time resulting in considerably inaccurate parameter configurations. We will show a solution, which can find near-optimal configuration in expected linear to quadratic time with respect to the number of input parameters.

This article is organised as follows. First, an overview of published works related to this topic will be given in section 2. A brief description of the compression algorithm we have been using in the optimisation process will follow in section 3. Next, we will describe our proposed method of rate-distortion optimisation of dynamic mesh compression in section 4 and show some results of the proposed method in 5. A conclusion will be drawn in 6 and some possibilities for future work will be suggested in 7.

1.1   Used Notation

F .... number of frames in the mesh animation
V .... number of vertices in each mesh of the animation
N .... truncated basis size
$\bar{\xi}$ .... decoded value of ξ
$\mathrm{pred}(\xi)$ ...... prediction of ξ
n .... number of input parameters of the compression algorithm
P .... set of input parameters, p_i is the i-th parameter
r .... bitrate, in the dynamic mesh case in bits per frame and vertex
d .... distortion of the compressed version from the original
H .... rate-distortion curve, $h = (r, d)$ is a point on this curve
O .... rate-distortion curve containing the optimal values
C .... compression projection from the space of parameter configurations to the rate-distortion space.

2   Related Work

The area of dynamic mesh compression has been thoroughly explored in the last decade and many compression techniques have been proposed. Some of them are mentioned below. First approach was published by Lengyel [1] and used a clustering of the animated mesh with movement of each cluster described by a single transformation matrix. Alexa and Müller [2] proposed using Principal Component Analysis to represent each frame as a combination of eigenframes. Mamou et al. [3] have proposed another approach called Frame-based Animated Mesh Coding (FAMC), which has been included in the second amendment to MPEG4 part 16 [4] as the MPEG standard for dynamic mesh compression. Váša and Skala [5] have published their Coddyac algorithm based on Rossignac's EdgeBreaker [6] and PCA in the space of trajectories.

So far, only a few papers have addressed the problem of rate-distortion optimisation in dynamic mesh compression. Payan and Antonini have proposed a bit allocation method for their wavelet-based compression algorithm in [7]. They are determining the optimal quantisation for different wavelet levels to minimise the distortion. Their work was extended to spatio-temporal wavelet coding in [8]. The same method was also used in [9] to optimise the FAMC algorithm [3,4]. Unfortunately, this approach is not applicable generally as there is no dependency between the coefficients in different wavelet levels and the problem is thus very simplified. It also exploits statistical properties of the wavelet coefficients, which makes this approach further unusable for our case.

Müller et al. [10] proposed a rate-distortion optimised version of their octree-based D3DMC algorithm [11]. In their approach, the octree is first subdivided to a given maximum level and the neighbouring cells are then merged back together, if the error introduced by the merge stays below a specified threshold. Moreover, each cell is encoded using the best fitting one of three possible methods. Again, this is an algorithm-specific brute-force approach that cannot be generalised to other compression methods.

3   Compression Algorithm

Although we would like to develop a general rate-distortion optimisation method for dynamic mesh compression algorithms, our initial goal is an optimiser for the *Coddyac* algorithm [5], as it is the only one, for which we have the complete implementation at the moment. We will now describe this approach in more detail.

The algorithm is based on representing dynamic meshes as a set of vertex trajectories of individual vertices. Trajectory of the i-th vertex is described by a vector T_i of length $3F$, consisting of XYZ coordinates of the given vertex in all the frames. Notice that for dense meshes, it is very likely that trajectory vectors of neighboring vertices will be similar. In other words, the trajectory vectors are not distributed evenly in the space of dimension $3F$, instead they are roughly located in a subspace of much lower dimension. This observation yields the first step of the Coddyac algorithm: finding the subspace and expressing the vertices in this subspace.

A straightforward way to find a subspace of a set of samples is using the PCA tool of linear algebra. The original animation is represented by a matrix B of size $3F \times V$, where the i-th column is the trajectory vector associated with the i-th vertex. First, an average trajectory vector A is computed and subtracted from each column of B, obtaining a matrix of samples S. Subsequently, the autocorrelation matrix $Q = S \cdot S^T$ of size $3F \times 3F$ is computed. Finally, the eigenvalue decomposition of the autocorrelation matrix Q gives a set of eigenvectors $E_i, i = 1 \ldots 3F$, and their corresponding eigenvalues. Of these eigenvectors, N most important ones are selected (according to their respective eigenvalues), N being a user-specified parameter. The selected eigenvectors form a basis of the subspace, and each trajectory vector can be expressed as:

$$T_i = A + \sum_{j=1}^{N} c_i^j E_j \qquad (1)$$

Since the basis is orthonormal it is possible to compute the matrix of combination coefficients c_i^j by matrix multiplication $C = S^T \cdot E$, where E is a matrix of size $3F \times N$ in which the i-th column is the i-th eigenvector E_i.

In order to transmit the mesh, the selected subset of eigenvectors (matrix E of size $3F \times N$) has to be transmitted along with the combination coefficients (matrix C of size $V \times N$) and the vector A representing the average trajectory. Details on how to efficiently encode the matrix of eigenvectors can be found in [12].

The other key observation of the Coddyac algorithm is that the PCA step can be interpreted as a simple change of basis, and therefore it should not have any influence on results of linear operators. This feature is employed for prediction of the values c_i^j at the decoder. In static mesh encoding, a very common prediction method is based on the parallelogram rule [13]. The idea is that the mesh is traversed progressively by growing an area of processed vertices by adding one adjacent triangle (with one adjacent vertex) at a time. The XYZ coordinates of the new vertex v_{new} are predicted to lie at the top of a projected parallelogram formed by the three known vertices v_{left}, v_{right} and v_{base} (see figure 1). The coordinate prediction is then defined as

$$pred(v_{new}^X) = \overline{v_{left}^X} + \overline{v_{right}^X} - \overline{v_{base}^X}$$
$$pred(v_{new}^Y) = \overline{v_{left}^Y} + \overline{v_{right}^Y} - \overline{v_{base}^Y} \tag{2}$$
$$pred(v_{new}^Z) = \overline{v_{left}^Z} + \overline{v_{right}^Z} - \overline{v_{base}^Z}$$

In dynamic mesh compression, these formulae may be applied on each element of the trajectory vectors. However, since the feature vectors are in fact linearly transformed trajectory vectors, it is possible to use the same formula also for the elements of feature vectors:

$$pred(c_{v_{new}}^j) = \overline{c_{v_{left}}^j} + \overline{c_{v_{right}}^j} - \overline{c_{v_{base}}^j} \, , \; j = 1 \ldots N \tag{3}$$

The Coddyac algorithm traverses the mesh, adding one triangle at the time, performs the prediction according to equation (3) and transmits the prediction residuals.

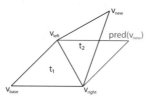

Fig. 1. Prediction of vertex v_{new} from the parallelogram created from vertices v_{left}, v_{right} and v_{base}

4   Proposed Approach

In the Coddyac compression algorithm (as well as in many others) the compression is divided to several stages, each with one or more input parameters. Here, we can simplify the compression algorithm into three basic stages. The first stage calculates and trims the PCA basis. This is controlled by one parameter – the number of the basis vectors N. During the second stage, the basis is encoded (and then decoded), which has an input parameter of the number of bits the basis vectors are quantised to. In the third stage, the feature vectors are calculated using the decoded basis, parallelogram prediction is performed and the prediction residual values are quantised to a certain number of bits, which is a third parameter.

Each one of the stages is controlled by at least one input parameter and, in most cases, *depends on the result of the previous stages*. If we, for example, decrease the number of basis vectors, the length of the residual vectors will decrease accordingly. In other words, a change of an input parameter not only influences the related compression stage, but also the subsequent ones. That is different e.g. from the wavelet coefficients quantisation where a complete wavelet transform is performed and the resulting values are then *independently* quantised. Our approach has proven so far to handle both dependent as well as independent parameters.

4.1   Principle of Equal Slopes

This is a common rate-distortion optimisation technique. If we run a (lossy) compressor on a given data with a fixed set P of n input parameters $P = p_1 \ldots p_n$, it will produce compressed data of a certain size with a certain error compared to the original data. These two values – size (bitrate, r) and error (distortion, d) – can be plotted on a rate-distortion (RD) chart H (figure 3). For a single input dataset, different parameter configurations will produce different points $h = (r, d)$ in this chart. In other words, the compression can be seen as a projection $C; C(P) \rightarrow H$. Assuming the parameters are continuous, there is an infinite number of such points. However, a lower bound can be found for each bitrate forming an envelope curve O of the chart:

$$O = \{o = (r_o, d_o) : \forall x = (r_o, d) \in H, d \geq d_o\} \tag{4}$$

This curve contains the parameter configurations that result in the lowest distortion for a given bitrate, which is exactly what we are looking for.

Now, let us choose an *optimal* configuration $P^j; C(P^j) \in O$ and change the value of a single parameter p_i while keeping the other parameters fixed. We will obtain an RD curve H_i^j. This way, we can construct curves for all the parameters. We will now exploit the fact that all these curves, as well as the envelope curve, are decreasing and convex.[1] As these curves are subsets of H, they lie above O – except for a single point, where they touch O and also one another. This point is the result point $C(P^j)$. Should any two of the curves *intersect* in that point, they would also intersect O meaning that a part of each of them would lie below O contradicting its definition, thus the configuration cannot be optimal.

---

[1] Rare exceptions can be found, e.g. for compression methods switching between several different algorithms during the compression.

The idea can be explained better using *slopes*. For each point h_i^j of a curve H_i^j we can calculate the slope value s_i^j of a tangent of the curve in that point. Two curves with a common point either have different slope values at that point (they are intersecting), or they have equal slopes in the common point (they are touching each other). We have already defined that in an optimal configuration all the curves are touching one another, and a configuration, in which the curves are intersecting, is not optimal. Hence we can say that *a parameter configuration P^j is optimal if and only if the slopes s_i^j of all rate-distortion curves H_i^j in the result point $C(P^j)$ are equal.* An example of such situation is shown in figure 2.

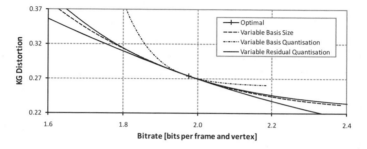

Fig. 2. RD curves of all three parameters of the compressor touching the optimal envelope in a single point

4.2   Iterative Rate-Distortion Optimisation

Based on the Principle of Equal Slopes, we can iteratively refine a parameter configuration until it gets close enough to an optimum.

In each iteration, the pair of r and d is evaluated in the current configuration, and two additional pairs of values for each parameter p_i: $r_i^{\text{left}}, d_i^{\text{left}}$ a small step to the left and $r_i^{\text{right}}, d_i^{\text{right}}$ to the right. From these values, we can calculate left and right slope $s_i^{\text{left}}, s_i^{\text{right}}$ and a relative change of slope (ds_i), bitrate (dr_i) and distortion (dd_i). These relative differences locally describe the behaviour of slope, bitrate and distortion in relation to a change in the parameter p_i. We can summarise it in this set of equations:

$$
\begin{aligned}
(r,d) &= C(p_1, \ldots, p_n) \\
(r_i^{\text{left}}, d_i^{\text{left}}) &= C(p_1, \ldots, p_i - \Delta p_i, \ldots, p_n) \\
(r_i^{\text{right}}, d_i^{\text{right}}) &= C(p_1, \ldots, p_i + \Delta p_i, \ldots, p_n)
\end{aligned}
\tag{5}
$$

$$
s_i^{\text{left}} \approx \frac{r - r_i^{\text{left}}}{d - d_i^{\text{left}}} \qquad s_i^{\text{right}} \approx \frac{r_i^{\text{right}} - r}{d_i^{\text{right}} - d}
\tag{6}
$$

$$
ds_i \approx \frac{s_i^{\text{right}} - s_i^{\text{left}}}{\Delta p_i} \qquad dr_i \approx \frac{r_i^{\text{right}} - r_i^{\text{left}}}{2\Delta p_i} \qquad dd_i \approx \frac{d_i^{\text{right}} - d_i^{\text{left}}}{2\Delta p_i}
\tag{7}
$$

Finally, a new configuration can be determined using these values. This configuration is then used as an input of the next iteration and so on, until a stop-condition is met. We have experimented with two different methods of determining the next configuration:

- **Changing All Parameters at Once**
  It is based on an idea that if we increase the value of a parameter by a certain amount and decrease the value of another one appropriately, we can keep the bitrate or the distortion value constant. The amounts of change can be approximately calculated using a system of linear equations. This method can be very fast, as it optimises all the parameters in each step, but does not adapt very well to curve changes. When one of the parameters is changed, the curves of the other parameters may also change, especially if there are dependencies between them and the changed parameter. This method calculates the next configuration from the knowledge of the local curve behaviour in all the parameters, i.e. expects the curves to stay invariant. That can lead to actually less optimal configurations and, subsequently, divergence, if the curves change too much.

- **Optimising One Parameter at a Time**
  This method yields a better, but also slower, solution. A parameter p_k with the most deviating slope is selected and its next value is determined using a linear function of the relative differences ds_k, dr_k or dd_k to match a target slope, bitrate or distortion depending on the current optimisation criterion. By changing only one parameter, we can reach more stable progress with a very high probability of convergence. Thus, this method has been selected to be used in our algorithm.

  To perform one step in each of the n parameters, n iterations are needed here, hence the expected complexity of the optimisation might be seen as $O(\alpha n)$, where α is a constant depending on the required precision and the starting configuration. In the case, where a change of one parameter causes changing of the curves of the other ones, experiments show that α is not constant anymore, but depends linearly on n making the complexity quadratic.

4.3   Optimisation Criteria

The optimisation process needs to be constrained to get a concrete result. Therefore, a certain criterion needs to be applied. This criterion also determines the stop-condition for the iterative configuration refinement. There are four criteria we have considered and implemented:

- **Fixed Slope**
  This criterion allows us to specify a target slope value s^* the final slopes should be equal to. The value of the most deviating parameter p_i in the j-th iteration is calculated using the following formula:

$$p_i^j = p_i^{j-1} + \frac{s^* - s_i^j}{ds_i^j} \tag{8}$$

The optimisation ends when the maximum of the distances between the specified slope and each parameter slope falls under a specified maximum deviation. This method is not very useful most times, since we usually do not know the magnitude of the bitrate and the distortion, and thus we cannot exactly determine the desired slope.

- **Fixed Bitrate**
  With this criterion applied, the algorithm tries to find an optimal configuration which results in the specified bitrate. It can be quite effectively used if we want to compare the compression algorithm with another one for which we know exact RD values. In this case, the calculation of the next value is more complex, as we need to reach the specified bitrate together with slope equality. Two potential parameter values are calculated:

$$\text{bitrate} : p_i^j = p_i^{j-1} + \frac{r^* - r^j}{dr_i^j} \tag{9}$$

$$\text{slopes} : p_i^j = p_i^{j-1} + \frac{s_{\text{avg}(i)}^j - s_i^j}{ds_i} \tag{10}$$

where r^* is the target bitrate and $s_{\text{avg}(i)}^j$ is the average slope not including the slope of parameter p_i. The final parameter value for the next iteration is then determined as a weighted average of these two values. If the current bitrate is close to the target bitrate, more weight is given on the slope prediction and vice versa.

  The stop-condition also depends on both bitrate and slope differences. The process is stopped when the overall deviation e^j gets smaller than a specified maximum deviation. The deviation e^j is evaluated using the maximum slope distance e_s^j (as in the fixed slope case) and the absolute deviation from the target bitrate e_r^j:

$$e^j = \sqrt{\left(e_s^j\right)^2 + \left(e_r^j\right)^2} \tag{11}$$

$$e_s^j = \max_{i=1...n} \left[\left(\frac{1}{n}\sum_{k=1}^n s_k^j\right) - s_i\right] \qquad e_r^j = r^* - r^j \tag{12}$$

- **Fixed Distortion**
  The idea here is the same as in the previous case, only the output configuration is bound to have a given distortion instead of bitrate, so the next value calculation and the stop-condition contain the deviation of the current distortion from the target distortion.

- **Fixed Parameter**
  This criterion drives the optimisation with respect to a given value of a specified parameter. It is a very useful method for constructing RD (envelope) curves, since we usually know the possible value range of the parameters, while we might not know the resulting bitrates, distortions and slopes. In

each iteration, the slope of the fixed parameter is evaluated and the rest of
the parameters is then optimised the same way as in the fixed slope case with
the target slope being the current evaluated slope of the fixed parameter.

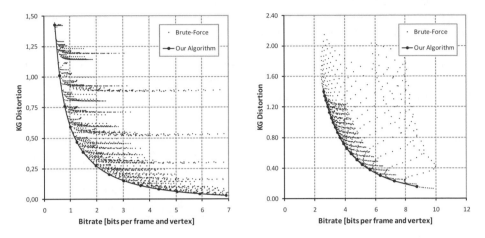

Fig. 3. The results of our method compared to the configurations evaluated during the
brute-force search on the Cow animation (left: Coddyac, right: D3DMC)

5   Experimental Results

Key input of the algorithm is the degree of suboptimality we allow in the resulting parameter configuration. This value is specified by the maximum deviation
parameter used in the stop-conditions of the optimisation criteria. The smaller
allowed deviation we set, the closer the configuration will be to an optimum, but
the more iterations the algorithm is likely to perform to reach such precision.

So far, we have not defined, what metric is used to measure the distortion of
the compressed animation. Generally, the algorithm can work with any distortion
metric, as long as it produces convex RD curves, which is the case of all the
commonly used methods. For the following results, we have used the Karni–
Gotsman (KG) distortion measure [14], which has been used by most authors in
the dynamic mesh compression.

We compared our algorithm to the commonly used brute-force approach on
many different mesh animations with very similar results. In the following part,
we show the results of finding the optimal envelope curve on the Cow animation
using Coddyac and D3DMC compression algorithms. For Coddyac, the fixed
parameter criterion was used in our method with 15 different numbers of basis
vectors. The same 15 values were set in the brute-force search together with
15 basis quantisation and 20 residual quantisation settings producing a total of
4500 configurations. With D3DMC, the optimiser was run the same way with
19 octree split threshold values, and 51 motion quantisation settings for the
brute-force search (969 configurations in total).

The resulting rate-distortion charts are shown in figure 3 and the results are summarised in table 1. For the Coddyac compressor with three input parameters, the proposed algorithm is significantly faster than the exhaustive search, while for D3DMC with only two parameters, the performance is roughly equal. This shows a decrease in complexity related to the number of parameters compared to the brute-force approach. With more than three optimised parameters, our method would probably be even more efficient. Note that most configurations evaluated during the brute-force search produce higher than optimal bitrates resulting in longer encoding times. Thus, the run-time difference between the algorithms is greater than the difference in the number of compressor runs.

Table 1. Construction of a curve of (nearly) optimal configurations for the Cow animation using 15 different numbers of basis vectors for Coddyac and 19 different split thresholds for D3DMC

	Coddyac		D3DMC	
	compressor runs	run time	compressor runs	run time
brute-force	4500	36:06:35.4	969	9:44:33.5
our method	612	1:19:03.7	859	8:02:42.6
speedup	**7.4**	**27.4**	**1.1**	**1.2**

6   Conclusion

We have proposed a rate-distortion optimisation method for a dynamic 3D triangle mesh compressor based on the Principle of Equal Slopes. Our main contribution is showing that using this principle, we can decrease the time needed to find the optimal configuration compared to the currently commonly used brute-force approach.

The key aspect of the algorithm will become apparent, if only a single configuration is needed. A single run of the optimiser is enough to find it, in contrast to the exhaustive search, where the same large number of configurations needs to be evaluated, no matter whether a single configuration or the whole curve is needed. Moreover, we show that even when constructing the optimal curve, our algorithm performs better, not only reaching shorter run times, but also finding more precise results. The search can also be constrained in four different ways, thus better fitting the current needs.

The implementation was carried out in the modular system MVE-2 which makes it possible to connect the optimiser to different compression modules and distortion evaluators in a straightforward way. Although we have developed the algorithm to be used with the Coddyac compression method, its nature should make it applicable to other methods as well with minimal additional effort. We have successfully run the algorithm with a D3DMC compression module.

7 Future Work

Currently, we are using a linear approximation of the slope values to calculate the parameter steps. We have recently found out that a rational function in the form of $f(x) = a \cdot b^x$ describes very well the dependency of slope on the related parameter value and thus could be used to improve the convergence probability and speed.

If run in a sequence, the current implementation has an option to use the previous result as the starting configuration. This option is useful when evaluating sequences of related configurations (e.g. with linear range of desired bitrates). We would like to further improve this idea by using a reduction approach, i.e. first evaluating configurations for only a few evenly distributed values in the sequence and then running the optimisation for the values in between while using an interpolation of the surrounding results as a starting configuration.

Acknowledgements

This work has been supported by the Ministry of Education, Youth and Sports of the Czech Republic under the research program LC-06008 (Center for Computer Graphics).

References

1. Lengyel, J.E.: Compression of time-dependent geometry. In: Proceedings of the 1999 symposium on Interactive 3D graphics, SI3D '99, pp. 89–95. ACM Press, New York (1999)
2. Alexa, M., Müller, W.: Representing animations by principal components. Computer Graphics Forum 19(3), 411–426 (2000)
3. Mamou, K., Zaharia, T., Preteux, F., Stefanoski, N., Ostermann, J.: Frame-based compression of animated meshes in MPEG-4. In: IEEE International Conference on Multimedia and Expo., ICME 2008, pp. 1121–1124 (June 2008)
4. International Organization for Standardization: ISO/IEC 14496 Part 16: Animation Framework eXtension (AFX), amendment 2: Frame-based Animated Mesh Compression (FAMC). International Organization for Standardization (2009)
5. Váša, L., Skala, V.: Coddyac: Connectivity driven dynamic mesh compression. In: 3DTV-CON, The True Vision - Capture, Transmission and Display of 3D Video, Kos, Greece. IEEE Computer Society Press, Los Alamitos (May 2007)
6. Rossignac, J.: EdgeBreaker: Connectivity compression for triangle meshes. IEEE Transactions on Visualization and Computer Graphics 5, 47–61 (1998)
7. Payan, F., Antonini, M.: An efficient bit allocation for compressing normal meshes with an error-driven quantization. Computer Aided Geometric Design 22(5), 466–486 (2005)
8. Kammoun, A., Payan, F., Antonini, M.: Bit allocation for spatio-temporal wavelet coding of animated semi-regular meshes. In: Huet, B., Smeaton, A., Mayer-Patel, K., Avrithis, Y. (eds.) MMM 2009. LNCS, vol. 5371, pp. 128–139. Springer, Heidelberg (2009)

9. Mamou, K., Zaharia, T., Preteux, F., Kamoun, A., Payan, F., Antonini, M.: Two optimizations of the MPEG-4 FAMC standard for enhanced compression of animated 3D meshes. In: 15th IEEE International Conference on Image Processing, ICIP 2008, pp. 1764–1767 (October 2008)
10. Müller, K., Smolic, A., Kautzner, M., Eisert, P., Wiegand, T.: Rate-distortion-optimized predictive compression of dynamic 3d mesh sequences. Signal Processing: Image Communication, Special Issue on Interactive representation of still and dynamic scenes 21(9), 812–828 (2006)
11. Müller, K., Smolic, A., Kautzner, M., Eisert, P., Wieg, T.: Predictive compression of dynamic 3d meshes. In: Proc. ICIP 2005, IEEE International Conference on Image Processing (2005)
12. Váša, L., Skala, V.: Cobra: Compression of the basis for the PCA represented animations. Computer Graphics Forum 28(6), 1529–1540 (2009)
13. Touma, C., Gotsman, C.: Triangle mesh compression. In: Graphics Interface, pp. 26–34 (June 1998)
14. Karni, Z., Gotsman, C.: Compression of soft-body animation sequences. Computers and Graphics 28, 25–34 (2004)

Silhouette Area Based Similarity Measure for Template Matching in Constant Time

Daniel Mohr and Gabriel Zachmann

Clausthal University
{dmoh,zach}@tu-clausthal.de

Abstract. In this paper, we present a novel, fast, resolution-independent silhouette area-based matching approach. We approximate the silhouette area by a small set of axis-aligned rectangles. This yields a very memory efficient representation of templates. In addition, utilizing the integral image, we can thus compare a silhouette with an input image at an arbitrary position in constant time.

Furthermore, we present a new method to build a template hierarchy optimized for our rectangular representation of template silhouettes. With the template hierarchy, the complexity of our matching method for n templates is $O(\log n)$. For example, we can match a hierarchy consisting of 1000 templates in $1.5ms$. Overall, our contribution constitutes an important piece in the initialization stage of any tracker of (articulated) objects.

Keywords: Pose estimation, tracking, template matching, rectangle packing problem.

1 Introduction

Most template-based object tracking systems compare a segmented input image with a set of templates at numerous positions in the input image, especially at initialization. The main focus of this paper is to present a novel, very fast algorithm for this stage of a complete tracking system. In a complete tracking system, this initial match would then be used by the next stage to estimate position, orientation and pose.

Usually, when a model of an articulated object is available, there is a large number of templates that must be compared with the input image. Since the template matching stage does very little besides the comparisons, it is crucial that each comparison can be performed extremely fast.

In this paper, we propose a novel method for very fast approximate area silhouette comparison between model templates and the segmented input image. For one template comparison, Stenger el al. [1] achieved a computation time proportional to the contour length of the template silhouette. We propose a new method, which reduces the computation time to be *constant* in the contour length and image resolution. To achieve this, we first approximate all template silhouettes by axis-aligned rectangles, which is done in a preprocessing step. In

F.J. Perales and R.B. Fisher (Eds.): AMDO 2010, LNCS 6169, pp. 43–54, 2010.

the online phase, we compute the integral image [2,3] of the segmented image. With this, the joint probability of a rectangle to match to an image region can be computed by four lookups in the integral image. Moreover, we present an algorithm to build a template hierarchy that can compare a large set of templates in sublinear time. The *main contributions* are:

An algorithm that approximates arbitrary shapes by a minimal set of axis-aligned rectangles. This results in a resolution-independent, very memory efficient silhouette area representation.

An algorithm to compare an object silhouette in $O(1)$. In contrast the algorithm proposed by [1] needs $O(\text{contour length})$.

We propose an algorithm to cluster templates hierarchically guided by their mutually overlapping areas. Our method builds on the recently developed batch neural gas clustering algorithm, which yields better results than more classical algorithms. This hierarchy further reduces the matching complexity for n templates from $O(n)$ to $O(\log n)$.

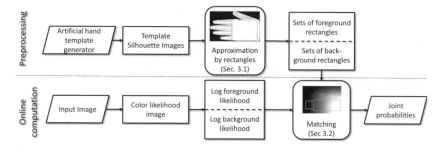

Fig. 1. Overview of our approach using rectangle sets to approximate a silhouette. This speeds up the matching by a factor 5–30 compared to the approach proposed by Stenger et al. [1].

Our approach only requires that binary silhouettes of the model in an arbitrary pose can be generated and that the input image can be segmented. The segmentation result does not necessarily need to be binarized. The approach can handle scalar segmentations as well.

It should be obvious that our proposed methods are suitable for any kind of template based matching of silhouettes. For sake of clarity, though, we will describe our novel methods in the following by the example of the human hand, since human hand tracking is our long-term target application. This includes the full 26 DOFs of the hand, not only a few poses or only the 2D position. To achieve this challenging task, we mainly use two different features for matching: edge gradients and skin color. In this paper, we focus on the skin color feature. We use a skin segmentation algorithm that computes for each image pixel the probability to represent skin or background, resp. We generate our templates by an artificial 3D hand model. This model can be rendered in any desired state, and it can be easily projected onto 2D and binarized to get the hand silhouette. Given an input image, the goal then is to find the best matching hand silhouette.

We use the joint probability as proposed by Stenger et al. [1] to compare the silhouettes with the segmentation result. A simple area overlap, of course, could be used, too. The only difference is that the sum instead of the product of probabilities would have be computed. For details, see Sec. 3.

2   Related Work

A lot of object tracking approaches based on silhouette comparison have been proposed. The approaches can be divided into two classes. The first class needs a binary silhouette of both, the model and the query image. The second class compare binary model silhouette area with the likelihood map of the query image.

A simple method belonging to the first class is used in [4,5]. The difference between the model silhouette and segmented foreground area in the query image is computed. The exponential of the negative squared difference is used as silhouette matching probability. A slightly different measure is used by Kato et al. [6]. First, they define the model silhouette area A_M, the segmented area A_I and the intersecting area $A_O = A_I \cap A_M$. The differences $A_I - A_O$, $A_M - A_O$ and $A_I - A_M$ are integrated in the same way, as described above, into the overall measure. In [7], the non-overlapping area of the model and the segmented silhouettes are integrated into classical optimization methods, e.g. Levenberg-Marquardt or downhill simplex. Nirei et al. [8] first compute the distance transform of both the input and model silhouette. Regarding the distance transformed images as vectors, they compute the normalized scalar product of these vectors. Additionally, the model is divided into meaningful parts. Next, for each part, the area overlap between the part and the segmented input image is computed. Then, a weighted sum of the quotient between this overlap and the area of the corresponding model part is computed. The final similarity is the sum of the scalar product and the weighted sum. In [9,10] a compact description of the hand model is generated. Vectors from the gravity center to sample points on the silhouette boundary, normalized by the square root of the silhouette area, are used as hand representation. During tracking, the same transformations are performed to the binary input image and the vector is compared to the database. A completely different approach is proposed by Zhou and Huang [11]. Although they extract the silhouette from the input image, they use only local features extracted from the silhouette boundary. Their features are inspired by the SIFT descriptor [12]. Each silhouette is described by a set of feature points. The chamfer distance between the feature points is used as similarity measure.

All the aforementioned approaches have the same drawback: to ensure that the algorithms work, a binary segmentation of the input image of high quality is necessary. The thresholds, needed for the binarization, are often not easy to determine.

To our knowledge, there are much less approaches working directly on the color likelihood map of a segmentation. In [13] the skin-color likelihood is used.

For further matching, new features, called likelihood edges, are generated by applying an edge operator to the likelihood ratio image. But, in many cases, this leads to a very noisy edge image. In [1,14,15], the skin-color likelihood map is directly compared with hand silhouettes. The product of all skin probabilities at the silhouette foreground is multiplied with the product of all background probabilities in the template background. Stenger et al. [14] proposed a method for the efficient computation of this joint probability. The row-wise prefix sum in the log-likelihood image is computed. The original product along all pixels in a row reduces to three lookups in the prefix sum. Thus, the complexity to compute the joint probability is linear in the number of pixels along the template border.

Nevertheless, the above mentioned approach has some disadvantages. First of all, the template representation is resolution dependent. Typically, the distance of the object from the camera is not constant, and thus different sizes of the templates need to be considered. Consequently, for each scale, an extra set of the templates has to be kept in memory. Also, the higher the resolution of the images, the higher is the matching cost.

Our approach does not have all these disadvantages.

3   Silhouette Representation

The key issue of our fast matching approach is the representation of the template silhouettes. Figure 1 shows an overview of our approach.

To avoid the issues mentioned in the previous section, we propose a novel *resolution-independent representation* of template silhouettes. With such a representation, one can perform silhouette matching at arbitrary resolutions in constant time with respect to the template size. We propose to approximate a silhouette by a set of axis-aligned mutually disjoint rectangles. In the remainder of this paper, we denote the integral image of a gray scale image I by II:

$$II(x, y) = \sum_{\substack{0 \leq i \leq x \\ 0 \leq j \leq y}} I(i, j) \tag{1}$$

Let R be an axis-aligned rectangle with upper left corner $\mathbf{u}$ and lower right corner $\mathbf{v}$, both inside I. The sum of the area R of all pixels in I is given by

$$\sum_{R} I(i, j) = II(\mathbf{v}_x, \mathbf{v}_y) + II(\mathbf{u}_x - 1, \mathbf{u}_y - 1) - II(\mathbf{v}_x, \mathbf{u}_y - 1) - I(\mathbf{u}_x - 1, \mathbf{v}_y) \tag{2}$$

Let T_S with $T_S(x, y) \in \{0, 1\}$ be a binary image representing a template T. Let S and $\bar{S}$ denote the set of foreground and background pixels in T_S, resp. We compute a set of n mutually non-overlapping rectangles $\mathcal{R} = \{R_i\}_{i=1\cdots n}$ that cover S. The number of rectangles n depends on the silhouette shape and thus varies slightly from silhouette to silhouette. Figure 2 shows some example silhouettes with their approximating rectangles.

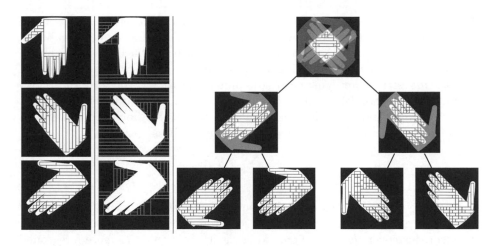

Fig. 2. Example silhouettes approximated by a set of rectangles (at 32×32 squares). The *left* column shows rectangles approximating the foreground, the *middle* one the rectangles approximating the background. The *right* one shows the template hierarchy generated by our approach in Sec. 3.3. For the sake of clarity, only the rectangles approximating the foreground are shown.

3.1   Rectangle Covering Computation

In the following, we denote a set of rectangles approximating S with $\mathcal{R}_S$. To obtain a good approximation, one has to minimize the non-overlapping area A of S and $\mathcal{R}_S$,

$$A = \min_{\mathcal{R}_S} \left| (S \cup \bigcup_{R_i \in \mathcal{R}_S} R_i) \setminus (S \cap \bigcup_{R_i \in \mathcal{R}_S} R_i) \right| \tag{3}$$

Obviously, there is a trade-off between A and $\mathcal{R}_S$. The smaller the number of rectangles, the faster the matching is, but also the more inaccurate.

A lot of work solving similar problems exists. One has to differentiate between rectangle covering [16,17,18] and partitioning [19,20] problems. Covering allows an arbitrary overlap between the rectangles in $\mathcal{R}_S$, partitioning does not. Most covering and partitioning algorithms compute solutions under the constraint that the rectangles lie completely inside the polygon to be covered. Our problem is similar to standard partitioning in that we do not allow overlaps between the rectangles $\mathcal{R}_S$, but it differs from partitioning because we do not need rectangles to lie completely in the silhouette S. In fact, we even encourage a solution where some rectangles lie slightly outside. The reason is that S never perfectly matches the observed real hand. Therefore, we can allow $A > 0$, which usually leads to solutions with much smaller numbers of rectangles $\mathcal{R}_S$. In the following, we present a simple algorithm to obtain a solution with $A < \delta$, where δ is application-dependent.

First, the model (here, the human hand) is rendered at a given state and rasterized at a high resolution. We obtain the resulting template T and, after thresholding, the binary image T_S. For simplification, we normalize the image dimensions to be in $[0,1]$. Next, we subdivide the image into $r \times s$ uniform boxes. The rectangles to cover S are oriented at the raster defined by these boxes. Basically, we compute the covering of an $r \times s$ image, which we denote by S_{rs}.

In the first step of our dynamic programming approach, we perform the following initialization: we define a benefit value $g_i = g(R_i)$ for each feasible rectangle R_i in S_{rs}, which indicates the benefit of a rectangle when included in the final set of covering rectangles $\mathcal{R}_S$. This value is computed as:

$$g(R_i) = -\theta + \sum_{(x,y) \in R_i} (T_S(x,y) - \tau) \tag{4}$$

The parameter $\tau \in [0,1]$ controls the penalty for covering a background box by a rectangle and the gain for covering a foreground box. For a value close to 0, the algorithm covers more background boxes in order to cover more foreground boxes as well. If τ is close to 1, the rectangles tend to cover no background rectangles and, thus, are nearly completely inside the silhouette. For now, we assume that $\tau = 0.5$. In Sections 3.2 and 3.3 we will need other values for τ.

The parameter θ adds a penalty to each rectangle R_i in the covering set $\mathcal{R}$. The parameter controls the aforementioned trade-off between the covering error A and the number of rectangles in $\mathcal{R}$. Because θ is a local control parameter, we cannot directly control the global error A. Instead, we set θ to an initial value, compute the covering, evaluate the error A and, if it is to high, we decrease θ and run the algorithm again.

We compute the optimal covering as follows. Let $\mathcal{R}^*$ denote the optimal covering for silhouette S. Let $R_{\mathbf{v}}^{\mathbf{u}} = R_{v_x,v_y}^{u_x,u_y}$ denote a rectangle with upper left corner $\mathbf{u}$ and lower right corner $\mathbf{v}$. Assume $R_{\mathbf{v}}^{\mathbf{u}}$ or a subset is part of the optimal covering, and let $\mathcal{D}(R_{\mathbf{v}}^{\mathbf{u}})$ denote the "benefit" value of this sub-covering. Then either $R_{\mathbf{v}}^{\mathbf{u}} \in \mathcal{R}^*$ or $R_{\mathbf{v}}^{\mathbf{u}}$ contains a number of non-overlapping rectangles that are in $\mathcal{R}^*$. Thus, the covering problem exhibits the *optimal substructure property* and dynamic programming can be applied. Therefore, we can compute

$$\mathcal{D}(R_{\mathbf{v}}^{\mathbf{u}}) = \max\Big\{ g(R_{\mathbf{v}}^{\mathbf{u}}), \max_{u_x < x < v_x} \big\{ \mathcal{D}(R_{x,v_y}^{u_x,u_y}) + \mathcal{D}(R_{v_x,v_y}^{x,u_y}) \big\},$$
$$\max_{v_x < y < v_y} \big\{ \mathcal{D}(R_{v_x,y}^{u_x,u_y}) + \mathcal{D}(R_{v_x,v_y}^{u_x,y}) \big\} \Big\} \tag{5}$$

Obviously, the optimal solution is obtained through $\mathcal{D}(R_{r,s}^{0,0})$ and the base case is $\mathcal{D}(R_{x+1,y+1}^{x,y}) = g(R_{x+1,y+1}^{x,y})$.

In our implementation, we try a number of different solutions $r \times s = 2 \times 2, \cdots, 32 \times 32$. As soon as the covering accuracy criterion is fulfilled, we terminate the computation.

3.2   Matching Silhouettes

In the previous section, we have developed an algorithm to compute for each template silhouette a resolution-independent compact representation consisting of axis-aligned rectangles. In the following, this representation will be used for fast silhouette area based template matching.

Our goal is to compare a silhouette S with an input image I at a given position $\mathbf{p}$ using the joint probability (see Stenger et al. [14]). The first step is the foreground/background segmentation. Due to its higher robustness compared to binary segmentation, we want to use the color likelihood. In the following, the color likelihood image of an input image I is denoted with $\tilde{L}$ with $\tilde{L}(x,y) \in [0,1]$. To convert the product in the joint probability into sums, we take the pixel-wise logarithm: $L(x,y) = \log \tilde{L}(x,y)$.

Utilizing Eq. 2, we can compute the joint probability at position $\mathbf{p}$ by:

$$P_S(\mathbf{p}) = \sum_{R_i \in \mathcal{R}_S} \left(IL\left(\begin{pmatrix} v_x^i \\ v_y^i \end{pmatrix} + \mathbf{p} \right) + IL\left(\begin{pmatrix} u_x^i \\ u_y^i \end{pmatrix} + \mathbf{p} \right) - IL\left(\begin{pmatrix} v_x^i \\ u_y^i \end{pmatrix} + \mathbf{p} \right) - IL\left(\begin{pmatrix} u_x^i \\ v_y^i \end{pmatrix} + \mathbf{p} \right) \right) \quad (6)$$

The rectangle set $\mathcal{R}_S$ approximates only the silhouette foreground. To get the appropriate match probability for a template, one has to take into account the background distribution, too.

Fortunately, the set of background pixels $\bar{S}$ of a silhouette image, obviously, can be approximated by a set of rectangles with the same algorithm described in the last section. Having computed $\mathcal{R}_{\bar{S}}$, we can compute $P_{\bar{S}}$.

P_S and $P_{\bar{S}}$ are resolution-dependent and need to be normalized. In the following, we explain the normalization for P_S. $P_{\bar{S}}$ can be normalized analogously. A naive approach is to normalize P_S. However, this fails in cases where the template is partially outside the input image. Therefore, we propose a "smart" normalization as follows.

For each pixel not covered by any rectangle, including *all* pixels of the template image that are outside the image borders, we assume a likelihood value of 0.5. The value is motivated by the assumption that at a pixel not yet observed, the probability to be foreground or background is equal. Lets denote the number of pixels of rectangle R_i inside the input image at position p in an input image by $N_{R_i}^{\mathbf{P}}$. Then we normalize P_S as follows:

$$P_S^N(\mathbf{p}) = \frac{1}{|S|} \left(P_S(\mathbf{p}) \cdot \log(0.5)(|S| - N_R^{\mathbf{P}}) \right) , \qquad \text{with } N_R^{\mathbf{P}} = \sum_{R_i \in \mathcal{R}_S} N_{R_i}^{\mathbf{P}} \quad (7)$$

To ensure, that $|S| - N_R^{\mathbf{P}}$ is positive, we set the parameter τ from Eq. 4 to 0.95. The final joint probability is

$$P^N = \exp\left(\frac{1}{2}(P_S^N + P_{\bar{S}}^N)\right) \quad (8)$$

where $P_{\bar{S}}^N$ is the normalized background joint probability. Treating the joint probabilities for the foreground and background equally takes care of the fact that different silhouette shapes have different area relative to their bounding box used in the template: in a silhouette with fewer foreground pixels, the matching of the background pixels should not have a bigger weight then the foreground pixels and vice versa.

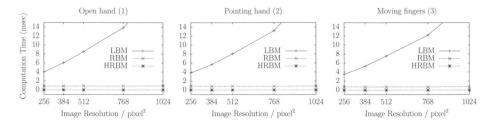

Fig. 3. Each plot shows the average computation time for all three approaches: LBM [1], RBM (our approach), HRBM (our approach incl. hierarchy). Clearly, our approaches are significantly faster and, even more important, resolution independent.

Using the same template at different sizes, i.e. when the distance from an object to the camera changes, is straight forward: simply scale the rectangles accordingly. No additional representation has to be stored. Comparability between the same template at different sizes is ensured by the normalization.

3.3   The Template Hierarchy

In the previous section, we have described a novel method to match an arbitrary template T to an input image I. In a typical tracking application, especially when dealing with articulated objects, a huge number of templates must be matched. A suitable approach to reduce the complexity from $O(\#templates)$ to $O(\log \#templates)$ is to use a template hierarchy. However, building a well working one is still a challenging task.

We propose an approach to build a hierarchy that naturally fits with our representation of the silhouettes by rectangles. In addition, it even further reduces the computational effort per template matching. We build the tree structure by utilizing a hierarchical clustering algorithm. Vectors, describing the similarity between templates, are computed and used as input for the clustering algorithm [21]. The output are k disjoint clusters, where k defines the number of children per tree node. At each node in the template tree, rectangles covering the intersection of all template silhouette of all children are pre-stored.

For matching n templates, we traverse the hierarchy. The rectangles from the root to one leaf constitutes a covering of that template, which is thus being matched incrementally during traversal. At the same time, we prune large parts of the hierarchy (i.e. large numbers of templates), because we descend only into those subtrees with largest probability. Figure 2 illustrates the basic idea of our template hierarchy. Due to space limitations, we can not provide a detailed description of the template tree generation and traversal.

4   Results

For all our experiments, we have chosen to set the silhouette image discretization to $r = s = 32$ boxes. The parameters in Eq. 4 were set initially to $\tau = 0.95$ and

$\theta = (1 - \tau) * 10^{-4}$. In order to achieve a small enough global error $A < \delta$, θ was halved successively. In our experience, 5 iterations were sufficient.

4.1   Rectangle Approximation

First, we evaluated the quality of our approach approximating silhouettes by axis-aligned rectangles. The two important criteria are the area of the covered silhouette and the number of rectangles needed. Let us denote the benefit value for the perfect covering (i.e. all foreground and no background pixels are covered) by $\mathcal{D}_P$ and its solution by $\mathcal{R}_P$. For an accuracy measure we use:

$$Q = \frac{\mathcal{D}(R_{r,s}^{0,0}) + \theta|\mathcal{R}^*|}{\mathcal{D}_P + \theta|\mathcal{R}_P|} \qquad (9)$$

In our experiments, where we have tried to cover a representative set of postures and orientations, we have observed that on average, we need about 20 rectangles to obtain a covering accuracy of $Q = 0.7$. In practice, we have observed that this value is appropriate for the similarity measure. Covering only a part of the silhouette can even increase the matching quality because we obtain a higher tolerance to slightly varying shapes in the input image.

4.2   Matching Quality

We compare our approach with a state-of-the-art approach proposed by Stenger et al. [1], because our approach was inspired by theirs and the application (hand tracking) is the same.

In the following, we will denote the algorithm from [1] as *line-based matching (LBM)*, ours as *rectangle-based matching (RBM)*, and ours including the hierarchy with *hierarchical matching (HRBM)*. It is not quite fair to compare a hierarchical approach to non-hierarchical ones. The reason for this is that, during the traversal, the decision which child nodes are visited is based only on the information of the children itself, not on the whole subtree. Thus, there is no guarantee that the subtree containing the best matching template is visited at all. Nevertheless, mostly HRBM provides a result very similar to the best matching template and, therefore, we add the results of the hierarchical match to our plots to analyze the potential of the hierarchy.

In the following, we will evaluate the difference between the methods with regard to resolution-independence, computation time, and accuracy. We generated templates with an artificial 3D hand model. We used the templates also as input images. There are two reasons to use such synthetic input datasets. First, we have the ground truth and second, we can eliminate negative influences like differences between hand model and real hand, image noise, bad illumination, and so on.

We generated three datasets for evaluation. Dataset 1, consisting of 1536 templates, is an open hand at different rotation angles. Dataset 2 is a pointing hand rendered at the same rotation angles as dataset 1. In dataset 3, consisting of 1080 templates, we used an open hand with moving fingers. Additionally, for each position of the fingers, we rendered the model at different rotations.

First, we examined the dependence between the resolution and computation time. We used input images at 5 different resolutions. We averaged the time to compute the joint probability for all frames at 49 positions. The result is shown in Figure 3. Clearly, LBM's computation time depends linearly on the resolution, while our approaches exhibit constant time.

Second, we compared the matching quality of the three approaches. We expect LBM to work best on the artificial datasets because, for each template, there is an exactly matching input image. Supposing the LBM templates are available at the same resolution than the hand found in the input image, there is a pixelwise identically template for each input image. For evaluation we used an input image resolution of 256×256 and compared the template at 5 different scalings (from 70×70 up to 200×200). The scalings are chosen such that one of the five scales matches to the hand in the input image with an accuracy of ± 1 pixel. All three approaches always found the correct location of the hand in the input image. Thus, for evaluation, we recorded at this position the 10 best matching templates (rank 0–9). Please see Fig 4 for the results. In the open-hand and pointing-hand datasets, LBM and RBM work nearly equally well. Apparently, all approaches have some difficulties to find the correct template in the moving-fingers dataset. The reason for that is that, in this set, there are many templates with nearly identical silhouette: they differ only by one finger flexed by a few degrees. Due to the difference in scale by one pixel, even the LBM can fail to find the best matching template.

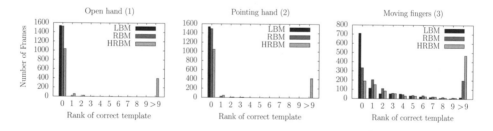

Fig. 4. The histograms show the matching accuracy for all three approaches: LBM [1], RBM (our approach) and HRBM (our approach incl. hierarchy). Rank k means that the correct template is found to be the k−th best match. Lower ranks are better.

5   Conclusions

In this paper, we have developed a silhouette area based *similarity measure* for template matching with constant time complexity. We get a significant increase in template matching speed and reduction of storage space by accepting a slight decrease of matching accuracy. We have also proposed a novel method to compute such a rectangle covering based on dynamic programming. Additionally, we have presented a template hierarchy, which exploits our representation of the silhouettes. This hierarchy reduces the computational complexity for a set of templates from linear to logarithmic time. Please remember that our contributions constitute just one of the many pieces of a complete hand tracking system.

Overall, we need about 0.7 ms on average to compare one template silhouette to one position in an input image at an arbitrary resolution. This is about a factor 25 faster than the state-of-the-art approach from [1] at a resolution of 1024×1024. Furthermore, the template representation is very memory efficient. For example, for 1500 templates, the complete hierarchy consumes less then 1 MByte storage space.

In the future, we plan to implement our approach in a massively parallel programming paradigm. Furthermore, we will extend our hierarchical approach to a random forest approach, which we expect to improve the template matching quality significantly. To get different classifiers at each node, one can choose a random subset instead of all covering templates to cluster a tree node for further subdivision. We also plan to build a hierarchy for our templates based on edge features and combine it with the one proposed in this paper.

References

1. Stenger, B., Thayananthan, A., Torr, P.H.S., Cipolla, R.: Model-based hand tracking using a hierarchical bayesian filter. IEEE Transactions on Pattern Analysis and Machine Intelligence (2006)
2. Crow, F.C.: Summed-area tables for texture mapping. In: SIGGRAPH: Proceedings of the 11th Annual Conference on Computer Graphics and Interactive Techniques (1984)
3. Viola, P., Jones, M.: Rapid object detection using a boosted cascade of simple features. In: IEEE Conference on Computer Vision and Pattern Recognition (2001)
4. Lin, J.Y., Wu, Y., Huang, T.S.: 3d model-based hand tracking using stochastic direct search method. In: International Conference on Automatic Face and Gesture Recognition (2004)
5. Wu, Y., Lin, J.Y., Huang, T.S.: Capturing natural hand articulation. In: International Conference on Computer Vision (2001)
6. Kato, M., Chen, Y.W., Xu, G.: Articulated hand tracking by pca-ica approach. In: International Conference on Automatic Face and Gesture Recognition (2006)
7. Ouhaddi, H., Horain, P.: 3d hand gesture tracking by model registration. In: Workshop on Synthetic-Natural Hybrid Coding and Three Dimensional Imaging (1999)
8. Nirei, K., Saito, H., Mochimaru, M., Ozawa, S.: Human hand tracking from binocular image sequences. In: 22th International Conference on Industrial Electronics, Control, and Instrumentation (1996)
9. Amai, A., Shimada, N., Shirai, Y.: 3-d hand posture recognition by training contour variation. In: IEEE Conference on Automatic Face and Gesture Recognition (2004)
10. Shimada, N., Kimura, K., Shirai, Y.: Real-time 3-d hand posture estimation based on 2-d appearance retrieval using monocular camera. In: IEEE International Conference on Computer Vision (2001)
11. Zhou, H., Huang, T.: Okapi-chamfer matching for articulated object recognition. In: IEEE International Conference on Computer Vision (2005)

12. Lowe, D.G.: Object recognition from local scale-invariant features. In: IEEE International Conference on Computer Vision (1999)
13. Zhou, H., Huang, T.: Tracking articulated hand motion with eigen dynamics analysis. In: IEEE International Conference on Computer Vision (2003)
14. Stenger, B.D.R.: Model-based hand tracking using a hierarchical bayesian filter. In: Dissertation submitted to the University of Cambridge (2004)
15. Sudderth, E.B., Mandel, M.I., Freeman, W.T., Willsky, A.S.: Visual hand tracking using nonparametric belief propagation. In: IEEE CVPR Workshop on Generative Model Based Vision (2004)
16. Kumar, V.A., Ramesh, H.: Covering rectilinear polygons with axis-parallel rectangles. In: Annual ACM Symposium on Theory of Computing (1999)
17. Wu, S., Sahni, S.: Covering rectilinear polygons by rectangles. IEEE Transactions on Computer-Aided Design of Integrated Circuits and Systems (1990)
18. Heinrich-Litan, L., Lübecke, M.E.: Rectangle covers revisited computationally. ACM Journal of Experimental Algorithmics 11 (2006)
19. Liou, W., Tan, J.J.M., Lee, R.C.T.: Minimum rectangular partition problem for simple rectilinear polygons. IEEE Transactions on Computer-Aided Design (1990)
20. O'Rourke, J., Tewari, G.: Partitioning orthogonal polygons into fat rectangles in polynomial time. In: Proc. 13th Canadian Conference on Computational Geometry (2001)
21. Cottrell, M., Hammer, B., Hasenfuß, A., Villmann, T.: Batch neural gas. In: 5th Workshop on Self-Organizing Maps (2005)

Analysing the Influence of Vertex Clustering on PCA-Based Dynamic Mesh Compression

Jan Rus and Libor Váša

University of West Bohemia, Univerzitní 22, Plzeň, CZ 30614, Czech Republic
jrus@kiv.zcu.cz, lvasa@kiv.zcu.cz

Abstract. The growth of computational power of contemporary hardware causes technologies working with 3D-data to expand. Examples of the use of this kind of data can be found in geography or gaming industry. 3D-data may not be only static, but also dynamic.

One way of animated 3D-data representation is expressing them by "dynamic triangle mesh". This kind of data representation is usually voluminous and needs to be compressed for efficient storage and transmission. In this paper, we are dealing with the influence of vertex clustering on dynamic mesh compression. The mesh is divided into vertex clusters based on the vertex movement similarity and compressed per-partes to achieve higher compression performance. We use Coddyac as a basic compression algorithm and extend it by adding well known clustering algorithms to demonstrate the efficiency of this approach. We also addres the choice of optimal clustering strategy for the Coddyac algorithm.

Keywords: 3D dynamic meshes, Data compression, Computer animation, Coddyac, Clustering.

1 Introduction

Data accuracy and quantity requirements are continually growing and similarly grows the volume of data structures which contain them. Because storage capacities and transmission speeds are limited we need to use compression algorithms to reduce data volume and reduce hardware requirements for storage and distribution of such data.

Unfortunately this kind of data includes a lot of complex information. Therefore it is very voluminous and needs to be compressed for efficient storage and transmission. ZIP and RAR are popular compression algorithms but they are not primarily intended for dynamic mesh compression. Specialised lossy compression algorithms can achieve better compression rates. One of the algorithms specialised for dynamic mesh compression is the Coddyac [1] algorithm. Unlike the ZIP compression Coddyac compression is a lossy compression algorithm but this may not be an obstacle due to the kind of data. Usual video compression algorithms are also lossy.

The more complex the movements of an animated model are, the less movement can be considered negligible and thus the length of the vectors of coefficients will have to be higher (decreasing compression ratio). Therefore, one

F.J. Perales and R.B. Fisher (Eds.): AMDO 2010, LNCS 6169, pp. 55–66, 2010.

possible way to improve the compression ratio is to reduce the movement complexity, which could be achieved by clustering the mesh vertices by similarity of their trajectories.

1.1   Related Work

Many algorithms have been proposed for dynamic mesh compression. There are also known various algorithms of mesh division into smaller parts (clusters) depending on the topology or geometry criteria, or division into logical parts. Similarly, as in the cases mentioned below, our method combines the compression algorithm and division of the mesh to increase compression ratio.

One such method is described by Amjoun and Straßer in [9]. This method extends the PCA based approach by Alexa [14] by introducing local principal component analysis (LPCA). It analyses the set of vertices for each frame and transforms their world coordinates into local coordinates of clusters. Local coordinate system of each cluster depends on the plane of it's seed triangle and the mesh is dividend into clusters using the motion of vertices in this system. Each cluster is finally encoded using PCA and compressed by arithmetic coding.

Similarly Sattler, Sarlette and Klein presented in [10] a compression method using clustering, but it is based on clustered principal component analysis (CPCA) analysing trajectories of all vertices throughout the animation time. Clustering of vertices here depends on similarity of their trajectories, which usually leads to meaningful clusters. Finally, clusters are separately encoded by PCA.

Frame-based Animated Mesh Compression (FAMC) method described in [5] by Mamou, Zaharia and Prêteux is also segmenting the mesh with respect to motion. Each segment is described by a single 3D affine transformation matrix. This algorithm is based on a hierarchical decimation strategy depending on topological simplifications: two neighbouring vertices are merged into single one (collapsed) if their affine motion is similar. Modification of this kind of clustering is described in section 4.3.

Our compression method uses similar procedures as the methods mentioned above, but achieves better compression ratios. Unlike the above-mentioned papers, we are dealing with deeper statement than how significant improvements in compression can be achieved through clustering. We will also show how clustering affects the Coddyac algorithm and what clustering is the most appropriate for this algorithm. We also examine what the optimal number of clusters is, and what impact their number has on the compressed data.

1.2   Notation

In this paper we use following notation:

F - number of frames of animation
V - number of vertices
B - matrix of original animation, size $3F \times V$
A - average trajectory vector

S - matrix of samples, contains substraction of A from each column of B
C - autocorrelation matrix
E_i - i-th eigenvector, made by eigenvalue decomposition of C
N - number of most important eigenvectors (components of PCA)
E - basis of the PCA subspace, size $3F \times N$

The rest of this paper is organised as follows: Section 2 gives an overview of the Coddyac algorithm; in Section 3 we present clustering modification of Coddyac and correction of possible problems; Section 4 contains brief description of the tested clustering algorithms; experimental results are presented in Section 5 and the paper is concluded in Section 6.

2   Coddyac Algorithm Overview

In this paper we examine the influence of vertex clustering on the Coddyac algorithm, which we will now describe in more detail. The algorithm is based on representing dynamic meshes as a set of vertex trajectories of individual vertices. Trajectory of the i-th vertex is described by a vector T_i of length $3F$, consisting of XYZ coordinates of the given vertex in all the frames. Notice that for dense meshes, it is very likely that trajectory vectors of neighbouring vertices will be similar. In other words, the trajectory vectors are not distributed evenly in the space of dimension $3F$, instead they are roughly located in a subspace of much lower dimension. This observation yields the first step of the Coddyac algorithm: finding the subspace and expressing the vertices in this subspace.

A straightforward way to find a subspace of a set of samples is using the PCA tool of linear algebra. We represent the original animation by a matrix B of size $3F \times V$, where the i-th column is the trajectory vector associated with the i-th vertex. First, we compute an average trajectory vector A, and subtract it from each column of B, obtaining a matrix of samples S. Subsequently, we compute the autocorrelation matrix $C = S \cdot S^T$ of size $3F \times 3F$. Finally, the eigenvalue decomposition of the autocorrelation matrix C gives us a set of eigenvectors $E_i, i = 1..3F$, and their corresponding eigenvalues. Of these eigenvectors we select N most important ones (according to their respective eigenvalues), N being a user-specified parameter. The selected eigenvectors form a basis of the subspace, and each trajectory vector can be expressed as:

$$T_i = A + \sum_{j=1}^{N} c_i^j E_j \qquad (1)$$

Since the basis is orthonormal it is possible to compute the matrix of combination coefficients c_i^j by matrix multiplication $C = S^T E$, where E is a matrix of size $3F \times N$ in which the i-th column is the i-th eigenvector E_i. In order to transmit the mesh we have to transmit the selected subset of eigenvectors (matrix E of size $3F \times N$), the combination coefficients (matrix C of size $V \times N$) and the vector A representing the average trajectory. Details on how to efficiently encode the matrix of eigenvectors can be found in [8].

The other key observation of the Coddyac algorithm is that the PCA step can be interpreted as a simple change of basis, and therefore it should not have any influence on results of linear operators. This feature is employed for prediction of the values c_i^j at the decoder. In static mesh encoding, a very common prediction method is based on the parallelogram rule [11]. The idea is that the mesh is traversed progressively by growing an area of processed vertices by adding one adjacent triangle (with one adjacent vertex) at a time. The XYZ coordinates of the new vertex are predicted to lie at the top of a projected parallelogram formed by the three known vertices v_left, v_right and v_base. The coordinate prediction is then expressed as:

$$
v_{predicted}^X = v_{left}^X + v_{right}^X - v_{base}^X
$$
$$
v_{predicted}^Y = v_{left}^Y + v_{right}^Y - v_{base}^Y \qquad (2)
$$
$$
v_{predicted}^Z = v_{left}^Z + v_{right}^Z - v_{base}^Z
$$

In dynamic mesh compression, these formulae may be applied on each element of the trajectory vectors. However, since the feature vectors are in fact linearly transformed trajectory vectors, we can use the same formula also for the elements of feature vectors:

$$
c_{predicted}^j = c_{left}^j + c_{right}^j - c_{base}^j \qquad (3)
$$

The Coddyac algorithm traverses the mesh, adding one triangle at the time, performs the prediction according to equation (3) and transmits the prediction residuals.

2.1   Number of Basis Vectors

When considering clustering as a means to improve efficiency of Coddyac compression, we have to change the approach to setting the number of basis vectors. Originally, the user has specified a single integer N which has influenced the quality of the output: higher value of N leads to higher data rates and lower errors, and vice versa.

The aim of clustering is to isolate parts of the mesh where the vertices move similarly, and therefore their movement can be expressed by lower number of basis vectors. However, the simplicity of motion might vary significantly between clusters, and therefore we should select a different number of basis vectors for each cluster.

In our solution the user specifies a scalar value of acceptable PCA-introduced error, and the algorithm selects the appropriate number of basis vectors automatically. We can express the average amount of PCA-introduced error using N basis vectors as:

$$
\triangle_{PCA}^N = \frac{1}{V} \sum_{j=1}^{V} \frac{1}{3F} \sum_{i=1}^{3F} \frac{|T_j^i - \bar{T}_j^i|}{l} \qquad (4)
$$

where l is the average edge length of the animation, T_j^i is the i-th component of the j-th original trajectory and $\bar{T}_j^i$ is the i-th component of the j-th trajectory reconstructed using N basis vectors. In order to select the number of basis vectors for a specific cluster, we select the smallest possible N for which this average PCA-introduced error falls below a user-specified value.

3 Clustering in Coddyac

The efficiency of the Coddyac compression algorithm directly depends on movements of the animated model. If different parts of the model move in a relatively orderly manner, but differently, the global movement of the model will be disorderly. Therefore, after application of PCA, all trajectories are described by vectors longer than necessary.

To restrict the length of the vectors (of coefficients after applying PCA), we must select those vertices of the mesh, whose trajectories are similar and include them in a common group - cluster. This way the movement complexity in individual clusters is reduced and so is the necessary length of PCA vectors.

After applying a clustering algorithm on the vertices and PCA on the input data we obtain an index for each vertex of the triangle mesh that determines to which cluster the vertex belongs. For reasons of topology compression, as indicated in [3] , it is necessary that the clusters are topologically compact. It means each cluster have to consists of triangles which are touching their neighbours by edges to enable Edgebreaker traverse the cluster topology by crossing edges of neighbouring triangles.

It is actually a projection from an n-dimensional space, in which the algorithm performs the clustering of the vertices of the model, on to the 2-dimensional space of the surface of an animated model. Unfortunately, after such projection individual clusters may overlap (fig. 1). It is therefore necessary to correct the clusters on the surface of the animated model.

It is also important to select number of clusters. The smaller clusters we choose to cover the surface of the model, the better complexity reduction can be

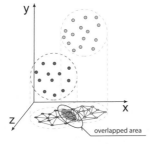

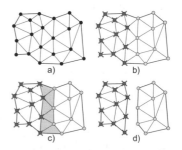

Fig. 1. Clusters separated in for example 3D space (xyz) can overlap after projection onto 2D surface(xz). This situation can be hard to solve for Edgebreaker compression.

Fig. 2. Topology of full mesh (a) is clustered (b) and stored. Triangles between clusters (c) are removed, and the mesh is divided into components (d).

achieved. However each cluster requires initialisation data (basis), which negatively affect the final compression ratio. Therefore, we try to find the optimal number of clusters, enough to ensure that movements of vertices included in them is as ordered as possible.

In our scheme, the full mesh (Fig. 2a) topology is compressed first and it is stored in a file together with the indices of clusters (Fig. 2b) for each vertex. As the number of clusters is relatively small (small variance of values), and their indices are often repeated, the set of indices can be efficiently compressed for example by an Arithmetic encoding. Before the next phase we remove those triangles, whose vertices belong to more than one cluster (Fig. 2c), and so the dynamic mesh is topologically and geometrically divided into smaller components (Fig. 2d).

The second phase is used only for compression of geometry, not topology. Geometry of the components is compressed by PCA separately by the Coddyac algorithm. Therefore each component has its set of PCA coefficients, basis and means vector, which PCA needs to decompress the original data. Therefore, with the increasing number of clusters decrease the volume of data for the PCA coefficients decreases, but the volume of data for basis and means vectors increases.

3.1 Cluster Correction

Due to the topology compression scheme it is necessary to achieve such shape of clusters, that the vertices of one n-dimensional cluster are in the common cluster on the 2-dimensional surface of the animated model. These clusters must not overlap.

There are two ways to resolve the situation. The first option is to connect remote cluster parts by "bridge", the second option is "drown" the remote cluster part. Both of these options lead to a situation when some vertices of a cluster are reassigned to a different cluster. This creates an error in the original assignment of vertices into clusters and leads to a reduction in the efficiency of compression algorithms.

If there is a separate part of a cluster on the surface of the model and it is sufficiently small, it is possible "drown" it. This means that all vertices of the small separate part of the cluster are connected to the cluster, which is adjacent or surrounding it. The greater the drowned part of this cluster is, the greater the error of its "drowning" arises. If the cluster is large enough, it is better to build a "bridge" between the two specific parts of the cluster by reassigning vertices between them. The farther away these parts are, the larger number of vertices have to be reassigned in building a "bridge", and the greater error occurs. Building a "bridge" raises a number of inconveniences and situations which are difficult to solve. One such situation is presented in figure 3.

To avoid these problems, we have chosen a possibility to build a "virtual" bridge. Such a bridge no longer consists of the triangles of the animated mesh. Such a bridge only carries information about the triangle from one part of cluster in which it starts and the second triangle, where it should end, and what is the relative position of these triangles. With this design we not only avoid the

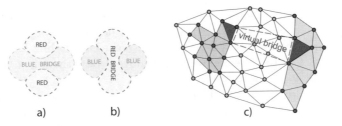

Fig. 3. Bridges. a) creation of blue bridge splits red cluster into two parts, b) creation of red bridge splits blue cluster into two parts and we need both bridges to solve this situation correctly. c) red virtual bridge over the blue cluster.

difficulties in the construction of "bridge", but also prevent the emergence of any errors that may occur by design.

4 Tested Clustering Algorithms

We have tested several methods of vertex clustering, whose functions and modifications are described below.

4.1 K-Means

K-means [4] is one of the distributive algorithms. The algorithm divides the given set of data into clusters. The clusters are iteratively refined according to the specified distribution criteria. Each k-means cluster is represented by its centre and the data points are usually assigned to clusters based on their distance to the centres of clusters.

To run the K-means algorithm we need to know in advance how many classes (clusters) will be used, i.e. the value k. The value varies according to the case of using k-means algorithm and may vary (as in this case) in dependence on the input data. We have modified the calculation of distance of trajectory vectors in clustering algorithms and in addition to Euclidean distance (L2 norm) we have experimented with calculation of the distance using any norm L_p by the following formula:

$$L_p = (\sum_i |x_i|^p)^{\frac{1}{p}} \tag{5}$$

4.2 Facility Location

Facility location [6] algorithm is similar to the algorithm mentioned above. The main difference is that the centres of clusters (called facilities) are always chosen from the set of input data. The algorithm tries to find a placement and number of facilities, to which it connects the other elements of initial set. Algorithm selects such locations of facilities to make the price of the connection of all elements minimal. Additionally, each facility needs to pay a constant opening price, which is one of the inputs of the algorithm and reduces the number of facilities.

The aim of the algorithm is to find a balance between the number of clusters and their sizes. Number of created clusters is thus dependent only on the specified facility cost and the input data-set. Like the k-means algorithm, Facility location is also iterative. Clusters are created and removed while there is a better overall price for the allocation of clusters.

In our case there is not big difference between k-means and facility location. If we use facility location algorithm with some facility cost and use the number of clusters as input k in k-means, then the location and size of clusters should be the same or very similar for both algorithms.

4.3   FAMC - Like Clustering

Unlike previous methods, this method is also influenced by the connectivity of the animated mesh. The clustering algorithm uses a priority queue, from which edges of the model are selected that have the best evaluation. Lowest cost edge is picked from the queue and collapsed into one vertex. Edges adjacent to this point are re-evaluated. The final number of clusters corresponds to the number of vertices resulting from collapsing the edges. Exact description of this algorithm can be found in [5].

This algorithm was also tested in combination with modified PCA coefficients vectors. The similarity of trajectories is no longer assessed on the basis of Euclidean distance of vectors, but by the number of important components of the vectors, which they have in common. The components which are zero after quantisation may be neglected by the compression algorithm. Therefore the similarity of trajectories is assessed by the number of zeros in specific common components. Now we do not want to cluster trajectories which are as similar as possible but those that allow us to maximise what can be neglected, see fig. 4. Trajectories were modified as follows:

0-trajectories: A threshold is given. Values in vectors, which are smaller than the threshold are rewritten to 0, the others are rewritten to 1. Parts of vectors with 0 are those parts which we want to discard. These vectors, that has the most of common 0, are therefore jointed to the common cluster.

!0-trajectories: Like the previous, except the common clusters are made of vectors, which have the most common non-zero components. Clusters should there-

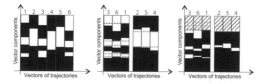

Fig. 4. Non-zero components of vectors are black, zero components are white. Modified vectors (left) are clustered by their common zero-components (middle). Zero-components common for all cluster (white between grey dotted lines) are moved to the end of the vectors. Sequences of zeros on the end of these vectors common for one cluster can be neglected (hatched area).

fore be designed so that it can be neglected as much of the vectors as possible, achieving a reduction of the resulting data stream.

5   Experimental Results

The algorithms mentioned above and their modifications have been implemented and subsequently we have measured the impact of vertex clustering on the selected dynamic meshes. The figure 5 shows the RD curves of clustering methods tested on Dance animation. The model was dividend into 8 clusters (provides the best results).

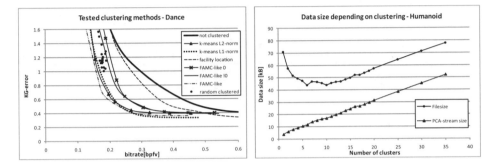

Fig. 5. Influence of tested clustering methods on Dance animation (left) and data size comparison of whole compressed file and including PCA-stream (mean vectors, basis and quantisation) of Humanoid animation (right)

To compare errors resulting from compression of 3D animated meshes we used KG-error [7] measure:

$$e = 100 \cdot \frac{\|B - \tilde{B}\|}{\|B - R(B)\|} \tag{6}$$

Where $\tilde{B}$ is matrix containing the animation after the compression and decompression steps and $R(B)$ is average matrix which contains average spatial value for each frame of animation. We have used Frobenius norm denoted by $\|x\|$.

The figure 5 shows that each method has brought some improvement of compression ratio. In the figure 5, comparing different methods of clustering, we can see that the largest improvement was brought by the FAMC-like method with original cost function, which is described in [5]. Unlike the original version, the algorithm improved by clustering can achieve significantly lower bitrate while maintaining the same error.

6   Conclusions and Future Work

In this paper we have examined the influence of clustering on the Coddyac algorithm. The improvement lies in the suitable division of compressed mesh into

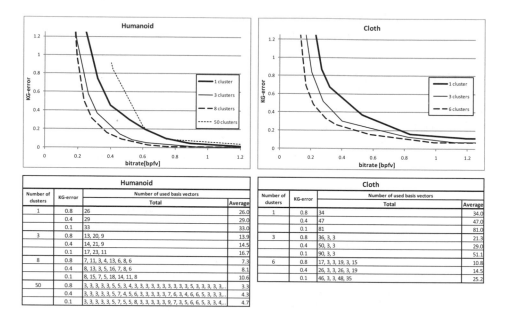

Fig. 6. Influence of clustering on Humanoid and Cloth animation

Humanoid			
Number of clusters	KG-error	Number of used basis vectors — Total	Average
1	0.8	26	26.0
	0.4	29	29.0
	0.1	33	33.0
3	0.8	13, 20, 9	13.9
	0.4	14, 21, 9	14.5
	0.1	17, 23, 11	16.7
8	0.8	7, 11, 3, 4, 13, 6, 8, 6	7.3
	0.4	8, 13, 3, 5, 16, 7, 8, 6	8.1
	0.1	8, 15, 7, 5, 18, 14, 11, 8	10.6
50	0.8	3, 3, 3, 3, 3, 5, 5, 3, 4, 3, 3, 3, 3, 3, 3, 3, 3, 3, 3, 5, 3, 3, 3, 3,...	3.3
	0.4	3, 3, 3, 3, 3, 5, 7, 4, 5, 6, 3, 3, 3, 3, 7, 6, 3, 4, 6, 6, 5, 3, 3, 3,...	4.3
	0.1	3, 3, 3, 3, 3, 5, 7, 5, 5, 8, 3, 3, 3, 3, 9, 7, 3, 5, 6, 6, 5, 3, 3, 4,...	4.7

Cloth			
Number of clusters	KG-error	Number of used basis vectors — Total	Average
1	0.8	34	34.0
	0.4	47	47.0
	0.1	81	81.0
3	0.8	36, 3, 3	21.3
	0.4	50, 3, 3	29.0
	0.1	90, 3, 3	51.1
6	0.8	17, 3, 3, 19, 3, 15	10.8
	0.4	26, 3, 3, 26, 3, 19	14.5
	0.1	46, 3, 3, 48, 35	25.2

smaller parts, which are then compressed separately. Purpose of this decomposition is to reduce the complexity of movement in animation which leads to a better compression ratio. The selection of the appropriate number of clusters depends on many aspects hence we use "try and error" method. But as can bee seen in figure 6, by the descent method we can quickly find a minimum of dependence of compressed animation size on the number of clusters and next find the best configuration in the meaning of RD curves. This optimal number of clusters is not dependent on the structure of animated model neither the complexity of vertex trajectories, but especially on the differences between trajectories of individual vertices, and for most tested meshes we have found that values of $8 - 12$ clusters provide good results.

We have tested several methods for clustering of dynamic meshes. Of these methods the best results are provided using FAMC-like with the original cost function. It should be noted that the improvement compared to the L1-norm k-means is negligible ($\simeq 5\%$), but the time complexity is several times larger. The figure 6 shows that the use of clustering in the original compression algorithm is able to improve the performance of the algorithm in terms of errors and data rate reduction. The bitrate can be reduced by $37\% - 46\%$ compared to the Coddyac output while maintaining the same KG-error.

Theoretically including clustering algorithm can improve the compression ratio without substantial increase in time complexity, because clustering algorithms are usually not too time-consuming. But since most of the clustering algorithms work with a trajectories processed by PCA for example to analyse movement of 3D-mesh, the resulting time required for compression can rise to twice the original time complexity of the Coddyac. However, the use of clustering has almost no effect on the decompression time, which is for a practical application of the algorithm more important.

In the future we would like to explore the possibility of avoiding the use of PCA in the stage of clustering, automatise the selection of the number of clusters and find more efficient clustering algorithms. Now is our work focused on clustering, where each vertex belongs to only one cluster so we also would like to try soften the transitions between clusters as for example in [13] to enhance the impression of animations compressed with lower quantizations. Another possible future improvement is clustering by using the time-line, i.e. not only examining the changes in position of vertices in time, but also the changes of movement complexity of individual trajectories depending on time. This could lead to more clusters but shorter vectors of PCA coefficients.

Acknowledgements

This work has been supported by the Ministry of Education, Youth and Sports of the Czech Republic under the research program LC-06008 (Center for Computer Graphics).

References

1. Váša, L., Skala, V.: CoDDyAC: Connectivity Driven Dynamic Mesh Compression. In: Proceedings of 3DTV Conference 2007 (2007)
2. Smith, L.I.: A tutorial on Principal Component Analysis (2002)
3. Rossignac, J.: Edgebreaker: Connectivity compression for triangle meshes. IEEE Transactions on Visualization and Computer Graphics 5(1) (January - March 1999)
4. Kanungo, T., Mount, D.M., Netanyahu, N.S., Piatko, C.D., Silverman, R., Wu, A.Y.: An Efficient k-Means Clustering Algorithm: Analysis and Implementation. IEEE Transactions on pattern analysis and machine inteligence 24(7) (July 2002)
5. Mamou, K., Zaharia, T., Prêteux, F.: FAMC: The MPEG-4 Standard for Animated Mesh Compression. ARTEMIS Department, Institut TELECOM
6. Charikar, M., Khuller, S., Mount, D.M., Narasimhan, G.: Algorithms for facility location problem with outliers. In: Symposium on Discrete Algorithms, pp. 642–651 (2001)
7. Karni, Z., Gotsman, C.: Compression of soft-body animation sequences. Elsevier Computer & Graphics 28, 25–34 (2004)
8. Váša, L., Skala, V.: COBRA: Compression of the Basis for PCA Represented Animations. Computer Graphics Forum 28, 1529–1540 (2009)
9. Amjoun, R., Straer, W.: Efficient Compression of 3D Dynamic Mesh Sequences. Journal of the WSCG (2007)
10. Sattler, M., Sarlette, R., Klein, R.: Simple and Efficient Compression of Animation Sequances. In: Proceedings of the 2005 ACM SIGGRAPH/Eurographics Symposium on Computer Animation (SCA 2005), pp. 209–217 (2005)

11. Gotsman, C., Touma, C.: Triangle Mesh Compression. In: Graphics Interface, pp. 26–34 (1998)
12. Skála, J., Kolingerová, I.: Clustering Geometric Data Streams. In: SIGRAD, pp. 17–23 (2007)
13. Kavan, L., Sloan, P., O'Sullivan, C.: Fast and Efficient Skinning of Animated Meshes. In: Eurographics 2010 (2010)
14. Alexa, M., Müller, W.: Representing Animations by Principal Components. Computer Graphics Forum 19(3) (2000)

Estimating 3D Pose via Stochastic Search and Expectation Maximization

Ben Daubney and Xianghua Xie

Department of Computer Science, Swansea University,
United Kingdom, SA2 8PP
{B.Daubney,X.Xie}@swansea.ac.uk

Abstract. In this paper an approach is described to estimate 3D pose using a part based stochastic method. A proposed representation of the human body is explored defined over joints that employs full conditional models learnt between connected joints. This representation is compared against a popular alternative defined over parts using approximated limb conditionals. It is shown that using full limb conditionals results in a model that is far more representative of the original training data. Furthermore, it is demonstrated that Expectation Maximization is suitable for estimating 3D pose and better convergence is achieved when using full limb conditionals. To demonstrate the efficacy of the proposed method it is applied to the domain of 3D pose estimation using a single monocular image. Quantitative results are provided using the HumanEva dataset which confirm that the proposed method outperforms that of the competing part based model. In this work just a single model is learnt to represent all actions contained in the dataset which is applied to all subjects viewed from differing angles.

Keywords: 3D Pose Estimation, Expectation Maximization, Stochastic Search, Rigid Joint, Loose Limbed.

1   Introduction

There is currently much interest in being able to extract the pose of a human from a single or sequence of images. A popular technique used to achieve this is to represent the human body as a probabilistic graphical model, where the nodes of the graph represent anatomical parts of the body and the edges represent the relationships between these parts [1,2,3,4,12,13,14]. However, a limitation with current part based methods is the use of the Loose Limbed model, which approximates the joint between two connected parts using a soft connection. This representation does not enforce the connecting joint between neighboring parts to coincide and is employed as the likelihood of two neighboring parts being detected independently, with their connecting joints exactly aligned, is very low. In this work a method is presented that uses ancestral sampling to generate a set of hypothesis locations where the connecting joint between neighboring parts is constrained to coincide.

F.J. Perales and R.B. Fisher (Eds.): AMDO 2010, LNCS 6169, pp. 67–77, 2010.

Forcing joints between connected parts to coincide will address one of the key limitations with the current Loose Limbed approach and will result in a model that is better constrained and is a more intuitive representation of the human body constructed of rigid parts with fixed joint locations. To achieve this, rather than defining a model over parts/limbs as is usual in current Loose Limbed approaches [1,2,3,4,12,14], we define a model where the hidden nodes of the graph represent joint locations. This proposed representation is referred to as a Fixed Joint model.

A further limitation with current Loose Limbed approaches is that typically the conditional probability distribution used to represent the relationship between neighboring parts, referred to as a limb conditional in this work for brevity, is approximated by learning a distribution over the relative state between connected limbs [1,2,3,14]. This is motivated by our knowledge of the human body; a given joint has a fixed and known range over which it can move. However, in order to learn approximate limb conditionals the original training data must be converted into a relative form. This process eliminates much of the original data's structure, therefore any model learnt using this will fail to capture its full complexity. In this work it is shown that learning a full conditional model between connected parts provides a richer and much more accurate description of the training set and therefore the object being modeled.

The principal reason that human pose estimation is difficult is the large number of degrees of freedom that the human body contains. Attempts to efficiently search this space using a graphical part based representation of the human body include Dynamic Programming [1] and Belief Propagation [4,13] for 2D pose estimation and stochastic methods such as the Pampas algorithm [6], Variational MAP [7] and Partitioned Sampling [8] for 3D pose estimation. These methods are iterative and require that a model must first be defined to propagate the particle set between iterations of the algorithm; how this model is defined is not intuitive and often the covariance of this model is simply initially overestimated and then shrunk at each iteration to force convergence [7,9]. A motivation for using full limb conditionals is that pose can then be efficiently estimated using Expectation Maximization (EM) and importance sampling. At each iteration samples are drawn from the prior which are then weighted to approximate the posterior distribution given the current observations, using this sample set the prior is then reestimated. In the following iteration a new set of samples are drawn from the reestimated prior and over a number of iterations the prior converges to a solution; empirically this solution appears to be global. Using this method samples are always drawn from the prior and an extra model to propagate samples between iterations is not necessary. A further advantage of this approach is that it results in a compact parametric description of the posterior distribution. This parametric representation is particularly advantageous in applications such as tracking where drift between frames could be added deterministically by scaling the resultant covariances.

In this work three principal claims are made: Firstly, compared to the Loose Limbed representation the proposed Fixed Joint model results in a prior that is far more representative of the original training set. Secondly, that the proposed Fixed Joint model results in faster convergence of the EM algorithm compared to the Loose Limbed model. Thirdly, that the Fixed Joint model outperforms that of the Loose Limbed model at estimating pose. These claims are supported by both quantitative and qualitative results using the HumanEva data set [5]. Whilst the presented approach is general enough that it could readily be applied to scenes captured from multiple views or employed in a tracking framework, here it is applied to single images and it is assumed that the position of the root node is fixed and known *a priori*. We employ this constrained scenario as the focus of this paper is on highlighting the limitations of existing representations and demonstrating the advantages of the proposed method through detailed analysis and comparison of performances. This is best achieved by constraining any experiments so that observed differences in performance can only be a direct result of the methodology used. However, the presented approach is adequately efficient such that uncertainty in the root node could be accommodated by sampling the root position multiple times, however, this is currently left for future work.

2   Pose Estimation

The problem of estimating pose of an articulated object can be defined over a probabilistic graph where the set of n hidden nodes $v_i \in \mathcal{V}$ represent the set of parts used to represent the object and $\{v_i, v_j\} \in \mathcal{E}$ represent the edges that connect the nodes of the graph. Given a set of proposal values for each node $X = \{\mathbf{x}_i, .., \mathbf{x}_n\}$ and a set of observations for each node $Z = \{z_i, .., z_n\}$ the posterior can then be calculated as

$$p(X|Z, \theta) = \prod_{\{i,j\} \in \mathcal{E}} p(\mathbf{x}_i|\mathbf{x}_j, \theta_{ij}) \prod_{i \in \mathcal{V}} p(z_i|\mathbf{x}_i) \tag{1}$$

where $\mathbf{x}_i$ is assumed to be the child of $\mathbf{x}_j$, $p(\mathbf{x}_i|\mathbf{x}_j, \theta_{ij})$ are limb conditionals which represent the model prior and θ_{ij} is a connection parameter, and $p(z_i|\mathbf{x}_i)$ are observational likelihoods. Pose can then be estimated by finding the configuration X^* that maximizes this equation. It is assumed that the graph used to represent the articulated object is a tree and therefore contains no loops.

The focus of this paper is on the comparison between using a Loose Limbed model defined over parts and a proposed Rigid Joint model defined over joint positions. As discussed in the proceeding section, whilst the Loose Limbed model approximates the limb conditional $p(\mathbf{x}_i|\mathbf{x}_j, \theta_{ij})$ from Equation 1 with a model learnt over $\mathbf{x}_i$ in the frame of reference of $\mathbf{x}_j$ denoted by $p(\mathbf{x}_{ij}|\theta_{ij})$, the Rigid Joint model uses full limb conditionals $p(\mathbf{x}_i|\mathbf{x}_j, \theta_{ij})$ which we show to be both far more representative of the original training set and result in faster convergence of the EM algorithm. In the following Sections we describe the limb conditionals learnt for each model, how samples can be generated from these models and how Equation 1 is maximized using EM.

2.1 Model Representation

Loose Limbed Model. The Loose Limbed model is based on that presented in [2] which we briefly describe. The model is defined over parts and each part has 6 degrees of freedom $\mathbf{x}_i = (\mathbf{r}_i, \boldsymbol{\Theta}_i)$, where $\mathbf{r}_i \in \mathbf{R}^3$ and $\boldsymbol{\Theta}_i \in \mathbf{SO}(3)$ which represent the global position of the proximal joint of the ith part and its rotation respectively, each part has a fixed length. The rotations are represented by unit quaternions, therefore $\mathbf{x}_i \in \mathbf{R}^7$. Rather than learning a conditional distribution over $\mathbf{x}_i$ and $\mathbf{x}_j$ directly a distribution is instead learnt over $\mathbf{x}_{ij}$, where $\mathbf{x}_{ij}$ is the position and orientation of the ith part described in the local frame of reference of the jth part. Given a set of training data the distribution $p(\mathbf{x}_{ij}|\theta_{ij})$ can be learnt directly for each part using a GMM. Following [2] each limb conditional is represented using three components.

Rigid Joint Model. The proposed Rigid Joint model is defined over joint positions, where the distance between neighboring joints is fixed. Conditional models $p(\mathbf{x}_i|\mathbf{x}_j, \theta_{ij})$ are learnt where $\mathbf{x}_i$ is the orientation of the ith joint defined in a global frame of reference (i.e. that of the root node). These models are also learnt using a GMM.

To create a conditional model a joint distribution $p(\mathbf{x}_i, \mathbf{x}_j|\theta_{ij})$ is first learnt from which the conditional distribution can be calculated during run time as described in Section 2.2. A prior distribution over the position of each joint is learnt over spherical coordinates (ρ, θ, ϕ), where ρ represents the length between the joint and the joint to which it is connected, $\theta \in [0, 2\pi]$ represents a rotation around the xy-plane and $\phi \in [0, \pi]$ represents the elevation measured relative to the z-axis. Since the length is fixed ρ is constant for each joint and we have only two free parameters θ and ϕ, which describe the orientation of each joint measured in the global frame of reference (i.e. that of the root node). We represent these two angles using polar coordinates (r, ω), where the rotation $\omega = \theta$ and the radius $r = \phi$, where $r \in [0, \pi]$.

The limitation with this representation is that a discontinuity occurs at $r = \pi$. To overcome this we also create a duplicate polar coordinate system where $r = \pi - \phi$ so that at the origin $\phi = \pi$. Each coordinate system is referred to using the suffixes 0 and π respectively as this indicates the value ϕ at the origin. Each position in the coordinate system also has a weight associated with it such that those nearer the origin are weighted higher that those near the outer edges (i.e. near the discontinuity) these weights are defined as $w_0 = \frac{r}{\pi}$ and as $w_\pi = 1 - w_0$. Hence, a measurement represented in 3D spherical coordinates $\mathbf{x} = (\rho, \theta, \phi)$ is thus represented as a set of 2D vectors and weights $\mathbf{x} = \{\mathbf{x}_0, w_0, \mathbf{x}_\pi, w_\pi\}$, where $\mathbf{x}_0 = (r_0, \omega_0)$. Using this representation a GMM could be learnt for each coordinate system independently and weighted proportional to the total weight of the training data used. These weights then describe whether the data was distributed near to the origin of the coordinate system, where it is better represented, or near the edge, where the discontinuity occurs and it is poorly represented.

Given training data for two connected joints i and j, $\mathbf{X}_i = \{[\mathbf{x}_i]_1, ..., [\mathbf{x}_i]_l\}$ and $\mathbf{X}_j = \{[\mathbf{x}_j]_1, ..., [\mathbf{x}_j]_l\}$, where $\mathbf{x}_i = \{\mathbf{x}_0^i, w_0^i, \mathbf{x}_\pi^i, w_\pi^i\}$ and l is the number of samples in the training set, a joint distribution is learnt by first concatenating the two sets of training data together so that $\mathbf{X}_{ij} = \{[\mathbf{x}_{ij}]_1, ..., [\mathbf{x}_{ij}]_l\}$ where $\mathbf{x}_{ij} = (\mathbf{x}_i, \mathbf{x}_j)$. Using this data the joint probability distribution $p(\mathbf{x}_i, \mathbf{x}_j | \theta_{ij})$ can be estimated, however, as each training point is represented by a set of two vectors and two weights, $\mathbf{x}_i = \{\mathbf{x}_0^i, w_0^i, \mathbf{x}_\pi^i, w_\pi^i\}$ and $\mathbf{x}_j = \{\mathbf{x}_0^j, w_0^j, \mathbf{x}_\pi^j, w_\pi^j\}$, when concatenating the data we must do so for each possible combination of the ordering of ϕ, i.e. $\mathbf{x}_{ij} = \{\mathbf{x}_{00}^{ij}, \mathbf{x}_{0\pi}^{ij}, \mathbf{x}_{\pi 0}^{ij}, \mathbf{x}_{\pi\pi}^{ij}\}$ where for example $\mathbf{x}_{0\pi}^{ij} = \{(\mathbf{x}_0^i, \mathbf{x}_\pi^j), w_{0\pi}^{ij}\}$ and the corresponding scalar weights are simply multiplied together so that $w_{0\pi}^{ij} = w_0^i w_\pi^j$. The consequence of this is that for each pair of connected joints we have four sets of training data, a GMM is learnt for each independently. Each GMM is assigned a weight proportional to the total weight of the training set (e.g. $W_{0\pi}^{ij} = \sum_{k=1}^l \left[w_{0\pi}^{ij}\right]_k$) so that GMM's with more data clustered near the origin have a higher weight since these will better represent the data. The prior of each individual GMM component is then scaled by this weight.

The number of components used to represent each distribution in the model is set to reflect the increasing complexity in the distribution at nodes located at a further depth from the root node. To represent this we employ the following scheme: Joints connected directly to the root node are given three components and at every subsequent increase in depth a further two components are added. Under our model the maximum number of components is assigned to the wrists with nine components. Whilst this may immediately seem advantageous since the Rigid Joint model is afforded a maximum of nine components compared to the Loose Limbed's three, it should be noted that the rigid model's distribution must represent a far larger space; it is likely the three component distribution of the Loose Limbed model is far more representative of the training data once it has been converted into a relative form. Our argument is that in the process of converting the original training set so that a Loose Limbed model can be learnt a large amount of information is being discarded from it.

2.2   Sampling

As the graphical model used to represent the articulated object is a tree and the root node is assumed to be fixed, samples can be generated using ancestral sampling [10]. Samples are drawn hierarchically starting from those nodes closest to the root node, then at each step down the tree, moving away from the root node, a further set of samples can be drawn conditioned on those samples generated for the parent node. To efficiently search the pose space the number of particles are exponentially grown moving out from the root node. This ensures that the location of less constrained joints are searched using more samples. For each sample $\mathbf{x}_j^m$, N child samples are drawn from the limb conditional $[\mathbf{x}_i^n]_{n=1}^N \sim p(\mathbf{x}_i | \mathbf{x}_j^m, \theta_{ij})$, N is referred to as the growth rate. As very few particles are needed to describe the prior distribution for nodes near the root this exponential growth is not problematic, for example setting $N = 8$ will result in

4096 samples being generated for each of the wrists. For efficiency all covariances used to represent limb conditionals are assumed to be diagonal.

Loose Limbed Model. As the Loose Limbed model only uses an approximated limb conditional a sample $\mathbf{x}_i^n$ can be generated from a parent sample $\mathbf{x}_j^m$ simply by drawing a sample $\mathbf{x}_{ij}^n \sim p(\mathbf{x}_{ij}|\theta_{ij})$, which can then be transformed into the global frame of reference through $M(\mathbf{x}_i^n) = M(\mathbf{x}_{ij}^n)M(\mathbf{x}_j^m)$, where $M(\mathbf{x}_i^n)$ represents the 3D object-to-world transform. To draw a sample from this distribution a GMM component k^* is sampled from the marginal distribution $p(m_{ij}^k) = \lambda_{ij}^k$, where the connection parameters $m_{ij}^k = \{\mu_{ij}^k, \Sigma_{ij}^k, \lambda_{ij}^k\}$ define the mean, covariance and weighting of the kth component of the GMM respectively, following which a sample for $\mathbf{x}_{ij}^n$ can be drawn from $\mathbf{x}_{ij}^n \sim \mathcal{N}(\mu_{ij}^{k^*}, \Sigma_{ij}^{k^*})$.

Rigid Joint Model. Given a sample for the jth node $\mathbf{x}_j^m$, a sample can be drawn conditioned on this by first calculating the marginal likelihood of observing this for each component in the GMM. Given that all covariance matrices are diagonal, i.e. $\Sigma_{ij}^k = diag(\Lambda_{ii}^k, \Lambda_{jj}^k)$, the marginal likelihood is given by $p(\mathbf{x}_j^m|m_{ij}^k) = \lambda_{ij}^k \mathcal{N}(\mathbf{x}_j^m; \mu_j^k, \Lambda_{jj}^k)$. Once this has been calculated for all components the resultant distribution is normalized to give the conditional distribution $p(m_{ij}^k|\mathbf{x}_j^m)$. A GMM component can then be sampled from this distribution $k^* \sim p(m_{ij}^k|\mathbf{x}_j^m)$, from which a sample $\mathbf{x}_i^n$ can be drawn from the selected component $\mathbf{x}_i^n \sim \mathcal{N}(\mu_i^{k^*}, \Lambda_{ii}^{k^*})$. Notice that in the case of the Loose Limbed model $p(m_{ij}^k|\mathbf{x}_j^m) = p(m_{ij}^k)$ i.e. is independent of $\mathbf{x}_j^m$.

2.3   Rigid Joint Model: Observing a Joint

The problem in defining a model over joints as apposed to parts is that there does not exist one-to-one correspondences between joints and observations; we can not directly observe a joint only the parts to which it is connected. To accommodate this we define a set of m observable parts $p_i \in P$, where $m \neq n$ and n represents the number of joints in the model. We further define $v_j \in p_i$ as being the set of joints defining the ith part and conversely $p_j \in v_i$ as being the set of parts of which the ith joint is a member. The set of observations made for the parts are defined by $Z = \{\mathbf{z}_i, .., \mathbf{z}_m\}$. The observational likelihood for the ith part can be written as $p(\mathbf{z}_i|\{\mathbf{x}_{j\in p_i}\})$, where this distribution is dependent on a number of joint positions. Intuitively, this represents that for example the appearance of the forearm must be dependent on the location of both the wrist and elbow. To estimate $p(\mathbf{z}_i|\mathbf{x}_j)$ from $p(\mathbf{z}_i|\{\mathbf{x}_j, \mathbf{x}_{k\in p_i|j}\})$ the nodes $\mathbf{x}_{k\in p_i|j}$ can be treated as nuisance parameters and marginalized over. In practice this is cumbersome to calculate and instead the following approximations are used: If the $\mathbf{x}_{k\in p_i|j}$ are child nodes to $\mathbf{x}_j$ we calculate $p(\mathbf{z}_i|\mathbf{x}_j)$ using the expectation of the set of particles drawn from $\mathbf{x}_j$ as $\mathbf{x}_{k\in p_i|j}$. If they are parent nodes we use the sample of $\mathbf{x}_{k\in p_i|j}$ from which $\mathbf{x}_j$ was drawn. For the torso we use the expectation of the shoulder and hips since these joints are not directly connected and do not share child/parent relationships. This method then allows an approximation of the term $p(\mathbf{z}_i|\mathbf{x}_j)$ to be calculated.

We further need to account for that a joint may be a member of several parts, for example the elbow defines both the upper arm and forearm. To accommodate this the likelihood terms $p(\mathbf{z}_i|\mathbf{x}_j)$ are combined for all parts to which that joint is a member $p_i \in v_j$. This can be calculated as

$$p(\mathbf{z}_{i\in v_j}|\mathbf{x}_j) = \prod_{i\in v_j} p(\mathbf{z}_i|\mathbf{x}_j). \tag{2}$$

This suggests that to infer the position of a joint all parts to which it is connected must be observed. Whilst in this section we have described how the observation likelihood is calculated for a joint we will write $p(\mathbf{z}_{i\in v_j}|\mathbf{x}_j)$ as $p(\mathbf{z}_j|\mathbf{x}_j)$ so that the same notation can be used when describing optimization of both the Loose Limbed and Rigid Joint model in the following section.

2.4   Maximization

Maximizing the posterior is achieved using EM where a new prior is estimated at each iteration given the posterior calculated using the old prior (M-step), a new set of particles is then generated from the prior and the posterior re-estimated (E-step). Given a set of M particles for the jth joint $\left[\mathbf{x}_j^m\right]_{m=1}^{M}$ each is assigned a weight proportional to the marginal likelihood $p(\mathbf{x}_j^m|\mathbf{z}_j)$. This can efficiently be calculated for each node using a simplified form of the Sum-Product algorithm. The outwards messages from the root node are represented by the generated set of samples and as such only backwards messages must be computed. Due to the ancestral sampling method used this can be efficiently calculated, the marginal for sample $\mathbf{x}_j^m$ is computed as

$$p(\mathbf{x}_j^m|\mathbf{z}_j) = p(\mathbf{z}_j|\mathbf{x}_j^m) \prod_{i\in C_j} \sum_{n=1}^{N} p(\mathbf{x}_i^n|\mathbf{z}_i) \tag{3}$$

where $i \in C_j$ is the set of nodes that are the children of the jth node and the summation is performed over the set of N samples that were drawn conditioned on the sample $\mathbf{x}_j^m$ under the ancestral sampling method.

At each iteration simulated annealing is used to ensure the distribution converges so that $w_j^m = p(\mathbf{x}_j^m|\mathbf{z}_j)^{\beta}$, where β is calculated at each iteration so approximately 60% of the particles would be discarded if resampling were performed [9]. Given the set of weighted samples the prior can then be reestimated.

2.5   Limb Likelihoods

A part is represented by a rectangular patch and defined by the joints that it is composed from (Rigid Joint) or the proximal/distal joint of the part (Loose Limbed). We use two image cues, edges and color. Edge cues are exploited using a set of M overlapping HOG features [11] placed along the edges of the part. Each feature is represented as a single normalized histogram of the local image gradients and are combined such that $p(\mathbf{z}_j|\mathbf{x}_j)_{edge} = \frac{1}{M}\prod_{m=1}^{M} H(\theta_\perp)$, where $H(\theta_\perp)$ returns the value in the histogram bin that is perpendicular to the edge of the proposed part.

Color is exploited by placing a bounding box at the location of the root node and then learning a foreground model using the pixel values within the box and a model for the background using pixels outside the box. The models are learnt using a GMM. This creates a very crude and noisy foreground probability map, the likelihood is then calculated as the average foreground probability value encompassed by the part. The individual likelihoods for each cue are then combined as $p(\mathbf{z}_j|\mathbf{x}_j) = p(\mathbf{z}_j|\mathbf{x}_j)_{edge}p(\mathbf{z}_j|\mathbf{x}_j)_{col}$.

3   Experiments

Both a Rigid Joint and Loose Limbed model were learnt using the Train partition of the HumanEva dataset using $\approx$ 4500 frames of data taken across all subjects and actions. Samples drawn from the prior of each model can be seen in Fig. 1 along with the training data from which the models were learnt. It is clear in this figure that the samples drawn from the Rigid Joint model much more closely resemble that of the training data, the samples from the Loose Limbed model are much more broad and shows less clear structure, this is particularly clear on the feet.

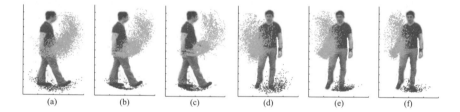

Fig. 1. Comparing samples of the left foot (green) and right wrist (blue) generated by each model representation and the training data. Side View: (a) Loose Limbed model (b) Rigid Joint model (c) Training data. Frontal view: (d) Loose Limbed model (e) Rigid Joint Model (f) Training data.

To compare the performance of both models a test set was created from the Validation partition of the HumanEva dataset. This was composed of 100 randomly selected frames from each action category (Box, Gesture, ThrowCatch, Walk, Jog) selected across all color views and all subjects, so that 500 frames were used in total. The root node and orientation was set using the pelvis marker data from the groundtruth provided and the scale was set as the maximum distance between the head and the feet. This scale is often inaccurate (e.g. if the subject was squatting) however, is used so all experiments are easily reproducible.

Both methods used the same settings so that the only difference in each experiment was the model used. Quantitative results can be see in Fig. 2 where it can be seen that the Rigid Joint representation outperforms the Loose Limbed model. We also experimented between updating the model by calculating marginals using Equation 3 or simply using local image evidence (i.e. setting $p(\mathbf{x}_j^m|\mathbf{z}_j) = p(\mathbf{z}_j|\mathbf{x}_j^m)$). As shown the use of marginals improves the error, this is because these allow information about observations being made at the extremities of the tree to influence the convergence of those parts nearer the root node.

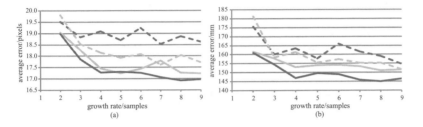

Fig. 2. Pose estimation errors as a function of growth rate (N) for 2D (a) and 3D (b) pose estimation after ten iterations of the algorithm. Dashed lines represent Loose Limbed model and solid lines Rigid Joint model. The green and purple line show the error using full marginals and the blue and red line shows the error using only local image evidence.

In Fig. 3 the expected pose and samples drawn from the prior are presented after each iteration for the example shown, as can be seen the Rigid Joint model converges much faster than the Loose Limbed model. Notice also the slip between the parts of the lower left leg in Fig. 3 (a) (v) this is as joint positions are not constrained to coincide in the Loose-Limbed representation.

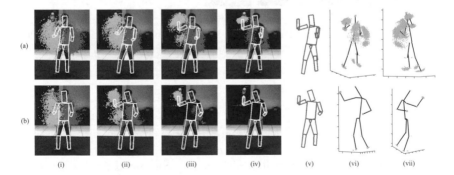

Fig. 3. Example of convergence for Loose Limbed model (a) and Rigid Joint model (b). (i) to (iv) shows iterations 1, 3, 5, 10 respectively. Samples for the left (red) and right (green) wrist drawn from each prior are also shown as is the expected pose. (v) shows the final expected pose. (vi) and (vii) show the final 3D reconstruction with samples that have been drawn from the final model.

To illustrate why a conditional model converges more efficiently than an approximated conditional model consider Fig. 4, which shows a hypothetical multimodal distribution. Whilst the full limb conditional model can converge, the relative limb conditional can not until its parent's limb conditional has converged to a single mode. In Fig. 5 an example is shown using a growth rate $N = 2$, this uses just a maximum of 16 samples for the wrists. However, as can be seen the presented method still finds the correct solution, it is the performance using very few samples that is particularly impressive and makes this approach of value.

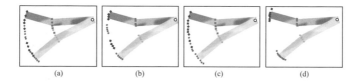

Fig. 4. Hypothetical two part example highlighting the difference in convergence between a relative limb conditional (a) and (b) and a full limb conditional (c) and (d). (a) and (c) show the prior model and (b) and (d) the model after a number of iterations. Both limb conditionals are represented by a two component GMM where each component is represented by different colors. Whilst the conditional model can represent each observational mode by a single Gaussian (d), the relative model can not and as such 'phantom modes' appear in the prior (b) slowing convergence.

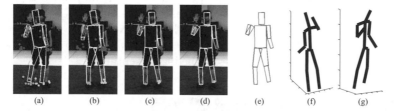

Fig. 5. Example of convergence and 3D pose estimation using a growth rate $N = 2$. (a) - (d) Iteration 1, 2, 4 and 10 respectively. (e) Expected pose as shown in (d). (f) and (g) final 3D expected pose.

4   Conclusions

A method has been presented to estimate 3D pose from single images using a stochastic search and Expectation Maximization. A novel part based representation has been defined over joint positions and compared against an existing method, it has been shown quantitatively that the presented method outperforms that of the Loose Limbed model. Furthermore, we have demonstrated qualitatively that using full limb conditionals results in a model that is more representative of the original training set and efficiently converges under the EM algorithm. Whilst in this paper it has been assumed the root node is fixed the approach can be generalized to account for uncertainty in this value by sampling multiple root node positions and will be the focus of future work.

References

1. Felzenswalb, P.F., Huttenlocher, D.P.: Pictorial Structures for Object Recogntion. International Journal on Computer Vision 61, 55–79 (2005)
2. Sigal, L., Bhatia, S., Roth, S., Black, M.J., Isard, M.: Tracking Loose-Limbed People. In: CVPR, pp. 421–428 (2005)
3. Andriluka, M., Roth, S., Schiele, B.: Pictorial Structures Revisited: People Detection and Articualted Pose Estimation. In: CVPR, pp. 1–8 (2009)
4. Ramanan, D.: Learning to Parse Images of Articulated Bodies. In: NIPS, pp. 1129–1136 (2006)
5. Sigal, L., Balan, A., Black, M.: HumanEva: Synchronized Video and Motion Capture Dataset and Baseline Algorithm for Evaluation of Articulated Human Motion. International Journal of Computer Vision 87, 4–27 (2009)
6. Isard, M.: PAMPAS: Real-Valued Graphical Models for Computer Vision. In: CVPR, pp. 613–620 (2003)
7. Hua, G., Wu, Y.: Variational Maximum a Posteriori by Annealed Mean Field Analysis. IEEE Transaction on Pattern Analysis and Machine Intelligience 27, 1747–1761 (2005)
8. Deutscher, J., Davidson, A., Reid, I.: Automatic Partitioning of High Dimensional Search Space associated with Articulated Body Motion Capture. In: CVPR, pp. 669–676 (2001)
9. Deutscher, J., Blake, A., Reid, I.: Articualted Body Motion Capture by Annealed Particle Filtering. In: CVPR, pp. 126–133 (2000)
10. Bishop, C.M.: Pattern Recognition and Machine Learning. Springer, Heidelberg (2006)
11. Dalal, N., Triggs, B.: Histogram of Orientated Gradients for Human Detection. In: CVPR, pp. 886–893 (2005)
12. Ferrari, V., Marin-Jimenez, M., Zisserman, A.: Progressive Search Space Reduction for Human Pose Estimation. In: CVPR, pp. 1–8 (2008)
13. Gao, J., Shi, J.: Multiple Frame Motion Inference using Belief Propagation. In: IEEE Conference on Automatic Face and Gesture Recognition, pp. 875–880 (2004)
14. Bernier, O., Cheung-Mon-Chan, P.: Real-Time 3D Articualted Pose Tracking using Particle filter and Belief Propagation on Factor Graphs. In: BMVC, pp. 27–36 (2006)

A Proposal for Local and Global Human Activities Identification

Antonio Fernández-Caballero,
José Carlos Castillo, and José María Rodríguez-Sánchez

Departamento de Sistemas Informáticos & Instituto de Investigación en Informática
Universidad de Castilla-La Mancha, Campus Universitario s/n, 02071-Albacete, Spain
`caballer@dsi.uclm.es`

Abstract. There are a number of solutions to automate the monotonous task of looking at a monitor to find suspicious behaviors in video surveillance scenarios. Detecting strange objects and intruders, or tracking people and objects, is essential for surveillance and safety in crowded environments. The present work deals with the idea of jointly modeling simple and complex behaviors to report local and global human activities in natural scenes. In order to validate our proposal we have performed some tests with some CAVIAR test cases. In this paper we show some relevant results for some study cases related to visual surveillance, namely "speed detection", "position and direction analysis", and "possible cashpoint holdup detection".

Keywords: Human activities, simple behaviors, complex behaviors.

1 Introduction

Detecting strange objects and intruders, or tracking people and objects, is essential for surveillance and safety in crowded environments [21], [9]. Much research has been dedicated to understanding human activities in the last decade (e.g. [10], [4]). Advanced visual surveillance systems not only need to track moving objects but also interpret their patterns of behavior [5]. Generally, these systems can detect a few simple concepts in video streams. The task of activity recognition is to bridge the gap between numerical pixel level data and a high-level abstract activity description. Activities analysis consists of feature extraction, basic activity description and complex activity description. Complex activities are composed of many single activities with their temporal relations. According to the features used for analysis, the activity analysis methods can be classified into three kinds, spatial based (such as shape), motion based (such as trajectory), and spatial-temporal based methods. Many techniques and methods have been used so far in human activity recognition and understanding. According to [12], shape features and spatial-temporal features are often used for single person activity analysis, and motion features can be used for interactive person activity.

F.J. Perales and R.B. Fisher (Eds.): AMDO 2010, LNCS 6169, pp. 78–87, 2010.

Bayesian networks have been used to recognize static postures or simple events. In [13] an activity recognition approach is proposed in which an activity is decomposed into multiple interactive stochastic processes, each corresponding to one scale of motion details. In [16] abnormal activities involving two persons using Recurrent Bayesian networks (RBNs) are detected. Recently, in [29] a novel unsupervised learning framework to model activities and interactions in crowded and complicated scenes is proposed. Inspired by the applications in speech recognition, the hidden Markov model (HMM) formalism has been extensively applied to activity recognition (e.g. [8]). In [2] an automatic technique is proposed for detection of abnormal events in crowds where the motion models are HMMs to cope with the variable number of motion samples that might be present in each observation window. In [25] a Bayesian computer vision system for modeling and recognizing human interactions using CHMMs and HMMs is described. Another approach [11] models scenario events from shape and trajectory features using a hierarchical activity representation, where events are organized into several layers of abstraction, providing flexibility and modularity in modeling scheme. In [1] a real-time system to detect context-independent events in video shots is proposed. In [15], recent approaches of video event understanding are presented. The importance of the two main component of the event understanding process – abstraction and event modeling– is also pointed out. Abstraction corresponds to the process of molding the data into informative units to be used as input to the event model [26,14,27,22] while event modeling is devoted to describing events of interest formally and enabling recognition of these events as they occur in the video sequence [28]. Our approach is closely related to the works of Ivanov and Bobick [13] and Hongeng et al. [11] in the sense that the external knowledge about the problem domain is incorporated into the expected structure of the activity model. Motion-based image features are linked explicitly to a symbolic notion of hierarchical activity through several layers of more abstract activity descriptions. Atomic actions are detected at a low level and fed to hand-crafted grammars to detect activity patterns of interest. Our inspiration also is close to the paper by [1], as we work with shape and trajectory to indicate the events related to moving objects.

2   Description of Local and Global Activities

Analyzing a video scene entails two large phases. On the one hand, we have the first phase in object detection [19], namely segmentation (e.g. [6], [20], [18]) and tracking o (e.g. [7], [17]). This phase consists of capturing images, analyzing them for shape interpretation and afterwards, recognizing them throughout the scene. On the other hand, we have the part this work focuses on, namely, scene interpretation (context recognition), made up of *basic actions* interpretation, *global behavior* interpretation and finally, interpretation of the *scene on a global scale*. In our proposal, the purpose of activity description is to reasonably choose a group of motion words or shout expressions to report activities of moving objects or humans in natural scenes.

2.1   Objects of Interest

From the ETISEO (see http://www-sop.inria.fr/orion/ETISEO/index.htm)
classification, four categories are established for dynamic objects and two for
static objects. As for the first, we distinguish between a *person*, a *group of people*
(made up of two or more people), a *portable object* (such as a brief case) and
other dynamic objects (able to move on its own), classified as *moving object*.
As for static objects, we will distinguish between *areas* and *pieces of equipment*.
The latter can be labeled as a portable object if a dynamic object, people or
group, interacts with it and it starts moving.

2.2   Description of Local Activities

In order to generalize the detection process we start with small functionalities
which detect simple actions of the active objects in the scene. Using these functions, we build behavior patterns much more complex and suited for the aims
of each video surveillance system. These small actions are defined by action
indicative queries about the actions performed by an active object (see Table 1).

Table 1. Local activities

Action	Origin vertex	Destination vertex
Object-like	Object speed	Makes it possible to define if an object is still, walking, running, going at great speeds, etc.
	Object trajectory	Apart from speed, we can obtain the direction and moving direction of an object.
Environment interaction	Direction	The system must determine if a person is approaching a specific area of the scenario. By taking the object's speed and trajectory as reference, the object's ultimate goal is inferred.
	Position	By knowing the important areas of the scenario, the system is capable of determining the relative position of dynamic objects. This way, it can detect if a person is standing in one of the areas.
Object inter-action	Proximity	The system must detect the distance between objects.
	Orientation	The system determines whether an object is approaching another or whether they are both approaching each other.
	Grouping	The system uses the parameters generated in the two previous points to detect object grouping (by taking into account its proximity and direction).

2.3   Description of Global Activities

Interpreting a visual scene is a task which, in general, resorts to a large body
of prior knowledge and experience of the viewer [23]. Through the actions or
queries described in the previous section, we can find out basic patterns (an
object speed or direction) and more complex patterns (e.g. the theft of a purse).
It is essential to define the desired behavior pattern in each situation, by using
the basic actions or queries from the previous section. For each specific scene, a
state diagram and a set of rules are designed to indicate the patterns.

The proposed video surveillance system will be able to detect simple actions
or queries and adapt to a great deal of situations. Also, it will be configured to
detect the behavior patterns necessary in each case and associate an alarm level
to each one which will enable them to be filtered and have a priority associated.

3   Image Preprocessing

Input image segmentation is not enough to detect the activities in the scene, other data which are not included (speed and direction) are necessary. Thus, the system takes the initial segmentation data and infers the new necessary parameters. For it, the preprocessing techniques described in Table 2 are necessary.

Table 2. Preprocessing techniques

Preprocessing	Details
Speed Hypothesis	The average speed for each object is calculated by dividing the displacement (Δx) by the time that has elapsed (Δt) in each frame.
Direction and Moving Direction Hypothesis	To find out the direction of objects, we calculate the angle of the straight line that passes through the positions of the previous and current instants in each object.
Image Rectification	Perspective distortion occurs because the distance between the furthest points from the camera is less than the distance between the closest points. The real position is measured through the weighted distance measure of the four manually placed points closest to the position we wish to interpolate.
Data Smoothing	The data taken at two time instants will be separated with enough time to avoid small distortions but this distance will be small enough to enable accurate results. We will call this distance between both consecutive time instants, interval analysis. At each interval analysis, the value of the hypotheses is updated, but the old value is not automatically substituted for the new one. To calculate the value at that instant, we calculate the means for both values.

4   Specification of Behaviors

4.1   Specification of Simple Behaviors

The system should be able to respond to a series of queries intended to find out behavior patterns of objects in the scene (see Table 3). These queries are defined as functions and return a logical value, which will be true if they are fulfilled for a specific object. They are represented in the following format:

$$query\ (parameter_1, parameter_2, ..., parameter_n)$$

4.2   Specification of Complex Behaviors

Patterns at a global level are used to analyze the scene from a general point of view without focusing on any specific object (detect patterns where more than one object intervenes).

Local Complex Behaviors. Objects in the scene are associated to a state machine that indicates the state they are in (what they are doing at that time instant). This state machine can be seen as a directed graph where the vertices are the possible states of the object and the edges are the basic functions or queries previously discussed. An edge has at least one associated outcome of the assessment (true or false) of a query, indicating an action of object, query q_i.

Table 3. Simple Queries

Type	Query	Description
Movement-based	*hasSpeedBetween (min, max)*	It is fulfilled if the object moves at a speed within the range [*min, max*].
	hasSpeedGreaterThan (speed)	It is fulfilled if the object moves at a speed greater than that indicated in the parameter *speed*.
Orientation-based Direction	*hasDirection (staticObject)*	It is fulfilled if the object is headed towards *staticObject*, being *staticObject* a static object in the scene.
	isFollowing ()	It is true if a dynamic object is following a non-dynamic object. We use the displacement angle.
Location-based	*isInsideZone (staticObject)*	It is true if a dynamic object is on the static object *staticObject*.
	isCloseTo (distance, staticObject)	It is fulfilled if the object is closer than distance from the static object *staticObject*.
	enterInScene ()	It is fulfilled when the object appears in the scene for the first time.

Therefore, an edge can have more than one query associated to it. For an edge with several actions to be fulfilled, all the associated queries have to be fulfilled. If a more complex rule is needed, where disjunctions also appear so that an object changes states, the rule must be divided into two edges.

Global Complex Behaviors. To detect global behavior patterns, more than just the local state machine from the previous section is needed since only the state of each object in that machine is reflected separately. These patterns are represented through state machines which vertices represent a possible state in the scene. Just like in the local state machine, the edges are made up of a series of queries that must be fulfilled at a certain time for the scene to change states.

5   Data and Results

In order to validate our proposal we have opted for working with the test cases that CAVIAR (coming from the EC Funded CAVIAR project/IST 2001 37540, found at URL: http://homepages.inf.ed.ac.uk/rbf/CAVIAR/) makes available for researchers. In fact, the test cases offer ground truth data; this enables bypassing the segmentation phase and only focusing on the problem of human activities identification. Of course, due to the limitation in pages of the current article, only a very limited set of examples may be provided. Concretely, in this paper we show some relevant results for the following study cases: "speed detection", "position and direction analysis", and "possible cashpoint holdup detection". This is a usual approach (e.g. [3], where the detection and classification of fighting and pre and post fighting events when viewed from a video camera is investigated).

5.1   Image Preprocessing

We select the first frame in any scene as backdrop image to make the placement of control points and fixed objects easier. Control points are used to compensate

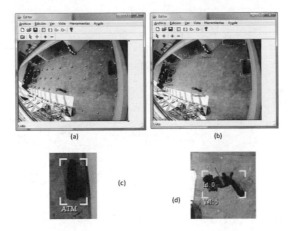

Fig. 1. Test environment for CAVIAR. (a) Position point maps. (b) Fixed objects in the scene. (c) Labeling of a static object in the scene. (d) Labeling of a dynamic object in the scene.

image distortion caused by the perspective and camera lens. Control points are interpolated using the four reference positions provided by CAVIAR (see Fig 1a). After creating the point map, we point out the fixed objects in the scene that will interact with the dynamic objects (as shown in Fig. 1b). In Fig. 1c and 1d, you may find examples of the labeling of a static object and a dynamic object, respectively, in the scene.

5.2   Speed Detection

In this case, we detect if the person starts running or moves slowly. To do this, we use the queries "hasSpeedBetween" and "hasSpeedGreaterThan" with their associated local state diagram (see Fig. 2a). When adjusting the alarm level to I and analyzing scene `Browse2` (series *Browsing*, case *Person browsing and reading for a while*), we get the output shown in Table 4. If the alarm level is adjusted to II and scene `Fight_RunAway1` (series *Two people fighting*, test case *Two people meet, fight and run away*) is analyzed, we get Table 5 as output. As shown, the application has detected the time when the two people started running.

5.3   Position and Direction Analysis

A configuration was designed for the purpose not only to analyze the position of people in a scene, but also to predict if someone is headed towards a specific position. Queries "isInsideZone" and "isCloseTo" are used to detect position and query "hasDirection" in order to generate a direction hypothesis. Fig. 2b shows the automaton that detects if someone is headed towards or is at the wastebasket, the leaflets, the seats or the cashpoint. Tests on three different scenes have been run. Table 6 shows the results from the analysis of scenes `Rest_InChair`, `Browse2`, and `Browse3`.

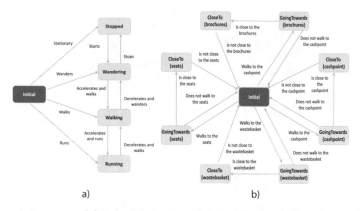

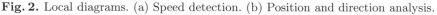

a)   b)

Fig. 2. Local diagrams. (a) Speed detection. (b) Position and direction analysis.

There are false positives in the last two tests. They are in the 14th second of test case `Browse2` and in the 15th second of test case `Browse3`. Indeed, object 3 was not going to the wastebasket but the direction of the object at that time made it seem like it could be going there. To avoid this, we could add another rule to edge direction to avoid predicting a possible target if the object is too far away. We could add an "isCloseTo" query to act along with queries "hasDirection" and "hasSpeedGreaterThan".

Table 4. Results of speed detection in scene "Browse2"

Time	Object	State	Alarm	Time	Object	State	Alarm
0:00:00	0	Stopped	I	0:00:12	3	Walking	I
	1	Stopped			3	Wandering	
	1	Wandering		0:00:13	3	Walking	I
0:00:01	1	Walking	I	0:00:14	3	Wandering	I
0:00:04	1	Wandering	I	0:00:15	3	Walking	I
0:00:05	1	Stopped	I	0:00:21	3	Wandering	I
	1	Wandering		0:00:22	3	Stopped	I
0:00:06	1	Walking	I	0:00:30	3	Wandering	I
0:00:07	2	Walking	I		3	Walking	
	2	Wandering		0:00:33	3	Wandering	I
	2	Stopped			3	Stopped	
0:00:09	1	Wandering	I				
	2	Wandering					

5.4   Possible Cashpoint Holdup Detection

It is also possible to design configurations able to detect suspicious behaviors. Here is an example pertaining to a situation related to a cashpoint. First, a local state diagram is created to detect the different ways of getting to the cashpoint. With this graph, we will be able to know if someone is going to the cashpoint, how fast he/she is going and if he/she is already next to the cashpoint. In the local state diagram shown in Fig. 3a, we see how a person can go into three states from the initial state: going towards the cashpoint slowly, walking or running.

Table 5. Results of speed detection in scene "Fight_RunAway1"

Time	Object	State	Alarm
0:00:15	7	Running	II
0:00:16	6	Running	II

Table 6. Results of position and direction analysis in scenes "Rest_InChair", "Browse2" and "Browse3"

Scene	Time	Object	State	Alarm
Rest_InChair	0:00:13	1	GoingTowards (seats)	II
	0:00:16	1	InsideZone (seats)	III
Browse 2	0:00:14	3	GoingTowards (wastebasket)	II
	0:00:16	3	GoingTowards (cashpoint)	II
	0:00:21	3	CloseTo (cashpoint)	III
Browse 3	0:00:15	3	GoingTowards (cashpoint)	II
	0:00:20	3	GoingTowards (leaflets)	II
	0:00:20	3	CloseTo (leaflets)	III

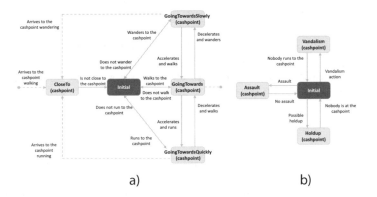

Fig. 3. Holdup at a cashpoint. (a) Local diagram. (b) Global diagram.

Thus two parameters are controlled, a person's speed and whether or not a person is going to the cashpoint.

Once the local state diagram has been created, we go on to behavior pattern specification at global level in the scene. Fig. 3b shows how the automaton is able to detect the suspicious behaviors described. Indeed, the diagram of Fig. 3b can detect suspicious behaviors, such as when there is someone at the cashpoint and someone else approaches him/her slowly. It can also detect if there is someone at the cashpoint and one or more people run towards him/her. Lastly, it can detect possible vandalism at the cashpoint. It will detect if one or more people run to the cashpoint and there is no one using it.

6   Conclusions

In this paper, an approach to human activities detection in complex scenarios has been presented. The approach describes two levels in which activities should be considered: local activities are necessary to generalize the detection process; and global activities are used to detect behavior patterns that involve not only a single object, but also groups of objects (or even the whole set of objects) in the scene. Some parameters must be inferred from the objects in the scene, such as speed or direction. The system takes the initial segmentation to calculate these parameters. Next, a set of queries are proposed in order to specify simple behaviors (to detect movement, orientation and location of the objects), and complex behaviors (where one or several objects intervenes).

In comparison to other approaches, such as Bayesian Networks or HMMs [24], our proposal is not able to model uncertainty in video events; but it is presented as a useful tool in video event understanding because of its simplicity, its ability to model temporal sequence and its ability to easily incorporate new actions. The results obtained so far are promising and we are currently engaged in performing test with real segmented data taken from different scenarios.

Acknowledgements

This work was partially supported by the Spanish Ministerio de Ciencia e Innovación under projects TIN2007-67586-C02-02 and TIN2010-20845-C03-01, and by the Spanish Junta de Comunidades de Castilla-La Mancha under projects PII2I09-0069-0994 and PEII09-0054-9581.

References

1. Amer, A., Dubois, E., Mitiche, A.: Rule-based real-time detection of context-independent events in video shots. Real-Time Imaging 11(33), 244–256 (2005)
2. Andrade, E.L., Blunsden, S., Fisher, R.B.: Modelling crowd scenes for event detection. In: 18th International Conference on Pattern Recognition, vol. 1, pp. 175–178 (2006)
3. Blunsden, S., Fisher, R.B.: Pre-fight detection - Classification of fighting situations using hierarchical AdaBoost. In: Fourth International Conference on Computer Vision Theory and Applications, vol. 2, pp. 303–308 (2009)
4. Bobick, A.F., Davis, J.W.: The recognition of human movement using temporal templates. IEEE PAMI 23(3), 257–267 (2001)
5. Buxton, H., Gong, S.: Visual surveillance in a dynamic and uncertain world. Artificial Intelligence 78(1), 431–459 (1995)
6. Fernández-Caballero, A., López, M.T., Saiz-Valverde, S.: Dynamic Stereoscopic Selective Visual Attention (DSSVA): Integrating motion and shape with depth in video segmentation. ESWA 34(2), 1394–1402 (2008)
7. Fernández-Caballero, A., Gómez, F.J., López-López, J.: Road-traffic monitoring by knowledge-driven static and dynamic image analysis. ESWA 35(3), 701–719 (2008)
8. Galata, A., Johnson, N., Hogg, D.: Learning variable-length Markov models of behavior. CVIU 81(3), 398–413 (2001)
9. Gascueña, J.M., Fernández-Caballero, A.: On the use of agent technology in intelligent, multi-sensory and distributed surveillance. In: KER (2009) (in press)
10. Gavrila, D.M.: The visual analysis of human movement: a survey. CVIU 73(1), 82–98 (1999)

11. Hongeng, S., Nevatia, R., Bremond, F.: Video-based event recognition: activity representation and probabilistic recognition methods. CVIU 96(2), 129–162 (2004)
12. Huang, K., Wang, S., Tan, T., Maybank, S.: Human behavior analysis based on a new motion descriptor. IEEE CirSysVideo 19(12), 1830–1840 (2009)
13. Ivanov, Y.A., Bobick, A.F.: Recognition of visual activities and interactions by stochastic parsing. IEEE PAMI 22(8), 852–872 (2000)
14. Laptev, I., Pérez, P.: Retrieving actions in movies. In: International Conference on Computer Vision, pp. 1–8 (2007)
15. Lavee, G., Rivlin, E., Rudzsky, M.: Understanding video events: a survey of methods for automatic interpretation of semantic occurrences in video. IEEE SMC-C 39(5), 489–504 (2009)
16. Loccoz, N.M., Bremond, F., Thonnat, M.: Recurrent Bayesian network for the recognition of human behaviors from video. In: 3rd International Conference on Computer Vision Systems, pp. 68–77 (2003)
17. López, M.T., Fernández-Caballero, A., Fernández, M.A., Mira, J., Delgado, A.E.: Dynamic visual attention model in image sequences. IMAVIS 25(5), 597–613 (2007)
18. López, M.T., Fernández-Caballero, A., Fernández, M.A., Mira, J., Delgado, A.E.: Motion features to enhance scene segmentation in active visual attention. Pattern Recognition Letters 27(5), 469–478 (2006)
19. López, M.T., Fernández-Caballero, A., Mira, J., Delgado, A.E., Fernández, M.A.: Algorithmic lateral inhibition method in dynamic and selective visual attention task: Application to moving objects detection and labelling. ESWA 31(3), 570–594 (2006)
20. López-Valles, J.M., Fernández, M.A., Fernández-Caballero, A.: Stereovision depth analysis by two-dimensional motion charge memories. Pattern Recognition Letters 28(1), 20–30 (2007)
21. Moreno-Garcia, J., Rodriguez-Benitez, L., Fernández-Caballero, A., López, M.T.: Video sequence motion tracking by fuzzification techniques. ASOC 10(1), 318–331 (2010)
22. Natarajan, P., Nevatia, R.: View and scale invariant action recognition using multiview shape-flow models. In: IEEE Computer Society Conference on Computer Vision and Pattern Recognition, pp. 1–8 (2008)
23. Neumann, B., Möller, R.: On scene interpretation with description logics. IMAVIS 26(1), 82–101 (2008)
24. Oliver, N.M., Horvitz, E.: A comparison of HMMs and dynamic Bayesian networks for recognizing office activities. User Modeling, 199-209 (2005)
25. Oliver, N.M., Rosario, B., Pentland, A.P.: A Bayesian computer system for modeling human interactions. IEEE PAMI 22(8), 831–843 (2000)
26. Shechtman, E., Irani, M.: Matching local self-similarities across images and videos. In: IEEE Conference on Computer Vision and Pattern Recognition, pp. 1–8 (2007)
27. Tran, S.D., Davis, L.S.: Event modeling and recognition using Markov logic networks. In: Forsyth, D., Torr, P., Zisserman, A. (eds.) ECCV 2008, Part II. LNCS, vol. 5303, pp. 610–623. Springer, Heidelberg (2008)
28. Ulusoy, I., Bishop, C.M.: Generative versus discriminative methods for object recognition. In: The 2005 IEEE Computer Society Conference on Computer Vision and Pattern Recognition, vol. 2, pp. 258–265 (2005)
29. Wang, X., Ma, X., Grimson, W.E.L.: Unsupervised activity perception in crowded and complicated scenes using hierarchical Bayesian models. IEEE PAMI 31(3), 539–555 (2009)

Skeleton and Shape Adjustment and Tracking in Multicamera Environments

Marcel Alcoverro, Josep Ramon Casas, and Montse Pardàs

Technical University of Catalonia, Barcelona, Spain
{marcel,josep,montse}@gps.tsc.upc.edu

Abstract. In this paper we present a method for automatic body model adjustment and motion tracking in multicamera environments. We introduce a set of shape deformation parameters based on linear blend skinning, that allow a deformation related to the scaling of the distinct bones of the body model skeleton, and a deformation in the radial direction of a bone. The adjustment of a generic body model to a specific subject is achieved by the estimation of those shape deformation parameters. This estimation combines a local optimization method and hierarchical particle filtering, and uses an efficient cost function based on foreground silhouettes using GPU. This estimation takes into account anthropometric constraints by using a rejection sampling method of propagation of particles. We propose a hierarchical particle filtering method for motion tracking using the adjusted model. We show accurate model adjustment and tracking for distinct subjects in a 5 cameras set up.

1 Introduction

The capture and analysis of the motion of a human body is applied in a variety of fields such as bio-mechanical analysis, human computer interaction, ergonomics or character animation in films or video games. Markerless human motion capture has been an active research area for the last decade due to an increasing interest for non intrusive methods, those not requiring markers or sensors, that may spread the use of motion analysis outside laboratory environments [1].

Markerless motion capture (MMC) systems use models composed by the body shape representation and an articulated skeleton. These models should fulfill the anthropometric profile (AP) of the specific subject tracked in order to achieve an accurate pose estimation.

On one side, some authors use models based on separate rigid shapes, as cylinders [2], ellipsoids [3], that depend on a few parameters. Then, these geometric primitives are adjusted to the specific subject AP. Mikić in [3] proposes a method of adjustment of the model using Bayesian networks to model body part proportions.

On the other side, surface-based models employ a single surface for the entire body. Triangular meshes are an efficient representation of surfaces and can describe the body shape with fidelity, making them a common choice for body representation in MMC systems [4],[5]. The surface mesh of the tracked subject may be acquired by either a laser scan [4] or a multiview reconstruction algorithm

F.J. Perales and R.B. Fisher (Eds.): AMDO 2010, LNCS 6169, pp. 88–97, 2010.

[5], and then a skeleton is attached to it, using an automatic rigging algorithm
[6]. An alternative, more suitable for certain applications or environments, is to
adjust a generic anthropomorphic mesh and skeleton to the specific subject, deforming the mesh according to a set of parameters related to distinct body parts.
Anguelov et al. [7] propose the SCAPE method to model deformable surfaces,
which is based on models of pose and body shape variation that are learned from
a database of 3D scans. The SCAPE model is used for human motion analysis
in [8], where it is also automatically adjusted to the specific subject. Bandouch
et al. [9] use the RAMSIS model, whose design has been guided by ergonomic
considerations, and it is adjusted manually to the specific subject.

Several approaches use silhouettes of the active people in the scene as image
descriptors to define the matching functions [2], [4], [10]. Silhouettes are insensi-
tive to variations in the surface such as color, and encode significant information
to recover 3D poses. Other methods use matching functions that account for the
intersection between the model and the visual hull of the individual [5], [8], [3],
or measurements based on optical flow [4].

Regarding the estimation method, we can distinguish estimation based on a
single hypothesis, focusing on the efficiency of a local search, or methods maintaining multiple hypothesis in order to add robustness to errors. Within single
hypothesis (or local optimization) methods, a common approach is to define an
objective function in a least-squares framework [4], and then minimize the function using a gradient descent approach. Multiple hypothesis based methods, are
generally inspired by particle filtering. In a particle filtering scheme, each particle or hypothesis has an associated weight, that is updated according to the cost
function. The particles are propagated in time according to certain dynamics and
including a noise component. In the case of human motion, the high dimensionality requires the use of many particles to sample with sufficient density the pose
space. A solution to deal with the high dimensionality is to spread the particles
efficiently where a local minimum is more likely. For example, Deutscher et al.
[2] use simulated annealing to focus the particles on the global maxima of the
posterior. Another solution to the problem of the dimensionality is to partition
the space into a number of lower-dimensional spaces [11], [12], [9], considering
the underlying hierarchical structure of the kinematic tree.

In this paper, we propose a method to automatically adjust a surface-based
human body model to a specific subject and then track, using image data captured by a low number of cameras. The proposal consists in:

- *Estimation of the anthropometric profile.* We adopt an analysis-by-synthesis
  approach, as in motion tracking techniques, but in our case we estimate the
  AP of the person together with the pose, which is also determined. To obtain
  distinct shape configurations, we propose a mesh deformation technique that
  is guided by parameters related to the skeleton bones. Parameter estimation
  is achieved by using a local optimization method together with a hierarchical
  sampling strategy where anthropometric constraints are taken into account.
- *Motion tracking.* We present a method for motion tracking using the adjusted
  model with a hierarchical particle filtering algorithm.

For both tasks, model adjustment and tracking, we use an observation model based on foreground silhouettes, as they provide good information about the body shape and the cost can be efficiently computed using GPU.

In section 2 we explain the technique used to deform the polygonal mesh according to the pose parameters and the shape parameters related to the skeleton bones. Next, in section 3 we describe the model adjustment and tracking method proposed. Finally, in sections 4 and 5, we present some results and conclusions.

2   Skeleton Based Deformation Framework

In our work, we adjust a generic body model to a specific subject using multi-camera information. The body model comprises two components: an articulated skeleton that describes the kinematic properties and a triangular mesh that describes the shape. Any mesh of human shape can be used to form the model surface. Then, the skeleton will be embedded into the mesh using the method presented in [6]. In this section we propose a method to deform the body model. Later we use this method to adjust the model to the subject anthropometry.

The body skeleton can be described by the *kinematic tree* concept, that has been recently formulated in the context of motion capture in [4]. A kinematic tree is a set of D reference systems organized in a tree structure, and it represents the connectivity of the joints and bones of the skeleton. A *kinematic chain* is an ordered subset of joints such that all joints are father and son of each other. We call Λ_j the kinematic chain that ends at joint j.

The rigid motions associated to each joint can be represented by twists ξ_j. The homogeneous matrix $\mathbf{M} \in SE(3)$, which represents the transformation from the *model reference system* to the *joint reference system*, may be constructed from a given twist by computing the exponential map as $\mathbf{M} = \exp(\theta\hat{\xi})$, where $\theta\hat{\xi}$ is the matrix representation of a twist ξ [13].

The rigid body motion associated to a joint can be obtained as the product of the exponential maps along the corresponding kinematic chain,

$$\mathbf{M}_j = \prod_{i=1}^{n_j} \exp(\theta_{\Lambda_j(i)}\hat{\xi}_{\Lambda_j(i)}) \tag{1}$$

where n_j is the number of joints involved in the kinematic chain Λ_j and $\Lambda_j(i)$ is a mapping that represents the order in the kinematic chain. The parameters of $\hat{\xi}_j$ are known, as the location of the rotation axes for each joint is part of the model. Thus, the state of the kinematic tree, i.e the pose of the body, is defined by the joint angles state vector $\mathbf{\Theta} := (\theta_1, \ldots, \theta_D)$ and the 6 parameters of the twist ξ_0 associated to the model reference system.

We model the skin with a 3D triangular mesh whose vertices can move in space according to weights assigned to each vertex. The mesh deformation is achieved with the *linear blend skinning* (LBS) technique [14]. If $\mathbf{v}_i$ is the position of the vertex i, $\mathbf{M}_j$ is the transformation of the bone j, and $w_{i,j}$ is the weight of the bone j for vertex i, the position of the transformed vertex is given according to LBS as

$$\mathbf{v}'_i = \sum_{j=1}^{D} w_{i,j}(\mathbf{M}_j \mathbf{v}_i) \tag{2}$$

The skinning weights $w_{i,j}$ are generated with the automatic rigging software Pinocchio [6]. The weights are proportional to the distance from the vertex to the bone, and vary smoothly along the surface. These weights are normalized such that $\sum_{j=1}^{D} w_{i,j} = 1$.

2.1 Shape Deformation

In order to obtain different configurations of the shape and pose of the model, the LBS technique for deformation of the skin mesh is applied for three types of transformations $\mathbf{M}$ (see Figure 1) related to the bones of the skeleton:

- *Pose deformation*: The mesh is deformed to achieve a specific pose represented by the state vector $\boldsymbol{\Theta}$, where the bone transformations $\mathbf{M}_j$ are obtained by the product of maps described in equation 1. Then the final position for each vertex can be computed using equation 2.
- *Scale deformation*: In this case, the mesh is deformed according to the scaling of a bone of the skeleton. Consider a bone j with length L that is scaled such that its final length is $L' = (1 + \alpha_j)L$. Then, the transformation associated to a bone $\mathbf{M}_j$ corresponds to a translation along the direction of the bone, by an amount of translation $L' - L$. Note that scaling a bone implies that the resulting translation must be applied also to the child joints along the corresponding kinematic chain. Once the translation matrices for each bone are already defined, the new position for the vertices of the mesh can be computed again as in equation 2.
- *Deformation in radial direction*: The mesh also can be deformed along the radial direction of the bone. In this case, we compute a translation direction $\mathbf{t}_{i,j}$ for each vertex of the mesh i and bone j, defined as the direction from the vertex position $\mathbf{v}_i$ to the closest point on the considered bone j. For each vertex and bone we obtain $\mathbf{M}_{i,j}$, as the transformation equivalent to the translation $\beta_j \mathbf{t}_{i,j}$. The parameter β_j is the *radial scale* associated to the bone j. In this case, the vertex positions are obtained in the same way than for LBS described in equation 2 but, in this case the transformation matrix $\mathbf{M}_{i,j}$ is specific for each vertex and bone.

  This type of deformation is slightly modified to account for radial deformations predominant along a certain direction. This is useful for example for the torso, where we can apply deformations along x or y independently, to describe torso width or depth. To obtain this type of deformation, the translation $\mathbf{t}_{i,j}$ is weighted by its scalar product with the main direction of the deformation.

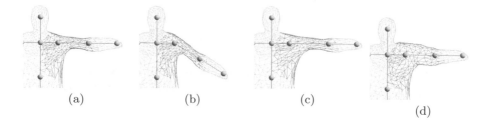

Fig. 1. Shape deformations associated with left upper arm bone (in red, edges whose vertices have $w_{i,j} > 0.1$) (a) Model at default configuration. (b) Pose deformation. (c) Scale deformation. (d) Deformation in radial direction.

3   Motion Capture Method

We propose a method for markerless motion capture with automatic model adjustment to the AP of the specific subject tracked. The model adjustment focuses on the estimation of the shape parameters for a single initialization frame, assuming that the pose is approximately known. Once the model is adjusted, the motion tracking is performed using this model. Both tasks, adjustment and tracking, have to deal with the high dimensionality of parameters to estimate and a multimodal observation model. Another important consideration is that the system has to deal with noisy measurements and ambiguities in the observation of the distinct body parts due to occlusions or misses of detection. For this reason, although we use a local optimization method for initialization, the estimation of the parameters is mainly performed with stochastic methods. Thus, formulated in probabilistic terms, the goal is to determine the posterior probability distribution over human poses and shape parameters, conditioned to the image measurements.

Several variations of particle filters have been demonstrated to cope well with the inference of the posterior distribution. A main drawback in particle filtering methods is that the amount of particles needed to achieve successful results grows exponentially with the number of dimensions, which make them computationally unfeasible. The hierarchical particle filter (HPF) [9], [12], also introduced as *partitioned sampling* [11], is based on a hierarchical decomposition of the pose space, so that different subparts are estimated independently. This approach aims to solve the mentioned problem of the dimensionality, and has been applied successfully for full body motion tracking. We propose hierarchical sampling strategies both for the model adjustment and for motion tracking. The same observation model is used for both tasks, modeled with the silhouette XOR cost function, described in following section.

3.1   Silhouette XOR Cost Function

The silhouette XOR cost function measures how close a given pose/shape hypothesis for the body is to the input foreground silhouettes. The number of

Table 1. Anthropometric entities size parameters (mean M_k and variance σ_k^2) used to model the probability of acceptance of a particle

	M_k	σ_k^2		M_k	σ_k^2
shoulder height	140.0	17.0	upperarms	25.5	4.0
head	25.0	5.0	lowerarms	30.5	10.0
clavicles	35.0	7.0	legs	90.5	17.0
arms	55.5	10.0	torso	52.0	8.0

evaluations of the cost function is very high, thus an efficient implementation of the cost function is decisive for system performance. The function we implement performs a pixel-wise XOR between the input image silhouettes and the rendered model silhouettes. This function is implemented in graphics hardware as proposed in [10].

First, the silhouettes of the input images are obtained by a background substraction technique. We use the *Running Gaussian Average* technique [15] to substract the background. Then, shadows and highlights are removed with the method proposed by Xu et al. [16]. Once foreground is detected, for each of the cameras we perform an XOR between the foreground silhouette from this camera and the model rendered on that view. The sum of all non-zero pixels resulting from this operation is the cost associated for this camera. We use the OpenGL stencil buffer and its associated operations to perform the XOR, so we can exploit the parallel processing of the GPU. Using an 8-bit stencil buffer we can perform the XOR operation for up to 8 cameras, obtaining the result with a single read of the stencil buffer. In this way, we can reduce the amount of memory transferred from the GPU to the CPU.

3.2 Model Adjustment

For the model adjustment we can use any generic mesh model of anthropomorphic shape with an attached skeleton previously rigged [6]. The number of parameters that conform the shape of the body is high, as they consist in the shape deformation parameters α_j, β_j for each bone, that we described in section 2.1. There is also a dependence of these parameters with the pose, in the way that the pose should be refined in order to obtain the optimal bone scale parameters. To tackle this estimation problem we combine a local optimization method with a hierarchical sampling strategy.

At the initial phase we perform a sequence of optimization steps using Powell's method [17] to adjust the pose and global scale of the model, assuming a known initial pose. In this case, we split the variables of each limb in separate optimization steps, which helps avoiding local minima, as proposed in [10].

Next, a hierarchical particle filter estimates the scale and radial deformation parameters (α_j, β_j) for each bone, starting with the skeleton and shape obtained by the local optimization explained above. The pose variables are also considered in the estimation, as a pose refinement is needed while estimating the scale of bones. The partition of the search space is designed such that the scaling of the bones does not affect hierarchically preceding scale parameters. Also the variables are grouped to conform meaningful anthropometric entities and to respect symmetry (see Table 1). For example, a meaningful anthropometric entity commonly considered in anthropometric studies is the *shoulders height*. To estimate the shoulders height all bones of the torso and legs are scaled together with the same parameter. In a similar manner, for example, variables are defined for clavicles, arms, legs and head scale. We denote by $\mathbf{\Phi}$ the anthropometric entities configuration vector, which consists of mappings to the variables α_j and β_j.

The hierarchical sampling method proposed is implemented as presented in previous works [9], [11], performing the *propagation, evaluation* and *resampling* steps for each of the levels of the hierarchy.

A particularity in our method is the propagation model we propose, which is based on the *rejection sampling* concept, and it is configured according to an anthropometric measurements database. The rejection sampling process operates as follows. Let us denote by $\{(\mathbf{s}, \pi)_i\}^h$ the set of N particles at the layer h, where $\mathbf{s}$ is an instance of the model configuration that consists of anthropometric entities and pose variables, $\mathbf{s} \in \{\mathbf{\Phi} \cup \mathbf{\Theta}\}$, and π is the particle weight.

At level h, candidate particles $\check{\mathbf{s}}_i$ are created from each particle $\mathbf{s}_i$ adding Gaussian noise as $\check{\mathbf{s}}_i = \mathbf{s}_i + \mathbf{N}$, where $\mathbf{N}$ is a multi-variate Gaussian random variable with mean $\mathbf{0}$ and diagonal covariance matrix $\mathbf{\Sigma} = diag\{\alpha^h \sigma_0, \alpha^{h-1}\sigma_1, \ldots, \sigma_h\}$. We denote by σ_h the variances associated to the variables considered at each level h, and α is a variance decay rate ($\alpha < 1$).

The probability of acceptance for a candidate particle is defined depending on the size of distinct anthropometric entities. The size of each anthropometric entity k is modeled with a Gaussian distribution $\mathcal{N}(M_k, \sigma_k^2)$ (see Table 1). For a given candidate particle $\check{\mathbf{s}}_i$ we calculate the actual sizes L_k for all the anthropometric entities $k \in \{0, \ldots, M-1\}$, and we compute a candidate probability,

$$P(\check{\mathbf{s}}_i) = \prod_{k=0}^{k=M-1} e^{-\left(\frac{(L_k - M_k)^2}{2\sigma_k^2}\right)} \tag{3}$$

Then, a candidate particle is accepted if

$$P(\check{\mathbf{s}}_i) > \tau P(\mathbf{s}_i) \tag{4}$$

where τ is the acceptance rate (experimentally, we set $\tau = 0.7$). We continue generating candidates until they fulfill the condition in equation 4, or we exceed a number of trials.

3.3   Motion Tracking

In order to track motion using the adjusted model, we implement the hierarchical particle filter, as already described above, but in this case only considering the pose space. We consider a partition of the pose space in 7 levels. The first layer estimates the global translation and rotation of the body. Next two layers estimate upper and lower leg joints. The rest four layers are dedicated to

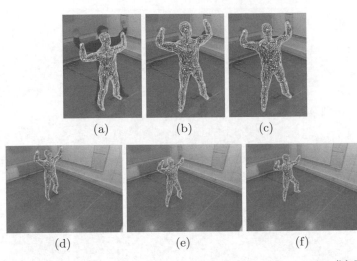

Fig. 2. Model adjustment. (a) Model set at the initial configuration. (b) Model after global scale and pose estimation using Powell method. (c) Model after shape and pose parameters estimation ($\{\boldsymbol{\Phi} \cup \boldsymbol{\Theta}\}$) using the hierarchical particle filter. (d,e,f) Model adjustment for distinct subjects.

the arms estimation, where we split the variables between upper and lower arm joints, and for the left and right arm independently. The propagation is modelled adding Gaussian noise as for model adjustment, but in this case we do not apply the rejection sampling approach, so all propagated particles are accepted.

4   Experimental Results

The method presented has been evaluated in a smart room environment with 5 cameras capturing at 25 fps. Ground truth data is not available, thus we cannot measure the model fitting quality or pose tracking errors, and we rely on visual inspection.

For the model adjustment, the subject is expected to adopt a pose with the hands up, the legs slightly open, looking at a predefined direction. The initial position is computed from the visual hull centroid (generated with the available silhouettes), and the model is scaled to fit the visual hull height. In figure 2.a we show the model set at the initial position and scale. Note that, as the initial pose is not exactly the subject pose, placing the model at the visual hull centroid is not accurate. After the optimization of the pose and global scale using Powell's method (Figure 2.b) the model is better adjusted, but for example, arms length and head size does not correspond with subject anthropometry. After the estimation of the shape parameters using the HPF (Figure 2.c) the model accurately fits the subject. Note that the model does not consider wrist joints and hands, thus those parts are less accurate. Figure 2(d,e,f) shows the adjusted model for different subjects.

With respect to the motion tracking, we tested the adjusted model for several subjects performing different activities in the smart room, as walking around,

Fig. 3. Motion tracking using the HPF with 500 particles and 7 layers

raising hands, jumping, crouching or sitting. We obtain successful results and the method performs accurately, except for fast movements, as in jumping actions, or when crouching, that several body parts appear self-occluded. The method is robust, recovers well from errors and the track is not lost in our tests for more than 3000 frames. In figure 3, we show several screenshots while performing some of those actions (each row shows a different subject)[1]. The processing time is ~ 25 sec. for a single frame, when using 500 particles.

5   Conclusion

We have introduced a mesh deformation framework that allows to adjust an anthropomorphic mesh to a specific subject shape. We have presented a method to automatically obtain the shape deformation parameters using foreground silhouettes. The hierarchical particle filtering method introduced allows to overcome the problem of the high dimensionality of the search space. Also, the anthropometric constraints introduced in the propagation of the particles allow to obtain feasible human shapes in case of ambiguities in the observation model, caused by self-occlusion or foreground detection misses. We have shown accurate model adjustment for several different subjects. These adjusted models allow for robust tracking using also HPF.

Future work involves testing the adjustment method with more subjects and different initial poses. The benefits can be twofold. On one side, more tests can provide information to reduce the set of parameters to estimate, by analysing the principal components over a population of AP's. On the other side, the study of

---

[1] Video available at http://gps-tsc.upc.es/imatge/_Marcel/adjustment.html

the adjustment with different initial poses will be useful to extend the presented method to perform the AP acquisition during motion sequences.

Acknowledgments. This work has been partially supported by the Spanish Ministerio de Educación y Ciencia, under project CENIT-VISION 2007-1007, and project TEC2007-66858/TCM. We would like to thank Adolfo López for his helpful suggestions on particle filtering and rejection sampling methods.

References

1. Poppe, R.: Vision-based human motion analysis: An overview. CVIU 108(1-2), 4–18 (2007)
2. Deutscher, J., Blake, A., Reid, I.: Articulated body motion capture by annealed particle filtering. In: IEEE CVPR '00, vol. 2, pp. 126–133 (2000)
3. Mikić, I.: Human Body Model Acquisition and Tracking using Multi-Camera Voxel Data. PhD thesis, University of California, San Diego (2002)
4. Ballan, L., Cortelazzo, G.M.: Marker-less motion capture of skinned models in a four camera set-up using optical flow and silhouettes. In: 3DPVT, USA (2008)
5. Vlasic, D., Baran, I., Matusik, W., Popović, J.: Articulated mesh animation from multi-view silhouettes. ACM TOG 27(3), 1–9 (2008)
6. Baran, I., Popović, J.: Automatic rigging and animation of 3d characters. In: SIGGRAPH '07, p. 72. ACM, New York (2007)
7. Anguelov, D., Srinivasan, P., Koller, D., Thrun, S., Rodgers, J., Davis, J.: SCAPE: shape completion and animation of people. In: SIGGRAPH '05, vol. 24(3), pp. 408–416 (2005)
8. Corazza, S., Mündermann, L., Gambaretto, E., Ferrigno, G., Andriacchi, T.: Markerless Motion Capture through Visual Hull, Articulated ICP and Subject Specific Model Generation. IJCV 87(1-2), 156–169 (2010)
9. Bandouch, J., Engstler, F., Beetz, M.: Accurate Human Motion Capture Using an Ergonomics-Based Anthropometric Human Model. In: Perales, F.J., Fisher, R.B. (eds.) AMDO 2008. LNCS, vol. 5098, p. 248. Springer, Heidelberg (2008)
10. Carranza, J., Theobalt, C., Magnor, M., Seidel, H.: Free-viewpoint video of human actors. ACM TOG 22(3), 569–577 (2003)
11. MacCormick, J., Isard, M.: Partitioned Sampling, Articulated Objects, and Interface-Quality Hand Tracking. In: Vernon, D. (ed.) ECCV 2000. LNCS, vol. 1843, pp. 3–19. Springer, Heidelberg (2000)
12. Canton-Ferrer, C., Casas, J.R., Pardàs, M.: Exploiting structural hierarchy in articulated objects towards robust motion capture. In: Perales, F.J., Fisher, R.B. (eds.) AMDO 2008. LNCS, vol. 5098, pp. 82–91. Springer, Heidelberg (2008)
13. Bregler, C., Malik, J., Pullen, K.: Twist based acquisition and tracking of animal and human kinematics. IJCV 56(3), 179–194 (2004)
14. Lewis, J., Cordner, M., Fong, N.: Pose space deformation: a unified approach to shape interpolation and skeleton-driven deformation. In: SIGGRAPH '00, pp. 165–172. ACM, New York (2000)
15. Piccardi, M.: Background subtraction techniques: a review. In: 2004 IEEE Conference on Systems, Man and Cybernetics, Vol. 4 (2004)
16. Xu, L., Landabaso, J., Pardas, M.: Shadow removal with blob-based morphological reconstruction for error correction. In: IEEE ICASSP '05, Vol. 2 (2005)
17. Press, W., Flannery, B., Teukolsky, S., Vetterling, W.: Numerical recipes in C: the art of scientific computing (1992)

Learning Generic Human Body Models*

Thomas Walther and Rolf P. Würtz

Institut für Neuroinformatik, Ruhr-Universität, 44780 Bochum, Germany
thomas.walther@ini.rub.de, rolf.wuertz@ini.rub.de

Abstract. We describe a posture estimation system based on Organic Computing concepts, which learns a generic body model from video input in a self-governed manner. We show experimentally that the constructed model generalizes well to different attire and persons.

1 Introduction

Analyzing human body poses by mere observation is a topic of growing interest in computer vision — with application potential ranging from surveillance over man-machine communication to motion picture animation. Yet, the artificial pose estimation (PE) approaches developed over the last two decades are nowhere close to matching human visual skills. This may be due to different working principles of artificial and biological vision systems. In the following, we aim at levelling these differences by Organic Computing (OC) concepts, in short, the attempt to make artificial systems more self-organized in their behavior [1]. In particular, we propose a PE system that acquires knowledge in a completely unsupervised manner directly from video input; this knowledge is then generalized to novel situations, mimicking human skills in 'non-trivial' and continuous learning [2]. We build on work done by [3,4] to assemble autonomously acquired visual data into a higher-level *meta model* for the acquired knowledge. After training on videos of a moving human's upper body the resulting model is shown to generalize well to different movements, attire, and individuals.

2 Method

In the following, we assume a *segmentation method* that reliably extracts non-rigid upper human body parts in a completely autonomous manner from simple, fronto-parallel, monocular input streams. The method is further presumed to extract connections between the single limbs (the upper body skeleton) coevally and to learn the distribution of relative body joint angles. We ignore the neck joint here, as rotational motion orthogonal to the image plane is hard to capture in a monocular setting and significant in-plane motion of the head relative to the torso is rare. Such a system has been proposed by [3] and [4]; other approaches (e. g. [5]) could, with modifications, also be employed for non-rigid limb segmentation and skeleton construction.

---

* Funding by the DFG (WU 314/5-2, WU 314/5-3) is gratefully acknowledged.

F.J. Perales and R.B. Fisher (Eds.): AMDO 2010, LNCS 6169, pp. 98–107, 2010.
© Springer-Verlag Berlin Heidelberg 2010

Let $\mathcal{M}_q = \{\mathcal{L}_q, \mathcal{J}_q, \mathcal{D}_q\}$ describe an upper body model extracted from input sequence q, where $\mathcal{L}_q = \{\mathbf{L}_q^l\}$ with $l = 0 \ldots N_L - 1$ represents the N_L body part appearance templates acquired from sequence q. Information concerning the kinematic skeleton structure of $\mathcal{M}_q$ (relative joint locations, connectivity) is stored in $\mathcal{J}_q$. Eventually, the distribution of relative joint angles for each skeleton joint (learned from all frames of sequence q) is stored in $\mathcal{D}_q$. Appearance models are retrieved from all input frames between an initial frame f_B and a stop frame f_E. Then each $\mathbf{L}_q^l$ holds a separate appearance representation of limb l for each valid frame f of video stream q, such that $\mathbf{L}_q^l = \left\{ \mathbf{l}_{q,f}^l \right\}$, $f \in [f_B, f_E]$. Moreover, $\mathbf{p}_{q,f}^l$ contains the pose (x, y, orientation, scale) of limb l in sequence q for frame f; stored in world coordinates. By letting $\mathbf{l}_{q,f}^l = \left\{ \mathbf{s}_{q,f}^l, \mathbf{c}_{q,f}^l \right\}$, we point out separation of limb appearance templates into a shape map $\mathbf{s}_{q,f}^l$ and an RGB color map $\mathbf{c}_{q,f}^l$ defined for each valid input frame of sequence q. The shape map with values in $[0,1]$ measures the relevance of each pixel to the limb's shape.

Assume that limb segmentation is applied to N_Q input video sequences, resulting in a data set $\mathfrak{M} = \{\mathcal{M}_0, \ldots, \mathcal{M}_{N_M-1}\}$ of $N_M = N_Q$ separate upper body models, which differ significantly w.r.t. clothing, motion patterns and slightly w.r.t. illumination. Self-occlusion of the limbs and variation of the depicted subject are not allowed in this segmentation stage of the learning algorithm.

In the following, we consolidate the models in data set $\mathfrak{M}$ into a single *meta model*, that represents the upper human body on a more abstract level while preserving *pertinent features* that characterize human appearance. Such a meta model is predestined to show good generalization during matching: it focuses on salient features typical for human beings (mean limb outline, persistent color patches on head and hands), while generalizing well across meaningless details like cloth color and deformation, illumination, and motion patterns.

Meta model generation is based on two subprocesses: *intra-sequence limb prototype generation* and *inter-sequence limb prototype construction*; borrowing from the biological paradigm [6], formulation of these prototypes is based on the evaluation of shape and color features in the input streams. Note that prototyping techniques are not unchallenged when it comes to body model construction and matching; [7] proposes, for instance, an interesting exemplar-based approach to detect animal or human body models in given image data. Furthermore, it is still discussed if human concept building capabilities foot on mental prototypes, exemplars or some different information management paradigm [8]. We decided in favor of the prototype approach here, as it principally allows to handle unlimited amounts of input data while keeping the memory footprint well-arranged and information retrieval times rather small.

2.1   Intra-sequence Limb Prototypes

Intra-sequence limb prototypes are rather straightforward to construct; for a dedicated limb $\hat{l}$ in input sequence $\hat{q}$, they unify the content of shape and color information memories $\mathbf{l}_{\hat{q},f}^{\hat{l}}$ from all valid frames $f = [f_B \ldots f_E]$.

Shape prototypes. Formulating a shape prototype for a structure that deforms as vividly as a dressed limb is not trivial. Landmark-based methods, which are quite standard to derive mean shapes and deformation modes from deformable objects (e. g. *point distribution models* [9]) are not applicable in the current context, as landmark finding would have to rely on human intervention, thereby spoiling any previous attempts to maximize system autonomy. Further, automatic landmark finding procedures are, due to significant deformation of the body parts, not reliable enough to replace manual annotation. For these reasons, we choose a different approach to arrive at a fuzzy 'mean' shape of the observed limb templates; our method is based on *Gaussian voting* and remotely inspired by the approach presented in [10]; inherently capitalizing on knowledge of limb poses in each valid input frame.

For the following discussion, focus, without loss of generality, on a single limb $\hat{l}$ in a given sequence $\hat{q}$; it is quite natural to treat $\mathbf{p}^{\hat{l}}_{\hat{q},f_B}$ as the *reference pose* of the processed limb. With that, set up two different operators: first, let $G\left(\cdot\right)$ define a Gaussian blur operator with standard deviation $\sigma_B = 5.0$. Applying this operator to an arbitrary shape map $\mathbf{s}^{\hat{l}}_{\hat{q},f}$ dilutes the formerly crisp body part outline. Additionally, install a *registration operator* $R\left(\cdot\right)$ that projects limb shape map $\mathbf{s}^{\hat{l}}_{\hat{q},f}$ from any valid frame f back to frame f_B.

Given this foundation, setting up the intra-sequence shape prototype $\mathbf{s}^{*\hat{l}}_{\hat{q}}$ for limb $\hat{l}$ in sequence $\hat{q}$ can be formulated as a 'Gaussianized voting' procedure:

$$\mathbf{s}^{*\hat{l}}_{\hat{q}} = G\left(\mathbf{s}^{\hat{l}}_{\hat{q},f_B}\right) + \sum_{f=f_B+1}^{f_E} G\left(R\left(\mathbf{s}^{\hat{l}}_{\hat{q},f}\right)\right). \tag{1}$$

While the 'voting' terminology had been lent from [10], the 'Gaussian' tag emphasizes our method of blurring the limb shapes prior to summation. This procedure to some degree compensates for the vivid cloth deformation behavior and results in smooth, naturally looking prototypical intra-sequence shapes. Eventually, the shape prototype is normalized (i.e., rescaled, such that the maximum summed voting value becomes 1.0), then the 25% weakest votes are removed to exclude spurious shape elements from further consideration. The resulting final intra-sequence shape prototype is re-normalized.

Color prototypes. To arrive at the intra-sequence color prototypes, a different strategy is employed: first, given the reference pose $\mathbf{p}^{\hat{l}}_{\hat{q},f_B}$, reuse registration operator $R\left(\cdot\right)$ to project a limb color map $\mathbf{c}^{\hat{l}}_{\hat{q},f}$ from any valid frame f back to frame f_B. Let the intra-sequence color prototype be

$$\mathbf{c}^{*\hat{l}}_{\hat{q}} = \frac{1}{(f_E - f_B + 1)} \left[\mathbf{c}^{\hat{l}}_{\hat{q},f_B} + \sum_{f=f_B+1}^{f_E} R\left(\mathbf{c}^{\hat{l}}_{\hat{q},f}\right)\right]. \tag{2}$$

i.e., the intra-sequence color prototype for limb $\hat{l}$ is the mean of all sampled color observations for this body part. Note that this procedure necessarily blurs the prototype, due to slight tissue and more significant cloth deformation. Yet, this blur does not severely distort the fundamental color distribution of the prototypical limb and is tolerated henceforth.

Given the intra-sequence limb prototypes, we combine these relatively specialized descriptors into more abstract inter-sequence body part prototypes that show better generalization capabilities.

2.2   Inter-sequence Limb Prototypes

We now return to the meta model announced above: the limbs of this generic body description essentially represent the sought-after inter-sequence prototypes. To avoid notational confusion, let these limbs henceforth be termed *meta limbs*, whereas the joints of the meta model are termed *meta joints* from here on.

Initially, the meta limbs are instantiated with the shape/color prototypes of the *primary model* $\mathcal{M}_0$; also the meta joint structure (i.e., the skeleton of the meta model) is copied from the primary model. With that, define a procedure that aligns every *subsequent model* $\mathcal{M}_n$, $n = 1 \ldots N_M - 1$ with the current meta model $\mathcal{M}_{\mathrm{meta}}$. For simplicity, we focus on a single subsequent model $\mathcal{M}_{\hat{m}}$ in the following. The alignment procedure first performs simple model matching (based on routines described in [4] and section 2.4) to identify limb correspondences between the meta limbs and the body part prototypes in $\mathcal{M}_{\hat{m}}$. Using these results, the limbs of $\mathcal{M}_{\hat{m}}$ are eventually aligned with the meta limbs; further, the skeleton structure of the subsequent model is rearranged to coincide with the skeleton structure of the meta model. Note that during these processes, limb and joint characteristics (i.e., limb orientations, relative joint angles) of $\mathcal{M}_{\hat{m}}$ are appropriately adopted. With both models completely aligned, information from $\mathcal{M}_{\hat{m}}$ can be used to update the current meta limbs and the skeleton structure of $\mathcal{M}_{\mathrm{meta}}$.

Shape prototypes.   To transfer limb appearance information from $\mathcal{M}_{\hat{m}}$ to the meta limbs, the approximate alignment established above is not sufficient; it, however, constitutes a good basis for further registration refinement: define an operator ICP $(\cdot)$ that applies the well-established 2D iterative closest point methods of [11] (accelerated according to [12]) to fine-register the limb shape prototypes of $\mathcal{M}_{\hat{m}}$ to their corresponding meta limbs. To keep computational effort at bay, we here perform shape registration on a thinned shape representation (thinning algorithm after [13]). With that, the inter-sequence shape prototype $\mathbf{s}^{*\hat{l}}_{\mathrm{meta}}$ for a certain meta limb $\hat{l}$ can be constructed from N_Q input sequences as follows

$$\mathbf{s}^{*\hat{l}}_{\mathrm{meta}} = \mathbf{s}^{*\hat{l}}_0 + \sum_{i=1}^{N_Q-1} \mathrm{ICP}\left(\mathbf{s}^{*\hat{l}}_i\right), \tag{3}$$

i.e., the meta limbs fuse shape information from the single models by plain superposition of the previously learned, registered intra-sequence prototypes. Normalization (s. above) and removal of the 25% weakest votes yields the final

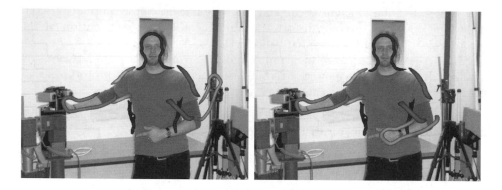

Fig. 1. Effect of limb flipping: the right image shows significantly better matching performance, as the left forearm is flipped orthogonally to the image plane

meta limb shape. Obviously, this procedure favors stable shape parts (which persist throughout all input sequences), whereas cloth induced deformations are largely suppressed.

Color prototypes. Deriving persistent color information from the captured models is somewhat more involved. First, assume that the above ICP operator results can be reused to register the color representation $\mathbf{c}^{*\hat{l}}_{\hat{q}}$ to its corresponding meta limb which had been learned from all sequences $0 \ldots \hat{q} - 1$. Derive a binary *persistent color mask* $P^{\hat{l}}_{\hat{q}}(\mathbf{x})$ that takes on values of 1 where color features within the current meta limb and the registered intra-sequence prototype coincide. We construct this mask by performing a windowed (15×15 pixels window size), color histogram-based correlation, setting mask pixels $\mathbf{x}$ to zero whenever correlation scores drop below 0.25. The resulting mask is then slightly eroded to prevent learning from border sites. Note that the histogram correlation presumes the limb color maps to be given in HSV color space. Choice of this color space allows to exclude the value (V) component from further consideration, rendering histogram-based processing more robust w. r. t. illumination variations [14].

Using $P^{\hat{l}}_{\hat{q}}(\mathbf{x})$, a *color prototype accumulator* $\mathbf{c}^{\hat{l}}_{\mathrm{acc}}$ is iteratively constructed from all models in $\mathfrak{M}$:

1. Primary model initialization:

$$\mathbf{c}^{\hat{l}}_{\mathrm{acc}} \leftarrow \mathbf{c}^{*\hat{l}}_{0} .$$

2. For each subsequent model $\mathcal{M}_i \in \mathfrak{M} : (i = 1 \ldots N_M - 1)$

$$\mathbf{c}^{\hat{l}}_{\mathrm{acc}}(\mathbf{x}) = \begin{cases} \mathbf{c}^{\hat{l}}_{\mathrm{acc}}(\mathbf{x}) + \mathrm{ICP}\left(\mathbf{c}^{*\hat{l}}_{i}\right)(\mathbf{x}) & \text{if } P^{\hat{l}}_{i}(\mathbf{x}) > 0 \\ 0 & \text{else} \end{cases} . \qquad (4)$$

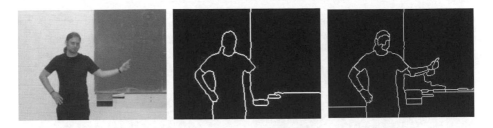

Fig. 2. Results of JSEG (center) and EDISON (right) edge segmenters on the image on the left; parameters are chosen according to [18] and [19], respectively

At each iteration i, prototypical color information $\mathbf{c}^{*\hat{l}}{}_{\text{meta}}$ for meta limb $\hat{l}$ can trivially be instantiated

$$\mathbf{c}^{*\hat{l}}{}_{\text{meta}} = \frac{\mathbf{c}^{\hat{l}}_{\text{acc}}}{i + 1} \tag{5}$$

and used for determining $P^{\hat{l}}_{i+1}(\mathbf{x})$. Note that the above correlation threshold is quite generous, allowing for a significant number of 'false positive' persistent color regions to evolve during each model update cycle. However, by learning from multiple limb instances displaying vividly varying cloth colors, the true persistent color patches (e. g. hands and head) will eventually pop out.

2.3 Meta Skeleton Retrieval

Compared to the prototyping approaches used for shape and color features, skeleton prototyping is straightforward. Whereas the overall *meta skeleton* is necessarily identical to the primary model's skeleton w.r.t. connectivity, relative locations of the meta joints are found by averaging the relative joint locations from all $\mathcal{J}_i$, with $i = 0 \ldots N_M - 1$. Similarly, the distribution of relative meta joint angles is learned by aggregating $\mathcal{D}_i$ for $i = 0 \ldots N_M - 1$.

2.4 Meta Model Matching

To match the fully evolved meta model to novel input images, we employ a *pictorial structure* (PS) matching scheme similar to the one proposed by [15]. Due to the tree-like structure of the learned models, this dynamic programming approach allows to speed up model matching significantly while guaranteeing to yield globally optimal results. [4] gives an overview of the employed baseline scheme; here we enhance their approach in several aspects: first, we allow the matching algorithm to not only find the location (shift, rotation, scale) of each meta limb, but also to infer if a body part is flipped or not. This enables the system to cope with *kinematic flips* (terminology chosen in allusion to [16]). Such flips occur due to the 3D nature of the captured scenario and have to be taken into account to allow analysis of a broader range of body postures. It is assumed that each body part can only be flipped orthogonal to the image plane (around

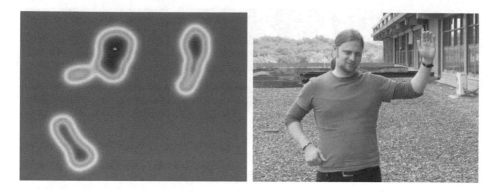

Fig. 3. Final color cue map produced by the left meta forearm for the input image on the right

the limbs' major principal axis); the limits and angular statistics of each joint attached to the flipped body part are updated automatically. Fig. 1 clarifies the importance of flipping capabilities in our system.

Second, matching reliability is increased by refining the matching cost function constructed in [4]: shape matching cost is now computed using the *oriented Chamfer* distance (cf. [17]) between the meta limb shapes and a line segmentation of the given query image. The stand-alone JSEG [18] algorithm utilized in [4] to generate this line segmentation has been replaced by the EDISON [19] image segmentation scheme that is fully integrated into our system. Quality of line images generated by EDISON perceptually compares to or even outperforms the JSEG output (cf. fig. 2). Note that we outsource oriented Chamfer calculations to the GPU (using a CUDA-based implementation), to compensate for the increased computational effort inherent to this more powerful approach. To save computation time, the above fuzzy meta shapes are thinned (as above, thinning algorithm from [13]) prior to being used for oriented Chamfer matching.

Adding up to the above, it is straightforward to exploit the persistent color feature stored in each meta limb for derivation of a per-limb *color cue* map: for that, we first transform the RGB representation of the query image to HSV color space. Let then $\mathbf{W}(\mathbf{x})$ define a window (7×7 pixels) centered at position $\mathbf{x}$ in the HSV representation of the query image. Assume that an HS-histogram can be derived (during a batch-processing step not described here due to the page limit) from the meta limb's persistent color regions. A similar histogram is deemed available for the window patch. We again drop the V-component during histogram construction for better invariance to illumination variation. The map value at $\mathbf{x}$ is then calculated as the correlation of the two HS-histograms. To get rid of spurious elements, we apply a threshold of 0.1, and a Gaussian with $\sigma = 5.0$ is centered at each surviving map entry, to account for possible wrong negative color detections. Loosely following [20], the final color cue map is used (after inversion and re-scaling) to define an additional *color matching cost* that backs up the shape cue described above and renders overall matching behavior more robust. An exemplary color map is shown in fig. 3.

3   Experimental Results and Discussion

After learning from different sequences of one person, we matched the model into still images of different persons under different lighting conditions and with different backgrounds. The results in figure 4 demonstrate the generalization capabilities of the model. The system is able to produce good inference of body posture even in situations it had never been intended for and shows good generalization capabilities in the presence of significant background clutter, regardless of subject identity. So far, we have demonstrated the successful analysis of still images. A quantitative analysis on the basis of hand-annotated images is currently under way.

Several 2D approaches for human posture identification have been employed. In [21] a cue combination similar to ours is used to achieve robust limb matching from a manually trained model. [22] and also [23] present learning-based approaches for posture estimation based on pictorial structures with model initialization as well as body predetection based on human hand-crafting and domain knowledge. Further, spatio-temporal constraints are exploited to make posture recognition more reliable, which prevents their systems from analyzing still images. [24] strive to solve the pose estimation problem on single, 2D input images; their technique shows impressive capabilities, yet also relies on higher level domain knowledge provided by human supervisors. In contrast, our system autonomously achieves acquisition of similar knowledge (e.g., color cues or kinematic constraints). [5] learns body models (of humans and animals) with occlusions in a fully autonomous way from video input. Their approach could serve for limb segmentation in our framework, but does not extract an explicit skeleton, and the tuning of a significant number of parameters appears tedious. In [25], a pictorial structure model is learned from input data, while the input is already hand-labeled (contradicting OC ideas) and the learned PS model's rectangular shapes inevitably display less detail than our meta limbs.

The system proposed in this work complies with Organic Computing directives in that all required model information is generated autonomously; achieved generalization performance is good, as demonstrated experimentally. These encouraging results notwithstanding several improvements are required. Creation of the meta model depends on the order of video presentation, an effect that needs to be quantified and eliminated by appropriate modifications to the learning scheme. Blandly using the thinned meta shapes for oriented Chamfer matching may be problematic – at least a weighting scheme projecting circumjacent values from the fuzzy meta shape maps to the thinned limb boundary representation is required. We also plan to replace thinning by weighted spline techniques. Eventually, to veer away from pure theory, we will use our system to render a humanoid robotic device capable of understanding and mimicking human upper body motion.

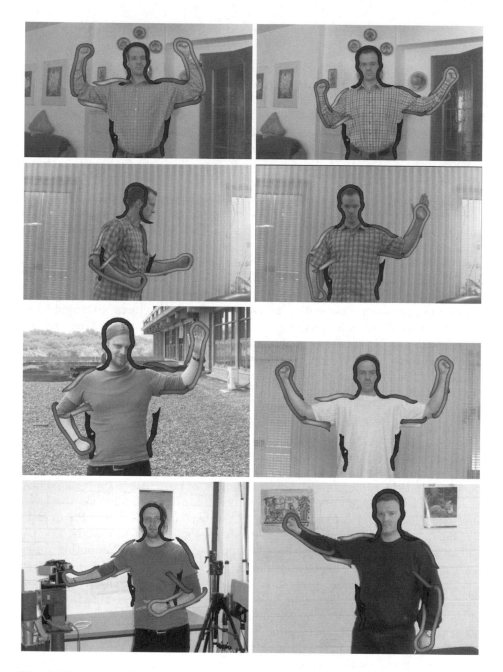

Fig. 4. Experimental results showing the range of applicability of the learned model (clockwise from upper left): Matching to the same person as in the model but wearing different shirts and with a variety of backgrounds and lighting conditions; different persons with different shirts and varying backgrounds; and finally, a side view, which was not seen at all during training.

References

1. Würtz, R.P. (ed.): Organic Computing. Springer, Heidelberg (2008)
2. Poggio, T., Bizzi, E.: Generalization in vision and motor control. Nature 431, 768–774 (2004)
3. Walther, T., Würtz, R.P.: Learning to look at humans - what are the parts of a moving body. In: Perales, F.J., Fisher, R.B. (eds.) AMDO 2008. LNCS, vol. 5098, pp. 22–31. Springer, Heidelberg (2008)
4. Walther, T., Würtz, R.P.: Unsupervised learning of human body parts from video footage. In: Proceedings of ICCV workshops, Kyoto, pp. 336–343. IEEE Computer Society, Los Alamitos (2009)
5. Kumar, M.P., Torr, P.H.S., Zisserman, A.: Learning layered motion segmentations of video. International Journal of Computer Vision 76(3), 301–319 (2008)
6. Bear, M.F., Connors, B.W., Paradiso, M.A.: Neuroscience – Exploring the Brain, 3rd edn. Lippinscott Williams & Wilkins (2006)
7. Kumar, M.P., Torr, P.H.S., Zisserman, A.: Objcut: Efficient segmentation using top-down and bottom-up cues. IEEE Trans. PAMI 32(3), 530–545 (2009)
8. Murphy, G.L.: The Big Book of Concepts. The MIT Press, Cambridge (2004)
9. Cootes, T.F., Taylor, C.J., Cooper, D.H., Graham, J.: Active shape models—their training and application. Comput. Vis. Image Underst. 61(1), 38–59 (1995)
10. Lee, Y.J., Grauman, K.: Shape discovery from unlabeled image collections. In: Proc. CVPR, pp. 2254–2261. IEEE, Los Alamitos (2009)
11. Besl, P.J., McKay, N.D.: A method for registration of 3-D shapes. IEEE Trans. PAMI 14(2), 239–256 (1992)
12. Rusinkiewicz, S., Levoy, M.: Efficient variants of the ICP algorithm. In: Proc. 3rd Intl. Conf. 3D Digital Imaging and Modeling, pp. 145–152 (2001)
13. Eriksen, R.D.: Image processing library 98 (2006), http://www.mip.sdu.dk/ipl98/
14. Elgammal, A., Muang, C., Hu, D.: Skin detection - a short tutorial (2009)
15. Felzenszwalb, P.F., Huttenlocher, D.P.: Pictorial structures for object recognition. Int. J. Comput. Vision 61(1), 55–79 (2005)
16. Sminchisescu, C., Triggs, B.: Kinematic jump processes for monocular 3D human tracking. In: Computer Vision and Pattern Recognition, pp. I:69–76 (2003)
17. Shotton, J., Blake, A., Cipolla, R.: Efficiently combining contour and texture cues for object recognition. In: British Machine Vision Conference (2008)
18. Deng, Y., Manjunath, B.: Unsupervised segmentation of color-texture regions in images and video. IEEE Trans. PAMI 23(8), 800–810 (2001)
19. Christoudias, C., Georgescu, B., Meer, P.: Synergism in low-level vision. In: Proc. ICPR, Quebec City, Canada, vol. 4, pp. 150–155 (2002)
20. Felzenszwalb, P.F., Huttenlocher, D.P.: Efficient matching of pictorial structures. In: Proc. ICPR, vol. 2, pp. 66–73 (2000)
21. Noriega, P., Bernier, O.: Multicues 2D articulated pose tracking using particle filtering and belief propagation on factor graphs. In: Proc. ICPR, pp. 57–60 (2007)
22. Ferrari, V., Marin-Jimenez, M., Zisserman, A.: Progressive search space reduction for human pose estimation. In: Proc. CVPR, pp. 976–983 (2008)
23. Niebles, J.C., Han, B., Ferencz, A., Fei-Fei, L.: Extracting moving people from internet videos. In: Forsyth, D., Torr, P., Zisserman, A. (eds.) ECCV 2008, Part IV. LNCS, vol. 5305, pp. 527–540. Springer, Heidelberg (2008)
24. Marcin, E., Vittorio, F.: Better appearance models for pictorial structures. In: Proc. BMVC (September 2009)
25. Kumar, M.P., Torr, P.H.S., Zisserman, A.: Efficient discriminative learning of parts-based models. In: Proc. ICCV (2009)

High-Realistic and Flexible Virtual Presenters

David Oyarzun, Andoni Mujika, Aitor Álvarez, Aritz Legarretaetxeberria,
Aitor Arrieta, and María del Puy Carretero

Vicomtech Research Centre
P. Mikeletegi, 57
20009 San Sebastián, Spain
doyarzun@vicomtech.org

Abstract. This paper presents the research steps that have been necessaries for creating a mixed reality prototype called PUPPET. The prototype provides a 3D virtual presenter that is embedded in a real TV scenario and is driven by an actor in real time. In this way it can interact with real presenters and/or public. The key modules of this prototype improve the state-of-the-art in such systems in four different aspects: real time management of high-realistic 3D characters, animations generated automatically from actor's speech, less equipment needs, and flexibility in the real/virtual integration. The paper describes the architecture and main modules of the prototype.

Keywords: 3D virtual presenters, mixed reality, real time animation.

1 Introduction

Television is a world where technologies with some level of maturity are sooner or later applied. And 3D computer graphics are not an exception. In fact, 3D virtual images have been appearing together with real ones during the last years. For example, they are very common in some weather reports.

In 2006, an Australian TV channel (Channel Ten) went a step forward and broadcasted a talk-show called 'David Tench Tonight show', which was conducted by a 3D virtual character. This character performed interviews to real people, in a mixed reality system shown on live [1].

Its conceptual way of working was very simple. A real actor drove the virtual presenter in real time. His voice caused a synchronized animation of the virtual presenter's lips and he drove the corporal animations by means of a motion capture system. The system was developed by Animal Logic.

Although the show was cancelled some months later, it was initially successful, being one of the 10 most watched programs in Australia[1].

Nowadays, the interest on this kind of mixed reality applications for TV is still alive. For example, companies like Nazooka have created 3D characters that have

---

[1] Statistics from eBroadcast:
http://www.ebroadcast.com.au/enews/
Third_Time_Lucky_for_Seven_180806.html

F.J. Perales and R.B. Fisher (Eds.): AMDO 2010, LNCS 6169, pp. 108–117, 2010.
© Springer-Verlag Berlin Heidelberg 2010

been broadcasted in different TV programs *via* mixed reality and focus its business model in this kind of technology [2].

However, the applicability of 3D real-time virtual presenters to the TV environment presents some lacks yet. Although most of these lacks are not appreciated by the audience, they imply costs that could be reduced, and interfaces that are not very comfortable for the actors. Concretely, some of the main lacks are:

— Character flexibility. Companies provide the whole system, including the character modeling. Costs would be considerably reduced if TV producers could (re)use characters not created exclusively for the mixed reality system.
— Actor's comfort. Some of current applications require the actor wear a motion capture system or s/he needs to memorize and launch in real time a lot of facial and corporal animations *via* joysticks or keyboards.
— Equipment needs. Apart from the possible motion capture system need, some applications require a chroma system for creating the mixed reality. It implies space, high cost equipment and time for setting up the TV program.
— Mixed reality flexibility. Real cameras are usually fixed when the 3D virtual presenter appears. Cameramen cannot make zoom or change cameras while virtual character is on-screen. Being able to *play* with camera parameters would increase the mixed reality illusion.

This work presents a research project, called PUPPET. Its main requisites are on the whole to improve current state-of-the-art on these applications. The initial prototype developed solves the lacks explained above and so, it provides a low-cost and very flexible solution.

Sections below explain the TV virtual presenter prototype in detail, going into development related research lines in depth. Section 2 present the state-of-the-art about systems related with this prototype and section 3 explains briefly our system architecture. Sections 4, 5 and 6 explain the main modules that solve the lacks mentioned above: section 4, the animation engine that provides character flexibility; section 5, the speech analyzer that improves the actor's comfort and section 6 the mixing module that reduces the equipment needs and improves the real/virtual flexibility. Finally, section 7 explains the resulting prototype tests and section 8 presents the conclusions and future work.

2   State of the Art

The prototype that is presented in this article involves several research fields like mixed reality, real time animation, speech technologies, etc.

Probably the applications that mix these fields in the most related way to this prototype are the works of Nazooka [2] and the David Tench Tonight show, developed by Animal Logic [1].

Nazooka presents some nice developments, however they present limitations regarding the change of camera parameters. That is, the camera remains fixed while the virtual presenter is visible.

On the other hand, David Tench Tonight was initially a successful TV program both from technological and audience level points of view. However, the actor had to use a motion capture system for reproducing all his/her movements in real time. It implied a complex setup and high hardware costs.

There is not many companies and prototypes for creating the mixed reality on TV, however, mixed reality applications are used in several fields such as marketing [3], leisure [4], medicine [5], education [6], etc.

In this way, techniques for obtaining realistic mixing between virtual and real world has been widely studied:

— Lighting, for achieving the shadows of virtual objects over the real world and *vice versa*. Methods like *shadow mapping* [7] or *shadow volumes* [8] are used frequently.

— Occlusions, for calculating virtual world elements occluding real ones and *vice versa*. Different models like a 3D representation of the real world [8], stereo vision-based depth maps [9] or multi-camera 3D reconstruction [10] are used. Each of them has their advantages and disadvantages.

Regarding speech driven animations, most of the previous works are related to the lip synchronization and coarticulation. Phoneme analysis has to transform the speech into phonetic sounds [11] and map them to visemes (the visual representation of each phoneme). However, most of them concerns English [12, 13]. On the other hand, some approaches have been presented for the generation of non-verbal facial expressions from speech. For example, works in [14, 15] generate head movements from fundamental frequency and real time speech driven facial animation is addressed in [16]. However, obtaining a coherent and realistic animation is a state-of-the-art field of research yet.

3 System Overview

The PUPPET prototype system architecture is designed for achieving independence among concrete input devices and the animation and mixed reality modules. In Fig. 1, the conceptual schema of the architecture is presented.

Basically, the input devices are on the one hand the microphone, command devices like keyboards, joysticks, data gloves… and, on the other hand, the cameras of the TV studio.

Microphone input, that is, the voice signal, is managed by the *Speech Analyzer* module. Command devices inputs are retrieved by the *Command Manager*. It is an abstraction layer that avoids device-related dependences in the Animation Engine.

The *Animation Engine* creates the 3D virtual scene that is sent to the *Positioning and Mixing Module*. This module creates the visually correct mixing between the virtual scene and the real image, taking into account real camera changes. Sections below detail the technical aspects about the modules that improve the current systems' lacks. They are:

— The *Speech Analyzer*, which provides not only the analysis for synchronizing the real speech with the virtual presenter lips, but facial animations and expressions too.

— The *Animation Engine*, which is able to load characters created by means of commercial tools like Maya or Poser and animate them through standard BVH files.

— The *Positioning and Mixing Module*, which receives the virtual scene and the real camera parameters in real time and creates a coherent real/virtual mixing.

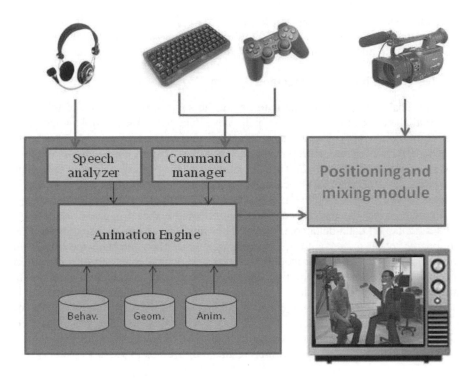

Fig. 1. Simplified architecture schema

4 Speech Analyzer

The Speech Analyzer provides the synchronization between the actor's voice and the avatar lips as well as some facial expressions and animations.

The analyzer captures the speech signal from the input using a microphone and identifies the appropriate phonemes. As phonemes are recognized, they are mapped to their corresponding visemes. In a parallel process, the speech signal is processed by a pitch and energy tracking algorithm, in order to analyze its behavior and decide non-verbal facial movements. The virtual character is then animated in real time and synchronized with the speaker's voice. Therefore, the speech analyzer developed in this paper is composed of four main sub-modules:

— The phoneme recognition system (described in the 4.1 subsection).
— The non-verbal facial animations sub-module (described in the 4.2 subsection).
— The sub-module that sends the input audio to the recognition system and to the pitch/energy tracking algorithm in real-time. To develop this interface we used the ATK API [17].
— The communication interface between the speech application and the animation platform that was developed with sockets, based on the TCP/IP communication protocol. Through this module we fed the animation module with the recognized unit and facial movements for realistic animation.

Using this module the actor has not to get worried about the facial animation of the virtual presenter. All the aspects including lips synchronization and facial expressions will be automatically and coherently launched by the prototype when s/he speaks.

4.1   Real-Time Phoneme Recognition System

The main goal of this sub-module is to obtain the suitable data to animate the lips of the virtual character in real time. To obtain these data, we trained a triphoneme model using HTK Toolkit [18]. The corpus used for training and testing was Albayzin [19], a phonetic database for the development and evaluation of speech recognition and processing systems. It consists of 6800 sentences and 204 speakers. We divided this corpus in two data sets, training (4800 recordings) and test (2000 recordings). All of them are in WAV format (16 kHz/ 16bits/ mono). The feature extraction was performed over 25 ms segments every 10 ms. The parametrization of the speech signal was based on MFCCs, delta and delta-delta coefficients. The Spanish version of SAMPA was used as phoneme set for the recognizer. This set contains 29 phonemes plus the silence and short pause ones. Thiphoneme models were created, which consisted of non-emitting start and end states and three emitting states (except from the short pause model) using Gaussian density functions. Their number of components of these functions was increased until no further recognition improvements were observed. The states are connected left-to-right with no skips. The models were trained iteratively using the embedded Baum-Welch re-estimation and the Viterbi alignment, while the resulting was tested using a Viterbi decoder. Algorithm results are resumed in Table 1.

Table 1. Experimental results (phoneme recognition rate)

Training		Testing	
Correctly Words	*Word Accuracy*	*Correctly Words*	*Word Accuracy*
90.41 %	**84.20 %**	**81.18 %**	**71.23 %**

4.2   Non-verbal Facial Animations Sub-module

The recognized phonemes are mapped in real-time to their corresponding visemes in order to make the lip-synchronization process. This is the first step for the facial animation, which has been enriched using prosodic information of speech. A statistical model adapted to current speaker is created during the first steps of the recognition, based on the fundamental frequency (pitch) and energy of the speech signal, in addition to some related statistics. According to the values given in real-time by both pitch and energy trackers, some facial animations are shot, mainly related to the head and eyebrows up and down movement, and eyes and mouth more or less expressively movements.

Fig. 2. Several facial expressions automatically generated from the actor's voice

5 Animation Engine

The animation engine has been designed in order to obtain high-quality real time animations and at the same time be able to load and animate characters not exclusively created for the PUPPET system.

The animation engine is divided in two main modules, the facial animation engine and the body animation engine.

— The facial animation engine uses advanced morphing techniques [20] for generating a high quality animation in real time. This technique is quite extended and it creates the resulting animation by means of the linear interpolation among a set of predefined key faces. The animation engine includes a technique to avoid tests among vertices that are equal to get a lower computational cost.

— The body animation engine implements a set of techniques that aim a realistic movements with a low computational cost. For obtaining realistic movements the engine supports the loading of animations created by professional animators. They are loaded in the system by means of BVH files [21], a semi-standard format to which almost all commercial modeling applications are able to export. Moreover, it includes a set of optimizations that achieve their execution in real time in a standard desktop computer.

The animation is based on smooth skinning techniques. That is, the vertices of the geometry (or geometries) that conforms the virtual presenter are affected by a virtual skeleton. Transformations over this skeleton influence each vertex taking into account weights assigned to this vertex. These weights provide a way for avoiding *cracks* in the geometry and achieving smooth deformations.

The conceptual equation for the animation is:

$$v_r = v + w_i * M_r * v_i$$

Where v_r is the resulting vertex, v is the vertex with the previous transformations in the hierarchy, w_i is the assigned weight, M_r is the rotation matrix corresponding to current node and v_i is the vertex in its initial position.

So as not to depend on specific modeling formats a separation has been established between the geometrical and the smooth skinning information.

— Geometrical information. The 3D character can be loaded in any common geometrical format (3ds, obj, vrml, etc.)

— Smooth skinning information. A new file format, called SHF (Simple Hierarchical Format), has been designed for storing the skeleton and weighting information (Fig. 3). A plug-in to *connect* Maya [22] to SHF has been developed. It allows designers to obtain this information from any Maya modeled character.

The animation engine relates both files in execution time and applies the BVH and morphing animations to them. This way, smooth deformations and high-realistic animations are obtained in real time over any virtual character designed with a standard modeling tool.

```
JessiCasual                              Node
0 101.194 3.16992                        Position
#
{
hip                                      Child node
0.0962168 102.182 2.18286                Position
428 0.139399                             Vertices: index-weight
429 0.182505
461 0.454841
432 0.298909


          . . .
```

Fig. 3. SHF format file description

6   Positioning and Mixing Module

The Positioning and Mixing Module is designed for creating the mixed reality in a coherent way, without need of physical chroma systems or similar. It works in the opposite way than chroma systems. The virtual presenter background is one uniform color and the real scene replaces directly that color.

Moreover, since our application will be used in television, it would be useful to allow the cameras to translate and zoom. Then, the cameras will be able to follow either the real presenters or the virtual characters and get a more detailed view of them, without losing synchronization between real world and virtual worlds.

The camera is motorized and can be handled remotely. With a remote control three parameters of the camera can be changed: pan, rotation with respect to the vertical axis; tilt, rotation that makes the camera look up and down and zoom.

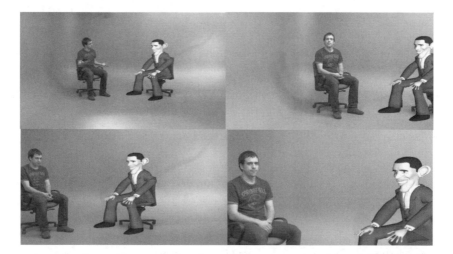

Fig. 4. Playing with the real camera parameters: changes in translation and zoom (chroma system is not necessary; it is just for having a clean background. Virtual character's chair is real, non virtual).

The robot that moves the camera is connected with the computer through a serial port and transmits the values of the parameters to the computer in real-time. The animation engine receives those values and with simple linear transformations parameters' values in degrees are calculated and transferred to the virtual camera.

In conclusion, the real camera is controlled remotely, but the virtual objects change their position in the screen coherently because of the information traffic between the real and the virtual camera. Fig. 4 shows some screenshots changing the camera parameters.

7 PUPPET Prototype Tests

Modules described before conforms the PUPPET prototype. It has been tested by professional actors and staff from a Basque TV production company called Pausoka[23]. They all agreed that the system is easy to use and avoids limitations and lacks found in the state-of-the-art.

The system has been tested in a standard desktop PC and using virtual characters from different sources. Concretely, along this paper, Fig. 2 shows some screenshots detailing the speech-based facial animation. The virtual character has been obtained from the Poser commercial tool [24].

Fig 4. showed changes in the parameters of the real camera, concretely translations and zooms, and the coherence between the virtual and real images. In this case, the virtual presenter, that is a caricature of Barack Obama, had been designed by a professional modeling company.

8 Conclusions and Future Work

This paper presents a prototype that provides a 3D virtual presenter that is immersed in a real TV scenario. It can be driven by an actor in real time and interact with real presenters and/or public.

The prototype solves some lacks existing in state-of-the-art similar developments. Concretely:

— Character flexibility. There is no need to model animations or virtual characters specifically for their use in the mixed reality platform. The platform supports standard file formats for animating the character and a new file format that supports the smooth skinning data store has been designed.
— Actor's comfort. The platform does not need motion capture systems. It can be handled just with a microphone and usual devices like keyboards or joysticks. Speech signal automates not only the lip animation but also some facial animations.
— Equipment needs. There is no need to use chroma systems or similar. The computer creates the real/virtual mix directly.

— Mixed reality flexibility. Almost all current platforms that do not use chroma systems need to fix the camera, without moving. The platform of this work allows the cameraman to change the camera parameters (zoom, movements…) in real time.

Next steps are to include lighting and occlusion techniques that improve the realism and possibilities of the virtual presenter.

References

1. Animal Logic web page, http://www.animallogic.com
2. Nazooka web page, http://www.nazooka.com/site/
3. Metaio Augmented Solutions, http://www.metaio.com
4. Oda, O., Lister, L.J., White, S., Feiner, S.: Developing an augmented reality racing game. In: Proceedings of the 2nd international conference on INtelligent TEchnologies for interactive enterTAINment (2008)
5. Carlin, A.S., Hoffman, H.G., Weghorst, S.: Virtual reality and tactile augmentation in the treatment of spider phobia: a case report. Behaviour research and therapy (1997)
6. Tan, K.T.W., Lewis, E.M., Avis, N.J., Withers, P.J.: Using augmented reality to promote an understanding of materials science to school children. In: International Conference on Computer Graphics and Interactive Techniques (2008)
7. McCool, M.D.: Shadow volume reconstruction from depth maps. ACM Transactions on Graphics (TOG) 19, 1–26 (2000)
8. Fuhrmann, A., Hesina, G., Faure, F., Gervautz, M.: Occlusion in collaborative augmented environments. Computers and Graphics 23 (1999)
9. Fortin, P., Herbert, P.: Handling occlusions in realtime augmented reality: Dealing with movable real and virtual objects. In: Proceedings of the Canadian Conf. on Computer and Robot Vision, Vol. 54 (2006)
10. Matusik, W., Buehler, C., McMillan, L.: Polyhedral visual hulls for real-time rendering. In: Proc. 12th Eurographics Workshop on Rendering EGWR '01, London (2001)
11. Lehr, M., Arruti, A., Ortiz, A., Oyarzun, D., Obach, M.: Speech Driven Facial Animation using HMMs in Basque. In: Sojka, P., Kopeček, I., Pala, K. (eds.) TSD 2006. LNCS (LNAI), vol. 4188, pp. 415–422. Springer, Heidelberg (2006)
12. Goldenthal, W., Waters, K., Van Thong, J.M., Glickman, O.: Driving Synthetic Mouth Gestures: Phonetic Recognition for FaceMe. In: Eurospeech, Rhodes, Greece (1997)
13. Massaro, D., Beskow, S., Cohen, M., Fry, C., Rodriguez, T.: Picture My Voice: Audio to Visual Speech Synthesis using Artificial Neural Networks. In: AVSP, Santa Cruz, California (1999)
14. Deng, Z., Busso, C., Narayanan, S., Neumann, U. : Audio-based Head Motion Synthesis for Avatar-based Telepresence Systems. In: ACM SIGMM Workshop on Effective Telepresence (ETP) (2004)
15. Chuang, E., Bregler, C.: Mood swings: expressive speech animation. ACM Transactions on Graphics (TOG) (2005)
16. Malcangi, M., de Tintis, R.: Audio Based Real-Time Speech Animation of Embodied Conversational Agents. LNCS. Springer, Heidelberg (2004)
17. Young, S., Kershaw, D., Odell, J., Ollason, D., Valtchev, V., Woodland, P.: The HTK Book
18. Young, S.: The ATK Real-Time API for HTK

19. Casacuberta, F., Garcia, R., Llisterri, J., Nadeu, C., Pardo, J.M., Rubio, A.: Development of Spanish Corpora for Speech Research (ALBAYZIN). In: Workshop on International Cooperation and Standardization of Speech Databases and Speech I/O Assesment Methods, Chiavari, Italy (1991)
20. Alexa, M., Behr, J., Müller, W.: The morph node. In: Proceedings of the fifth symposium on Virtual reality modeling language (Web3D-VRML), Monterey, California, United States, pp. 29–34 (2000)
21. Meredith, M., Maddock, S.: Motion Capture File Formats Explained. Department of Computer Science, University of Sheffield (2001)
22. Maya Home Page, `http://usa.autodesk.com/adsk/servlet/pc/index?siteID=123112&id=13577897`
23. Poser Home Page, `http://my.smithmicro.com/win/poser/`

Model-Based Hand Gesture Tracking in ToF Image Sequences

Sigurjón Árni Guðmundsson[1,2], Jóhannes R. Sveinsson[1], Montse Pardàs[3],
Henrik Aanæs[2], and Rasmus Larsen[2]

[1] University of Iceland, Department of Electrical and Computer Engineering
{sag15,sveinsso}@hi.is
[2] Technical University of Denmark, DTU Informatics
{sag,haa,rl}@imm.dtu.dk
[3] UPC-Barcelona Tech, Department of Signal Theory and Communications
montse.pardas@upc.edu

Abstract. This paper presents a Time-of-Flight (ToF) camera based system for hand motion and gesture tracking. A 27 degree of freedom (DOF) hand model is constructed and fleshed out by ellipsoids. This allows the synthesis of range images of the model through projective geometry. The hand pose is then tracked with a particle filter by statistically measuring the hypothetical pose against the ToF input image; where the inside/outside alignment of the hand pixels and the depth differences serve as classifying metrics. The high DOF tracking problem for the particle filter is addressed by reducing the high dimensionality of the joint angle space to a low dimensional space via Principal Component Analysis (PCA). The basis vectors are learned from a few basic model configurations and the transformations between these poses. This results in a system capable of practical hand tracking in a restricted gesture configuration space.

1 Introduction

Recovering the complex motions and poses of a human hand from camera observations is one of the more challenging problems in computer vision. A hand gesture tracker has many uses in the modern computer applications, to name a few: Sign language recognition, gaming interfaces where the hand gestures are used as input, navigation by pointing and special computer interfaces where no physical touching is required such as for medical applications [1].

Numerous computer vision researchers have addressed the hand tracking problem. A good review is given in Erol et al. [2]. There approaches can be roughly divided into two categories appearance-based vs. model-based. Appearance-based methods strive at mapping image features to hand poses using e.g., clustering and fast search methods [3]. Model-based approaches use a deformable model, where the model's configuration space is searched for parameters that maximize the similarity between groups of features in the input image and the model. Particle Filters

F.J. Perales and R.B. Fisher (Eds.): AMDO 2010, LNCS 6169, pp. 118–127, 2010.

(PF) have been thoroughly applied to model-based hand and human body analysis due to their abilities in non-linear estimation. In particular, PF variants that deal with high degree of freedom (DOF) of the model configuration space, are of high interest. Methods such as annealed particle filtering [4], hierarchical methods [5] and manifold methods where lower dimensional pose spaces are learned from training pose data [6].

Most of the research mentioned in [2] is based on input from a single CCD camera approaches using features such as color, edges etc. Others use multiple cameras and include depth features into the tracking.

Time-of-Flight (ToF) sensors are camera like depth measuring devises built on an active illumination modulation principle [7]. ToF cameras offer real-time simultaneous amplitude images and range images (depth measurement in each pixel).

The Swissranger SR3000 [8] used in this paper is designed to be a cost-efficient and eye-safe range imaging solution. Basically, it is an amplitude modulated near infra-red light source and a specialized 176×144 two dimensional sensor built in a miniaturized package. ToF cameras have been found increasingly useful for solving various computer vision applications as is reviewed in [7].

Using ToF sensors for tracking purposes has many interesting benefits. They are free from some of the problems that are present in standard intensity images such as lighting changes with shadows and reflections, color similarity and clutter. Depth is a more natural foreground / background separator than intensity and color. On the other hand the current ToF cameras' main disadvantages is the low spatial resolution, the low quality intensity image and the depth accuracy, that may have systematic errors and errors that depend on the scene. Human body tracking using ToF cameras has been studied in a few papers(cf. [7]) and one where an articulated model of the upper body is fitted to the data [9]. Hand gestures have also been studied in [10,11,1], the first attempts to fit an static computer graphics model to the ToF data and the latter two strive at recognizing static hand gestures by analyzing the segmented hands in the ToF images.

Here, a novel approach to hand gesture tracking is presented using a model-based particle filter tracker with ToF-data. By representing the models pose as range images a simple and straight forward comparison to the ToF images can be made leading to robust tracking results. We will show that the search space can be limited to chosen poses by generating instances of poses of interest and reducing the dimensionality of the joint angle space to only a few dimensional pose space via Principle Component Analysis (PCA), yielding a fast and practical hand gesture tracker.

2   The System

Fig. 1 shows an overview of the proposed system. The grey arrow path, inside the particle filter blue box, shows the path of the particles and the black arrows that come into the box are the input data and parameters, and finally the arrow out of the box is the output: the hand pose estimation for frame t. The input

ToF frame t is preprocessed and sent to the PF. In PF the posterior probability distribution is approximated by a weighted particle set, where the particles are instances of the state space. In our case, the state vector describes instances of a hand model, i.e. vector descriptions of the position in space (translation and rotation) and the joint angles of the hand (the pose). Additionally, each particle bears a weight that is updated according to how well the particle matches the input. These weights are then used to make the weighted average of the particles generating the estimate. In the remainder of this section the input and preprocessing are described, then the hand model, followed by the particle filter and pose estimation.

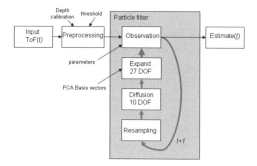

Fig. 1. Overview of the system pipeline.

2.1   Input and Preprocessing

ToF cameras have systematic depth errors that can be resolved to an extent by depth calibration [12]. Here we use the multi-camera ToF-CCD rig calibration method and tool described by Schiller et al. [12]. The tool finds an optimal higher order polynomial to compensate for the depth error and also provides the camera calibration parameters needed later for the ToF camera's projection matrix. After undistorting the input frame the hand is segmented by thresholding. Here we simply find the closest pixel, assume that it belongs to the hand and throw everything that is farther than 20 cm away from this closest pixel. This works in this "man in front of a camera scenario", but can easily be replaced by, e.g., a fast foreground segmentation algorithm [13] or hand detection algorithm [1] for different scenarios.

2.2   The Hand Model

The hand is modelled as a kinematic chain skeleton model similar to many other studies in hand and human body analysis [2]. The hand position and pose is described by a 27 dimensional vector where 6 dimensions are the global position (translations and rotations along and around the X, Y and Z axes) and then 5 dimensions for the thumb and 4 dimensions for the joint angles of the other

Fig. 2. The Hand model. *Left:* The kinematic chain model. Red signifies 6 DOF movement, blue 2 DOF angle movement and white 1 DOF. *Right:* A synthesized range image of a hand model instance fleshed out with ellipsoids. Darker pixels are closer to the camera.

fingers. Fig. 2 illustrates the joint DOF. Each joint 3D position in a kinematic chain is found by exponential maps and twists, i.e., simple multiplications of rotational matrices and translations as has been described in various robotics and human analysis literature, cf. [14,15].

Synthesizing Range Images of the Model Poses. A quadric is a 4×4 matrix $\mathbf{Q}$ which describes a surface in 3D so that all points $\mathbf{X}$ on this surface fulfill:

$$\mathbf{X}^T \mathbf{Q} \mathbf{X} = 0. \tag{1}$$

The points inside the normalized quadric give a negative result and positive on the outside. A conic is a 3×3 matrix $\mathbf{C}$ that has the same properties in the plane as quadrics have in 3D. A projective camera or pinhole camera model is $\mathbf{P} = \mathbf{K}[\mathbf{I}|\mathbf{0}]$, where $\mathbf{K}$ is the calibration matrix of the camera. $\mathbf{P}$ maps a 3D point $\mathbf{X} = [X, Y, Z, 1]^T$ to the pixel positions $\mathbf{x} = [x, y, 1]^T$ in the image plane by $\mathbf{x} = \mathbf{P}\mathbf{X}$.

The projective camera furthermore maps quadrics to conics in the image plane. This can be shown using the duality property of quadrics in projective geometry [16]. If the dual quadric of $\mathbf{Q}$ is mapped to $\mathbf{Q}^*$ and the dual conic of $\mathbf{C}$ is mapped to $\mathbf{C}^*$, then: $\mathbf{C}^* = \mathbf{P}\mathbf{Q}^*\mathbf{P}^T$.

The mapping of the dual conic to the conic is straight forward.

Here the skeletal hand model is fleshed out by ellipsoids which are quadrics that are thus mapped to ellipses on the ToF cameras image plane. The ellipsoids are constructed so that the axes of the ellipsoid is seen as a covariance matrix $\mathbf{V}$ with the main axis length l_1 and thickness l_2 and l_3 on the other axes, the covariance matrix is thus:

$$\mathbf{V} = \begin{bmatrix} l_1^2 & 0 & 0 \\ 0 & l_2^2 & 0 \\ 0 & 0 & l_3^2 \end{bmatrix}. \tag{2}$$

The kinematic model provides the 3D endpoint positions of the ellipsoid which give the center-point position and the 3D rotation of the ellipsoid. The quadric is thus rotated by a 3×3 rotation matrix $\mathbf{R}$ and translated from the origin by the 4×4 translation matrix $\mathbf{M}$. The ellipsoid is constructed as:

$$\mathbf{Q} = \mathbf{M}^T \begin{bmatrix} \left(\mathbf{R}^T \mathbf{V} \mathbf{R}\right)^{-1} & \mathbf{0} \\ \mathbf{0} & 1 \end{bmatrix} \mathbf{M}. \tag{3}$$

For a range image representation of the hand model configuration, the depth from the camera for each of the pixels inside the ellipses $\mathbf{C}$ need to be found. This is done by stepping along the ray towards the pixel $\mathbf{x}$. Solving the projection equation for X and Y for each Z along the ray:

$$\begin{bmatrix} X \\ Y \\ Z \end{bmatrix} = \mathbf{K}^{-1}(\begin{bmatrix} x \\ y \\ 1 \end{bmatrix} \cdot Z). \tag{4}$$

These points $\mathbf{X}$ for each step on the ray are tested with the quadric equation (1) thus finding the zero crossing which is at the desired surface depth Z.

An initial point on the ray is found by using the ellipsoids center-point and main axis-length so that the surface depth is found in only few steps. Occlusion (overlapping ellipsoids) is simply handled by saving the smallest Z.

2.3   The Particle Filter

Particle filters, or often called CONDENSATION in visual tracking [17], are sequential Monte Carlo methods based on *particle* representations of probability densities. They are powerful in solving estimation and tracking problems where the variables are non-linear and non-Gaussian. In this paper the Sample Importance Resampling (SIR) approach is followed as, e.g., is described in [18]. The PF can be summarized into 3 steps: *1. Resampling* of particles, *2. Observation* of particles (weighting function) and *3. Diffusion* of particles (propagation in search space).

The resampling step is done to avoid degeneracy of the particles and here the standard procedure is followed as described in, e.g. [18]. The observation and diffusion steps are described in the following sections.

Observation: The purpose of the observation step is to find the observation likelihood of the particles: $p(X|Z_k)$, i.e., the probability of the observation X given the kth particle Z_k. In our case X is the depth image after preprocessing. The observation step is usually the most expensive in the PF. A full Bayesian solution is often difficult to model so that all the aspects of the data are taken into account. Often the likelihood is replaced by more intuitive weighting function $w(X, Z_k)$. Here, the function is modelled by general statistical metrics: correct, false, missed pixel detections and an F-measure (cf. [19]). The pixels obtained with the projection of the hand model with the parameters corresponding to a given particle Z_k are here referred to as Z_k pixels.

Correct pixels: The number of Z_k pixels for which $e^{-\gamma|d_X - d_{Z_k}|} > \alpha$, where d_X and d_{Z_k} are the pixel depth values for input X and particle Z_k. The threshold α

and γ are chosen so that the pixel is classified correct if the distance is smaller than 2 cm.

False pixels: The number of Z_k pixels for which $e^{-\gamma|d_X - d_{Z_k}|} \leq \alpha$.

Missed pixels: The number of input image pixels that are in a neighbourhood region of Z_k pixels. The neighbourhood region, as shown in Fig. 3, is defined by the binary distance transform of Z_k; $DT(Z_k)$. The size of the region is controlled so that it is in proportion to the fingers length. The arm does not fall into the neighbourhood region as it is removed from the region by projecting an ellipsoid onto the wrist in $DT(Z_k)$, the wrist position is given by the kinematic model.

Fig. 3 illustrates the measurement principle and the three classes for one particle instance.

Fig. 3. The measurement of one particle hypothesis. *Left to right:* The preprocessed input X, The particle Z_k range image, Z_k's neighbourhood region in grey and classified image with correct, false and missed pixels indicated with red, green and blue.

The particles performance is measured for precision and recall. The precision is given by: $w_{prec}(X, Z_k) = \frac{\text{correct}}{\text{correct+missed}}$, and measures the exactness of the fit, while the recall; $w_{rec}(X, Z_k) = \frac{\text{correct}}{\text{correct+false}}$, measures the completeness. The final weight is then the F-measure:

$$w(X, Z_k) = \frac{(1 + \beta^2) \cdot w_{prec}(X, Z_k) \cdot w_{rec}(X, Z_k)}{\beta^2 \cdot w_{prec}(X, Z_k) + w_{rec}(X, Z_k)}. \tag{5}$$

Here β controls the balance between w_{prec} and w_{rec}, and is chosen ad-hoc to be 1.5 thus giving the recall more weight. It was seen in most typical scenes, that the missed detections were usually much fewer than the false ones and therefore needed extra penalization.

Diffusion in Subspace: It has been shown in [20] that the required number of particles for standard PF probability density estimation increases exponentially with the variable dimensionality. Standard PF can thus not handle 27 DOF hand tracking effectively. Here a reduction of dimensionality approach is followed, where a low dimensional pose space is learned from pose data. In a "proof of concept"-experiment, synthetic data is used: The model joint angle dimensions are set to three basic poses: flat palm (or "high 5"), fist, and pointing index finger (or "gun"), also the basic transformations between these poses with some

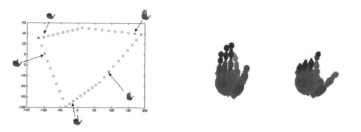

Fig. 4. *Left:* The 2 first PCs of the learning data. The 3 first PC describe 97.4% of the variance and the 6th PC added 0.1% but captured some important thumb motions. *Middle and right:* Extreme boundary poses using the maximum (middle) and minimum (right) value in all PCA basis directions. These are unlikely poses but show in a way that the poses within the subspace boundaries are not that far off.

additional thumb configurations; in total 79 poses. A PCA model was trained on these 79 points in the 21 dimensional joint angle space. Fig. 4 shows the first 2 PCs of the training data. Here, 4 PC basis vectors were used describing 97.5% of the covariance in the data.

The maximum and minimum values of the training points in each of the four dimensions, bound the pose space. Within these boundaries the particles propagate randomly according to a Gaussian density. The points, that are far off the path the training points lie on, can generate unnatural hand poses. Fig. 4 shows two of the extreme corners of the 4 dimensional hypercube. One of these poses is an unlikely pose (index finger bending backwards) but not that far from possible poses or from the poses that were used for the training.

After the propagation in the low dimensional space the particles are expanded via the 4 PC basis vectors to the full 21 dimensions where they are synthesized for the observation step.

3   Hand Tracking Results

Experiments were performed where the hand was tracked through poses in the predefined pose space. The initialization is done by a rough "manual" positioning, and 300 particles were used in all experiments.

The results in Fig. 5 show that the tracker does a good job at catching the pose changes and out of image plane rotations, although the estimation lags somewhat. Also note that the index finger is slightly bent when it should be straight: This might be caused by the fact that this position is close to the boundary and thus the diffusion of the particles is truncated, which gives this tendency to move slightly from the boundary. Furthermore, Fig. 5 illustrates how the tracker recovers from self occlusion in large motion situations. The thumb is occluded and then it reappears and the PF detects it in the next frame. In the end of the sequence; part of the hand goes out of the frame, here the PF recovers correctly.

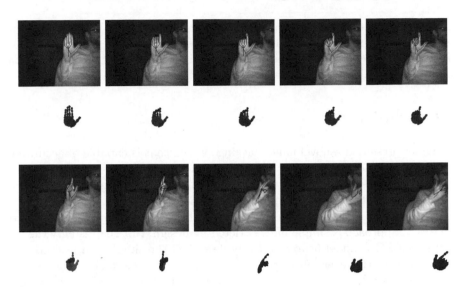

Fig. 5. 10 frames of tracking a "high 5" gesture transformed to "gun" with rotation, translation, self- and object-occlusion. *Top and 3rd row:* ToF amplitude images with superimposed skeleton estimation. *2nd and bottom row:* Corresponding range image of the estimated model. The transformation is successful although the model estimation is slightly lagging, i.e., the fingers should be more bent in the 2nd and 3rd frame . In the 8th frame the PF has not recovered the thumb, but it reappears in the next frame. Here the PF had no problems when the hand partially exited the cameras field of view.

Fig. 6 shows that out of pose space gestures give of course false estimations. The weight measurement however gives a strong indication of a poor match so these cases can be classified as lost or out of limits. A recovering system can then be triggered where the PF is helped back on track by a larger number of particles and wider diffusion variance. More video examples are available on this projects homepage[1].

Fig. 6. Out of pose space gestures are incorrectly estimated. *Left:* ToF amplitude image with superimposed skeleton estimation. *Right:* Corresponding range image.

Currently the system runs at about 2 seconds per frame on a standard laptop PC (Core Duo 1.66 GHz, 1 Gb RAM). The implementation is done by using C++

---

[1] http://www.hi.is/~sag15/handtracking.html

libraries and has not been optimized for higher performance. We are confident that the performance can be enhanced greatly with, e.g., faster implementations of the range image construction and particle weighting. Then, the real-time goal should be achievable on newer hardware.

4 Conclusion

This paper presented a novel hand tracking system that is capable of accurately capturing the hand pose in a restricted pose space. A ToF real-time range imaging device was used so that the surface of the hand and a kinematic model were matched using 3D features in a quick and simple manner.

The main obstacle of hand pose tracking is the high DOF problem. The proposed PCA approach is simple but restricted by design. Not surprisingly the low dimensional PCA model nearly perfectly described the simple synthesized pose data used here. However, unrestricted hand motion is extremely complex, and the proposed method with manually synthesized hand pose configurations with linear transformations is not prone for success. Several researchers have used data-gloves for hand-motion capture and trained models on this data. Some have used PCA on such data ([21]), while others ([3]) have shown how natural hand motions lie on low dimensional non-linear manifolds. Then, a methodology similar to what is proposed in [22], might be used: First, learn the manifold using Locally Linear Embedding, or other manifold learning method, and then map back to the original dimensionality using, e.g. a kernel method. Such a method can be incorporated directly into the framework described here; replacing the PC basis with the kernel basis.

On the other hand, for many applications non-restricted hand motion is not required. E.g., applications like human computer interfaces, navigation, and games; where the simplicity of this system can be an asset. The results presented here show that this tracker is robust to difficult scenarios, self occlusion and complex global motions, and can therefore suit perfectly for such an application. In the near future our research will include expanding this approach to a more multi-pose gesture tracking for practical interfacing purposes.

References

1. Soutschek, S., Penne, J., Hornegger, J., Kornhuber, J.: 3-D Gesture-Based Scene Navigation in Medical Imaging Applications Using Time-Of-Flight Cameras. In: Proc. Conference on Computer Vision and Pattern Recognition Workshops (2008)
2. Erol, A., Bebis, G., Nicolescu, M., Boyle, R.D., Twombly, X.: Vision-based hand pose estimation: A review. Computer Vision and Image Understanding 108 (2007)
3. Stenger, B., Thayananthan, A., Torr, P.H.S., Cipolla, R.: Model-Based Hand Tracking Using a Hierarchical Bayesian Filter. Trans. on Pattern Analysis and Machine Intelligence 28(9), 1372–1384 (2006)
4. Deutscher, J., Reid, I.: Articulated body motion capture by stochastic search. International Journal of Computer Vision 61(2), 185–205 (2005)

5. Canton-Ferrer, C., Casas, J.R., Pàrdas, M.: Exploiting structural hierarchy in articulated objects towards robust motion capture. In: Perales, F.J., Fisher, R.B. (eds.) AMDO 2008. LNCS, vol. 5098, pp. 82–91. Springer, Heidelberg (2008)
6. Kato, M., Chen, Y.W., Xu, G.: Articulated hand motion tracking using ICA-based analysis and particle filtering. Journal of multimedia 1(3) (2003)
7. Kolb, A., Barth, E., Koch, R., Larsen, R.: ToF-Sensors: New Dimensions for Realism and Interactivity. Computer Graphics Forum (2009)
8. MESA Imaging AG, http://www.mesa-imaging.ch/
9. Zhu, Y., Dariush, B., Fujimura, K.: Controlled human pose estimation from depth image streams. In: Proc. Conference on Computer Vision and Pattern Recognition Workshops (2008)
10. Breuer, P., Eckes, C., Müller, S.: Hand gesture recognition with a novel ir time-of-flight range camera-a pilot study. In: Gagalowicz, A., Philips, W. (eds.) MIRAGE 2007. LNCS, vol. 4418, pp. 247–260. Springer, Heidelberg (2007)
11. Kollorz, E., Hornegger, J.: Gesture recognition with a time-of-flight camera. Int. J. on Intell. Systems and Techn. and App. (IJISTA), Issue on Dynamic 3D Imaging (2007)
12. Schiller, I., Beder, C., Koch, R.: Calibration of a PMD-Camera Using a Planar Calibration Pattern Together with a Multi-Camera Setup. In: The International Archives of the Photogrammetry, Remote Sensing and Spatial Information Sciences, pp. 297–302 (2008)
13. Guðmundsson, S.A., Larsen, R., Aanæs, H., Pardás, M., Casas, J.R.: ToF imaging in smart room environments towards improved people tracking. In: Proc. Conference on Computer Vision and Pattern Recognition Workshops (2008)
14. Bregler, C., Malik, J.: Tracking people with twists and exponential maps. In: Proc. Conference on Computer Vision and Pattern Recognition, pp. 8–15 (1998)
15. Mikic, I.: Human body model acquisition and tracking using multi-camera voxel data. PhD Thesis, University of California, San Diego (2002)
16. Kanatani, K.: Statistical optimization for geometric computation: theory and practice. Elsevier Science Ltd., Amsterdam (1996)
17. Isard, M., Blake, A.: CONDENSATION - Conditional density propagation for visual tracking. International Journal of Computer Vision 29(1), 5–28 (1998)
18. Arulampalam, M., Maskell, S., Gordon, N., Clapp, T.: A tutorial on particle filters for online nonlinear/non-gaussian bayesian tracking. IEEE Transactions on Signal Processing 50(2), 174–188 (2002)
19. van Rijsbergen, C.J.: Information Retrieval. Butterworths, London (1975)
20. MacCormick, J., Isard, M.: Partitioned sampling articulated objects and interface quality hand tracking. In: Vernon, D. (ed.) ECCV 2000. LNCS, vol. 1843, pp. 3–19. Springer, Heidelberg (2000)
21. Wu, Y., Lin, J., Huang, T.S.: Capturing natural hand articulation. In: Proc. Intl Conf. Computer Vision, ICCV, pp. 426–432 (2001)
22. Jaeggli, T., Koller-Meier, E., Gool, L.V.: Multi-activity tracking in lle body pose space. In: ICCV workshop: 2nd Workshop on Human Motion - Understanding, Modeling, Capture and Animation, pp. 42–57 (2007)

An Evaluation of Wavelet Kernels for Palmprint Based Recognition

Atif Bin Mansoor[1,2], Hassan Masood[2], Mustafa Mumtaz[2],
Sameem Shabbir[2], and Shoab A. Khan[1,2]

[1] Center for Advanced Studies in Engineering, University of Engineering
and Technology, Taxila, Pakistan
[2] National University of Sciences and Technology, Pakistan
atif.mansoor@gmail.com, hassan13204@yahoo.com, mustafa672@ieee.org,
sameemshabbir@yahoo.com, shoab@case.edu.pk

Abstract. Palmprint based Identification is gaining popularity due to its traits like user acceptance, reliability and ease of acquisition. The paper presents a recognition method which extorts textural information obtainable from the palmprint, utilizing different filters of wavelet transform. Palmprint center has been computed using the chessboard metric of Distance Transform whereas the strictures of best fitting ellipse help resolve the alignment of the palmprint. Region Of Interest of 256×256 pixels is clipped around the center. Next, normalized directional energy components of the decomposed subband outputs are computed for each block. Biorthogonal, Symlet, Discrete Meyer, Coiflet, Daubechies and Mexican hat wavelets are investigated on 500 palmprints acquired from 50 users with 10 samples each for their individual and concatenated combined features vectors. The performance has been analyzed using Euclidean classifier. An Equal Error Rate (EER) of 0.0217 and Genuine Acceptance Rate (GAR) of 97.12% with combined feature vector formed by Bior3.9, Sym8 and Dmeyer wavelets depict better performance over individual wavelet transforms and combination of coiflet, Daubechies and Mexican hat wavelets.

1 Introduction

Biometrics is identification of individual on the basis of unique physiological and behavioral patterns. It is fast replacing other means of authentication like passwords and keys due to the inherent drawbacks in them and increased effectiveness and reliability of the biometric modalities. The passwords can be forgotten or hacked, while keys can be lost or compromised. The individual's unique physiological or behavioral characteristics, on the other hand are hard to forged or lost. Fingerprint and face are the common biometrics being used nowadays, but they have inherent problems. The illumination variations affect the performance of face recognition algorithms, while fingerprint, along with technological challenges, has less user acceptability due to the historical use in crime investigations. In future, a considerable number of consumer electronics

F.J. Perales and R.B. Fisher (Eds.): AMDO 2010, LNCS 6169, pp. 128–137, 2010.
© Springer-Verlag Berlin Heidelberg 2010

devices will be personalized. We already see fingerprint identification replacing passwords in personal computers and laptops. This requirement driven usage is predicted to increase manifold in coming years. Biometrics using physiological features is a prime candidate for use in such applications.

1.1 Significance/Research Challenges

Palmprint's information content includes wrinkles, creases, delta points, minutiae and principal lines. Palmprint has also been used in conjunction with hand shape biometric so as to form a more reliable biometric based individual identification system. This type of identification has become an increasingly active research topic. Formally, palmprint analysis is divided into four main specialized categories [1], [2]. A brief description of these categories is given as under:-

1. Ridgeology analyzes friction ridges found on palmprint, and also weighs up point features and minutiae which is quite similar to fingerprint minutiae.

2. Edgeoscopy examines characteristics of ridge edges and take stock of ridges, ridge endings, bifurcation and dots.

3. Palmer flexion crease identification assesses creases on palm formed by flexing the hand. It also involves analysis of line feature, principal lines and wrinkles.

4. Geometric features, like the width, length and area of the palm.

Palm images have been analyzed for discriminating features like principal lines [3], [4], appearance based [5], [6], [7], [8], [9] and texture based [10], [11], [12], [13], [14], [15] and [16]. This paper investigates and enhance our previous work on different filters of wavelet transform and their combination for palmprint identification [17].

1.2 Algorithm Development

The development stages of palmprint identification algorithm consist of development of image acquisition platform, image registration, drawing out the Region of Interest (ROI), extraction of distinctive feature from the ROI and categorization or classification.

2 Development of Image Acquisition Platform

Scanners and pegged systems are currently in vogue as palmprint acquisition setups, [13], [18]. Scanners are hygienically susceptible, while systems with pegs are not very user friendly since they have pegs fixed at certain locations and cause inconvenience to user as they are required to clamp their hands inside the pegs. We, therefore, developed a peg free system that is more acceptable to users as it is non invasive and user friendly, Fig. 1. It is an enclosed black box, simple in construction and draws on ring shaped lighting tube to ensure uniform illumination. The image acquisition setup is provided with two flat plates. The camera and the light source are fixed on the upper plate while the bottom plate is used to place the hand for image acquisition. To shun any mismatch due to scale invariance the distance between these two plates is kept constant. After empirical testing the distance between the plates is kept at 14 inches. 10 images from 50 male individuals have been collected making a total of 500 images as the experimental dataset. The age distribution of individuals is between 22 to 56 years, with high percentage between 22 to 25 years. SONY DSC W-35 cyber shot camera has been utilized for imaging the palmprint.

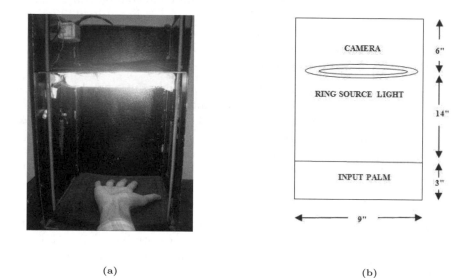

(a)   (b)

Fig. 1. (a) Image Acquisition Platform (b) Dimensions of Image Acquisition Platform

3   Image Registration

We utilised the approach proposed by [11] in which the captured palmprint images were color images having RGB as the parameters. These parameters were changed to HSI parameters. The palmprint has been analyzed for its texture by means of its gray level or intensity values (I) available in the HSI parameters. The obtained gray level images are normalized and then hysteresis thresholding is used to obtain a binarized image. In order to cater for inadvertent rotations rotational alignment has been incorporated using the second order moments. Second order statistical moments have been utilized to obtain the parameters of best fitting ellipse in which the major axis of the ellipse corresponds to the longest line in the image and was assumed to be passing through the middle finger. Ratios between eigen values help examine the shape of an object whereas direction of elongation is evaluated using the direction of the eigenvector

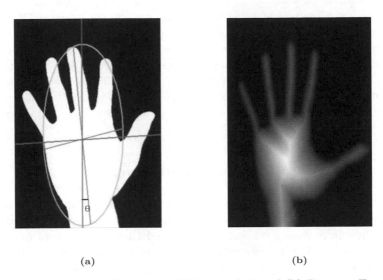

(a)   (b)

Fig. 2. (a) Calculation of alignment of Palm by finding θ (b) Distance Transformed Palmprint

corresponding to highest eigen value. Subsequently, the offset θ between the normal axis and the major axis of the ellipse is calculated, Fig. 2(a). The following equation has been used for the computation of theta:

$$\theta = [\frac{1}{2} \arctan[\frac{2c}{a-b}]] \tag{1}$$

where a, b and c are the second order normalized moments of the pixels and are calculated using the following equations:

$$a = \frac{\sum\limits_{(x,y)\epsilon P} (y-v)^2.P(x,y)}{\sum\limits_{(x,y)\epsilon P} P(x,y)} \tag{2}$$

$$b = \frac{\sum\limits_{(x,y)\epsilon P} (x-u)^2.P(x,y)}{\sum\limits_{(x,y)\epsilon P} P(x,y)} \tag{3}$$

$$c = \frac{\sum\limits_{(x,y)\epsilon P} (x-u).(y-v).P(x,y)}{\sum\limits_{(x,y)\epsilon P} P(x,y)} \tag{4}$$

In above equations, P(x,y) are the pixels in the image, while u and v are locations of centeroids. The palmprint is then vertically aligned using Affine transformation after which morphological operations are employed to remove noise in the binary image. The image is further complemented and distance transform is applied in conjunction with the chessboard metric to evaluate the center of palmprint, Fig. 2(b). Distance transform valuates the pixels having a gray level value of zero from their nearest non-zero neighbours and the maximum value obtained from the transform is estimated to be the center of palmprint. Further, taking coordinates of the center of palmprint a fixed square region is cropped which is of the size of 256×256.

4   Feature Extraction and Classification

Wavelets have been used as a tool so as to extract the textural information of palmprint images, we calculated the horizontal, vertical and diagonal normalized energy values from each level and concatenated these values to form a feature vector for classification between intra and inter class images. Five images out of a total dataset of 10 images from each user are utilized for training while the rest five are used for validation. Textural analysis has been carried out on extracted Region of interest, ROI using different wavelet families namely Biorthogonal 3.9, Symmlet 8, Demeyer 5, Coiflet, Daubechies and Mexican hat. ROI has been decomposed into three scales using each wavelet type. Using this procedure ten directional details are obtained for each wavelet. We further calculated the directional energy in each level and normalized it so as to reduce variation in the gray levels of palmprint images due to illumination variance. Normalized energy minimizes feature variance due to non-uniform illumination, as it brings the extreme values down by calculating the average and thus help lower intensity variations due to illumination [19].

As for the extraction of distinctive features we adopted two different approaches, these two approaches are explained below:-

Approach-1: The energy estimated from each block for the three wavelet types (Biorthogonal 3.9, Symmlet 8, Demeyer 5) is concatenated to form a characteristic vector comprising 27 values for an individual palmprint. The lowpass version of the decomposition is excluded from the feature vector. The same principle applied for other three types of wavelet families (Coiflet, Daubechies, Mexican hat).

$E_{k\theta}$, defined as the Energy value in directional sub-band $S_{k,\theta}$ at k^{th} resolution level is given by:

$$E_{k\theta} = \sum_{S_{k,\theta}} |F_{k,\theta}(x,y) - \overline{F}_{k,\theta}| \qquad (5)$$

where $\overline{F}_{k,\theta}$ is the mean of pixel values of $F_{k,\theta}(x,y)$ in the sub-band $S_{k,\theta}$. $F_{k,\theta}(x,y)$ is the contourlet coefficient value at position (x,y). Additionally, the directional sub-bands vary from 0 to $2^n - 1$. The normalized energy value $\hat{E}_{k\theta}$ of subband θ at k^{th} resolution level is defined as:

$$\hat{E}_{k\theta} = \frac{E_{k\theta}}{\sum\limits_{\theta=0}^{2^n-1} E_{k\theta}} \tag{6}$$

where 'n' presents the total number of blocks present in the image. Matching is performed by calculating the Euclidean distance between the energy features of registered palm image and the test palm image. Euclidean distance between two point p(a,b) and q(x,y) is defined as:

$$Eu\_Dist = [(a - x)^2 + (b - y)^2]^{\frac{1}{2}} \tag{7}$$

It was revealed that rotating an image causes a considerable blur in it due to interpolation which is not affordable in case of textural analysis of palmprint. Thus instead of rotating palmprint image for vertical alignment we have rotated the axis of region instead of the palm. A reverse transformation is computed from the Affine transform, as following:

$$X(new) = X\cos(\theta) - Y\sin(\theta) \tag{8}$$

$$Y(new) = X\sin(\theta) + Y\cos(\theta) \tag{9}$$

Using the above equations, a rotation invariant region of interest is obtained. Although the approximation or interpolation error still exists since the coordinates obtained would still be rounded off but the results show improved performance and accuracy.

Approach-2: In this approach, we opted to analyze the individual performance of the individual wavelet by calculating the block level energies and constructing a feature vector of the same length 27. The individual wavelets were used for 9 decomposition levels and normalized energies were found for each individual block. The individual results for Bior 3.9, Symlet, Demeyer, Coiflet, Daubechies and Mexican hat wavelet kernels are shown in Fig. 3(a), 3(b), 4(a), 4(b), 5(a) and 5(b) respectively. Fig. 6(a) gives the Genuine and impostor distribution for the combined approach for Bior 3.9, Symlet and Demeyer wavelet families whereas Fig. 6(b) gives combined approach for Coiflet, Daubechies and Mexican hat wavelet kernels. Fig. 7(a) gives Threshold Vs FMR and FNMR graph for the first three filters and their Combined approach, while 7(b) is of next three kernels. Fig. 8(a) gives Receiver Operating Curve for first three filters and their Combined approach, while Fig. 8(b) for the next three.

Table-1 summarizes the Equal Error Rate, EER, Decidability Index and Genuine Acceptance Rate, GAR, for the different wavelets for their individual and combined performance. The wavelets combination (Bior 3.9, Symlet, Demeyer) gives GAR of 97.12% and EER of 0.0217, better than individual wavelets.

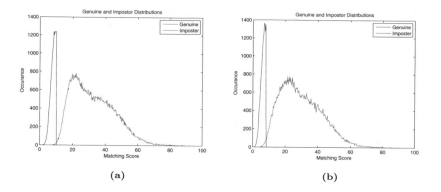

Fig. 3. (a) Genuine and Imposter Distribution Curve for Bior 3.9 (b) Genuine and Imposter Distribution Curve for Symlet 8

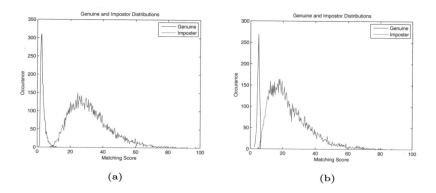

Fig. 4. (a) Genuine and Imposter Distribution Curve for Demyer (b) Genuine and Imposter Distribution Curve for Coiflet

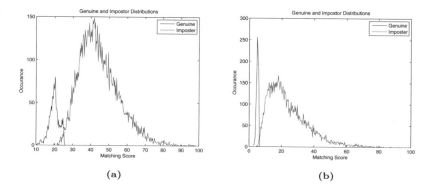

Fig. 5. (a) Genuine and Imposter Distribution Curve for Daubechies (b) Genuine and Imposter Distribution Curve for Mexican hat

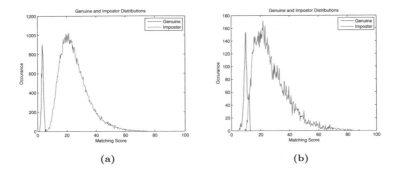

(a)   (b)

Fig. 6. (a) Genuine and Imposter Distribution Curve for Combined Approach of Bior 3.9, Symlet, Demeyer Kernels (b) Genuine and Imposter Distribution Curve for Combined Approach of Coiflet, Daubechies and Mexican hat kernels

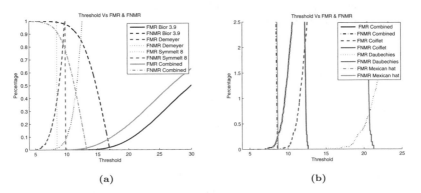

(a)   (b)

Fig. 7. (a) Threshold Vs FMR and FNMR for Bior 3.9, Symlet, Demeyer filters and their Combined Response(b) Threshold Vs FMR and FNMR for Coiflet, Daubechies, Mexican hat filters and their Combined Response

Table 1. Performance Characteristics of Different Wavelets

Wavelet	EER	Decidability Index	GAR (%)
Bior3.9	0.0322	2.6411	76.23
Sym8	0.0821	2.6987	84.45
Dmeyer	0.3833	2.5677	71.1
Coiflet	2.0643	2.1320	65
Daubechies	0.7082	2.3413	70
Mexican hat	0.2296	2.4559	73
Combination of wavelets (Bior3.9 + Sym8 + Dmeyer)	0.0217	3.1275	97.12
Combination of wavelets (Coiflet + Daubechies + Mexican hat)	0.2255	2.7834	80

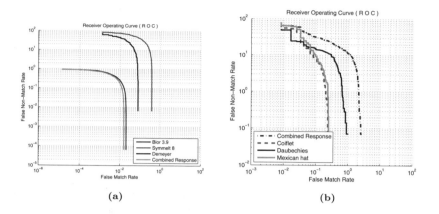

Fig. 8. (a) Receiver Operating Curve for Bior 3.9, Symlet, Demeyer filters and their Combined Response(b) Receiver Operating Curve for Coiflet, Daubechies, Mexican hat filters and their Combined Response

5   Conclusion

This paper presents individual and combination of multiple wavelets at feature level for palmprint based authentication system using the developed peg-free image acquisition platform. Six different wavelet kernels and their combination are investigated for palmprint identification application. Various quantitative measures like Equal Error Rate, Decidability Index and Genuine Acceptance Rate are calculated. Among the three individual wavelet kernels, Bior3.9 gives the best Equal Error Rate while combined wavelets approach outperforms the individual wavelet feature for the palmprint identification.

References

1. Roberts, C.: Biometric-Palm and Hand. Centre for Critical Infrastructure Protection (May 2006),
   http://www.ccip.govt.nz/newsroom/information-notes/2006/
   biometrics-technologies-palmhand.pdf
2. Shu, W., Zhang, D.: Palmprint Verification: An implementation of Biometric Technology. In: International Conference on Pattern Recognition, ICPR, vol. I, pp. 219–221 (1998)
3. Wu, X., Zhang, D., Wang, K.: Palm Line Extraction and Matching for Personal authentication. IEEE Trans. Systems, Man, and Cybernetics-Part A: Systems and Humans 36(5), 978–987 (2006)
4. Kumar, A., Wong, D.C.M., Shen, H.C., Jain, A.K.: Personal Verification using Palmprint and Hand Geometry Biometric. In: Kittler, J., Nixon, M.S. (eds.) AVBPA 2003. LNCS, vol. 2688. Springer, Heidelberg (2003)
5. Ekinci, M., Aykut, M.: Palmprint Recognition by Applying Wavelet Subband Representation and Kernel PCA. In: Perner, P. (ed.) MLDM 2007. LNCS (LNAI), vol. 4571, pp. 628–642. Springer, Heidelberg (2007)

6. Tao, J., Jiang, W., Gao, Z., Chen, S., Wang, C.: Palmprint Recognition Based on Improved 2DPCA. In: Shi, Z.-Z., Sadananda, R. (eds.) PRIMA 2006. LNCS (LNAI), vol. 4088, pp. 455–462. Springer, Heidelberg (2006)
7. Shang, L., Huang, D.-S., Du, J.-X., Huang, Z.-K.: Palmprint Recognition Using ICA Based on Winner-Take-All Network and Radial Basis Probabilistic Neural Network. In: Wang, J., Yi, Z., Żurada, J.M., Lu, B.-L., Yin, H. (eds.) ISNN 2006. LNCS, vol. 3972, pp. 216–221. Springer, Heidelberg (2006)
8. Connie, T., Teoh, A., Goh, M., Ngo, D.: Palmprint Recognition with PCA and ICA. In: Image and Vision Computing, New Zealand 2003, Palmerston North, New Zealand, vol. 3, pp. 232–227 (2003)
9. Lu, G., Zhang, D., Wang, K.Q.: Palmprint recognition using eigenpalms features. Pattern Recognition Letters 24(9-10), 1473–1477 (2003)
10. Mumtaz, M., Masoor, A.B., Masood, H.: Directional Energy Based Palmprint Identification using Non Subsampled Contourlet Transform. In: IEEE International Conference on Image Procesing, ICIP 2009, Egypt (2009)
11. Kumar, A., Zhang, D.: Personal Recognition Using Hand Shape and Texture. IEEE Trans. Image Processing 15, 2454–2461 (2006)
12. Zhou, X., Peng, Y., Yang, M.: Palmprint Recognition Using Wavelet and Support Vector Machines. In: Yang, Q., Webb, G. (eds.) PRICAI 2006. LNCS (LNAI), vol. 4099, pp. 385–393. Springer, Heidelberg (2006)
13. Zhang, L., Zhang, D.: Characterization of Palmprints by Wavelet Signatures via Directional Context Modeling. IEEE Trans. on SMC-B 34(3), 1335–1347 (2004)
14. Zhang, D., kong, W.-k., You, J., Wong, M.: Online Palmprint Identification. IEEE Trans. Pattern Analysis and Machine Intelligence 25(9), 1041–1050 (2003)
15. Li, W., Zhang, D., Xu, Z.: Palmprint identification by Fourier transform. International Journal of Pattern Recognition and Artifical Intelligence 16(4), 417–432 (2002)
16. Kumar, A., Shen, H.C.: Recognition of Palmprints Using Wavelet-based Features. In: Proc. Intl. Conf. Sys., Cybern., SCI 2002, Orlando, Florida (2002)
17. Masood, H., Mumtaz, M., Butt, M.A.A., Mansoor, A.B., Khan, S.A.: Wavelet based Palmprint Authentication System. In: IEEE International Symposium on Biometrics and Security System, ISBAST 2008, Islamabad, Pakistan, April 23-24 (2008)
18. Zhang, D., Lu, G., Kong, A.W.-K., Wong, M.: A Novel Personal Authentication System Using Palmprint Technology. In: Pal, S.K., Bandyopadhyay, S., Biswas, S. (eds.) PReMI 2005. LNCS, vol. 3776, pp. 40–49. Springer, Heidelberg (2005)
19. Masood, H., Asim, M., Mumtaz, M., Mansoor, A.B.: Combined Contourlet and Non Subsampled Contourlet Transform based Approach for Personal Identification using Palmprint. In: Digital Image Computing: Techniques and Applications, DICTA 2009, Melbourne, Australia (December 2009)

Real-Time Motion Transition by Example

Cameron Egbert[1], Parris K. Egbert[2], and Bryan S. Morse[2]

[1] Microsoft Corp, 1 Microsoft Way, Redmond, Washington, USA, 98052
[2] Brigham Young University, 3361 TMCB, Provo, UT, USA 84602
cegbert@microsoft.com, egbert@cs.byu.edu, morse@cs.byu.edu

Abstract. Motion transitioning is a common task in real-time applications such as games. While most character motions can be created a priori using motion capture or hand animation, transitions between these motions must be created by an animation system at runtime. Because of this requirement, it is often difficult to create a transition that preserves the feel that the actor or animator has put into the motion. In addition, transitions must be created in real-time. This paper describes a method of creating motion transitions that is computationally feasible for interactive speeds and preserves the feel of the original motions. We do this by using both a procedural motion and a motion segment taken from the motions being transitioned between.

Keywords: Computer animation, articulated objects, motion transition.

1 Introduction

Realistic character motion is a necessity for computer graphics applications such as movies and games. Three main methods exist to create motion for a virtual character—*motion capture*, *hand animation*, and *simulation*. *Motion capture* is the process of recording the motion of a human actor. *Hand animation* refers to the use of a software package to manipulate a 3D model of a character to achieve an animation. In *simulation*, the motion of the character is computed using a physical model.

Simulation methods are generally thought to be too unrealistic for games. In addition, since an interactive application, such as a game, must generate animation on the fly, and both motion capture and hand animation produce pre-made motion, these methods can only be used if further processing is done.

The method most commonly used in games is to create several base motion segments (i.e., walking, running, jumping, etc.) using motion capture or hand animation, and transition between these motions on the fly [1, 2].

The goal of this research is to find a method to create plausible transitions for interactive applications. Since the point of transition is not known ahead of time, these transitions must be created dynamically. This puts more severe constraints on the transitioning method than would be needed for an offline method.

Ideally, the method of creating the transition should have the following properties, in order of decreasing necessity: 1) Computing the transition should be efficient enough to run in real time, 2) Transitioning should be responsive, 3) The transitioning method should not require excessive space resources (disk space, memory, etc.), 4) The motion created should be continuous and believable.

F.J. Perales and R.B. Fisher (Eds.): AMDO 2010, LNCS 6169, pp. 138–147, 2010.
© Springer-Verlag Berlin Heidelberg 2010

These are the basic criteria for any algorithm that creates a transition. The first three are hard constraints for real-time applications. The fourth is a softer constraint and is somewhat subjective. At the very least, the algorithm should produce a motion for which C^1 continuity is preserved for the position and rotation of the joints.

2 Related Work

Currently, the most widely used method of creating transitions involves linearly interpolating between two motions. A pre-determined number of frames at the end of the first motion are overlapped with the first frames of the second motion, and the values of each are linearly interpolated, creating a smooth transition between the motions. Unfortunately, this transition may not be realistic, especially in the case of extremely dissimilar motions. Even when the motions are similar, the problem of synchronizing motions is not addressed using this method alone. Transitioning between two walking motions that are at different points in their cycle will give an unrealistic transition, even though the motions are similar.

This problem is addressed by using *dynamic timewarping* [3, 4]. Dynamic timewarping creates a function that synchronizes both motions to be at similar poses at any given time by first determining the similarity of each pair of frames for both motions. The synchronization function is determined by finding the best path through these similarity values. While timewarping alleviates the problem of unsynchronized motions, it doesn't address the problem of two dissimilar motions.

Park et al. [5] use dynamic timewarping to align clips of motion before interpolating between them. In addition, the motion clips are parameterized to provide a method for controlling the synthesized motion. Their approach allows for specification of locomotion over a range of directions and speeds. Unfortunately, this method is geared toward generating motion from a set of similar motions, and not between two arbitrary (possibly different) motions.

Physically-based motion synthesis is another method of synthesizing motion [6, 7]. In these methods, motion is generated from a dynamic simulation of the character. However, it is difficult to produce realistic motion using physically-based approaches. Additionally, these approaches fail to capture the small nuances of human motion.

Another approach that has been taken is to construct a mathematical model from a set of motion capture data. Hidden markov models [8] and switched linear dynamic systems [9] are among the most popular approaches. These methods can produce arbitrary motion that resembles the pre-existing cache of motion capture data, but at the cost of low control and high processing requirements.

Arikan and Forsyth [10] apply a randomized algorithm to search for motions from a hierarchy of transition graphs. In later work, Arikan et al. [11] create motion by using a similar graph structure but satisfy user-specified annotations in the creation of the resulting motion. When the number of example motions becomes too large, it becomes prohibitively time-consuming to search through these graph structures for a suitable motion. Follow-on work by Arikan et. al. [12] uses physical models with motion to create transitions between motions.

Ikemoto et. al. [13] create a cache of transitions by searching through motion clips and saving clips that give good transitions for each frame of motion. This cache is then accessed to retrieve the best transition clips for a given motion.

Pullen and Bregler [14] use motion capture to assist an artist in creating an animation. In their method, the artist creates a rough animation using conventional keyframing, and motion capture data is used to enhance the animation in order to make it look more lifelike.

Rose et al. [15], use spacetime constraints to create transitions. In their method, a combination of dynamic and kinematic constraints is placed on the skeleton, and a transition is generated using these constraints. This method gives realistic motion for short transitions but is not computationally efficient enough for real-time applications.

Kovar, et al. [16] use a method they call a Motion Graph, which is a way of arranging motion data into a graph. Each node of the graph corresponds to a common pose, such as standing. Traversing an edge corresponds to playing a short motion segment between two poses. However, motion graphs are not suitable for interactive applications because of the computation time needed to find a traversal of the graph.

Snap-together motion [1] processes a corpus of motion into a graph similar to a motion graph. Instead of computing an entire traversal through the graph, each edge traversal is determined at run-time from the user's input. The downfall of this method is that once an edge is taken, no further input can be given until the motion reaches the next node. While this is sufficient for some real-time applications, more interactivity is required. In follow-on work, Heck and Gleischer [17] apply example based motion synthesis in which motion graphs are used to generate motion transitions by blending together example motions from the space.

Peng et. al. [18] also use an example based motion synthesis technique. Similar animations are clustered together and then bundled into a motion graph. Transitions are generated by traversing the graph.

Wang and Bodenheimer [19, 20] study the appropriate length of time for transitions between motions. Their studies discuss how much time should be devoted to transitions, and the point at which the transition time becomes distracting to the animation.

This paper proposes a method feasible for real-time applications that gives more believable motion than a simple linear transition. Specifically, the motion for the transition is adapted from a segment of motion from one of the two motions being transitioned between, and can be chosen to resemble any specific motion. This ability is leveraged to choose a segment that resembles the desired transition. The segment chosen is then warped to match this transition even more closely. In this way the method enables the synthesis of a transition that preserves the same "feel" of the original motion while producing a motion that is feasible as a continuous transition.

3 Real-Time Motion Transition by Example

In order to produce a method of creating transitions that meet the four proposed goals, we propose a new method that is both feasible for real-time applications and produces more believable motion than a simple linear transition. The "feel" of the motion is preserved by adapting pre-existing motion from the two motions being transitioned between.

This approach at producing real-time motion transitions is encapsulated in a 4-step process: 1) Find transition points, 2) Align motions, 3) Search for an example, and 4) Motion modification.

In the following discussion, M_0 is the motion that is being transitioned from, M_1 is the motion that is being transitioned to, T is the transition, and t is the length of the transition (in frames).

3.1 Finding Transition Points

First, since the start of the transition is a frame from M_0, and the end of the transition is a frame from M_1, transition points are found for M_0 and M_1. The transition point for M_0 is the frame at which the transition is initiated. For example, if the character is on frame 10 of a walking animation when the user initiates the transition, the transition point for M_0 is frame 10. The transition point of M_1 is either set manually, or found using a method similar to *dynamic timewarping*. Motions that should be played from start to finish (jumping, kicking, punching, etc.) have their "transition to" frame set manually to the first frame, while the transition point for two similar motions (walking to running) is computed using *dynamic timewarping*. These transition points are kept in a lookup table for use at runtime.

Keeping a lookup table of the matching frames requires storage space to hold the frame of each motion that could be transitioned to, for each frame in each motion. Therefore, if there are n motions, and each motion has m frames, the space required to store these values is $n*m*n$. Typically a character will have up to 50 motions, at about 200 frames per motion. Since each value of a table is a frame index, these values can be stored in 1 byte, which requires 500,000 bytes (479 kB) to store all of the tables, which is not an excessive space requirement. Since we want the transition to look natural, we find the transition point in M_1 which matches what the frame from M_0 would have been had there been no transition. For example, if a 30 frame transition is initiated on a walk cycle when the left foot is forward, and at the end of 30 frames, the character would have had its right foot forward, we want to transition to a frame in M_1 that is similar to the right foot forward pose. Specifically, given frame i in M_0, to find the correct "transition to" frame j in M_1 (after a transition of length t), just read the lookup table value for $M_0(i+t)$, instead of simply $M_0(i)$.

3.1.1 Dynamic Timewarping

To determine a timewarp, we use the same distance metric as in [16]. Specifically, to compute the distance between two frames F_i and F_j, two point clouds representing each frame are compared. The point clouds are created from the joint positions of the skeleton. In order to take into account derivative information, a small neighborhood of frames about F_i and F_j are used to create the point clouds. Finally, the optimal sum of squared distances is computed between the two point clouds, allowing for rigid 2D transformations. The distance metric is defined as:

$$D(F_i, F_j) = \min_{\theta, x_0, z_o} \sum_k w_k \left\| p_{i,k} - T_{\theta, x_o, z_0} \, p_{j,k} \right\|^2 \tag{1}$$

where $p_{i,k}$ is the kth point in the cloud generated from frame i and $T_{\theta, x0, z0}$ is a linear transformation consisting of a rotation of θ degrees about the vertical axis followed by a translation of (x_0, z_0). w_k are weights that sum to one and give more importance to F_i and F_j, and less importance to the frames at the edges of the neighborhoods.

This has the following closed form solution:

$$\theta = \arctan \frac{\sum_i w_i (x_i z_i' - x_i' z_i) - (\overline{xz'} - \overline{x'z})}{\sum_i w_i (x_i x_i' - z_i z_i') - (\overline{xx'} - \overline{zz'})}$$

$$x_0 = (\overline{x} - \overline{x'} \cos\theta - \overline{z'} \sin\theta)$$

$$z_0 = (\overline{z} - \overline{x'} \sin\theta - \overline{z'} \cos\theta)$$

(2)

where $\overline{x} = \sum_i w_i x_i$ and the other barred terms are similar.

This distance metric is calculated for each pair of frames, which produces a distance array. Figure 1 shows an example distance array for the *weak kick* and *strong kick* actions.

Matching frames are calculated from this array. The idea is to create a minimum cost connecting path through the array, and use this path to determine which frames best match. This path is determined by stepping through the array one frame at a time, choosing one of the neighbors of the current position as the next step in the path. The neighbor chosen is the neighbor with the least cost value. The path is also restricted to be continuous, causal (i.e., to always move forward), and to have a slope limit (i.e., a limit to the number of consecutive horizontal or vertical steps). The slope limit is somewhat arbitrary, but in practice a slope limit of 3 steps works well.

This path is calculated for every possible starting point, and the path that yields the minimum average cost is saved. From this path, the matching frames are determined.

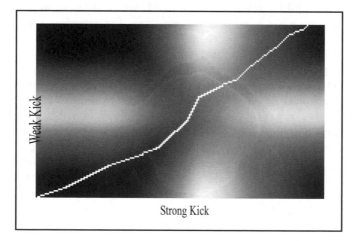

Fig. 1. The distance array for two similar motions. The white line represents the minimum cost path connecting frame 0 and frame n of the weak kicking motion.

3.2 Aligning Motions

After the transition points for the motions are determined, $\mathbf{M}_1$ is aligned to $\mathbf{M}_0$. The starting position of $\mathbf{M}_1$ is found from the Newtonian motion formula:

$$\mathbf{p}_1 = \mathbf{p}_0 + \mathbf{v}*t + \tfrac{1}{2}\,\mathbf{a}*t^2$$

(3)

where $\mathbf{p}_1$ is the starting position of $\mathbf{M}_1$, $\mathbf{p}_0$ is the position of the final frame of $\mathbf{M}_0$, $\mathbf{v}$ is the velocity of the final frame of $\mathbf{M}_0$, t is the time length of the transition, and $\mathbf{a}$ is the constant acceleration needed to achieve the velocity of the starting frame of $\mathbf{M}_1$ in the time of the transition. The rotations of the root joint of $\mathbf{M}_1$ are found in a similar way.

3.3 Searching for an Example

At this point the endpoints for the desired transition are known, and hence we are ready to create the transition. In order to preserve the "feel" of the motion, a segment of either $\mathbf{M}_0$ or $\mathbf{M}_1$ is used to build the transition. The third step of creating the transition is to find this segment. Both $\mathbf{M}_0$ and $\mathbf{M}_1$ are searched to find the motion segment that most closely matches the desired transition according to a "closeness" metric. The metric we use is a measure of change in value from the start of the transition to the end of the transition, and the velocity at both endpoints. Specifically,

$$\mathbf{C} = (\mathbf{m}_0 - \mathbf{m}_{0\text{TARGET}})^2 + (\mathbf{m}_1 - \mathbf{m}_{1\text{TARGET}})^2 + (\mathbf{ds} - \mathbf{ds}_{\text{TARGET}})^2 \qquad (4)$$

where $\mathbf{m}_0$ is the slope of the start of the motion segment, $\mathbf{m}_1$ is the slope at the end of the motion segment, $\mathbf{ds}$ is the change in value of the motion segment, and $\mathbf{m}_{0\text{TARGET}}$, $\mathbf{m}_{1\text{TARGET}}$, and $\mathbf{ds}_{\text{TARGET}}$ are the values of the desired transition. The number of frames between $\mathbf{m}_0$ and $\mathbf{m}_1$ equals the number of frames between $\mathbf{m}_{0\text{TARGET}}$ and $\mathbf{m}_{1\text{TARGET}}$. In other words, time scaling is disallowed.

For each degree of freedom, the motion segment that produces the minimum value for $\mathbf{C}$ is used as the example segment in creating the final transition. This process is repeated for each degree of freedom.

3.4 Motion Modification

The final step is to modify the motion to resemble the desired transition. The previous step yielded a motion segment that roughly matches what the transition should be at the endpoints. This is necessary for the transition to be continuous with the original two motions, but so far no constraint has been made for the motion between the endpoints. What is really desired is a motion that behaves relatively well but looks like what the character would have done if it had chosen the transition. In other words, we want to control the general motion yet have it resemble the pre-existing motions. In order to accomplish this, we construct the motion from both a smooth transition and the example motion. High frequency information, which gives the motion its character, is taken from the example motion, while low frequency information is taken from the smooth transition. The signal is reconstructed from this frequency information into the final signal.

In order to accomplish this, we use a Laplacian pyramid decomposition, first introduced to motion signal processing in [3]. Each level of the Laplacian pyramid can be thought of as containing frequency information for the signal, where $\mathbf{L}_1$ contains the highest frequencies.

Now, for each degree of freedom of each joint in the transition, the new motion segments are decomposed using a Laplacian pyramid, and the lowest level is replaced by a 3rd degree Bezier curve that is $\mathbf{C}^1$ continuous with both $\mathbf{M}_0$ and $\mathbf{M}_1$. The signal is then reconstructed from the Laplacian pyramid to give a function which transitions with C^1 continuity from the end of $\mathbf{M}_0$ to the beginning of $\mathbf{M}_1$ while having the same "feel" as $\mathbf{M}_0$ and $\mathbf{M}_1$.

The level to which the signal is decomposed before substitution and reconstruction can vary. Substitution at the first level is equivalent to using none of the sample signal, while substitution at higher levels introduces more and more of the sampled signal. Practice has shown that substitution at about the third level usually produces the best results.

4   Experiments and Results

The method has been tested on a set of seven motions, some similar, others dissimilar. These motions include walking, running, jumping, skipping, weak kicking, strong kicking, and punching. Computing transition points between pairs of motions typically takes about 20 seconds of pre-runtime computation.

Actual motion transitions are created at runtime in response to user input. Calculating the transitions is virtually instantaneous and causes no noticeable delay in frame rate. Figures 2-5 show the results of the method in creating a few different transitions.

5   Discussion and Further Work

The goal of this research was to provide a method for creating a motion transition in real time that is both believable and consistent with the motions being transitioned between. Previous methods for creating transitions are either too compute intensive for real time, or lack the nuances that make the motion appealing. Our method attempts to meet these goals by modifying motion from a pre-existing source, using computationally simple transformations.

We will now attempt to evaluate the strengths and weaknesses of this technique based on the criteria established at the beginning of the paper.

First, the transition is efficient enough to run in real time. The timewarps are computed as a pre-processing step, and the transitions are created in real time.

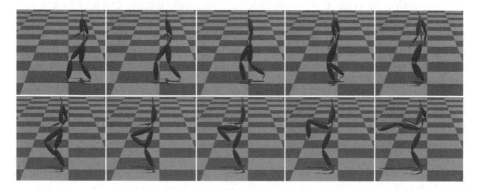

Fig. 2. Walking to kicking

Second, transitioning is responsive. The transitions happen instantaneously when the user presses a button.

Third, this algorithm doesn't require excessive space resources. The lookup table for the transition points of the test set of seven motions took 40 kB in ASCII text format. The space required to store this table is $O(mn^2)$, where m is the number of frames in each motion, and n is the number of motions. Since there were 7 motions, of approximately 200 frames each, and each entry in the table took approximately 4 bytes, the expected table size is 200*7*7*4 = 38.2 kB. For a motion set containing 50 motions, this table would take 200*50*50*4 = 1.9MB. This space could be further reduced by using a binary representation, reducing the size required for the set containing 50 motions down to 200*50*50*1 = 479 kB.

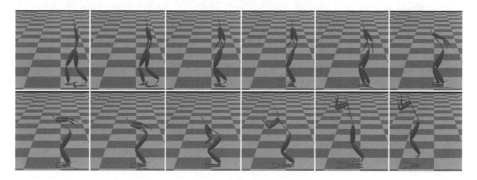

Fig. 3. Walking to jumping

Fig. 4. Jumping to skipping

Fourth, the motion created is arguably continuous and believable. For transitions between similar motions, the effect is at least as good, and for transitions between dissimilar motions, the method produces motion superior to linear transitioning, though it is not always perfect.

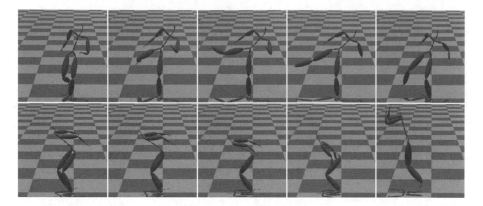

Fig. 5. Kicking to jumping

There are some limitations to the algorithm. Since this method deals only with forward kinematics, it is inherently susceptible to foot-skate and other artifacts. An inverse kinematic solution should fit well within this framework, and the addition of IK would alleviate foot-skate and other problems.

6   Summary and Conclusions

This paper has presented a method of creating motion transitions that are both realistic and computable in real time. Previous methods either were too compute-intensive to run in real time, or sacrificed motion quality to be feasible for real time.

The method presented in this paper accomplishes both goals of motion quality and ease of computation. By using a pre-existing motion segment to construct the motion transition, the quality of the motion is preserved. At the same time, no extraordinary computation is required, making this method feasible for real-time. The transitioning mechanism has low latency and is therefore quite responsive. Additionally, the method requires only a modest amount of space resources.

Acknowledgements

This work was made possible through a donation from Electronic Arts. The data used in this project was obtained from mocap.cs.cmu.edu. The database was created with funding from NSF EIA-0196217.

References

1. Gleicher, M., Shin, H., Kovar, L., Jepsen, A.: Snap-together motion: Assembling Run-Time Animation. In: Symposium on Interactive 3D Graphics (2003)
2. Mizuguchi, M., Buchanan, J., Calvert, T.: Data driven motion transitions for interactive games. In: Eurographics 2001 Short Presentations (2002)

3. Bruderlin, A., Williams, L.: Motion signal processing. In: Proceedings of ACM SIG-GRAPH 1995, pp. 97–104 (1995)
4. Kovar, L., Gleicher, M.: Flexible automatic motion blending with registration curves. In: Proceedings of ACM SIGGRAPH/Eurographics Symposium on Computer Animation, pp. 214–224 (2003)
5. Park, S., Shin, H., Shin, S.: On-line locomotion generation based on motion blending. In: ACM Symposium on Computer Animation (2002)
6. Hodgins, J.K., Wooten, W.L., Brogan, D.C., O'Brien, J.F.: Animating human athletics. In: Proceedings of ACM SIGGRAPH 1995, pp. 71–78 (1995)
7. Liu, C., Popović, Z.: Synthesis of complex dynamic character motion from simple animations. In: Proceedings of ACM SIGGRAPH 2002, pp. 408–416 (2002)
8. Brand, M., Hertzmann, A.: Style machines. In: Proceedings of ACM SIGGRAPH 2000, pp. 183–192 (2000)
9. Li, Y., Wang, T., Shum, H.: Motion texture: A two-level statistical model for character motion synthesis. ACM Transactions on Graphics 21(3), 465–472 (2002)
10. Arikan, O., Forsythe, D.A.: Interactive motion generation from examples. ACM Transaction on Graphics 21(3), 483–490 (2002)
11. Arikan, O., Forsyth, D.A., O'Brien, J.: Motion synthesis from annotations. ACM Transactions on Graphics 22(3), 402–408 (2003)
12. Arikan, O., Forsythe, D.A., O'Brian, J.F.: Pushing People Around. In: SCA 2005, pp. 59–66. ACM Press, New York (2005)
13. Ikemoto, L.K.M., Arikan, O., Forsyth, D.: Quick Motion Transitions with Cached Multi-way Blends. University of California, Berkeley Technical Report No. UCB/EECS-2006-14 (2006)
14. Pullen, K., Bregler, C.: Motion capture assisted animation: Texturing and synthesis. In: Proceedings of ACM SIGGRAPH 2002, pp. 501–508 (2002)
15. Rose, C., Guenter, B., Bodenheimer, B., Cohen, M. F.: Efficient generation of motion transitions using spacetime constraints. In: Proceedings of SIGGRAPH '96, Computer Graphics Proceedings. Annual Conference Series, pp. 147–154 (1996)
16. Kovar, L., Gleicher, M., Pighin, F.: Motion graphs. ACM Transactions on Graphics 21(3), 473–482 (2002)
17. Heck, R., Gleicher, M.: Parametric Motion Graphs. In: Proceedings of Symposium on Interactive 3D Graphics and Games 2007 (April 2007)
18. Peng, J., Lin, I., Chao, J., Chen, Y., Juang, G.: Interactive and Flexible Motion Transition. Journal of Visualization and Computer Animation (2007)
19. Wang, J., Boednheimer, B.: The Just Noticeable Difference of Transition Durations. In: SIGGRAPH poster, Los Angeles, CA (July 2005)
20. Wang, J., Bodenheimer, B.: Computing the Duration of Motion Transitions: An Empirical Approach. In: SCA 2004, pp. 335–344. ACM Press, New York (2004)

Novel Representations, Techniques and Error Evaluation for 3D Reconstruction

Sidharth R.Varier, Amey Vaidya, and K.S.Venkatesh

Department of Electrical Engineering,
Indian Institute of Technology Kanpur,
Kanpur-208016 (U.P.) India
sidvarier@gmail.com, ameynvaidya@gmail.com, venkats@iitk.ac.in

Abstract. Silhouette and laser based techniques have been widely used for 3D reconstruction of objects. We propose a Multiple Axis Object Centered Cylindrical Coordinate System (MAOCCCS) for the representation of 3D models reconstructed by silhouette based technique. A single axis cylindrical coordinate system is insufficient for representing objects with multiple auxiliary components because it leads to unequal distribution of points over the object. We also propose a camera calibration method using meshgrid patterns for laser based technique. Using this method we are able to achieve sub-millimeter accuracy in the reconstructed 3D models. It is difficult to qualitatively ascertain the accuracy of any reconstruction method by measuring the various dimensions of the object and comparing them with that of the reconstructed model as this is a very tedious process. A novel technique for the error evaluation of a reconstruction method, which is closely related to the conventional concept of visual hull, has been introduced in this paper.

Keywords: 3D reconstruction, silhouette, visual hull, laser profile, thresholding, pixelisation.

1 Introduction

3D reconstruction is a process of obtaining 3D geometrical and texture information of a real-world object. 3D object reconstruction from multiple 2D images is a well known problem in computer vision. It has got applications in 3D animations, virtual reality, visual metrology, 3D scanner, 3D fax, terrain reconstruction. In [1] volume segment models are constructed using orthographic projections of silhouettes of an object. These volume segment models approximate the visual hull of the target object. This method is well known as volume intersection in computer vision literature. In [2] an octree based representation of an object is generated using its three standard orthographic projections. [3] gives a theoretical foundation for the geometric concept of visual hull. Most of the laser based reconstruction methods use a camera, a laser ray or plane, and a motion platform which is usually a linear slide or a turn-table. An automated scanning system based on orthogonal cross-sections is presented in [4]. This system utilizes an intermediate data model that consists of three orthogonal cross-sections and is built from the triangulated scan data. The resultant model is

F.J. Perales and R.B. Fisher (Eds.): AMDO 2010, LNCS 6169, pp. 148–161, 2010.
© Springer-Verlag Berlin Heidelberg 2010

easily visualized, which facilitates further interactive operation on the data. In [5] two laser sources aligned to project the same plane are used along with a camera and a turn-table. Usage of two laser sources eliminates some light occlusions but not camera occlusions.

A hybrid surface reconstruction method that fuses geometrical information acquired from silhouette images and optical triangulation is presented in [6]. Silhouette based reconstruction is unable to reconstruct the concavities on the object surface. Optical triangulation can detect concavities, but has several shortcomings due to occlusion and laser reflectance properties of the object surface, that often lead to holes and inaccuracies on the recovered surface. So, when both the methods are combined they tend to compensate for the errors produced by the other. A similar fusion of shape from silhouette and shape from laser methods is presented in [7]. In [7] an octree based model is used to represent objects. A calibration technique proposed by Roger Y. Tsai is used in [7]. In [8], a two-stage camera calibration technique is introduced for computing the camera external position and orientation, relative to object reference coordinate system, by using off-the-shelf TV cameras and lenses. An automatic distortion calibration method is presented in [9], which makes use of only images of scenes containing 3D segments, like interior scenes or city scenes.

In this paper the two techniques, silhouette and laser based, are discussed independently and a comparison is presented at the end. In silhouette based technique we use a *multiple axis object centered cylindrical coordinate system* for representing objects with multiple auxiliary components. A camera calibration method using mesh-grid patterns is introduced for the laser based technique which can provide an accurate reconstruction. Apart from the silhouette and the laser based techniques, a method for the qualitative analysis based on the accuracy associated with both the reconstruction methods is introduced. Error in reconstructing an object using any of the two methods can be calculated by this new error evaluation technique.

The remaining paper is organized as follows. In *Section 2* the setup used for object reconstruction is described. *Section 3* discusses the silhouette based reconstruction. *Section 4* describes laser based reconstruction using mesh-grid pattern for camera calibration. *Section 5* introduces the method for calculating the error in reconstruction of 3D objects. Finally conclusion is given in *Section 6*.

2   Setup

The acquisition system is a compact setup in which both the reconstruction techniques can be carried out. In some 3D reconstruction techniques hand-held scanners are used [11, 12]. We have used a hands free setup which is completely automatic. The setup consists of a wooden platform with a rotating platform placed at the center, on which the object to be reconstructed is placed. The rotating platform is driven by a stepper motor with a minimum angular rotation of 1.8 °. In front of the rotating platform, a camera and a laser source are mounted on a raised platform. The laser source is a simple arrangement of a key-chain laser (point laser source) and a cylindrical lens. This laser source emits a laser plane. The camera and the laser source are fixed and they are not moved throughout the experiment.

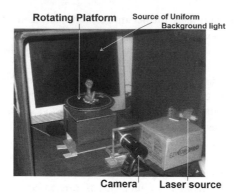

Fig. 1. An image of the setup

Behind the rotating platform a source of uniform background light is kept, so that when viewed from the position of the camera, silhouettes of the object will be seen. The centre of rotation, the camera optical center and the laser source form a triangle. The angle between the laser plane and the camera optical axis is fixed to be 22 °. The camera used in the setup is a 640x480 resolution Enter webcam. The rotation of the platform and the capturing of images are controlled by a computer. Thus the entire setup is automatic. The reconstructed 3D model is displayed in the computer using OpenGL toolkit. Fig.1 shows the image of the setup that is used.

3   Silhouette Based Reconstruction

For the silhouette based reconstruction the object is placed on the rotating platform and the source of uniform background light is turned on. The object is rotated and images of the silhouettes are captured simultaneously. The silhouette images of the object will contain different views of the object. It is same as viewing the object from different viewpoints, relatively speaking.

Fig. 2. The figure in the left is the image of an object. The figure in the right is its cross-section at a certain height.

The silhouette images are next subjected to cropping, contrast enhancement and thresholding to generate images with white background and sharp edged black foreground. The resultant images are subjected to edge detection. Considering the edges of only one side, for example right hand-side, they are sampled along the vertical height at regular intervals. Thus we have the locations of the edge points at all heights and at all angular views of the object. Using this data set, horizontal cross-sections at all heights are generated using a space carving algorithm.

Fig.2 shows the image of an object and its horizontal cross-section at a certain height, generated by employing the space carving algorithm. Here the silhouette images are strictly assumed to be orthographic images. Now to represent any object in a cylindrical coordinate system, there are two important requirements at all heights, firstly a suitable center for the axis (origin) and secondly the set of 3-d coordinates of the points on the surface of the object measured at fixed intervals of angle.

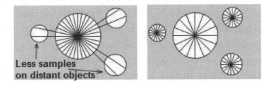
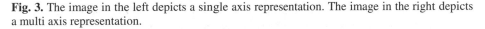

Fig. 3. The image in the left depicts a single axis representation. The image in the right depicts a multi axis representation.

Since a general object, possibly having auxiliary components is being dealt with here, it will have cross-sections with multiple disconnected segments, such as in the example shown in Fig.3. So, single axis cylindrical coordinate system is used, as shown in the left hand-side image of Fig.3, the number of sample points obtained on the distant object is very sparse as compared to the sample points obtained on the object component closer to the centre. But when a *multiple axis object centered cylindrical coordinate system* is used, as shown in the right hand-side image of Fig.3, sample points are obtained which are more equally distributed over the object's surface. In this approach, connected component labeling of the cross-section image is carried out to determine the number of disjoint segments present in the image. In connected component labeling, subsets of connected components in the image are uniquely labeled. This algorithm traverses the image, labeling the pixels based on the connectivity and relative values of its neighbors. Then for every segment its centroid is calculated and centroid is considered as the center for the cylindrical coordinate system for that particular component of the object. Among the group of segments, the one that is nearest to the center of rotation is chosen to be the primary object component, the rest are the secondary object components. The cylindrical coordinate system of the primary object component is fixed to be the global coordinate system. After evaluating centers for all the object components, individual component is sampled using its own local cylindrical coordinate system. This approach is carried out on the cross-section images of all the heights. The positions of the centers of a particular object

Fig. 4. The set of two images in the left-hand side shows the first object in the extreme left and its reconstructed model in the right. Similarly the second object and its reconstructed model are shown in the set of two images in the right hand-side.

component at different heights may vary. Using the set of coordinates of the surface points calculated w.r.t the global coordinate system, the wireframe model of the object is displayed using OpenGL toolkit. Some results are shown in Fig.4.

4   Laser Based Reconstruction

The laser source used for this technique is a simple arrangement of a key-chain laser and a cylindrical lens, as mentioned before. The key-chain laser by itself is a point source laser which emits a laser beam. The cylindrical lens kept in front of it diverges the laser beam into a plane of laser in the direction perpendicular to the axis of the cylindrical lens. This plane is referred to as *laser plane*. This laser falls on the target object forming a curve that lies in this *laser plane*. The image of this curve captured by a camera from a certain viewpoint is known as a *laser profile* image. So *laser profile* can be better defined as the intersection of the *laser plane* and the target object, captured by a camera. Fig.5 shows a target object and its *laser profile* image from a certain viewpoint. In our setup the angle between the laser plane and the camera optical axis is fixed to be 22 °, as mentioned before.

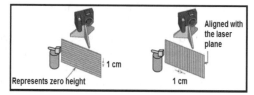
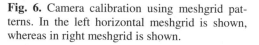

Fig. 5. The image in the left is the target object. The image in the right is its laser profile w.r.t a particular viewpoint.

Fig. 6. Camera calibration using meshgrid patterns. In the left horizontal meshgrid is shown, whereas in right meshgrid is shown.

The procedure for the laser based reconstruction of an object is described as follows:

Steps taken for Camera Calibration. In the beginning, two patterns of meshgrid are placed in the laser plane one at a time, and images are captured. One pattern consists of horizontal lines, which are 1cm apart from each other. Whereas, the second pattern is a set of vertical lines which are 1 cm apart from each other. This is illustrated in Fig.6. Due to the short range, the depth of the field of the camera is small. Therefore the meshgrid images are not focused and the images are blurred out. To obtain single pixel thick meshgrid patterns, these blurred images are subjected to thresholding and pixelisation.

The horizontal meshgrid measures height above the plane containing the rotating platform while the vertical meshgrid measures the distance away from the central axis of rotation. A significant positive of our method is that this approach of empirical meshgrid formation automatically accounts for all the optical distortional aberrations in the system. The two pixelised meshgrid patterns are superimposed to locate the *corner-points*. The resultant image is the complete meshgrid pattern. The corner-points are the points of intersection of the horizontal and vertical lines. These corner-points and their coordinates (p, q), w.r.t the image plane are grouped as a set T. Following this, the number of horizontal gridlines are increased by a factor of 50, by inserting 50 more virtual lines in between each consecutive pair of captured lines.

It is important to note that the captured lines may not be straight, due to optical system defects during capture; we therefore take care to further resolve the vertical measurements by ensuring the new virtual gridlines follow the contours of the visually captured coarse gridlines. With this, now the lines are 0.2 mm apart from each other in real-world coordinates. This is depicted in Fig.7. Thus the improved horizontal mesh-grid pattern has a vertical resolution of 0.2 mm and it helps to obtain the vertical measurements with good accuracy.

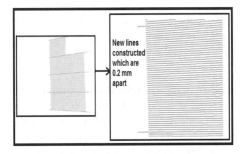

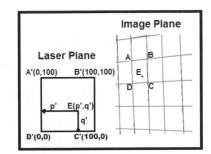

Fig. 7. In the left an image of the improved horizontal meshgrid is shown. The image in the right shows its zoomed view in which the new lines constructed are 0.2 mm apart.

Fig. 8. Mapping of *ABCD* to *A'B'C'D'*. Polygon *ABCD* is in image plane and *A'B'C'D'* is in laser plane. Point *E* is mapped to point *E'* using DLT algorithm.

Capturing laser profile images of the object. The object is placed on the rotating platform of the setup and the source of uniform background light is turned off and the laser source is turned on. The object is rotated and the images are captured at periodic intervals of the object rotation. Each captured image depicts a laser profile of the object, viewed from a different viewpoint.

Mapping of laser profile from the image plane to the laser plane. The laser profile images undergo thresholding and pixelisation. The pixelised laser profile is superimposed over the improved horizontal meshgrid pattern. This results in sampling of the laser profile images at heights of 0.2 mm in real-world coordinates. This assures the capturing of minute surface details, in the vertical direction, present on the object which are of the order of sub-millimeter. The height h of each sampled point can be measured using the improved horizontal meshgrid pattern. In the following discussion, the points on the image plane are denoted by alphabets, for example P, and the points on the laser plane are denoted by alphabets followed by an apostrophe, for example P'. Let a point E (p, q) be one of the sampled points on the laser profile, where (p, q) are the coordinates of the point E w.r.t the image plane. Firstly, the four closest corner-points A $(p1, q1)$, B $(p2, q2)$, C $(p3, q3)$ and D $(p4, q4)$ of point E are found, that forms a polygon $ABCD$. The points A, B, C and D (and their respective coordinates) are obtained from the set of corner-points T which was formed during the camera calibration. Point E is either completely inside or on one of the sides of $ABCD$. Each side AB, BC, CD and AD is 1 cm wide in the laser plane. Therefore the polygon $ABCD$ is mapped to a 100 units sided regular square $A'B'C'D'$ with vertices A' *(0,100)*, B' *(100, 100)*, C' *(100, 0)* and D' *(0, 0)*. This is illustrated in Fig.8. If point E maps to point $E'= (p', q')$ on the regular square then, the actual distance of the point in the laser plane can be determined using Direct Linear Transformation (DLT) [10].

Suppose homogeneous vectors P_i for $1 \le i \le 4$ represent four corner points of polygon $ABCD$ in the image plane and homogeneous vectors P'_i for $1 \le i \le 4$ represent four corner points of regular square $A'B'C'D'$ in the laser plane. Then, if H is the homography matrix which converts P_i to P'_i, then

$$P'_i \times HP_i = 0 \tag{1}$$

Once H is computed by Direct Linear Transformation [10], the coordinates of the point $E'(p', q')$ is calculated as,

$$P' = HP \tag{2}$$

where $P'= (p', q', 1)$, $P=(p, q, 1)$ (point E) and H is the computed homography matrix. The coordinates (p',q') of the point E' are local w.r.t the polygon $A'B'C'D'$. The global coordinates (r',s') w.r.t the laser plane are calculated using the location of the polygon $A'B'C'D'$ in the laser plane. Thus using DLT method the 2-d coordinates of all sample points of all laser profile images have been mapped from the image plane to the laser plane. The r'-coordinate calculated signifies the distance of the sampled point from the central axis of rotation in the laser plane, whereas the s'-coordinate calculated signifies the height of the sampled point in the laser plane.

Transforming from 2-d coordinates to 3-d coordinates. Each laser profile is captured after rotating the object by an angle θ. So, for each pair of adjacent laser profiles, their corresponding planes which contain them are separated in space by an angle θ. Now the 2-d coordinates (r', s') corresponding to each laser profile can be converted into 3-d coordinates (x, y, z). In the 3-d coordinate system, the x-axis is the camera optical axis, the y-axis is the line perpendicular to x-axis in the plane containing the rotating platform, the z-axis is the central axis of rotation and the origin is the centre of rotation of the platform. The new 3-d coordinates can be calculated as follows:

$$x = r' \times \cos(n\theta) \tag{3}$$

$$y = r' \times \sin(n\theta) \tag{4}$$

$$z = s' \tag{5}$$

In the above equations, θ represents the smallest angle by which the object is rotated in the anti-clockwise direction to get a particular laser profile image. n represents the number of times the object has to be rotated by steps of the angle θ to get a particular laser profile image. After this, z-coordinate is replaced by the height h of point E measured using the improved horizontal meshgrid pattern. Using the set of 3-d coordinates of all the sampled surface points, the wireframe model of the object is displayed using OpenGL toolkit. A resultant wireframe model is shown in Fig.9 (b).

The object used for reconstruction in Fig.9 (a), is a clay object on which the thread (grooves) of a screw with a pitch length of 1 mm as shown in Fig.9 (c). The Fig.10 shows the profile of the reconstructed model with measurements at the top and it shows the zoomed profile in the bottom. The 1 mm pitch is visible along with the depth of the groove which is found out to be 0.4 mm. This is clearly shown in the Fig.10. The detailed reconstruction of the grooves of the screw confirm that the sub-millimeter accuracy is achieved using improved meshgrid patterns. This method of camera calibration could be very valuable for visual metrology where the measurements of objects require high precision.

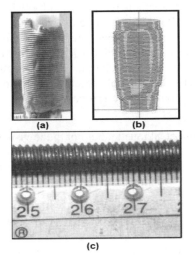

(a)   (b)

(c)

Fig. 9. The image in (a) is a clay object. The image in (b) is the reconstructed model. The image in (c) shows the lead screw used for imprinting on the clay model.

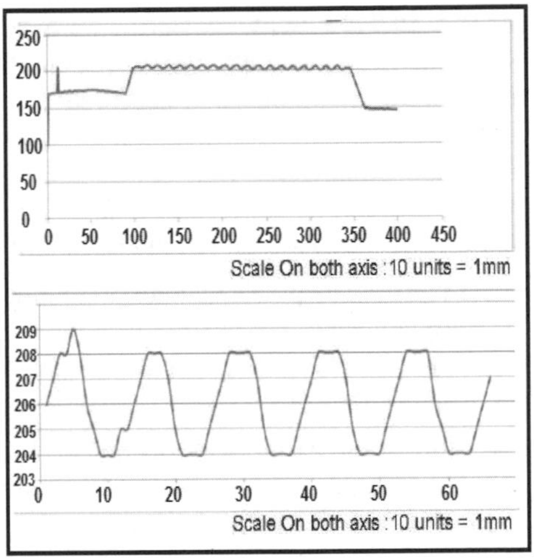

Fig. 10. The profile of the reconstructed model using a graph is shown in the image in the top. A zoomed view of the same profile is shown in the image in the bottom.

5   Error Evaluation of 3D Reconstruction

It is difficult to establish whether a reconstructed model is an exact replica of its target object, qualitatively. Comparing the measurements of various dimensions of both becomes a tedious process. An optimum method in terms of time and memory is presented here.

5.1   Error Evaluation for Silhouette Based Technique

The method for the error evaluation for 3D reconstruction, is derived from the concept of *visual hull*, as explained in [3]. Let R be the set of points from where the object is being viewed. But in case of our setup the camera is fixed and the object is being rotated. But relative to the object it can be said that the viewing points of the camera is changing. So, these pseudo viewing points make up the set R in our case. Let S be the object to be reconstructed. And V is any viewpoint such that $V \in R$. In [3] a simple geometric definition for visual hull is given, which is as follows:

The visual hull VH(S, R) of an object S relative to viewing region R is a region of E^3 such that for each point $P \in VH(S, R)$ and each viewpoint $V \in R$, the half-line starting at V and passing through P contains at least one point of S.

The following propositions are made in [3]:

Proposition 1: *VH(S, R)* is the maximal object silhouette equivalent to *S* with respect to *R*. (i.e., that gives the same silhouette as *S* when observed from any $V \in R$).

Proposition 2: *VH(S, R)* is the closest approximation of *S* that can be obtained using volume intersection techniques with viewpoints $V \in R$.

From the above discussion it can be inferred that the silhouette generated by the visual hull *VH(S, R)* with respect to a viewpoint $V \in R$ should be same as the silhouette generated by the object *S* with respect to the same viewpoint *V* and this must hold true for each $V \in R$. Using this idea, firstly the visual hull of the object is reconstructed. Then the silhouettes of the visual hull are generated by computation. The silhouettes of the visual hull are compared with the original silhouettes of the object. The comparison of the two silhouette images is done by counting the erroneous pixels. The erroneous pixels can be classified into two categories:

- **Type A:** The pixels that are present in the object silhouette, but not in the visual hull silhouette.
- **Type B:** The pixels that are present in the visual hull silhouette, but not in the object silhouette.

The ratio of the count of erroneous pixels, of both the types (A & B), with the total number of pixels present in the object silhouette gives the percentage of error with respect to one viewpoint. This comparison is carried out for the silhouettes with respect to all the viewpoints. The percentage of error for all viewpoints is averaged out. The percentage of error w.r.t one viewpoint *V*, (P.E(V)) would be given as:

$$P.E(V) = \frac{Number\ of\ deviating\ pixels \times 100}{Number\ of\ pixels\ present\ in\ the\ object\ silhouette} \tag{6}$$

The total percentage of error in reconstruction of the object is given as:

$$Error\ (\%) = \frac{\sum_{V \in R} P.E(V)}{|R|} \tag{7}$$

where |R| represents the total number of viewpoints. Here error evaluation is carried out on 7 test objects. Their images are shown in the Fig.11. The silhouette based reconstruction of the test object is done first and the silhouettes of their respective visual hulls is generated.

Fig. 11. The objects are denoted by O1-O7 from left to right

Some differences between the two silhouette images, as shown in the Fig.12, are visually evident like the visual hull silhouette looks a little thinner than the object

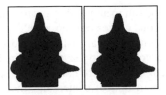

Fig. 12. Object (O2) Silhouette in the left and Visual Hull Silhouette in the right

Table 1. Error in Reconstruction for Objects O1-7

Test Object	% Type A error in reconstruction	% Type B error in reconstruction
O1	2.166059	1.796690
O2	1.635022	2.654316
O3	4.87001	1.065532
O4	3.557686	3.155562
O5	2.363172	5.307045
O6	3.885849	3.908471
O7	22.397410	11.021011

silhouette. After the generation of visual hull silhouette images, error evaluation is performed. The total error (%) in reconstruction for each test object is given in Table 1.

The error in reconstruction in silhouette based method appears essentially because of the assumption that the silhouettes are orthographic projections. By assuming orthographic projections, the space carving technique that is employed, generates incorrect cross-sections. Thus the reconstructed model slightly deviates from the original object. If perspective projection is assumed instead, which is the actual case, then true convex cross-sections will be generated.

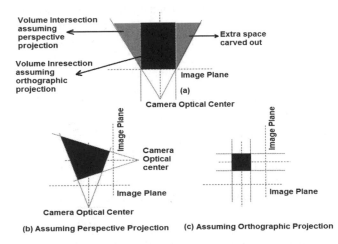

Fig. 13. Difference between volume intersection methods. Perspective projection is considered in the cross-section of figure (b), whereas orthographic projection is considered in figure (c).

In Fig.13 it is shown through an example that performing volume intersection considering orthographic projections carves out too much space (shaded in grey), which, on the other hand, actually remains intact when perspective projection is assumed. The grey region may have a cross-section segment which is being lost when orthographic projection is assumed. In figure (b) considering perspective projection and by knowing the position of camera optical center and the focal length, the true cross-section after space carving w.r.t two viewpoints is obtained. The cross-section generated (that is to say, by perspective, rather than orthographic carving) is a polygon. As even more viewpoints are used for carving, correspondingly more matter is carved out. But in case of orthographic projections that is shown in figure (c) the cross-section obtained is a square, which is incorrect. True orthographic projections of the object silhouette can be obtained using *telecentric lenses*. Then the horizontal cross-section obtained by volume intersection method, considering orthographic projections, will indeed be the correct cross-section. Consequently, the reconstructed visual hull will be exactly same as the original object. Thus there will be no error in reconstruction. But this error evaluation still notifies the error in reconstruction due to other causes such as incorrect knowledge of the center of rotation, uneven sampling, etc.

It is seen that the reconstruction error for the silhouette method never exceeds 6% except for O7, which suffers due to the presence of the auxiliary components. This suggests that the orthographic assumption, though invalid, is approximately upheld when the camera optical center is sufficiently distant from the object.

5.2 Error Evaluation for Laser Based Technique

The error evaluation for the laser based technique is similar to that of the silhouette based technique. After constructing the 3D model of the object, it should produce the same laser profile images as the original object for the respective view point, theoretically speaking, but in practice there could be some deviations. So, in this method the 3D model of the object is constructed first. Then the laser profile images of the 3D model are generated by computation and then they are compared with the laser profile images of the original object. Comparison is done by counting the erroneous pixels. As explained in *Section 5.1* there are two types of errors A and B:

- **Type A:** The pixels that are present in the object laser profile, but not in the 3D model laser profile.
- **Type B:** The pixels that are present in the 3D model laser profile, but not in the object laser profile.

The ratio of the count of erroneous pixels, of both types (A & B), with the total number of pixels present in the object laser profile gives the percentage of error with respect to one viewpoint. This comparison is carried out for the laser profiles with respect to all the viewpoints. The percentage of error for all viewpoints is averaged out. The percentage of error w.r.t one viewpoint V, (P.E(V)) would be given as:

$$P.E(V) = \frac{Number\ of\ deviating\ pixels \times 100}{Number\ of\ pixels\ present\ in\ the\ object\ laser\ profile} \tag{8}$$

The total percentage of error in reconstruction of the object is given by equation (7). Error evaluation is carried out for the test objects shown in the Fig.14. Not many differences are visible in Fig.15, except for the gap that is present in the object laser profile and the interpolation in the 3D model laser profile. The total error (%) in reconstruction for each test object is given in Table 2.

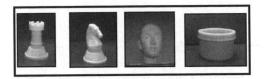
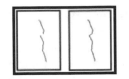

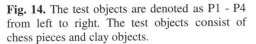

Fig. 14. The test objects are denoted as P1 - P4 from left to right. The test objects consist of chess pieces and clay objects.

Fig. 15. Laser profile of the original object P2 in the left and laser profile of its 3D model in the right.

The error in reconstruction is appearing at the stage of calculating the 3-d world coordinates of the sampled surface points. By finding the projections on x- and y-axis the floating point numbers are getting rounded up. In spite of this, the error is consistently less than 3 %.

Table 2. Error in reconstruction for object P1-P4

Test Object	% Type A error in reconstruction	% Type B error in reconstruction
P1	1.222864	2.847844
P2	1.390640	2.699499
P3	1.341192	1.146823
P4	1.568747	1.568747

5.3   Comparison of Both Techniques

For comparison we have chosen the common objects used for the error in reconstruction for both the techniques. So object O3 & P4, O5 & P3 and O6 & P2 are same. The percentage error calculated for both the techniques for the common objects is presented in the Table 3.

Table 3. A comparison of silhouette and laser based reconstruction techniques

Test Object	% Error in Silhouette techniques		% Error in Laser techniques	
	Type A	Type B	Type A	Type B
O3 or P4	4.87001	1.065532	1.568747	1.568747
O5 or P3	2.363172	5.307045	1.341192	1.146823
O6 or P2	3.885849	3.908471	1.390640	2.699499

From the table it is evident that laser based reconstruction is more accurate as compared to the silhouette based reconstruction. Laser based technique can also reconstruct certain kinds of concavities. But it cannot reconstruct an object with multiple auxiliary components using a single set of camera and laser source, which the Silhouette based technique can. Laser based technique is also faster, considering that the silhouette based technique carries out cross-section generation.

6 Conclusions

The multiple axis object centered cylindrical coordinate system representation is found to be better than single axis representation of objects in terms of uniformity in the distribution of points on the surface of the object. It is very useful for reconstructing objects with multiple auxiliary components. However the object registration requires a lot of time. Using mesh-grid patterns gives a new technique for camera calibration. The camera calibration has to be done only once. The laser based reconstruction is faster as compared to silhouette based reconstruction and sub-millimeter accuracy is achieved using enhanced mesh-grid patterns. Better accuracy can still be achieved if, a camera with better resolution and a laser-source which diverges less, are used. The error evaluation method turns out to be a good way of finding the error in reconstructing an object. This gives a technique to analyze how close is the reconstructed model to the original object. Using this performance analysis, we could establish that the laser based reconstruction is superior to silhouette based reconstruction when the target object does not contain concavities.

Acknowledgments. The authors of this paper would like to thank Dept. of Atomic Energy, Govt. of India, for their support for the project.

References

[1] Martin, W.N., Aggarwal, J.K.: Volumetric Descriptions of Objects from Multiple Views. PAMI 5(2), 150–158 (1983)
[2] Chien, C.H., Aggarwal, J.K.: Volume/surface octrees for the representation of three-dimensional objects. Computer Vision, Graphics, Image Processing 36(1), 100–113 (1986)
[3] Laurentini, A.: The Visual Hull Concept for Silhouette-Based Image Understanding. PAMI 16(2), 150–162 (1994)
[4] Milroy, M.J., Bradley, C., Vickers, G.W.: Automated laser scanning based on orthogonal cross-sections. Mach. Vision Appl. 9(3), 106–118 (1996)
[5] Liska, C.: Estimating the Next Sensor Position Based on Surface Characteristics. In: ICPR '00: Proceedings of the International Conference on Pattern Recognition, Washington, DC, USA, p. 1538. IEEE Computer Society, Los Alamitos (2000)
[6] Yemez, Y., Wetherilt, C.J.: A volumetric fusion technique for surface reconstruction from silhouettes and range data. Computer Vision and Image Understanding 105, 30–41 (2007)
[7] Tosovic, S., Sablatnig, R., Kampel, M.: On Combining Shape from Silhouette and Shape from Structured Light. Technical report, Vienna University of Technology, Vienna University of Technology, Institute of Computer (2002)
[8] Tsai, R.Y.: A versatile camera calibration technique for high-accuracy 3D machine vision metrology using the off-the-shelf TV cameras and lenses. IEEE Journal Robotics and Automation RA-3(4), 323–344 (1987)

[9] Devernay, F., Faugeras, O.: Straight lines have to be straight: Automatic calibration and removal of distortion from scenes of structured environments. Machine Vision and Applications 13, 14–24 (2001)

[10] Hartley, R., Zisserman, A.: Multiple view geometry in computer vision, pp. 87–92. Cambridge University Press, Cambridge

[11] Winkelbach, S., Monkelstruck, S., Wahl, F.M.: Low-cost Laser Range Scanner and Fast Surface Registration Approach. In: Franke, K., Müller, K.-R., Nickolay, B., Schäfer, R. (eds.) DAGM 2006. LNCS, vol. 4174, pp. 718–728. Springer, Heidelberg (2006)

[12] Zagorchev, L., Goshtasby, A.: A paintbrush laser range scanner. Comput. Vis. Image Underst. 101(2), 65–86 (2006)

Inelastic Deformation Invariant Modal Representation for Non-rigid 3D Object Recognition

Dirk Smeets*, Thomas Fabry, Jeroen Hermans,
Dirk Vandermeulen, and Paul Suetens

K.U. Leuven, Faculty of Engineering, ESAT/PSI
Medical Imaging Research Center, UZ Gasthuisberg,
Herestraat 49 bus 7003, B-3000 Leuven, Belgium
dirk.smeets@uz.kuleuven.be

Abstract. Intra-shape deformations complicate 3D object recognition and retrieval and need therefore proper modeling. A method for inelastic deformation invariant object recognition is proposed, representing 3D objects by diffusion distance tensors (DDT), i.e. third order tensors containing the average diffusion distance for different diffusion times between each pair of points on the surface. In addition to the DDT, also geodesic distance matrices (GDM) are used to represent the objects independent of the reference frame. Transforming these distance tensors into modal representations provides a sampling order invariant shape descriptor. Different dissimilarity measures can be used for comparing these shape descriptors. The final object pair dissimilarity is the sum or product of the dissimilarities obtained by modal representations of the GDM and DDT. The method is validated on the TOSCA non-rigid world database and the SHREC 2010 dataset of non-rigid 3D models indicating that our method combining these two representations provides a more noise robust but still inter-subject shape variation sensitive method for the identification and the verification scenario in object retrieval.

Keywords: Intra-subject deformation, 3D object recognition, geodesic distance, diffusion distance.

1 Introduction

During the last decades, developments in 3D modeling and 3D capturing techniques caused an increased interest in the use of 3D objects for a number of applications, such as CAD/CAM, architecture, computer games, archaeology, medical applications and biometrics. In many of these fields, an important research problem is 3D shape retrieval, in which an object needs to be recognized or classified from a large database of objects. The success of the yearly SHape REtrieval Contest (SHREC) [1], organized with the objective to evaluate the

---

* Corresponding author.

F.J. Perales and R.B. Fisher (Eds.): AMDO 2010, LNCS 6169, pp. 162–171, 2010.
© Springer-Verlag Berlin Heidelberg 2010

effectiveness of 3D shape retrieval algorithms, proves the increasing interest in shape retrieval.

The challenge of 3D shape recognition and retrieval becomes even harder when intra-shape deformations are present in the database, as is often the case for articulating objects. Figure 1(a), for example, shows some shape deformations in the TOSCA database [2], due to articulated motion. Since articulating objects deform mostly in an inelastic way, we will focus on 3D object recognition in the presence of inelastic deformations.

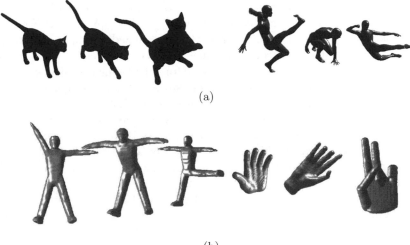

(a)

(b)

Fig. 1. Intra-shape deformations occur in the TOSCA database [2] (a) and in the McGill database [3] (b)

In this paper, an inelastic deformation invariant object recognition method is presented, not requiring explicit point correspondences for shape comparison. First, the object is represented by a geodesic distance matrix (GDM) and, for the first time, by a diffusion distance tensor (DDT), both invariant for inelastic deformation. The GDM is more sensitive to small shape variations, while the DDT is more robust to small topological variations that can occur in the database. Both the GDM and DDT are transformed into modal representations, which are invariant to the sampling order. As such, object recognition reduces to direct comparison of the modal representations without the need to establish explicit point correspondences.

After the discussion of the related work in section 1.1, the method is described in more detail in sections 2 and 3 and validated, leading to the results shown in section 4. At the end, we draw some conclusions and make some suggestions for future work.

1.1   Related Work

In literature, geodesic distance matrices have already been used to tackle 3D recognition problems involving non-rigid objects. Probably the best known of these contributions is the algorithm of Elad and Kimmel [4]. Here, the GDM is computed using the fast marching on triangulated domains (FMTD) method. Subsequently, the GDM is processed using a multidimensional scaling (MDS) approach, converting non-rigid objects into their rigid, isometric deformation-invariant signature surfaces. These can be compared using standard algorithms for rigid matching. This method has also been used in expression-invariant 3D face recognition by Bronstein et al. [5]. An extension of the method is the partial embedding of one surface into another surface using generalized MDS (GMDS) [6,7]. GMDS maps the probe image on the model by minimizing the generalized stress, i.e. the weighted sum of differences between corresponding geodesic distances. The three-point geodesic distance approximation is developed for calculating the geodesic distance between points originally not on the model surface. Shape comparison is using the generalized stress as dissimilarity measure. The GMDS framework is also validated and extended with diffusion distances in [8] for reasons of robustness against topological changes. However, the generalized stress is computed using only one, experimentally determined, diffusion time to compute the diffusion distances. We, on the other hand, propose an approach using distances computed for several diffusion times allowing multi-scale recognition.

The *Geodesic Object Representation* of Hamza and Krim [9] is another 3D object recognition method relying on geodesic distance matrices. In [9], GDMs are used to determine global geodesic shape functions. This global shape descriptor is defined in each point of the surface and measures the normalized accumulated squared geodesic distances to each other point on the surface. Using kernel density estimation (KDE), the global geodesic shape functions of a particular object are transformed into a geodesic shape distribution. For the actual recognition, these KDEs are compared using the Jensen-Shannon divergence.

In [10], the modal representation approach is already applied on geodesic distance matrices for isometric deformation invariant object recognition. It was proved that decomposing the GDM using singular value decomposition provides a sampling order invariant shape descriptor. In this paper, the isometric deformation invariant method without need for correspondences is further extended with diffusion distances and to tensor representations (instead of matrix representations) allowing a multi-scale recognition approach and a higher robustness against noise.

2   Inelastic Deformation Invariant Representations

Since many intra-shape deformations, e.g. the deformations in Fig. 1, are approximately inelastic, the non-rigid object recognition method should be invariant for those deformations. We present the combination of two inelastic deformation invariant object representations: the geodesic distance matrix and the diffusion distance tensor.

2.1   Geodesic Distance Matrix

The geodesic distance matrix (GDM) contains the geodesic distance between each pair of points on the surface. An example is shown in Fig. 2. The geodesic distance is the length of the shortest path on the object surface between two points on the object. It is calculated by solving the Eikonal equation,

$$|\nabla T(\mathbf{P})| = V, \tag{1}$$

on the surface, with T the traveling time on the surface to $\mathbf{P}$ starting from $\mathbf{P_0}$ and V the velocity. Choosing $V = 1$, the travel time is equal to the distance of the shortest path between $\mathbf{P}$ and $\mathbf{P_0}$.

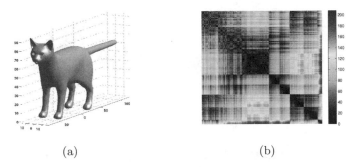

(a)   (b)

Fig. 2. 3D mesh of an object (a) and its geodesic distance matrix representation (b)

The computation can be achieved with a fast marching algorithm for triangulated meshes [11,12]. Isometric deformations, and thus also inelastic deformations, leave these geodesic distances unchanged. Therefore, the GDM is an appropriate representation for isometrically deformed objects.

2.2   Diffusion Distance Tensor

The diffusion distance tensor (DDT) is a third order tensor containing the average diffusion distance between each pair of points on the surface for different diffusion times. An example is shown in Fig. 3. The average diffusion distance is related to the probability that a particle, started in one point, arrives at the other point after a diffusion process ran for a certain time t_D (random walk). This distance is calculated by solving the heat equation i.e. diffusion equation with constant diffusion coefficient α,

$$\frac{\partial u}{\partial t} = \alpha \Delta_X u, \tag{2}$$

obtaining the distribution of temperature (density of the diffusing material) u on the surface. Δ_X denotes the Laplace-Beltrami operator, a generalization of the

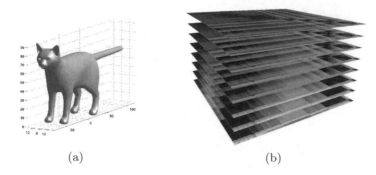

(a)   (b)

Fig. 3. 3D mesh of an object (a) and its diffusion distance tensor representation (b)

Fig. 4. The average diffusion distance for the tip of the nose to all other points is shown for different diffusion times

Laplace operator for non-Euclidean domains [8]. The average diffusion distance for all points is shown for different diffusion times in Fig. 4 when diffusion started at the nose tip.

Practically, the average diffusion distance computation can be achieved by solving the generalized eigendecomposition problem of the discretized Laplace-Beltrami operator L [13],

$$L\Phi = \lambda A\Phi, \tag{3}$$

with A a diagonal matrix containing numbers a_i proportional to the sum of the areas of the triangles sharing the vertex i (with proportionality constant: 5/average triangle area). Different discretizations of the Laplace-Beltrami operator are found in literature (see [8]). We used the cotangent weighting scheme in which $L = diag(\sum_{l \neq i} w_{il}) - w_{ij}$ and $w_{ij} = \cot\alpha_{ij} + \cot\beta_{ij}$ (α_{ij} and β_{ij} are the two angles opposite to the edge between vertices i and j in the two triangles with shared edge between i and j). The discrete average diffusion distance between points i and j is then approximated by

$$d_{X,t_D}(i,j) \approx \sqrt{\sum_{l=1}^{k} e^{-2\lambda_l t_D} (\Phi_{l;i} - \Phi_{l;j})^2}. \tag{4}$$

Since the average diffusion distance is the average length of paths connecting two points on the shape, also this distance is intrinsic and thus invariant to inelastic deformations. Because of the implicit averaging, the (average) diffusion distance is expected to be less sensitive to noise and more robust against small topological changes than the geodesic distance. On the other hand, this robustness implies a lower sensitivity for small inter-subject shape variations.

3   A Modal Representation

The GDMs and DDTs are uniquely defined up to a random simultaneous permutation of the first and second mode vectors due to the arbitrary sampling order of the surface points, mathematically expressed as

$$\mathcal{D}' = \mathcal{D} \times_1 P \times_2 P, \tag{5}$$

with $\mathcal{D}$ the distance matrix or tensor and P an arbitrary permutation matrix.

Provided that two instances of the same object are represented by surface meshes containing an equal number of sufficiently dense sampled surface points, an approximate one-to-one correspondence map can be assumed to exist between both surface representations. Hence, point correspondences are mathematically characterized by a permutation matrix and the distance tensors of these surface meshes are approximately related by eq. (5). Hence, shape comparison reduces to verifying the extent to which eq. (5) holds. However, in practice the point correspondences between the objects compared are generally not known.

Since establishing explicit point correspondences between surfaces is far from trivial, this work proposes the use of a modal representation of the distance tensors which is invariant for simultaneous permutation of their first and second mode vectors. The singular value decomposition (SVD) of the distance tensors transforms them into permutation-variant matrices of singular vectors and a permutation-invariant core tensor (2D for DDM and 3D for DDT). For the 3D case, the higher order SVD [14], also known as Tucker decomposition [15], of tensors $\mathcal{D}$ and $\mathcal{D}'$ coming from the same object, can be written as

$$\mathcal{D} = \Sigma \times_1 U^{(1)} \times_2 U^{(2)} \times_3 U^{(3)}, \tag{6}$$

$$\mathcal{D}' = \mathcal{D} \times_1 P \times_2 P = \Sigma \times_1 PU^{(1)} \times_2 PU^{(2)} \times_3 U^{(3)}. \tag{7}$$

When the core tensor is ordered according to a decreasing Frobenius norm, it is uniquely determined by the decomposed tensor (cfr. decreasing singular values in 2D case) [14]. The latter is therefore an excellent shape descriptor. For computational reasons, dimension reduction is performed meaning that only the largest singular values are computed in 2D and a core tensor that is much smaller than the original tensor in 3D.

As such, shape comparison comes down to comparing the modal representations, reshaped as vectors, using an appropriate dissimilarity measure. For this purpose, the mean normalized Manhattan distance

$$D_1 = \sum_{i=1}^{M} \frac{2|S_i^k - S_i^l|}{S_i^k + S_i^l} \tag{8}$$

and the normalized Euclidean distance

$$D_2 = \sqrt{\sum_{i=1}^{M} \frac{(S_i^k - S_i^l)^2}{\sigma_i^2}} \tag{9}$$

are used, with S^k and S^l the shape descriptors of the two objects to compare and M the number of used singular values or elements in the core tensor.

4   Experimental Results

The proposed method is validated using standard recognition experiments, i.e. the verification and the identification scenario. The performance of those scenarios is measured with the receiving operating characteristic (ROC) curve and the cumulative matching curve (CMC), respectively. The former is a curve plotting the false rejection rate (FRR) against the false acceptance rate (FAR), while the latter gives the recognition rate for several ranks. Characteristic points on these curves are the equal error rate (EER) and the rank 1 recognition rate (R1RR). The percentage of correct nearest neighbor (NN) in the all-to-all experiment (verification), is a frequently used statistic in shape retrieval.

For the validation of the proposed approach, we use the TOSCA non-rigid world database [2] as well as the dataset of "SHREC 2010 - Shape Retrieval Contest of Non-rigid 3D Models" [16], which is a subset of the McGill 3D Shape Benchmark [3].

4.1   The TOSCA Non-rigid World Database

The TOSCA non-rigid world database consists of various 3D non-rigid shapes in a variety of poses and is intended for non-rigid shape similarity and correspondence experiments. We use 112 objects, including 9 cats, 6 centaurs, 11 dogs, 3 wolves, 6 seahorses, 17 horses, 1 shark, 24 female figures, and two different male figures, containing 15 and 20 poses. Each object contains approximately 3000 vertices. Therefore and because the objects have already the same scale, no surface preprocessing is needed before GDM and DDT computation. The (higher order) SVD provides shape descriptors which are compared using the mean normalized Manhattan distance and fused using the sum rule.

The results are tabulated in Tab. 1, showing a high performance of the proposed method, in particular for the GDM representation. This can be explained by the good quality of the meshes which permits the more shape sensitive GDM approach to be more distinguishing. The lower noise sensitivity and the higher robustness against topological changes of the DDT approach are not needed for this database.

Table 1. Results of the inelastic deformation invariant recognition method on the TOSCA non-rigid world dataset

representation	R1RR	EER	NN
GDM	100.0%	1.87%	100.0%
DDT	100.0%	9.77%	100.0%
GDM + DDT	100.0%	2.67%	100.0%

Compared to results found in literature and validated on the same database –although we use another subset– [8] we see that the results presented here are slightly better than those of the diffusion distance based method using the Gromov-Hausdorff framework, obtaining an EER of 2.22% and 2.02% for different subsets. The authors compare with the same method but using geodesic distances, obtaining an EER of 4.95% and 15.49% respectively.

4.2   SHREC Non-rigid 3D Models

The dataset of "SHREC 2010 - Shape Retrieval Contest of Non-rigid 3D Models" contains 200 non-rigid objects, including 20 ants, crabs, hands, humans, octopuses, pliers, snakes, spectacles, spiders and teddies each. The objective of this 3D Shape Retrieval Contest is to evaluate the effectiveness of 3D-shape retrieval algorithms for non-rigidly deformed 3D objects. Unlike the object instances of TOSCA non-rigid world database, the different instances of the same object do have some small intrinsic shape and scale variations in the SHREC dataset. Therefore, all meshes are resampled keeping 2500 points. After computation of the GDM and the DDT, these tensors are normalized by dividing each element by the sum of all distances of one slice in the tensor, compensating the meaningless scale variations. For the DDT, 5 different diffusion times are combined in one tensor, namely $t_D = 100, 200, 400, 800, 1500$. The (higher order) SVD results in modal representations which are compared using the normalized Euclidean distance and fused using the product rule. For the GDM approach, the 19 largest singular values are kept, while for the DDT core tensor is $20 \times 20 \times 5$.

The results of the validation are shown in Fig. 5 and the main characteristic points are listed in Tab. 2. We see a lower performance compared to the TOSCA database, which can be explained by the small intrinsic shape variations that occur in this dataset. Unlike for the TOSCA database, there is a clear improvement by combining the GDM approach with the DDT approach. This can be explained by the need for noise robustness and robustness against topological changes for the more imperfect data together with the need for a shape sensitive representation.

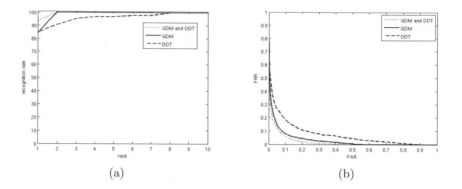

(a)   (b)

Fig. 5. Validation of the proposed method for the SHREC 2010 dataset, with the CMC (a) and the ROC (b)

Table 2. Results of the inelastic deformation invariant recognition method on the SHREC Non-rigid 3D Models dataset

representation	R1RR	EER	NN
GDM	84.21%	8.86%	99.5%
DDT	84.74%	14.22%	97.5%
GDM × DDT	93.68%	7.96%	100%

When these results are compared with other methods on the same dataset [16], also here we see a better performance for the described method based on the nearest neighbor (NN) criterion.

5   Conclusion and Future Work

As a conclusion, we can state that the fusion of two inelastic deformation invariant recognition approaches provides a noise robust and a inter-subject shape sensitive object recognition method, leading to excellent results for the "TOSCA non-rigid world" database and especially for the "SHREC 2010 Non-rigid 3D Models" dataset. The first approach is based on the geodesic distance matrix as object representation, the second is built upon the diffusion distance tensor. Because of the implicit averaging of distances on the surface, the (average) diffusion distance is more robust for noise and topological changes. On the other hand, geodesic distance is more sensitive for small inter-subject variations.

Depending on the dataset and its noise content, the fusion of both approaches could be done in a smarter way by giving one approach a higher weight than the other. As future work, we want to evaluate this weighting.

References

1. AIM@SHAPE: SHREC - 3D shape retrieval contest,
   `http://www.aimatshape.net/event/SHREC`
2. Bronstein, A.M., Bronstein, M.M., Kimmel, R.: Numerical Geometry of Non-Rigid Shapes. Springer, Heidelberg (2008)
3. Siddiqi, K., Zhang, J., Macrini, D., Shokoufandeh, A., Bouix, S., Dickinson, S.: Retrieving articulated 3D models using medial surfaces. Machine Vision and Applications 19(4), 261–274 (2008)
4. Elad, A., Kimmel, R.: On bending invariant signatures for surfaces. IEEE Transactions on Pattern Analysis and Machine Intelligence 25(10), 1285–1295 (2003)
5. Bronstein, A.M., Bronstein, M.M., Kimmel, R.: Three-dimensional face recognition. Intl. Journal of Computer Vision 64(1), 5–30 (2005)
6. Bronstein, A.M., Bronstein, M.M., Kimmel, R.: Generalized multidimensional scaling: A framework for isometry-invariant partial surface matching. PNAS
7. Bronstein, M.M., Bronstein, A.M., Kimmel, R.: Robust expression-invariant face recognition from partially missing data. In: Leonardis, A., Bischof, H., Pinz, A. (eds.) ECCV 2006. LNCS, vol. 3953, pp. 396–408. Springer, Heidelberg (2006)
8. Bronstein, A.M., Bronstein, M.M., Kimmel, R., Mahmoudi, M., Sapiro, G.: A Gromov-Hausdorff framework with diffusion geometry for topologically-robust nonrigid shape matching. Intl. Journal of Computer Vision (2009) (published online)
9. Hamza, A.B., Krim, H.: Geodesic object representation and recognition. In: Nyström, I., Sanniti di Baja, G., Svensson, S. (eds.) DGCI 2003. LNCS, vol. 2886, pp. 378–387. Springer, Heidelberg (2003)
10. Smeets, D., Fabry, T., Hermans, J., Vandermeulen, D., Suetens, P.: Isometric deformation modelling for object recognition. In: Jiang, X., Petkov, N. (eds.) CAIP 2009. LNCS, vol. 5702, pp. 757–765. Springer, Heidelberg (2009)
11. Kimmel, R., Sethian, J.A.: Computing geodesic paths on manifolds. PNAS
12. Peyré, G., Cohen, L.D.: Heuristically driven front propagation for fast geodesic extraction. Intl. J. for Computational Vision and Biomechanics 1(1), 55–67 (2008)
13. Levy, B.: Laplace-Beltrami eigenfunctions towards an algorithm that "understands" geometry. In: SMI '06, p. 13 (2006)
14. De Lathauwer, L., De Moor, B., Vandewalle, J.: A multilinear singular value decomposition. SIAM J. Matrix Anal. Appl. 21(4), 1253–1278 (2000)
15. Tucker, L.: Some mathematical notes on three-mode factor analysis. Psychometrika 31(3), 279–311 (1966)
16. Lian, Z., Godil, A.: SHREC 2010 - shape retrieval contest of non-rigid 3D models (February 2010),
   `http://www.itl.nist.gov/iad/vug/sharp/contest/2010/NonRigidShapes/`

Cyclic and Non-cyclic Gesture Spotting and Classification in Real-Time Applications

Luis Unzueta and Jon Goenetxea

Vicomtech. Mikeletegi Pasealekua 57, Parque Tecnológico 20009,
Donostia-San Sebastián, Spain
{lunzueta,jgoenetxea}@vicomtech.org
http://www.vicomtech.es

Abstract. This paper presents a gesture recognition method for detecting and classifying both cyclic and non-cyclic human motion patterns in real-time applications. The semantic segmentation of a constantly captured human motion data stream is a key research topic, especially if both cyclic and non-cyclic gestures are considered during the human-computer interaction. The system measures the temporal coherence of the movements being captured according to its knowledge database, and once it has a sufficient level of certainty on its observation semantics the motion pattern is labeled automatically. In this way, our recognition method is also capable of handling time-varying dynamic gestures. The effectiveness of the proposed method is demonstrated via recognition experiments with a triple-axis accelerometer and a 3D tracker used by various performers.

Keywords: Human-Computer Interaction, Gesture Spotting, Gesture Recognition, Motion Pattern, Motion Capture.

1   Introduction

The semantic interpretation of human motion [1] is a key research topic in various fields, such as human-computer interaction, video-surveillance, robotics, biomechanics, biometric systems, or multimedia content analysis, amongst others. Thus, gesture recognition allows us to communicate with computers at a higher level of abstraction, adding more intelligence to motion capture and computer vision systems. Moreover, combining such semantic motion information with other communication channels such as voice or touch, i.e. multimodal interfaces, would lead to a more natural interaction [2]. To achieve the goal of recognizing motion patterns, three steps must be carried out: (1) the selection of meaningful motion-features, (2) potential gesture spotting and (3) gesture classification.

The first step consists of deciding which features derived from the data being tracked will be used for a semantic interpretation. Depending on the motion capture or computer vision system, these data could be obtained directly from sensors or images, but also from the reconstruction of the user's kinematic body

F.J. Perales and R.B. Fisher (Eds.): AMDO 2010, LNCS 6169, pp. 172–181, 2010.

structure (e.g, temporal joint positions, angles, velocities, etc). These are usually chosen beforehand, but there are also some sophisticated approaches that can make this selection (semi)automatically [3,4]. Then, motor actions are represented by *templates* [5,6,7] or *state-space models* [8,9,10,11,12] using these selected data. The former are static shape patterns containing motion information, while the latter define the considered instantaneous motion-features as a *state*, and therefore a sequence is considered as a tour going through various states.

The second step consists of segmenting the continuous data stream into temporal regions that might possibly be gestures with a meaning. As stated in [1], the main difficulties come from the segmentation ambiguity and the spatio-temporal variability involved. Additionally, gesture spotting is more challenging when both cyclic and non-cyclic gestures are considered during the interaction, because cyclic gestures may be performed with a different starting direction and number of cycles keeping the same meaning (e.g., *waving*). Hence, there are methods explicitly designed for non-cyclic gestures which require start and end pauses [11] and others for cyclic [13] which focus on motion periods.

Finally, the third step consists of labeling the segmented motion with one of the categories of the knowledge database, or as an *unknown* motion pattern. The typical classification procedures found in the literature for motor action recognition are hidden Markov models (HMMs) [8], dynamic time warping [17], nearest neighbors [5], dynamic Bayesian networks [10], neural networks [14] and kernel methods such as support vector machines (SVMs) [15] and relevance vector machines [16].

In this is work we propose a method for gesture spotting and classification that can cope with both cyclic and non-cyclic time-varying human motion patterns in real-time applications. Both objectives are achieved with a semantic observation of the performance's temporal advance, as once the computer *knows* that the user is making a certain gesture it can segment the dataflow accordingly. Unlike other approaches (especially those based on HMMs), our method does not transform motion into symbols, and allows a measure of the proximity of new performances to those in the database. This can be useful for motion style learning tasks, which can lead to motor skills transfer through imitation.

2   Cyclic and Non-cyclic Gesture Spotting

A system designed for coping with both cyclic and non-cyclic gestures should label the observed motion patterns after each period of cyclic gestures, and after each non-cyclic gesture has been performed, even if the user keeps moving, ignoring other transition movements. Ramanan and Forsyth [15] use joint trajectories per second as motion-features, in order to obtain a continuous stream of descriptive annotations (one per frame). Their experiments reveal that in this way choppy annotation streams are produced. Therefore, they need to apply a smoothing technique, once the observed bit strings are known, obtaining automatic action descriptions quite close to real (no quantitative results are provided for comparison). Kang et al. [17], whose work is focused on videogame control, segment potential gestures by detecting abnormal velocities, frames classified as static gestures, or frames in which the tracked trajectories have severe curvatures, attaining a reliability of 93.36%. However, in this method those gestures that may include one of these events during its performance cannot be considered. Stiefmeier and Rogen [18] transform the data stream and gestures into strings encoding motion vectors and apply an approximate string matching procedure for the spotting and classification task. They achieved a correct spotting rate of 82.7% with users performing bicycle maintenance tasks including cyclic and non-cyclic gestures.

These approaches transform movements into symbol sequences before spotting and classification tasks. Symbols are obtained by clustering neighboring positions and trajectories in order to define a finite set of possibilities with which motions can be modeled. This *grid* allows a higher generality in order to label different performances of the same gesture in the same way, however at the same time it may prevent the system from measuring the proximity of different performance styles.

On the contrary, we propose to measure the spatio-temporal consistency of the data stream with respect to each of the known gestures, and once a "clear" semantic match is obtained, label the period in which this observation has been made with the corresponding meaning. Thus, the core of our approach relies on the concept *Temporal Advance Counting Algorithm* presented by Mena et al. [12], but goes beyond it by analyzing the advance through a dynamic time buffer which is increased until the decision is taken, instead of observing a constant number of recent frames for labeling the most recent one at each time instant. In this paper we focus on the recognition of gestures performed by a single "rigid" body (e.g., one hand, the head, etc). The combination of semantic body part motion descriptions in a multibody structure (i.e., a full human body) is beyond this scope.

The motion of a body part is defined as a temporally ordered sequence of motion-features, i.e. vectors containing relevant information for further gesture classification (e.g., velocities, accelerations, angular variations, etc). Therefore, the knowledge database is constituted by a set of labeled motion patterns represented as connected states. The number of states will be the same for all of them in order to make a balanced computation of the *temporal advance* in all gesture candidates. Hence, even though this normalization is obtained through a postprocessing step (concretely adjusting a cubic-spline), the number of states of the original gestures should not be too different from each other, so that they do not get too distorted. This may appear to be a major restriction on the kind of actions that can be modeled together (even after the cubic spline fitting), but the complexity of these can be higher than those presented in previous approaches in the field [15,17,18]. However, there is a restriction that must be accomplished and it is that gestures must be independent one of each other, i.e. there must not be gestures whose complete shape is similar to the part of another.

Algorithm 1 shows how the temporal advance is computed for a motion sequence of size p with respect to a gesture candidate C. This advance takes into consideration the proximity of the recent dataflow states with respect to those of the gesture. Hence, we call it a *weighted temporal advance*, where the weight comes from the inverse of the mean distance of advancing states with respect to their corresponding nearest ones in the gesture. A higher weighted temporal advance count means a more accurate approximation to the gesture candidate, and thus can be used as a quantitative measure for motor skills transfer through imitation. However, it must be taken into account that in order to avoid a division by zero this proximity must be limited to a certain minimal value. Note that multiple states in the observed motion sequence can get matched to the same state in gesture model, which would mean that there would not be advance in that case, but this feature is precisely the one that allows to handle time warping in performed gestures.

Algorithm 1. Weighted Temporal Advance Algorithm

1: **procedure** WEIGHTEDTEMPORALADVANCE($sequence, gesture_C$)
2:    $nVotes_C \Leftarrow 0$
3:    $nearestStateIndex_C \Leftarrow -1$
4:    $previousIndex_C \Leftarrow -1$
5:    $sumDistances_C \Leftarrow 1$
6:    $nearestStateDistance_C \Leftarrow 0$
7:    **for** $i = 1$ to p **do**
8:        $nearestStateIndex_C \Leftarrow$ getNearestStateIndex($sequence_{[i]}$)
9:        $nearestStateDistance_C \Leftarrow$ getNearestStateDistance($sequence_{[i]}$)
10:       **if** $nearestStateIndex_C > previousIndex_C$ **then**
11:           $nVotes_C \Leftarrow nVotes_C + 1$
12:           $sumDistances_C \Leftarrow sumDistances_C + nearestStateDistance_C$
13:       **end if**
14:       $previousIndex_C \Leftarrow nearestPoseIndex_C$
15:   **end for**
16:   **return** $nVotes_C/(sumDistances_C/nVotes_C) = nVotes_C^2/sumDistances_C$, where $sumDistances_C > 0$
17: **end procedure**

---

3   Semantic Observation of Temporal Advance

The weighted temporal advance will allow to compute the level of confidence in the continuous data stream for a semantic gesture spotting. Firstly, we spot when occurs a variation in the state sequence higher than a certain threshold, and start the observation from the instant in which that variation was zero. To do so we apply the algorithm used in [11] for the starting point determination. Having this threshold allows us to filter small state variations due to noise. Then, we can start the semantic observation from that point until the system takes a decision, which could be a gesture detection or doing a reset. Therefore, the observed segment, i.e. the buffer, increases its size dynamically as new motion-features are being obtained from the motion capture system. Hence, gesture spotting and classification are solved in parallel. There are six conditions that the observation must accomplish so that a data stream segment is labeled with a gesture candidate:

(a) It has the highest weighted temporal advance.
(b) The weighted temporal advance is over a threshold.
(c) The number of temporal advances without the distance weight is at least a certain portion of the number of gesture states.
(d) The observed data stream has at least a certain number of states.
(e) The dataflow has not been still for at least a certain time.
(f) The number of frames in the buffer is not excessive.

If all these conditions are met, apart from labeling the segment, the system also resets the weighted temporal advance counting and *forgets* the previous data, which means that in case a cyclic gesture is being done, when the system tries to detect again the starting point of the new cycle, the lastest instant that it may take into consideration will be the latest of the previous segment. On the contrary, if the system accomplishes conditions (c) and (d), but not (b), or it does not satisfy conditions (e) or (f), the counting is reset, but no answer is delivered, because there was not enough confidence on the best candidate. Meanwhile, while these situations are not met algorithm 1 is applied to the increasing buffer. The matching procedure is not sensitive to the starting location, which is of special interest especially for cyclic actions, which can start at any state, because the weighted temporal advance will be increased independently of it.

This algorithm is fast enough for human-computer interaction with off-the-shelf equipment, but in case it would be necessary, it may also be possible to alleviate the computational cost by applying the counting every N frames while the buffer is increasing and not every frame. Alternatively, taking advantage of current GPU and multi-core CPU platforms, it is also possible to parallelize the measurements with respect to gesture candidates, to attain faster framerates, or otherwise for increasing the database size with a higher number of candidates.

4   Experimental Results

In order to evaluate the presented gesture spotting and classification method, a set of continuous dataflow captures containing a series of hand gestures performed several times is used. The number of correct spotting and classifications are computed, but also the number of *deletions, insertions* and *substitutions*. Deletions occur when a gesture has not been spotted, insertions when the system has spotted a gesture when it should not, and substitutions when it has spotted a gesture correctly but it has not classified it with the right label. We build the continuous data streams by concatenating previously segmented gestures so that the obtained results can be visualized in an easier way (otherwise the continuous dataflows should be segmented manually afterwards). In this way we exactly know when start and end real gestures and which they are. There may appear unnatural discontinuities at the boundaries of actions, especially for non-cyclic actions, but these are not relevant for this test because, as stated in Section 3, the weighted temporal advance will be increased independently of the gesture starting point.

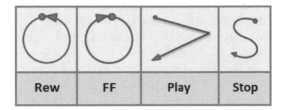

Fig. 1. The dynamic gestures to be performed

Both a triple-axis accelerometer (Wiimote: http://www.nintendo.com/wii) and a 3D tracker (Flock of Birds: http://www.ascension-tech.com) are used for the experiment with the same gestures in order to compare results with different motion-features. The motion-features used in the triple-axis accelerometer are directly the data coming from the sensor, while in the case of the 3D tracker the velocity vectors derived from captured 3D positions are used. Fig. 1 shows the gesture classes to be performed in the experiment. For each device, four users perform 20 times these four gestures and therefore there are $20 \times 4 \times 4 = 320$ samples in total (80 repetitions per gesture). The two confusion matrices obtained from the leave-one-out training validation method [19] with all these samples are shown in table 1. It can be seen that gesture classification using the weighted temporal advance algorithm obtains very high rates: 98.75% using the triple-axis accelerometer and 100% with the 3D tracker.

Table 1. Confusion matrices of the labeled gestures captured with the triple-axis accelerometer and the 3D tracker respectively, using leave-one-out

Assigned Class	Real Class (3-Axis Accel.)				Assigned Class	Real Class (3D Tracker)			
	Rew	FF	Play	Stop		Rew	FF	Play	Stop
Rew	80	0	2	0	Rew	80	0	0	0
FF	0	80	0	0	FF	0	80	0	0
Play	0	0	78	2	Play	0	0	80	0
Stop	0	0	0	78	Stop	0	0	0	80

For the dataflow automatic segmentation, for each device, a part of the recorded samples is used to build the knowledge database and the rest to build the continuous data streams to be evaluated, one for each performer. During the database training it is possible to obtain the most suitable parameter values for gesture spotting according to it. These parameters are: (a) normalized number of states per gesture in the database (NNS), (b) weighted temporal advance threshold (WTAT) and (c) temporal advance number with respect to the number of states

(TANS). In order to obtain the optimal parameter values, a continuous dataflow with the database gestures (without resampling) is evaluated with different parameters combinations until the one with the highest recognition rate is obtained. In our experiments we obtain, with slight variations from case to case, NNS=12, WTAT=10 and TANS=70% for the triple-axis accelerometer and NNS=19, WTAT=5 and TANS=70% for the 3D tracker. On the other hand, the threshold of sequence variation for determining the observation starting point is set manually for each device through experimentation, so that slight movements are filtered. In this experiment we test two different alternatives for evaluating the system: (1) using only one database of 80 samples (5 performances per gesture and user) to evaluate the continuous dataflows of all users with the same gesture spotting parameter values and (2) using 4 databases of 20 samples (one per user, 5 performances per gesture) to evaluate the continuous dataflows of the corresponding users that trained the system.

Table 2. Spotting and classification results with the triple-axis accelerometer for different subjects using (1) an overall auto-generated configuration and (2) their own databases and auto-generated configurations respectively

Case 1	Correct	Deleted	Inserted	Substituted	Ground Truth
Subject 1	58 (96.67%)	1 (1.67%)	3 (5%)	1 (1.67%)	60
Subject 2	57 (95%)	3 (5%)	6 (10%)	0 (0%)	60
Subject 3	53 (88.33%)	3 (5%)	13 (21.67%)	4 (6.67%)	60
Subject 4	51 (85%)	3 (5%)	16 (26.67%)	6 (10%)	60
Total	**219 (91.25%)**	**10 (4.16%)**	**38 (15.83%)**	**11 (4.58%)**	**240**
Case 2	Correct	Deleted	Inserted	Substituted	Ground Truth
Subject 1	60 (100%)	0 (0%)	6 (6.67%)	0 (0%)	60
Subject 2	56 (93.33%)	3 (5%)	12 (20%)	1 (1.67%)	60
Subject 3	56 (93.33%)	2 (3.33%)	6 (10%)	2 (3.33%)	60
Subject 4	50 (83.33%)	8 (13.33%)	13 (21.67%)	2 (3.33%)	60
Total	**222 (92.25%)**	**13 (5.41%)**	**35 (14.58%)**	**5 (2.08%)**	**240**

Table 2 shows the obtained spotting and recognition results of this test using the triple-axis accelerometer. It can be seen that in both cases remarkable recognition rates are obtained (above 91%), and also that using the overall database of 80 samples a slightly lower rate (91.25%) than using smaller (20 samples) but more user oriented ones (92.25%) is achieved. Table 3 shows the obtained results with the 3D tracker and the user oriented databases (we omit the overall database results because similar conclusions to those with the tripe axis accelerometer are deduced). In this case the obtained results are even better (94.58%). This improvement is also related to the employed motion-features. In this case, these have a more direct relation with the performed movements, while in the case of the triple-axis accelerometer the captured data are influenced by gravity apart from the movements themselves. Regarding the computation time, the heaviest system, i.e. the one using the 80 sample database, runs at 82-98 Hz which is above real-time performance even if the implementation has not been parallelized. The system was implemented using C++, and tested on a 2.00 GHz Intel Celeron 1 GB RAM.

Finally, Fig. 2 shows close-ups of how the semantic observation of the temporal advance segments the data stream with respect to the true start and end points of gestures being performed one after the other for both motion capture devices. It can be seen how both the temporal advance and the weighted temporal advance increase their values while the gestures are being recognized and how the system resets to zero once it has met the necessary conditions to take a decision. It can also be observed how the decision is taken a few frames before the real transition from gesture to gesture (marked with vertical dashed lines). It occurs this way because it has been determined during the training that the answer should be given when the number of temporal advances without the weight is a bit less than the total number of states per gesture in the database, in order to obtain better recognition rates.

Table 3. Spotting and classification results with the 3D tracker for different subjects using their own databases and auto-generated configurations

	Correct	Deleted	Inserted	Substituted	Ground Truth
Subject 1	58 (96.67%)	2 (3.33%)	5 (8.33%)	0 (0%)	60
Subject 2	58 (96.67%)	2 (3.33%)	9 (15%)	0 (0%)	60
Subject 3	56 (93.33%)	3 (5%)	5 (8.33%)	1 (1.67%)	60
Subject 4	55 (91.67%)	4 (6.67%)	4 (6.67%)	1 (1.67%)	60
Total	**227 (94.58%)**	**11 (4.58%)**	**23 (9.58%)**	**2 (0.83%)**	**240**

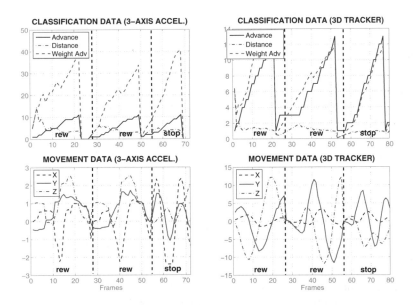

Fig. 2. Close-up of the semantic gesture spotting and classification using the triple-axis accelerometer and the 3D tracker respectively

5   Conclusions and Further Work

In this is work we have presented a method for gesture spotting and classification that can cope with both cyclic and non-cyclic time-varying human motion patterns in real-time applications. The spatio-temporal consistency of the data stream with respect to each of the known gestures is measured with a weighted temporal advance counting, where the weight comes from the inverse of the mean distance of advancing states with respect to their corresponding nearest ones in the gesture. A higher weighted temporal advance count means a more accurate approximation to the gesture candidate, and thus can be used as a quantitative measure for motor skills transfer through imitation. This weighted temporal advance allows to compute the level of confidence in the continuous data stream for a semantic gesture spotting.

The semantic observation starts from the instant when a variation in the state sequence higher than a certain threshold occurs until the system takes a decision, which could be a gesture detection or doing a reset, depending on certain conditions related with the temporal advance, the segment size and the state sequence variation. Hence, gesture spotting and classification are solved in parallel. Experimental results with gestures performed by various users with a triple-axis accelerometer and a 3D tracker show the potential of this approach for human-computer interaction.

Future work will focus on automatizing the selection of the optimal motion-features for the spotting and recognition of gestures involving different body parts. Additionally, it will also be explored the combination of semantic body part motion descriptions in a multibody structure, extending the work done in this subject in previous approaches such as [15,20].

References

1. Mitra, S., Acharya, T.: Gesture Recognition: A Survey. IEEE Transactions on Systems, Man, and Cybernetics, Part C: Applications and Reviews 37(3), 311–324 (2007)
2. Jaimes, A., Sebe, N.: Multimodal Human Computer Interaction: A Survey. Computer Vision and Image Understanding 108(1-2), 116–134 (2007)
3. Lösch, M., Schmidt-Rohr, S.R., Knoop, S., Dillmann, R.: Feature Selection for Human Activity Recognition Using Feature Taxonomies and User Comments. In: Proceedings of the International Conference on Cognitive Systems, Karlsruhe, Germany (2008)
4. Liu, G., Zhang, J., Wang, W., McMillan, L.: Human Motion Estimation from a Reduced Marker Set. In: Proceedings of the 2006 Symposium on Interactive 3D Graphics and Games, Boston, MA, USA (2006)
5. Masoud, O., Papanikolopoulos, N.: A Method for Human Action Recognition. Image and Vision Computing 21(8), 729–743 (2003)
6. Weinland, D., Ronfard, R., Boyer, E.: Motion History Volumes for Free Viewpoint Action Recognition. In: Proceedings of the Workshop on Modeling People and Human Interaction, Beijing, China, vol. 104, pp. 249–257 (2005)

7. Rahman, M.M., Robles-Kelly, A.: A Tuned Eigenspace Technique for Articulated Motion Recognition. In: Leonardis, A., Bischof, H., Pinz, A. (eds.) ECCV 2006. LNCS, vol. 3954, pp. 174–185. Springer, Heidelberg (2006)
8. Ahmad, M., Lee, S.-W.: Human Action Recognition Using Multi-View Image Sequences Features. In: Proceedings of the International Conference on Automatic Face and Gesture Recognition, Southampton, UK, pp. 523–528 (2006)
9. Rittscher, J., Blake, A., Roberts, S.J.: Towards the Automatic Analysis of Complex Human Body Motions. Image and Vision Computing 20, 905–916 (2002)
10. Ren, H., Xu, G., Kee, S.: Subject-Independent Natural Action Recognition. In: Proceedings of the International Conference on Automatic Face and Gesture Recognition, Seoul, Korea, pp. 523–528 (2004)
11. Unzueta, L., Mena, O., Sierra, B., Suescun, Á.: Kinetic Pseudo-Energy History for Human Dynamic Gestures Recognition. In: Perales, F.J., Fisher, R.B. (eds.) AMDO 2008. LNCS, vol. 5098, pp. 390–399. Springer, Heidelberg (2008)
12. Mena, O., Unzueta, L., Sierra, B., Matey, L.: Temporal Nearest End-Effectors for Real-Time Full-Body Human Actions Recognition. In: Perales, F.J., Fisher, R.B. (eds.) AMDO 2008. LNCS, vol. 5098, pp. 269–278. Springer, Heidelberg (2008)
13. Kubota, N., Abe, M.: Computational Intelligence for Cyclic Gestures Recognition of A Partner Robot. In: Proceedings of the International Conference on Knowledge-Based Intelligent Information & Engineering Systems, Melbourne, Australia, pp. 650–656 (2005)
14. Yu, H., Sun, G.-m., Song, W.-x., Li, X.: Human Motion Recognition Based on Neural Network. In: Proceedings of the International Conference on Communications, Circuits and Systems, Hong Kong, China, vol. 2, p. 982 (2005)
15. Ramanan, D., Forsyth, D.A.: Automatic Annotation of Everyday Movements. In: Proceedings of the Neural Information Processing Systems Conference, Vancouver, BC, Canada (2003)
16. Guo, F., Qian, G.: Dance Posture Recognition Using Wide-Baseline Orthogonal Stereo Cameras. In: Proceedings of the International Conference on Automatic Face and Gesture Recognition, Tempe, AZ, USA, pp. 481–486 (2006)
17. Kang, H., Lee, C.W., Jung, K.: Recognition-Based Gesture Spotting in Video Games. Pattern Recognition Letters 25(15), 1701–1714 (2004)
18. Stiefmeier, T., Roggen, D.: Gestures Are Strings: Efficient Online Gesture Spotting and Classification Using String Matching. In: Proceedings of the International Conference on Body Area Networks, Florence, Italy (2007)
19. Stone, M.: Cross-Validation Choice and Assessment of Statistical Procedures. Journal of Royal Statistical Society 36, 111–147 (1974)
20. Unzueta, L.: Markerless Full-Body Human Motion Capture and Combined Motor Action Recognition for Human-Computer Interaction. PhD Thesis, Tecnun, University of Navarra, Donostia-San Sebastián, Spain (2009)

Automatic Motion Segmentation for Human Motion Synthesis

Sebastian Schulz and Annika Woerner

Group on Human Motion Analysis, Institute for Anthropomatics,
Faculty of Informatics, Karlsruhe Institute of Technology,
Kaiserstrasse 12, 76131 Karlsruhe, Germany
{s.schulz,woerner}@kit.edu

Abstract. Motion segmentation is one of the key techniques in the context of motion analysis and generation. The basic idea is to split motion capture data into continuous segments that can be used to generate new motion sequences. For most applications, this segmentation is done manually leading to inaccurate and inconsistent results. This makes it difficult to conceive general methods for subsequent reassembly.

This paper proposes an automatic segmentation of motion capture data that results in deterministic segmentation points. The method can be considered as an advanced zero crossing segmentation technique. As zero crossing performs poorly on weak motion, a threshold is defined detecting phases of week motion. We distinguish two states: One for the resting phase and one for phases of movement. Splitting this second phase again, the presented approach leads to a symbolic level allowing later steps to be carried out without the need of considering spatio-temporal dependencies.

1 Introduction

The idea of motion capturing has been in the focus of research for a long time. The interest in human and animal motion goes back very far in human history [14]. Today most of the human motion capture data is used in the field of entertainment as well as in the film industry. Computer animation is most popular. But, with the integration of humanoid robots in society, another challenging aim is the design of human-like motion for service robots. The development of a service robot within the scope of the special research area 588 has the objective of generating motion for a machine that closely cooperates with humans.

Using motion capture (mocap) data is common for motion analysis, e.g. body tracking [6], segmentation [16] or activity recognition [10]. In humanoid robotics and film industries the data is used also for transferring motion to the actors. Usually mocap data is directly mapped to the robot or film characters, so it is just the replay of predefined motions or live motions from an human actor. With the assignment of the robot to new tasks or in new situations it would be desirable and necessary to be able to act and cooperate in a complex environment.

In this paper, we are focusing on a method to autonomously extract motion segments from mocap data to provide a basis for the synthesis of new motion.

F.J. Perales and R.B. Fisher (Eds.): AMDO 2010, LNCS 6169, pp. 182–191, 2010.

Achieving good results in human motion recognition does not necessarily mean that the underlying segmentation is automatically sufficient to provide a basis for the synthesis of human motion. For both, analysis and synthesis of human movements, it is necessary to split motion sequences into meaningful time periods in order to associate them to partial actions. The same segmentation approach can be applied to get motion primitives for analysis, learning and generation of human movement [19] [18]. But segmenting mocap data for motion synthesis can be different compared to the conventional methods of segmenting the captured data for analysis [4]. So the aim will be to develop a suitable segmentation approach and to adapt it to the needs of the motion synthesis. A comparison of the present literature on hand shows that only in a minority of cases a new segmentation approach is used for motion generation.

The segmentation presented in this work can be used for learning systems and the synthesis of generalized motion. For motion synthesis, we present a suitable procedure that also handles motion without a-priori knowledge and allows to generate motion according to modular design principles, that can be customized or modified to the application's needs.

2   Related Work

This work focus mainly on trajectory based methods using representations of a human action as a collection of significant trajectories. Trajectory based methods are primarily used for movement imitation and learning from observation [2] [1].

Imitation of human motion can be divided into movement reproduction and imitation learning. Imitation learning comprises deriving a set of primitives directly from the mocap data and representing the human motion. Movement reproduction transfers human motion to an actor and gets by without motion primitives. A transformation fits the joint angle configuration of a human movement to the less complex kinematic structure of e.g. a humanoid robot and retains thereby the human characteristics. An example of an application is given in [7].

Instead of using mapped motion data or offline trajectory planning, imitation learning is based on observing human motion. A pre-requisite for this is a similar structure between human and actor. Imitation learning uses motion primitives constituted by motion segmentations as a key requirement.

In Kulic et al. [16] the existing segmentation algorithms are classified based on whether previous knowledge of the motion primitives to be segmented is required. In the first class of approaches, motion primitives are preset, e.g. via short HMMs, by an expert a-priori. The algorithms are based on the comparison between the known motions and the data to be segmented. The second class of approaches conducts segmentation without prior information about the motion primitives. The first class of approaches belongs to the class of top-down strategies. They are usually not able to handle new motions patterns and generalization of motion. Because of this limitations we consider only the second class, that is based on velocity information of the joint angles. The second class of approaches can be subdivided further using velocity properties for segmentation with and without considering individual degrees of freedom. Kulic et al. [15] and Koenig and Mataric [22] created segmentations without considering an individual degree of freedom.

Other approaches, which deliver key decisive factors for our own approach, usually consider individual degrees of freedom and typically work only on an subset of the human body, e.g. the arm or the torso. The first to mention are Pomplum and Mataric [21]. They use the root square value of the joint velocities. A threshold of that root square value determines if a new segment is recognized. The approaches of Fod et al. [8] and Ilg et al. [23] are based on zero velocity crossing. A boundary of a segment (segmentation point) represents a change in the direction of movement. It is set when there are zero point crossings in a sufficient number of dimensions. The human action language (HAL) [11] as representation of human motion also makes use of velocity and, in addition, of acceleration. To segment human movement it considers each angle joint independently and splits the motion depending on these values.

In summary it can be stated that we need an autonomous segmentation, whose motion primitives must not been specified manually and that works without a-priori knowledge and uses trajectory based data providing a fine granular basis for the generation of all new motion data.

3   Segmentation Strategy

3.1   Theoretical Approach

In this section, we describe a method for automatically deriving segmentation points from continues mocap data that can be considered as an advanced zero crossing segmentation technique. Zero crossing segmentation is performed by analyzing the zero-crossing of the second derivatives. The zero-crossing method is simple to implement and fast, however, it performs poorly in the presence of noise. To avoid such failures, we define a threshold ϵ instead of a simple zero-crossing. The threshold parameter ϵ characterizes a range where subjectively no movement is detectable but in fact the human subject moves slightly. So no motion is detected until the threshold value exceeds the parameter. We thus create two states: One for the resting phase, nearly zero velocity within the threshold and for the phases of movement lying outside that range. Finally, we split the second state again. This leads to five classes which can be use to generate combinations of these classes, so called state sequences.

The representation of mocap data as state sequences makes joint-angle trajectories comparable to each other. The superior temporal aspects are eliminated. Similar motions result in the same motion state sequences. One single state represents the most granular motion primitive in our approach. We call it micro motion. So we are dealing with a bottom-up strategy. In our case the execution speed or characteristic of the motion has no influence on the state sequences.

3.2   Segmentation Algorithm

In the following section, the baseline procedure of our segmentation approach is introduced. The aim of our algorithm is to analyze the complex motion sequences and divide them into subsequences. The proposed system consists of four major components. For automatically deriving segmentation points and representing them in state sequences, the consecutive execution of four steps is needed, as depicted in 1.

The four processing steps are: (1) adaptation; (2) filtering; (3) segmentation; (4) clustering. Each box of the diagram can be assigned to one step of the algorithm.

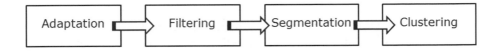

Fig. 1. The four stages of the algorithm

The first and the second step can be considered as preprocessing, the third as the core issue of this approach and the last one as knowledge builder. Further details about every step are described in the following paragraphs.

Adaption to reference model. Human models are the basis of every motion capture, reconstruction or analysis system. We use a static rigid upper body model of the human skeleton based on the mean proportions of the human body representing the kinematics of the human anatomy with up to 108 DOFs. In the adaption process, the marker positions captured by a Vicon infra-red camera system are translated to corresponding joint angles of the model. For the adaption of the model structures to the individual kinematics we are using marker-based optimization and motion-based estimation of joint rotation centers [20].

Filtering. The zero crossing approaches are sensitive to noise. Hence, it is necessary to filter the reconstructed kinematic data. We correct the data using established filter methods. A Gaussian filter ($\sigma = 15$ $n = 5$) already outperformed the original baseline on the noisy data. As can be seen in Figure 2, the noise is eliminated almost completely.

Segmentation. The now following segmentation converts the original motion data into a sequence of states by using a five-state machine to split the filtered joint angle data. This can be seen as a method for representing the joint angles of human motion very compactly. In comparison to plain segmentation, our representation in states allows a comparison of time series of various lengths. All spatio-temporal aspects are compensated and in all future steps of processing we use the new representation of sequences by states. As a result the state transitions settle the temporal boundaries for a sub-motion.

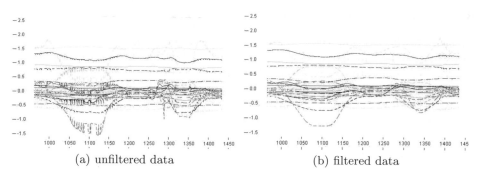

(a) unfiltered data   (b) filtered data

Fig. 2. Example of joint angle series

In the following this characteristic is explained in more detail. For the extraction of primitives we take advantage of the first and second derivatives, using

position,
$$x(t) \tag{1}$$

velocity,
$$\dot{x}(t) = v(t) = \frac{dx}{dt} \tag{2}$$

and acceleration
$$\ddot{x}(t) = a(t) = \frac{dv}{dt}. \tag{3}$$

In accordance to the structure proposed by Guerra e. t. al. [11] , we use four states to model positive and negative velocity and acceleration. We extended this approach by a fifth state, in case the mean velocity falls below a certain value (ϵ). The following function $f(t)$ specifies the segmentation for the different cases:

$$f(t) = \begin{cases} 2 : \text{if } v(t) > \epsilon \text{ and } a(t) > 0 \\ 1 : \text{if } v(t) > \epsilon \text{ and } a(t) < 0 \\ 0 : \text{if } v(t) < \epsilon \\ -1 : \text{if } v(t) < -\epsilon \text{ and } a(t) > 0 \\ -2 : \text{if } v(t) < -\epsilon \text{ and } a(t) < 0 \end{cases} \tag{4}$$

The combination of these states can be use to generate so called state sequences. The idea was that certain movements lead to characteristic sequences, even in motion in various directions.

According to the idea of bottom-up approaches a very high degree of granularity is desirable. However, the already filtered motion data still sets clear limits. By using the fundamental theorem of calculus, we can rewrite the above equations to

$$v(t) = \int_{T_1}^{T_2} v(t) \, dt = x(T_2) - x(T_1) \tag{5}$$

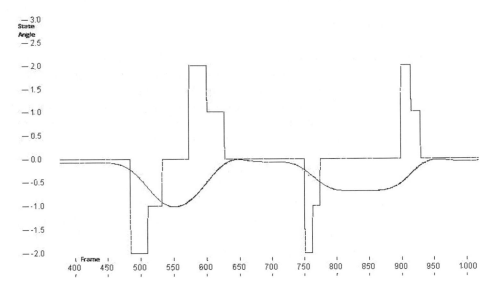

Fig. 3. Example of joint angle and its states

$$a(t) = \int_{T_1}^{T_2} a(t) \; dt = \; v(T_2) \; - \; v(T_1) \tag{6}$$

We can choose the accuracy of the calculation model by choosing the displacement

$$x(T_2) \; - \; x(T_1) \tag{7}$$

To ensure that the joint-angle time series were converted to a continuous gapless function, the method is completed by applying a median filter.

Clustering. In order to create a uniform characterization which facilitates transparency and allows comparisons to be made, the extracted motion states are represented in sequences. These allow further processing without observing the spatial-temporal dependencies at a symbolic level. Joint-angles will be compared in just considering its state sequence. Certain movement leads to a characteristic of a particular joint-angle. The importance of certain joint-angles correspond to the relative frequency density of a particular state sequence and could be put into adaptive training methods.

4   Evaluation

In this section, we evaluated our approach by comparing the results of our algorithm with manual segmentation. We tested the accuracy of the boundaries and the influence of ϵ as well. In order to evaluate the accuracy of the automatic partition algorithm, the boundaries were compared to each other by capturing ground truth data with manual annotations of video footage. Altogether we evaluated the data sets of nine people with twenty motion sequences per person.

4.1   Data Acquisition

We investigated different motion sequences consisting of motion units e. g. pointing gestures. For the data acquisition a test person performs the motion sequence while standing at a fixed position in a kitchen. At the beginning and after the motion sequences the subject takes a neutral position with both hands resting on fix positions. For the tracking of the human motions reflecting markers were attached to the person's body. Ten Vicon infra-red cameras were used to track the marker positions in space.

First, the motion sequences are divided manually into submotions by an expert. Here, only sections of zero velocity can be recognized by an human expert. Additional, boundaries for sections of positive or negative velocity and acceleration will mostly become too imprecise to be used as the ground truth. The deviation between the manually segmented and automatically determined boundaries is calculated as a sum of mean square errors.

4.2   Segmentation Units

The rotation of the arm has turned out to be a good feature, as the most relevant joint angle of a pointing gesture. So we will look at the outcome of our algorithm for this joint angle. The following sequence of segmentation states can be seen as an example of this outcome: (0) (-2) (-1) (0) (2) (1) (0). An example for the sequences with $\epsilon = 0.01$ is given in table 1. The human expert detected three phases of zero velocity and four associated state transitions. So this sequence can be transferred to a annotation such as the one of the expert and can be clustered in (0) (-2 -1) (0) (2 1) (0). The importance of a state sequence can be measured by its occurrence divided by the total number of observations. This corresponds to the relative frequency density. Important features reach a relative frequency density with $h_n(A) \geq 0.8$.

Table 1. Example sequences

Trial 1	0 2 1 0 -2 -1 0	Trial 11	0 2 1 0
Trial 2	0 -2 -1 0 2 1 0	Trial 12	0 2 1 0 -2 -1 0
Trial 3	0 -2 -1 0 2 1 0	Trial 13	0 2 1 0 -2 -1 0
Trial 4	0 2 1 0 -2 -1 0 -2	Trial 14	0 2 1 0 -2 -1 0
Trial 5	0 -2 -1 0 2 1 0	Trial 15	0 2 1 0
Trial 6	0 -2 -1 0 2 1 2 1 0	Trial 16	0 -2 -1 0 2 1 0
Trial 7	0 2 1 0 -2 -1 0	Trial 17	0 -2 -1 0 2 1 0
Trial 8	0 1 2 1 0 -2 -1 0	Trial 18	0 2 1 0
Trial 9	0 -1 -2 -1 0 2 1 0	Trial 19	0 2 1 0 -2 -1 0 2 1 0
Trial 10	0 2 1 0 -2 -1 0	Trial 20	0 2 1 0 -2 -1 0

4.3   Comparison with Manual Segmentation

The same joint angle is used to evaluate our approach by comparing the manual segmentation μ and the algorithm results x_i with the parameters $\epsilon = 0.003$. and $\epsilon = 0.01$. using the mean squared error $\sigma = \sqrt{\frac{1}{N} \sum_{i=1}^{N}(x_i - \mu)^2}$,

We can see that the result for the boundaries gets imprecise if the value for ϵ increases. This is due to the fact that the resting phases (phases of zero velocity) between two states are extended by a greater value of ϵ. Small values for ϵ lead to a miss of the resting phases.

Table 2. The accuracy of the segmentation

actor	$\sigma_{\epsilon=0.003}$	$\sigma_{\epsilon=0.01}$
Person 1	9,47	28,45
Person 2	5,56	13,26
Person 3	9,19	26,53
Person 4	9,21	22,19
Person 5	10,24	110,57
Person 6	5,01	22,42
Person 7	6,76	22,32
Person 8	9,64	51
Person 9	8,1	
$\frac{1}{n}\sum_{i=1}^{n}(\sigma_i)$	8,13	37,07

5   Conclusion

We introduced a method for segmenting joint-angle trajectories and applied it to articulated human motion. The trajectories were segmented in state sequences, leading to a symbolic representation of motion units. This allows concatenation of motion segments to complex motions, as well as their comparability. All this post-processing steps can be carried out without the need of considering spatio-temporal dependencies. First results are shown in our experiments on pointing gestures. We segmented joint angles in sequences of unconstrained human motion showing a relative frequency of 80 percent for a certain task on the same joint-angle. Further work will focus on the application on the proposed method onto larger motion databases. We think that the proposed method can provide a basis for consecutive methods for the generation and recognition of motion sequences.

Acknowledgments

This work has been supported by the German Research Foundation (DFG) within the Collaborative Research Center 588 "Humanoid Robots – Learning and Co-operation Multimodal Robots".

References

1. Al-Zubi, S., Sommer, G.: Imitation learning and transfering of human movement and hand grabbing to adapt to environment changes. In: Reinhard Klette, B.R., Metaxas, D. (eds.) 13th Workshop on Human Motion - Understanding, Modeling, Capture and Animation. LNCS. Springer, Heidelberg (2006)
2. Bakker, P., Kuniyoshi, Y.: Robot see, robot do: An overview of robot imitation. In: Fogarty, T.C. (ed.) AISB-WS 1996. LNCS, vol. 1143, pp. 3–11. Springer, Heidelberg (1996)
3. Barbic, J., Safonova, A., Pan, J.-Y., Faloutsos, C., Hodgins, J.K., Pollard, N.S.: Segmenting motion capture data into distinct behaviors. In: Graphics Interface, pp. 185–194 (2004)
4. Bouchard, D.: Automated time series segmentation for human motion analysis. Technical report, Philadelphia: Center for Human Modeling and Simulation University of Pennsylvania (2006)
5. Gehrig, D., Kuehne, H., Woerner, A., Schultz, T.: Hmm-based human motion recognition with optical flow data. In: IEEE International Conference on Humanoid Robots (Humanoids 2009), Paris, France (2009)
6. Demirdjian, D., Ko, T., Darrell, T.: Constraining human body tracking. In: ICCV '03: Proceedings of the Ninth IEEE International Conference on Computer Vision, Washington, DC, USA, p. 1071. IEEE Computer Society, Los Alamitos (2003)
7. Do, M., Gehrig, D., Azad, P., Pastor, P., Asfour, T., Warner, A., Dillmann, R., Schultz, T.: Transfer of human movements to humanoid robots (2008)
8. Fod, A., Matari, M.J., Jenkins, O.C.: Automated derivation of primitives for movement classification. In: Proc. of First IEEE-RAS International Conference on Humanoid Robots (2000)
9. Gehrig, D., Fischer, A., Kuehne, H., Stein, T., Woerner, A., Schwameder, H., Schultz, T.: Online recognition of daily-life movements (2008)
10. Gehrig, D., Kuehne, H., Woerner, A., Schultz, T.: Hmm-based human motion recognition with optical flow data. In: 2009 9th IEEE-RAS International Conference on Humanoid Robots (2009)
11. Guerra-Filho, G.: The morphology of human action: Finding essential actuators, motiom patterns, and their coordination. International Journal on Humanoid Robotics (2009)
12. Guerra-Filho, G., Aloimonos, Y.: A sensory-motor language for human activity understanding. In: 2006 6th IEEE-RAS International Conference on Humanoid Robots, pp. 69–75 (2006)
13. Kahol, K., Tripathi, P., Panchanathan, S.: Automated gesture segmentation from dance sequences. In: Proceedings of Sixth IEEE International Conference on Automatic Face and Gesture Recognition, pp. 883–888 (2004)
14. Klette, R., Tee, C.: Understanding human motion: A historic review, p. 1 (2008)
15. Kulic, D., Lee, D., Ott, C., Nakamura, Y.: Incremental learning of full body motion primitives for humanoid robots. In: 2008 8th IEEE-RAS International Conference on Humanoid Robots, Humanoids, pp. 326–332 (2008)
16. Kulic, D., Nakamura, Y.: Comparative study of representations for segmentation of whole body human motion data. In: IROS, pp. 4300–4305 (2009)
17. Musto, A.: A fuzzy-based, qualitative representation of movement. Technical report (2008)
18. Nakazawa, A., Nakaoka, S., Ikeuchi, K., Yokoi, K.: Imitating human dance motions through motion structure analysis. In: Proc. of International Conference on Intelligent Robots and Systems, pp. 2539–2544 (2002)

19. Rizzolatti, G., Craighero, L.: The mirror-neuron system. Annu. Rev. Neuroscience (2004)
20. Simonidis, C., Gaertner, S., Do, M.: Spezifikationen zu den ganzkoerpermen-schmodellen im sfb 588. Technical report, Universitaets Verlag Karlsruhe (2009)
21. Pomplun, M., Matarić, M.: Evaluation metrics and results of human arm movement imitation. In: Proceedings of the 1st IEEE-RAS International Conference on Humanoid Robotics (2000)
22. Koenig, N.: Behavior-based segmentation of demonstrated task (2006)
23. Ilg, W., Bakir, G., Mezger, J., Giese, M.: On the representation, learning and transfer of spatio-temporal movement characteristics (2003)

Multiple-Activity Human Body Tracking in Unconstrained Environments

Loren Arthur Schwarz, Diana Mateus, and Nassir Navab

Computer Aided Medical Procedures, Technische Universität München, Germany
{schwarz,mateus,navab}@cs.tum.edu
http://campar.cs.tum.edu/

Abstract. We propose a method for human full-body pose tracking from measurements of wearable inertial sensors. Since the data provided by such sensors is sparse, noisy and often ambiguous, we use a compound prior model of feasible human poses to constrain the tracking problem. Our model consists of several low-dimensional, activity-specific motion models and an efficient, sampling-based activity switching mechanism. We restrict the search space for pose tracking by means of manifold learning. Together with the portability of wearable sensors, our method allows us to track human full-body motion in unconstrained environments. In fact, we are able to simultaneously classify the activity a person is performing and estimate the full-body pose. Experiments on movement sequences containing different activities show that our method can seamlessly detect activity switches and precisely reconstruct full-body pose from the data of only six wearable inertial sensors.

Keywords: Human pose tracking, manifold learning, wearable sensors.

1 Introduction

Approaches for human full-body pose tracking have mostly been studied in the field of computer vision, where observations are typically image features, such as human silhouettes [1,2,3,4]. Vision-based methods depend on illumination, viewpoint and line of sight between the tracked person and one or more cameras. In applications where long-term tracking is addressed or when everyday-life activities need to be studied, such constraints are not practicable. Typical cases are motion analysis for ergonomic studies of factory workers or for medical diagnosis of diseases involving motion-disorders, e.g. Multiple Sclerosis [5]. These applications require the recovery of full-body motion for a set of activities of interest, while subjects move freely. We take an alternative to using vision-based observations for full-body pose estimation and rely on measurements from wearable inertial sensors. Our proposed method allows us to capture full-body motion data in situations where visual tracking systems cannot be used.

Tracking human motion using inertial sensors is challenging, since the measurements provided by such sensors are sparse, noisy and often ambiguous. Prior models of human motion are therefore a prerequisite for achieving satisfactory

F.J. Perales and R.B. Fisher (Eds.): AMDO 2010, LNCS 6169, pp. 192–202, 2010.
© Springer-Verlag Berlin Heidelberg 2010

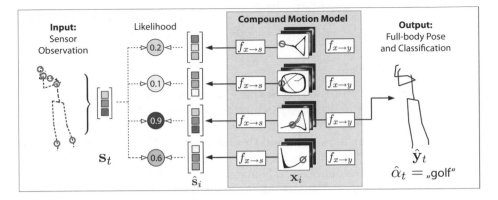

Fig. 1. The proposed compound motion model is comprised of several activity-specific models. Each of these consists of a manifold embedding of feasible poses, pose likelihood priors and learned mappings to sensor space ($f_{x \to s}$) and full-body pose space ($f_{x \to y}$). We use a particle filter in embedding space to track multiple pose hypotheses x_i and select the hypothesis that best matches the true sensor observation s_t.

tracking results. We rely on identifying the low-dimensional *manifold of feasible human poses* inside the high-dimensional space of pose parameters [2]. In particular, we use Laplacian Eigenmaps [6], a manifold learning technique, to create a prior motion model from full-body pose training data. Manifold learning methods are known to produce meaningful embeddings that efficiently parameterize human poses for single activities, e.g. walking [7,2]. Unfortunately, the generalization to multiple activities, as required by the above-mentioned applications, is not straightforward [8]. In fact, a global embedding including all activities will be dominated by inter-activity differences and characteristics of individual activities will be represented inadequately. We propose to address the multiple-activity tracking problem by means of a *compound motion model* comprised of several activity-specific models and an efficient *activity switching mechanism*.

The activity-specific motion models consist of separate low-dimensional manifold embeddings generated from full-body pose training data. Together, the embeddings provide a compact representation of likely poses for multiple activities and allow us to significantly restrict search space during tracking. Additionally, we learn kernel regression mappings for each activity, which relate the low-dimensional embeddings both to observation space and to full-body space (Figure 1). We formulate the tracking problem within the Bayesian framework and use a particle filter for efficient inference. This way, we are able to track multiple pose hypotheses and select the one that best explains the sensor observations. Since a pose hypothesis in our case consists of both, a pose in embedding space and an activity index identifying the most likely motion model, we can simultaneously estimate full-body pose and classify performed activities.

Our tracking method is at the same time *general*, in that motions corresponding to multiple activities can be tracked, and *specific*, since our compound model provides specialized motion models for each activity of interest. The cost of a one-time training phase is compensated by the ability to faithfully track full-body pose from simple and limited wearable sensor observations.

1.1 Related Work

Generative full-body pose tracking methods are based on modelling the mapping from poses to observations and searching for the most likely pose, given new observations. The major difficulty is the high dimensionality of full-body pose space. Several authors have addressed this issue by sampling pose space using a particle filter [3,9]. Computation cost can also be reduced by restricting search space using learned low-dimensional human motion models [1,7,10]. For instance, Gaussian Process Latent Variable Models (GP-LVM) can provide a compact representation of human motion from training data [1,11].

With a similar purpose, our method uses a spectral embedding technique [6] for obtaining prior motion models. Spectral embeddings are low-dimensional and, as opposed to GP-LVMs, reflect local structural properties of the high-dimensional training data. Approaches using spectral embedding methods for human tracking commonly rely on a single motion model [12,7] and the generalization to various activities is not straightforward. We propose to employ a compound model built from separate, activity-specific manifold embeddings, making it possible to track various types of motions.

Mechanisms for using multiple specialized motion models for tracking can be found in several domains. The classical particle filter algorithm was extended in [13] to handle multiple, discrete dynamics models. An efficient approach for full-body tracking using multiple low-dimensional motion models is proposed in [10]. The authors demonstrate a switching mechanism for the two actions of running and walking. Unfortunately, the computational cost of their method grows significantly with the number of considered activities. In contrast, our method can be trained on a potentially arbitrary number of activities.

Most of the methods estimate pose from visual cues. Since our final goal is long-term motion analysis, where visual features are hard to obtain, we focus on mobile inertial sensors. However, sensor data is typically less informative and suffers from issues, such as drift. Existing approaches for full-body tracking using inertial sensors [14,15] recover the pose directly from the measurements. To the authors' knowledge, learning prior constraints for tracking full-body pose from sensor data is new. In [16], accelerometer measurements are compared to a database of poses and motion sequences matching the measurements are replayed in an approximation of the true motion. The method proposed in [15] is able to track full-body pose using ultrasonic sensors and accelerometers. However, their approach is computationally expensive. Our method uses a low-dimensional, efficient parameterization of human poses for reducing search space.

2 Full-Body Tracking Method

We address the problem of human full-body tracking from measurements of inertial orientation sensors. Given a set of M activities of interest, we start by building a compound motion model from training data containing both full-body poses $\mathbf{y} \in \mathbb{R}^{d_y}$ and sensor readings $\mathbf{s} \in \mathbb{R}^{d_s}$. Then, during testing, we estimate the full-body pose $\hat{\mathbf{y}}_t$ at each time step t only from sensor observations $\mathbf{s}_t$.

Our compound motion model contains multiple activity-specific motion models, each of which consists of (1) a low-dimensional manifold embedding of the full-body pose training data, (2) predictive mappings from the embedding to full-body pose space and to observation space, (3) a pose likelihood prior in embedding space and (4) an activity switching prior. We formulate the tracking problem in the Bayesian framework and estimate the system state at each time step t. The system state is given by an activity index $\alpha \in \{1, \ldots, M\}$ and a pose $\mathbf{x} \in \mathbb{R}^{d_x}$ in low-dimensional embedding space ($d_x \ll d_y$). Applying a particle filter allows us to seamlessly evaluate multiple pose hypotheses and to select the most appropriate motion model for each new sensor observation. The learning tasks are described in section 2.1, the tracking approach in sections 2.2 and 2.3.

2.1   Learning Multiple Low-Dimensional Motion Models

In a training phase, we learn activity-specific motion models from full-body pose data and corresponding sensor measurements. Each motion model consists of the following components (see Figure 2 for an illustration):

Manifold Embedding. Let the set of N_α full-body training poses for activity α be denoted by $\mathbf{Y}^\alpha = [\mathbf{y}_1^\alpha \ldots \mathbf{y}_{N_\alpha}^\alpha]$. We obtain a corresponding set of dimensionality-reduced points $\mathbf{X}^\alpha = [\mathbf{x}_1^\alpha \ldots \mathbf{x}_{N_\alpha}^\alpha]$ by applying Laplacian Eigenmaps, a spectral embedding technique [6]. The low-dimensional points $\mathbf{x}_i^\alpha$ efficiently represent the *manifold of feasible poses* for activity α. Using this representation for tracking, we are able to restrict search space to likely poses, instead of exhaustively searching the high-dimensional full-body pose space.

Predictive Mappings. In order to relate poses in low-dimensional embedding space to sensor measurements and to full-body poses, we learn predictive mappings from training data. We follow the approach in [12,7] and use nonlinear kernel regression, with the difference that we learn separate mappings from each of the activity-specific manifold embeddings. The mapping $f_{x \to y}^\alpha(\mathbf{x})$ for *prediction of full-body poses* is learned from corresponding training pairs of embedding points $\mathbf{x}_i^\alpha$ and full-body poses $\mathbf{y}_i^\alpha$ for an activity α. Similarly, the mapping $f_{x \to s}^\alpha(\mathbf{x})$ is learned from training pairs of embedding points and sensor measurements $\mathbf{s}_i^\alpha$ and allows *predicting sensor values*.

Pose Likelihood Prior. Using the training data for each activity, we can derive the likelihood for arbitrary poses in low-dimensional embedding space. Intuitively, poses $\mathbf{x}$ that are close to the embedding points $\mathbf{x}_i^\alpha$ learned from training data should have the highest likelihood. The pose likelihood prior for activity α is obtained using a kernel density estimate [12,7] as $p_{\text{pose}}^\alpha(\mathbf{x}) = \frac{1}{N_\alpha} \sum_{i=1}^{N_\alpha} k(\mathbf{x}, \mathbf{x}_i^\alpha)$, where $k(\cdot, \cdot)$ is a Gaussian kernel function.

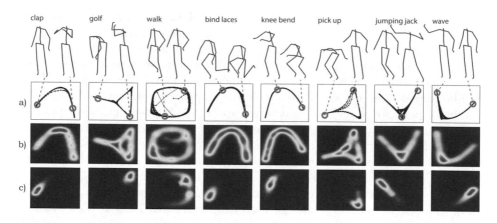

Fig. 2. Learned motion models for 8 different activities. a) Two-dimensional manifold embeddings obtained using Laplacian Eigenmaps on full-body pose training data. Each point on the manifolds corresponds to a valid full-body pose, a few examples are shown above. b) Static pose priors in latent space. c) Activity switching priors in latent space.

Activity Switching Prior. We also define a prior distribution $p^\alpha_{\text{switch}}(\mathbf{x})$ for every motion model that describes how likely a switch of activity is, given a pose $\mathbf{x}$ in embedding space. To ensure generality, we allow activity switching from any pose with constant minimum probability p_k. However, we let the probability of switching increase for poses that typically occur between subsequent activities. In our experiments, the upright standing pose was used as an intermediate pose that encourages activity switching. We model the switching prior with a normal distribution $p^\alpha_{\text{switch}}(\mathbf{x}) = \mathcal{N}(f^\alpha_{x \to y}(\mathbf{x}); \mathbf{y}_0, \mathbf{\Sigma}^\alpha_y) + p_k$, where $\mathbf{y}_0$ represents the intermediate pose in full-body space, $f^\alpha_{x \to y}(\mathbf{x})$ is a predicted full-body pose and $\mathbf{\Sigma}^\alpha_y$ is the diagonal covariance matrix of the training data $\mathbf{Y}^\alpha$.

2.2 Bayesian Tracking Using Multiple Motion Models

The testing phase of our method consists of tracking pose in low-dimensional embedding space. In a standard Bayesian tracking formulation, we wish to find the optimum of the posterior $p(\mathbf{x}_t|\mathbf{s}_t) = p(\mathbf{s}_t|\mathbf{x}_t)p(\mathbf{x}_t|\mathbf{s}_{t-1})$, with $p(\mathbf{x}_t|\mathbf{s}_{t-1}) = \int p(\mathbf{x}_t|\mathbf{x}_{t-1})p(\mathbf{x}_{t-1}|\mathbf{s}_{t-1})d\mathbf{x}_{t-1}$. In other words, we seek the most likely pose $\mathbf{x}_t$ in embedding space at time t, given the observations up to $\mathbf{s}_t$. The *dynamics model* $p(\mathbf{x}_t|\mathbf{x}_{t-1})$ determines how pose estimates are updated from one time step to the next and the *observation model* $p(\mathbf{s}_t|\mathbf{x}_t)$ links poses in embedding space to observations. Since we are using multiple motion models for tracking, we need to include the discrete activity index $\alpha_t \in \{1, \ldots, M\}$, leading to the posterior

$$\underbrace{p(\mathbf{x}_t, \alpha_t|\mathbf{s}_t)}_{\text{posterior}} = \underbrace{p(\mathbf{s}_t|\mathbf{x}_t, \alpha_t)}_{\text{observation model}} \underbrace{p(\mathbf{x}_t, \alpha_t|\mathbf{s}_{t-1})}_{\text{prior}}. \tag{1}$$

Following [13], we also augment the dynamics model $p(\mathbf{x}_t|\mathbf{x}_{t-1})$ with an activity index, yielding the factored model

$$\underbrace{p(\mathbf{x}_t, \alpha_t|\mathbf{x}_{t-1}, \alpha_{t-1})}_{\text{dynamics model}} = \underbrace{p(\mathbf{x}_t|\mathbf{x}_{t-1}, \alpha_t, \alpha_{t-1})}_{\text{pose dynamics}} \underbrace{p(\alpha_t|\mathbf{x}_{t-1}, \alpha_{t-1})}_{\text{activity dynamics}}. \qquad (2)$$

The pose dynamics model governs the evolution of poses in embedding space and the activity dynamics model describes the activity switching process.

Pose Dynamics Model. We define the new pose dynamics model as follows:

$$p(\mathbf{x}_t|\mathbf{x}_{t-1}, \alpha_t, \alpha_{t-1}) = \begin{cases} p(\mathbf{x}_t|\mathbf{x}_{t-1}) & \text{if } \alpha_t = \alpha_{t-1}, \\ p_{\text{pose}}^{\alpha_t}(\mathbf{x}_t) & \text{else.} \end{cases} \qquad (3)$$

When there is no switch of activity ($\alpha_t = \alpha_{t-1}$), dynamics are governed by a random walk, modeled as a normal distribution centered at the previous pose in embedding space, $p(\mathbf{x}_t|\mathbf{x}_{t-1}) = \mathcal{N}(\mathbf{x}_t; \mathbf{x}_{t-1}, \Sigma_x^{\alpha_t})$. Here, $\Sigma_x^{\alpha_t}$ is the diagonal covariance matrix of the low-dimensional training data $\mathbf{X}^{\alpha_t}$. In the case of activity switching ($\alpha_t \neq \alpha_{t-1}$), the dynamics model follows the pose likelihood prior $p_{\text{pose}}^{\alpha_t}(\mathbf{x})$ of activity α_t (section 2.1). In other words, the most likely poses after switching to activity α_t are those learned from the training data.

Activity Dynamics Model. We assume that all sequences of consecutive activities are equally likely, i.e. $p(\alpha_t = j|\mathbf{x}_{t-1}, \alpha_{t-1} = i)$ is equal for all activity indices $j \neq i$. The probability of switching from a given activity α_{t-1} to any other activity then only depends on the previous pose $\mathbf{x}_{t-1}$ in embedding space. Thus, we state our activity dynamics model using the activity switching prior defined in section 2.1 as $p(\alpha_t|\mathbf{x}_{t-1}, \alpha_{t-1}) = p_{\text{switch}}^{\alpha_{t-1}}(\mathbf{x}_{t-1})$.

Observation Model. Our observation model $p(\mathbf{s}_t|\mathbf{x}_t, \alpha_t)$ relates observations to the learned embedding space. We define it as a product of three terms:

$$p(\mathbf{s}_t|\mathbf{x}_t, \alpha_t) = \underbrace{\mathcal{N}(\mathbf{s}_t; f_{x \to s}^{\alpha_t}(\mathbf{x}_t), \Sigma_s^{\alpha_t})}_{\text{prediction term}} \underbrace{\mathcal{N}(\mathbf{y_{t-1}}; f_{x \to y}^{\alpha_t}(\mathbf{x}_t), \Sigma_y^{\alpha_t})}_{\text{full pose smoothness term}} \underbrace{p_{\text{pose}}^{\alpha_t}(\mathbf{x}_t)}_{\text{prior}}. \qquad (4)$$

The prediction term uses the learned mapping $f_{x \to s}^{\alpha}(\mathbf{x})$ to predict sensor observations from a pose $\mathbf{x}_t$. The likelihood of $\mathbf{x}_t$ based on this term is maximal if the prediction perfectly matches the true observation $\mathbf{s}_t$. In order to reduce the influence of outlier observations, the smoothness term penalizes embedding locations if their predicted full-body pose differs strongly form the previous pose $\mathbf{y}_{t-1}$. The pose likelihood prior encourages poses that are likely with respect to the training data. $\Sigma_s^{\alpha_t}$ and $\Sigma_y^{\alpha_t}$ are the diagonal covariance matrices of the training observations $\mathbf{S}^{\alpha_t}$ and full-body poses $\mathbf{Y}^{\alpha_t}$ belonging to activity α_t.

2.3   Particle Filtering and Full-Body Pose Inference

We employ a particle filter [17,13] to sample the posterior density in Eq. 1. The particle filter, adapted to use our compound motion model, allows simultaneously evaluating pose hypotheses of different motion models and selecting the most appropriate model. Particle filtering is computationally efficient in our setting, since it is applied in the low-dimensional space of manifold embeddings.

We initialize n particles $(\mathbf{x}_0^i, \alpha_0^i)$, $i \in \{1 \ldots n\}$, with locations across all manifold embeddings of our compound model. At each time step t, we first resample the particles according to their weights w_{t-1}^i. Each particle is then updated by sampling from the dynamics model $p(\mathbf{x}_t, \alpha_t | \mathbf{x}_{t-1} = \mathbf{x}_{t-1}^i, \alpha_{t-1} = \alpha_{t-1}^i)$. This implies switching the i-th particle to a randomly chosen other activity with probability $p_{\text{switch}}^{\alpha'}(\mathbf{x}_{t-1}^i)$, where $\alpha' = \alpha_{t-1}^i$. The weights are re-computed using the observation model, $w_t^i = p(\mathbf{s}_t | \mathbf{x}_t = \mathbf{x}_t^i, \alpha_t = \alpha_t^i)$. We then determine the estimated activity $\hat{\alpha}_t$ as the most frequent activity among the highest-weight particles. The pose estimate $\hat{\mathbf{x}}_t$ in low-dimensional space is computed as a convex combination of the positions of the highest-weight particles with activity $\hat{\alpha}_t$. The full-body pose at time t is finally obtained as $\hat{\mathbf{y}}_t = f_{x \to y}^{\hat{\alpha}_t}(\hat{\mathbf{x}}_t)$.

3   Experiments and Results

We acquired a synchronized dataset of full-body poses $\mathbf{Y}^\alpha$ and sensor values $\mathbf{S}^\alpha$, $\alpha \in \{1 \ldots M\}$, using a motion capture system and six wearable inertial *orientation* sensors. A full-body pose is given by a vector of $d_y = 35$ dimensions representing the joint angles of our skeleton body model. An observation vector has $d_s = 12$ dimensions, representing pitch and roll for each of the sensors. The yaw values were omitted for independence of magnetic north. We placed sensors on the wrists, upper arms and shinbones of each person. In the training phase, we learned a manifold embedding $\mathbf{X}^\alpha$ of $d_x = 2$ dimensions for each activity.

We considered $M = 10$ activities: clapping, golfing, hurrah (arms up), jumping jack, knee bends, binding laces, picking something up, scratching head, walking and waving. Each of the movements was recorded 6 times with 9 actors. Every movement recording has a length of ~ 600 frames. The testing data consists of 5 sequences per actor containing all activities (~ 2000 frames each). See Figure 3

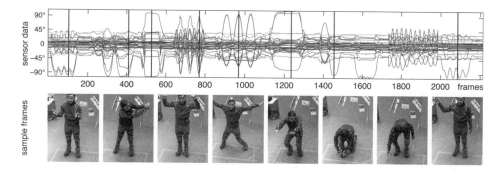

Fig. 3. *Top:* Inertial sensor data for a sequence of 10 activities in a row. *Bottom:* Pictures of the person at the time instants marked above with vertical lines. The person is equipped with motion capture markers and six wearable inertial sensors.

for an illustration. For tracking, only the inertial sensor values were used, the motion capture data served as ground truth. All experiments were performed in a cross-validation scheme, i.e. each testing sequence was generated from one of the recordings per activity and actor, using the remaining five for training.

Full-body Pose Tracking. Noting that the appropriate number of particles grows *linearly* with the number of considered activities, we used $n = 400$ particles. Figure 4 illustrates how particles sample the activity-specific manifold embeddings (only two are shown for clarity) for a testing sequence switching from *waving* to *golfing*. Initially, the person is waving and most particles are concentrated around a pose on the *waving* embedding. A small number of particles also samples all other manifolds. As the person leans forward for golfing, particles quickly accumulate on the *golfing* manifold, since the sensor predictions of these particles increasingly match the real observations. Subsequent resampling steps cause the majority of particles to follow.

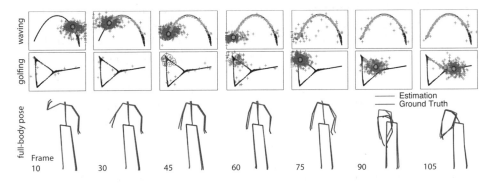

Fig. 4. The particle filter-based activity switching mechanism on a sample sequence. Two of the ten activity manifold embeddings (*waving* and *golfing*) are displayed for several frames. Particles are shown as red crosses. The particles used for predicting full-body pose are circled in dark color. Green crosses indicate the trace of previous frames. Shown below are the corresponding predicted and ground-truth body poses.

Activity Classification. The number of particles per activity manifold is an indicator of activity class membership. Figure 5.(a) shows classification results for the testing sequence in Figure 3. The particle count over time for four of the manifold embeddings is displayed, along with predicted and true activity classifications. Misclassifications mainly occur at the beginning and end of activities. In fact, these frames can be classified as any activity, since the person is standing idle. The confusion matrix in Figure 5.(b) gives the classification rates for all activities over all testing sequences. On average, we achieved a correct classification rate of 89% for all non-idle frames. The matrix is mostly diagonal, significant confusion only occurs between *waving* and *scratching head*, which both consist of raising the right arm close to the head. Misclassification in this case therefore does not necessarily affect the precision of full-body pose estimation.

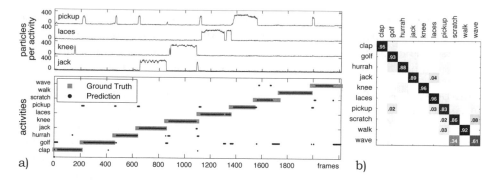

a)   b)

Fig. 5. (a) Activity classification results for the sequence shown in Fig. 3. *Top:* Number of particles per frame sampling four of the activity manifolds. *Bottom:* Ground truth classification and predicted activities for each frame of the sequence. (b) Confusion matrix computed from the classification results for all testing sequences.

Pose Estimation Accuracy. We measured how precisely the poses estimated by our method match the ground truth using two metrics. The angular error e_{ang} gives the deviation from the ground truth in terms of joint angles. The distance error e_{dist} is the difference in 3D space between predicted joint locations and the ground truth. Averaged over all frames of the testing sequences, we achieved $\bar{e}_{\mathrm{ang}} = 6.23°$ per joint and $\bar{e}_{\mathrm{dist}} = 45.2$mm. As shown in Table 1, the deviation from the ground truth only increases for fast movements with a large variability, such as *jumping jack* or *walking*. Our results are comparable to other state-of-the-art methods that use visual observations [4,15].

Table 1. Pose estimation accuracy for all considered activities. Deviations from ground truth poses are provided as joint angles (e_{ang} in degrees per joint) and as distances (e_{dist} in millimeters per joint), averaged over all experiments.

	clap	golf	hurrah	jack	knee	laces	pickup	scratch	walk	wave
e_{ang}	4.95	6.10	6.79	8.80	4.87	5.90	5.90	4.43	9.65	4.93
e_{dist}	37.8	51.2	40.4	58.1	45.6	60.5	51.4	27.7	50.7	28.5

4   Discussion and Conclusion

The learned compound model of feasible poses provides a reliable framework for multiple-activity tracking from limited, low-dimensional observations. Apart from wearable sensor data, other observations can also be used, such as sparse visual features. A requirement of our method is that the motion model is initially trained on a set of activities. While the model allows stylistic variation between instances of the same motion, completely unseen movements will not be reconstructed precisely. However, our method will still provide a pose estimate that matches the new observations as close as possible. The multiple-hypothesis tracker will furthermore quickly recover the correct pose, as soon as a known movement is performed. We also do not require pose initialization, since when tracking begins, particles are distributed to sample all learned feasible poses.

Since inertial sensors only measure relative movement, we do not track the global position of a person. However, integrating global tracking can be easily achieved using conventional positioning systems. We particularly target scenarios where the focus lies on the movement itself, not the person's location. An application of interest to us is medical motion analysis for Multiple Sclerosis patients [5]. Currently, physicians evaluate the disease state by analyzing patient motion in a short protocol including movements such as walking and jumping. Training our method on the movements of the protocol would allow acquiring motion data over longer periods of time in the patient's everyday environment. We currently investigate how to extend the method for being able to detect anomalies (i.e. unknown activities) in such scenarios.

In conclusion, we have presented a method for tracking human full-body pose given only limited observations from wearable inertial sensors. For dealing with the sparse and often ambiguous sensor data, we learn a compound model of human motion from full-body pose training data. The method is efficient, since we track poses in a low-dimensional space of manifold embeddings and use sparse non-linear regression to relate the embedding space to observations and to full-body poses. Our experiments showed that we can reliably recognize motions of multiple activities and precisely track human full-body pose.

References

1. Urtasun, R., Fleet, D., Fua, P.: 3d people tracking with gaussian process dynamical models. In: CVPR (June 2006)
2. Elgammal, A., Lee, C.: The role of manifold learning in human motion analysis. In: Human Motion Understanding, Modeling, Capture and Animation, pp. 1–29 (2008)
3. Bandouch, J., Engstler, F., Beetz, M.: Accurate human motion capture using an ergonomics-based anthropometric human model. In: Perales, F.J., Fisher, R.B. (eds.) AMDO 2008. LNCS, vol. 5098, pp. 248–258. Springer, Heidelberg (2008)
4. Agarwal, A., Triggs, B., Montbonnot, F.: Recovering 3d human pose from monocular images. PAMI 28(1), 44–58 (2006)
5. Weikert, M., Motl, R.W., Suh, Y., McAuley, E., Wynn, D.: Accelerometry in persons with multiple sclerosis: Measurement of physical activity or walking mobility? Journal of the neurological sciences 290(1), 6–11 (2010)
6. Belkin, M., Niyogi, P.: Laplacian eigenmaps for dimensionality reduction and data representation. Neural Computation 15(6), 1373–1396 (2003)
7. Lu, Z., Carreira-Perpinan, M., Sminchisescu, C.: People tracking with the laplacian eigenmaps latent variable model. In: NIPS (January 2007)
8. Datta, A., Sheikh, Y., Kanade, T.: Modeling the product manifold of posture and motion. In: THEMIS Workshop (2009)
9. Deutscher, J., Reid, I.: Articulated body motion capture by stochastic search. IJCV 61(2), 185–205 (2005)
10. Jaeggli, T., Koller-Meier, E., van Gool, L.: Learning generative models for multi-activity body pose estimation. IJCV 83, 121–134 (2009)

11. Wang, J., Fleet, D., Hertzmann, A.: Gaussian process dynamical models for human motion. PAMI, 283–298 (2008)
12. Kanaujia, A., Sminchisescu, C., Metaxas, D.: Spectral latent variable models for perceptual inference. In: ICCV, pp. 1–8 (2007)
13. Isard, M., Blake, A.: A mixed-state condensation tracker with automatic model-switching. In: ICCV, pp. 107–112 (1998)
14. Roetenberg, D., Slycke, P., Veltink, P.: Ambulatory position and orientation tracking fusing magnetic and inertial sensing. IEEE Transactions on Biomedical Engineering 54(4), 883–890 (2007)
15. Vlasic, D., Adelsberger, R., Vannucci, G., Barnwell, J.: Practical motion capture in everyday surroundings. In: ACM TOG (2007)
16. Slyper, R., Hodgins, J.: Action capture with accelerometers. In: ACM SIGGRAPH Symposium on Computer Animation, pp. 193–199 (2008)
17. Isard, M., Blake, A.: Condensation—conditional density propagation for visual tracking. IJCV (1998)

Identity Recognition-Based Correction Mechanism for Face Tracking

Łukasz A. Stasiak[1,2] and Raul Vicente-Garcia[1]

[1] Fraunhofer IPK, Pascalstrasse 8-9, 10587 Berlin, Germany
[2] Warsaw University of Technology, Nowowiejska 15/19, 00-665 Warsaw, Poland
{lukasz.stasiak,raul.vicente}@ipk.fraunhofer.de

Abstract. A system for parallel face detection, tracking and recognition in real-time video sequences is being developed. The particle filtering is utilized for the purpose of combined and effective detection, tracking and recognition. Temporal information contained in videos is utilized. Fast, skin color-based face extraction and normalization technique is applied. Consequently, real-time processing is achieved.

Implementation of face recognition mechanisms within the tracking framework is used not only for the purpose of identity recognition, but also to improve the tracking robustness in case of multi-person tracking scenarios. In such scenarios, face-to-track assignment conflicts can often be resolved with the use of motion modeling. However, in case of close trajectories, motion-based conflict resolution can be erroneous. Identity clue can be used to improve tracking quality in such cases.

This paper describes the concept of face tracking corrections with the use of identity recognition mechanism, implemented within a compact particle filtering-based framework for face detection, tracking and recognition.

Keywords: Face tracking, particle-filtering, face recognition, biometrics.

1 Introduction

The automatic detection, tracking, and analysis of faces offer new application possibilities in a wide range of automated systems, including security solutions (e.g. biometric authentication, abnormal activity detection), entertainment industry (e.g. analysis of face expressions with the use of a webcam) or tools supporting marketing policy analysis (e.g. customer behavior analysis, visitor track analysis). The issues of face detection and tracking have been addressed for a long time now [7, 18, 4, 9, 16, 17]. However, a generic solution, applicable for all real-world scenarios, still does not exist. In particular, changing environmental conditions, such as illumination, or head posing and non-rigid face motions, can seriously deteriorate the quality of face detection, face tracking and face analysis methods [1, 10, 15, 14]. Many sophisticated methods are also not able to process input images in real-time. Additionally, most of the existing face recognition solutions require the images to be frontal and of good quality, with controlled

F.J. Perales and R.B. Fisher (Eds.): AMDO 2010, LNCS 6169, pp. 203–212, 2010.
© Springer-Verlag Berlin Heidelberg 2010

illumination. However, images of such quality cannot usually be acquired with the use of the existing surveillance infrastructure, such as closed-circuit television (CCTV), and without a high level of cooperation from a human user. On the other hand, existing infrastructure can usually easily provide video sequences instead of single still images. Video sequences may then be processed with the use of video-oriented face analysis systems [8].

To address these specific needs we are developing a framework for parallel face detection, tracking and recognition in real-time video sequences. The motivation is to build a system capable of recognizing people from low-resolution videos and with the use of popular, easily available hardware (such as PC and webcam), i.e. the system having low computational requirements. The subjects' behavior should not be constrained in any way: they are allowed to behave naturally. Multiple persons in the scene are allowed. By utilizing video sequences, these requirements can be met, even if single frame analysis would result in poor performance (due to poor quality of single frames, large face image deviations in single frames, and/or simplified and thus fast per-frame analysis). By means of score cumulation over a sequence of video frames, weak *per-frame* classification decisions are cumulated to obtain *strong* classification decision over a sequence. All stages in the proposed framework, i.e. face detection, tracking and recognition, are based on the particle filtering approach. As a result, computational requirements are minimized.

Face-based identity recognition from videos is the main aim of the proposed framework. The face tracking module of the framework provides normalized face images for the recognition module. However, since identity relevant information is processed and available, a feedback from the recognition module can additionally support the tracking module in order to resolve some specific face-to-track assignment conflicts. In this paper, we present a conceptual extension of the previously presented face tracking approach [12]. The extension is achieved by utilizing identity relevant information for the purpose of improving tracking robustness.

2   Particle Filtering-Based Face Detect-Track-Recognize Framework

2.1   Structure of the Framework

Face detection is a task typical for still image input data, whereas face tracking is often applied to sequences of images (videos), where some temporal information can be utilized. Face tracking usually consumes the results of face detection to initialize the tracker or to improve its accuracy by correcting locations of tracked faces. However, some tracking mechanisms can also be applied for the purpose of detection. We proposed [13] a particle filtering-based [5] framework, which utilizes local face features for the purpose of face detection, tracking and recognition from videos. In particular, we defined a process of *detection by tracking*. Steps of the process can be summarized as follows:

1. Randomly spread particles over a region (or regions) of interest.
2. Relocate and re-weight particles by means of diffusion (as in the Condensation framework [5]). Particles are expected to converge to face areas over a few video frames.
3. Automatically cluster the particles after some given number of frames.
4. Evaluate particle clusters as face candidates.
5. Assign faces to existing tracks or launch new tracks.

The resulting detection by tracking is a process that extends over a few video frames, as opposed to classical detection approaches, which operate on a single frame. For the purpose of initializing the face detector, regions of interest can be pre-defined accordingly to a specific application. They could be defined, e.g. adjacently to entrance areas of a building etc. In particular, regions of interest may cover the whole video frame. Particle spread (initialization) can be triggered off by an external event, e.g. with the use of a door-open sensor or cyclically, e.g. every 5 seconds. For the purpose of automatic clustering, we applied a modified X-Means algorithm. For the purpose of face image normalization, we proposed a fast *dust filtering* procedure. More details on the processes of face detection and face tracking within the proposed framework can be found in [12, 13]. The process of face recognition was mainly described in [13].

The detected and track-assigned faces are tracked over a sequence. The problem of initial face-to-track assignment will be discussed later. The tracking process is realized within the Condensation framework [5] and with the use of motion modeling. Particles assigned to a given cluster, i.e. particles tracking a single given face, share a motion model. The primary role of the tracker is to provide normalized face regions to the recognition module and provide track consistency, i.e. ensure that faces extracted from successive frames are linked to each other as belonging to the same individual moving in the video. Providing track consistency in case of single person in the scene is straightforward. However, when multiple persons are considered and track crossing and mutual occlusions occur, the tracks are likely to *skip* between the individuals. Such problems should be automatically resolved, as described further. The tracker can be initialized by means of the detection by tracking or by any external face detector.

Within the proposed framework, the tracked faces are subject to a face recognition procedure that utilizes particle-related local face features previously extracted for the purpose of tracking. The recognition procedure is applied in a closed-set identification scenario, i.e. it is assumed that all individuals present in the input video are registered users of the system. The recognition procedure outputs a ranking of identities for each tracked face. Identities are sorted by the level of similarity to the tracked faces on a per-frame as well as multiple-frame basis. These rankings can then be used as a supporting clue for tracking corrections, as presented in the following sections of this paper. The general structure of the detect-track-recognize framework is depicted in Fig. 1.

The proposed framework achieved the maximal speed of 31 ms per frame when one individual in an identity verification scenario was considered. Tracking and recognition in a 10-user closed set experiment required 85 ms per frame.

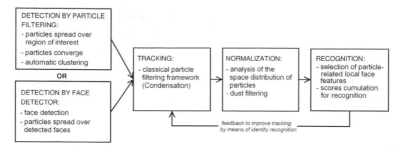

Fig. 1. Structure of the particle filtering-based face detect-track-recognize framework. Particle related information is utilized throughout the sequence: from the detection phase, through the tracking and normalization phases, to the recognition phase. The feedback from recognition can be used to improve tracking quality.

The minimum speed of 5 fps is regarded as sufficient for handling *normal* head motions [7]. The given processing times were achieved with input frames of size 320×240 pixels on a PC Intel Core 2 Duo E6750, 2.67 GHz with 2.00 GB RAM. Further optimizations, particularly by means of parallelization, are possible.

2.2   Motion Modeling

In the simple case of one face in the scene, the initialized particle filtering-based tracker is able to track a face without a deterministic motion model and random diffusion suffices. However, in order to provide tracking consistency in more demanding situations, the tracker should utilize a motion model. Tracking of face candidate regions within our framework is based on a tracking history and predictions of the candidate locations in successive video frames. Predictions are derived from the motion model with the use of the tracking history, which stores face regions previously normalized with the use of the dust filtering procedure, namely

$$\hat{R}(0) = \hat{R}(-1) + (\hat{R}(-1) - \hat{R}(-2)) + \varepsilon(0), \tag{1}$$

where $\varepsilon(t)$ is an i.i.d. zero-mean noise, and new location of a candidate region $\hat{R}(0)$ is based on past locations of the respective (dust filtering-normalized) face region $\hat{R}(t)$, where $t < 0$ denotes previous frames. This simple prediction procedure is sufficient to overcome the problem of face-to-track assignment in many cases of crossing tracks. It has been shown [6], that using e.g. high order autoregressive models may lead to over-fitting, which deteriorates tracking quality.

2.3   Face-to-Track Assignment and Track Management

Multi-face scenarios result in additional difficulty of assigning detected faces to tracks. It must be decided whether the detected faces are re-detections of already tracked faces or they are new faces for which new tracks should be created (initialized). To solve the face-to-track assignment problem optimally, all detected faces must be compared to all existing tracks. We applied the auction algorithm by Bertsekas [2] to solve this task. It has been found that the auction algorithm is the most efficient method so far to reach the optimal or sub-optimal solution *without any practical difference* [3]. However, in our application, where the number of new faces detected over a sequence is low, and thus assignment conflicts appear rarely, simple cross-comparison between faces and tracks is on average as computationally expensive as the auction algorithm.

For the purpose of assignment, a match score between a face and a track must be defined. We utilize rectangle bounding box as a representation of a face area and define the face-to-track match score as the normalized overlap area between normalized detected face area (*where the face is observed to be*) and the predicted position of the face (*where the face is expected to be*). The match scores determine a ranking of face-to-track assignments. If the match score is above a pre-defined threshold, the detected face is considered a re-detection and used to refine a respective track. If the match score falls below the threshold, the face is considered a new face appearing in the scene and a new track is created.

As a result of such procedure, some false tracks, i.e. duplicated tracks for already tracked faces, may be created. This may particularly happen when the tracker prediction or the face detection is inaccurate (e.g. due to a rapid motion change). In such cases, the track duplications should shortly get merged with the *correct* tracks, since successive measurements (in particular, the dust filtering normalization procedure) will operate on the same image regions for both the correct tracks and the duplicated tracks. Track merging is constantly monitored over a sequence and if the merge lasts *long enough,* one of the tracks – the track with a shorter history – is erased.

In ideal conditions, faces detected in a video sequence are *observed* in every successive video frame until they leave the scene. However, due to tracking errors and/or other scene interference such as occlusions, faces can become temporarily unobservable. This leads to *disruptions* of the tracks, i.e. situations, when the actual face location cannot be retrieved (measured) from the frame and thus only the predicted location can be used. Each track must be sustained over the disruptions, so that, after the face reappears in the video, it can be correctly tracked without loosing all its track history. How long may the track exist before erasing – without actual feedback measured from the video – is a track property, which we simply call *time-to-live* (TTL). The maximal TTL value is an application dependent parameter. We propose a simple policy of TTL management: a new track (at its creation) is given a TTL equal to some allowed period of disruption of a track. When new frames are available, each track is getting *older* and thus its TTL is, by default, decreased by 1. Only when a valid face region is found by the tracker, i.e. the dust filtering procedure returns a valid normalized face area, the track is *revitalized* by increasing TTL by 2 as long as the maximal TTL value is not reached. If TTL falls to 0, the track is erased (*killed*) and its descriptor may be used in the future without any reference to the historical descriptor (i.e. reusing the descriptor does not mean that the same individual is tracked). The initial TTL value is not the maximal TTL value. This realizes the idea that the more track measurements are available, the more *disruption-resistant* the track should be. If the track creation is based only on a single measurement it is not likely to be persistent, unless confirmed by new measurements. Consequently, falsely created tracks that are not duplications of actual tracks (e.g. tracks created as a result of false face detection) are sustained only for a short period of time, since their initial TTL quickly falls to 0. *Cycle of life* used for the track management by means of TTL is depicted in Fig. 2.

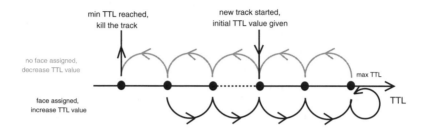

Fig. 2. The track life cycle driven by TTL parameter

3   Tracking Corrections by Means of Identity Recognition

3.1   Considered Scenario

The following target scenario of the proposed system is considered: a camera is installed over a security gate and observes persons approaching the gate-secured zone. The approaching persons are automatically tracked and their identities are recognized. If the recognition is successful and an individual is recognized as permitted to cross the gate, the gate opens automatically for the individual. If the recognition fails, the individual must use another authentication method to open the gate, e.g. use his/her chip card, enter a PIN or be subject to a precise biometric recognition (including face recognition from a still image). Groups of individuals are allowed. Individuals can behave naturally and should only not be intentionally uncooperative, e.g. by turning their heads away or by obscuring the face [8].

3.2   Tracking Corrections Mechanism

The tracking module is responsible for providing consistent tracks of individuals, which are then subjected to the recognition process [13]. Track consistency is provided by means of motion modeling and face-to-track assignments. However, there exist possible face-to-track assignment conflicts which cannot be correctly resolved by means of motion analysis only. Such conflicts may occur when different tracks cross each other resulting in occlusions and, particularly, when the motion pattern of the occluded individual changes rapidly during the occlusion. The output of the recognition module can then be used to support the tracking module in order to restore correct tracking after the occlusion.

The described type of conflicts may appear frequently in the considered scenario of a group of individuals moving toward a camera and along the camera's view axis. When the occluded subject reappears in the camera view, but does not actually cross the track of another individual (motion pattern change), motion-based prediction is likely to swap tracks. Note that in some applications, tracking is employed as an effective way to detect subjects, e.g. to detect whether an individual entered a restricted zone. In such cases, frame track swapping may not pose a problem. However, when the track history is to be kept, e.g. for analyzing visitor/customer motion patterns or to cumulate identity-relevant data for the purpose of *strong* identification from video, track swapping may lead to false conclusions.

Here we propose an identity-based support mechanism to resolve face-to-track assignment conflicts. The mechanism can be applied within the previously proposed face detect-track-recognize framework [13]. As it was described above, face-to-track assignment is based on the ranking of face-to-track match scores, which are a result of utilizing a motion model. When face-to-track assignment is not obvious, i.e. multiple faces *compete* for a given track (typical for new face appearing or reappearing in the scene) or multiple tracks *compete* for a given face (typical for occlusion), then several face-track pairs take close positions in the ranking. If the scores of successive face-track pairs in the ranking are *too close* to each other a reliable assignment cannot be done. In such cases, the supporting mechanism of identity-based conflict resolution can be launched, namely

$$\text{for any } i, j \ (i \neq j):$$
$$M(track_*, face_i) - M(track_*, face_j) < th_M$$
$$\Downarrow$$
$$\text{assign } track_* \text{ with the use of identity clue,}$$

where $track_*$ is the track to be assigned, $face_i$ and $face_j$ are (competing) face candidates to be assigned to the track, $M(track_*, face_i)$ is the *match score* for the given track-face pair, and th_M is the threshold for launching identity-based assignment resolution mechanism. The analogous rule is applied for the case of multiple tracks competing for one face.

Identity-based assignment consists in building a subranking of faces (face identities) per given track. Subranking positions are determined by a distance between the currently extracted face (to be assigned to a track) and the template corresponding to the last validly assigned face for the given track, namely

$$face \text{ position in subranking for } track \propto D(face, track_{\text{last}}), \qquad (2)$$

where $D(f_1, f_2)$ is a distance between two face representations f_1 and f_2, $face$ is the currently extracted face, which is to be assigned to a track, and $track_{\text{last}}$ denotes the stored template corresponding to the last validly assigned face for the given track. Unassigned faces are used to initialize new tracks.

As a result of applying identity-based correction, the average tracking quality (tracking consistency) is improved. Cost of the improvement is extension of processing time whenever conflicts occur – identity-based resolution is launched only when motion-based assignment cannot be done reliably. In the case of conflict, identity-based face-to-track assignment precedes identity score cumulation for the purpose of identity recognition over a video sequence. The idea of the identity-based face-to-track assignment mechanism applied to a sample video is depicted in Fig. 3.

(a) Three individuals approach camera. Subject *A* is going to hide behind subject *B*.

(b) Tracks *A* and *B* compete for face in the frame. By motion analysis two subjects are almost equally probable at this position. Identity-clue results in assigning track *B*.

(c) Subject *A* reappears from behind subject *B*. By identity-based assignment tracks *A* and *B* are correctly restored/continued.

(d) All subjects are further tracked with the use of motion modeling only.

Fig. 3. Identity recognition-supported tracking. With the use of identity clue, faces can be correctly assigned to their tracks even when motion-based assignment may fail.

4   Conclusions

The conceptual extension of the previously presented [13] face detect-track-recognize framework is proposed. The particle filtering-based framework provides mechanisms of face detection, tracking and building identity rankings in closed set scenario for every face in every video frame. The extension proposed in this paper utilizes results of face recognition for the purpose of improving tracking quality in case of multiple persons in the scene. This is opposed to classical approaches, where the recognition module consumes output of the tracking module, but not conversely. As a result, the tracking module and the recognition module operate in a feedback loop.

Future research on the proposed approach includes the statistical evaluation of tracking corrections by means of identity recognition and the possibilities of implementing the method within other track-recognize frameworks. Other frameworks would particularly mean non particle filtering-based solutions and classical face recognition approaches, such as e.g. principal component analysis [11,15], which are known to provide good recognition results [7], but, on the other hand, require well aligned input data and are more computationally demanding than the proposed framework. The use of last validly assigned faces extracted directly from the processed video, instead of using the corresponding stored templates, should also be considered. Such approach imposes additional difficulties about providing good face image quality, but can result in straightforward extension of the solution beyond the closed-set scenario, namely tracked individuals would not have to be registered users of the system and a *self-similarity* based approach could be employed to improve tracking quality.

References

1. Acosta, E., Torres, L., Albiol, A., Delp, E.: An automatic face detection and recognition system for video indexing applications. In: Proc. IEEE International Conference on Acoustics, Speech, and Signal Processing, vol. 4, pp. 3644–3647 (2002)
2. Bertsekas, D.P., Castanon, D.A.: The auction algorithm for the transportation problem. Technical report LIDS-P-1850, Laboratory for Information and Decision Systems, M.I.T. (February 1989)
3. Cai, Y., de Freitas, N., Little, J.J.: Robust visual tracking for multiple targets. In: Leonardis, A., Bischof, H., Pinz, A. (eds.) ECCV 2006. LNCS, vol. 3954, pp. 107–118. Springer, Heidelberg (2006)
4. Hjelmas, E., Low, B.K.: Face detection: A survey. Computer Vision and Image Understanding 83, 236–274 (2001)
5. Isard, M., Blake, A.: Condensation-conditional density propagation for visual tracking. International Journal of Computer Vision 29, 5–28 (1998)
6. Lei, Y., Ding, X., Wang, S.: AdaBoost tracker embedded in adaptive particle filtering. In: Proc. 18th International Conference on Pattern Recognition (ICPR '06), pp. 939–943 (2006)
7. Li, S.Z., Jain, A.K. (eds.): Handbook of Face Recognition. Springer, Heidelberg (2005)

8. McKenna, S., Gong, S.: Non-intrusive person authentication for access control by visual tracking and face recognition. In: Bigün, J., Borgefors, G., Chollet, G. (eds.) AVBPA 1997. LNCS, vol. 1206, pp. 177–184. Springer, Heidelberg (1997)
9. Moeslund, T.B., Granum, E.: A survey of computer vision-based human motion capture. Computer Vision and Image Understanding 81, 231–268 (2001)
10. Rowley, H.A., Baluja, S., Kanade, T.: Neural network-based face detection. IEEE Transactions on Pattern Analysis and Machine Intelligence 20(1), 23–38 (1998)
11. Shlens, J.: A tutorial on principal components analysis. Technical report, Institute for Nonlinear Science, University of California, San Diego (December 2005)
12. Stasiak, L., Pacut, A.: Particle filtering in multilevel color context for face detection and tracking in real-time video sequences. In: Proc. 42nd Annual IEEE International Carnahan Conference on Security Technology, ICCST, Prague, Czech Republic (October 2008)
13. Stasiak, L., Pacut, A., Vincente-Garcia, R.: Face tracking and recognition in low quality video sequences with the use of particle filtering. In: Proc. 43rd Annual 2009 IEEE International Carnahan Conference on Security Technology, ICCST, Zurich, Switzerland (October 2009)
14. Sung, K.-K., Poggio, T.: Example-based learning for view-based human face detection. IEEE Transactions on Pattern Analysis and Machine Intelligence 20, 39–51 (1998)
15. Turk, M.A., Pentland, A.P.: Eigenfaces for recognition. Journal of Cognitive Neuroscience 3(1), 71–86 (1991)
16. Viola, P., Jones, M.: Rapid object detection using a boosted cascade of simple features. In: Proc. IEEE International Conference on Computer Vision and Pattern Recognition, vol. 1, pp. 511–518 (2001)
17. Yang, J., Waibel, A.: Tracking human faces in real-time. Technical report, CMU-CS-95-210, School of Computer Science, Carnegie Mellon University, Pittsburgh (November 1995)
18. Yang, M.-H., Kriegman, D.J., Ahuja, N.: Detecting faces in images: A survey. IEEE Transactions on Pattern Analysis and Machine Intelligence 24, 34–58 (2002)

Analytical Simulation of Non-planar B-Spline Surfaces Deformation

Manuel González-Hidalgo, Antoni Jaume-i-Capó,
Arnau Mir, and Gabriel Nicolau-Bestard

Computer Graphics, Vision and Artificial Intelligence Group. Maths. and Computer
Science Dept. University of the Balearic Islands, Spain
manuel.gonzalez@uib.es, antoni.jaume@uib.es, arnau.mir@uib.es,
gabriel.nicolau@gmail.com
http://dmi.uib.es/~ugiv/

Abstract. A method to deform non-planar parametric surfaces based
on B-splines is presented. To develop this method, an energy functional
and its variational formulation are introduced. The deformation of the
non-planar surface is made moving the control points of the surface. In
order to do that, the space will be discretized and a ordinary differential
equation has to be solved. To do it, an analytical solution will be used
taking into account the features of B-splines as a finite elements. Our
method will be fast because only a reduced number of control points will
be moved instead of all the surface points. So, our method can be used
to make simulations.

Keywords: Computer graphics, surface deformation, finite elements,
B-splines.

1 Introduction

The deformation models include a large number of applications, and they have
been used in fields as edge detection, computer animation, geometric modelling,
and so on.

This work can be viewed as a continuation of the work [5] where the deformation of a planar surfaces, using an analytical solution of the associated ststem
of differential equations, is introduced and developed. So, the same deformation
model of the work [5] is used in this work. The main difference between the two
works is the type of deformed surfaces we perform. In this previous work, a planar surfaces are deformed but in this work, we will deform non-planar surfaces
as a half sphere.

First of all, a deformation model will be introduced that uses B-splines as
finite elements. The model includes deformation equation, its analytical solution,
examples of deformations and computational cost.

Höllig was the first that introduces the use of B-splines and their properties as
finite elements. Our deformation model is similar to the model introduced in [1].
In that work, the deformation model is solved using classical finite elements
(triangles and squares). In our work, we use B-splines finite elements instead.

F.J. Perales and R.B. Fisher (Eds.): AMDO 2010, LNCS 6169, pp. 213–223, 2010.

Classical finite elements are commonly used to solve models that involves partial differential equations but it implies big data structures. On the other hand, the use of B-splines as finite elements reduces the data structure of the model. Moreover, our model has the advantage that we can solve it analitically.

2   B-Splines

The B-splines are piecewise polynomial functions with a good local aproximations for smooth function and local support [11]. Uniform B-splines are introduced in [3], [4], [11] and [9]. The chosen definition is given in [9]:

Definition 1. *An uniform B-spline of degree* n, b^n, *is defined by the following recurrence formula:*

$$b^n(x) = \int_{x-1}^x b^{n-1}(t)dt$$

starting with $b^0(x) = \begin{cases} 1, & x \in [0,1), \\ 0, & otherwise. \end{cases}$ *[9]*

To evaluate the B-splines in a simple form and fast computationally, we use the following recurrence equation (De Boor [3] and Cox [2]).

$$b^n(x) = \frac{x}{n}b^{n-1}(x) + \frac{(n+1-x)}{n}b^{n-1}(x-1) \tag{1}$$

The finite element base of B-splines is defined upon a grid $h\mathbb{Z} = \{..., -2h, h, 0, h, 2h, ...\}$, where h is the scaled step:

Definition 2. *The transformation for* $h > 0$ *and* $k \in \mathbb{Z}$ *is* $b^n_{k,h}(x) = b^n(\frac{x}{h} - k)$. *The support of this function is* $[k, k+n+1)h$

The generalization to more dimensions can be performed in the following way: The N-variate B-spline of degree $\mathbf{n} = (n_1, ..., n_N)$, of index $\mathbf{k} = (k_1, ..., k_N)$ and the space discretization $\mathbf{h} = (h_1, ..., h_N)$ is defined as

$$B^{\mathbf{n}}_{\mathbf{k},\mathbf{h}}(\mathbf{x}) = \prod_{i=1}^N b^{n_i}_{k_i,h_i}(x_i). \tag{2}$$

The support of this function is $\prod_{i=1}^N [k_i, k_i + n_i + 1)h_i$.

The derivatives of B-splines can be computed easily as it is shown in [5].

A B-spline parametric surface is a linear combination function of the B-spline functions base: $S : \Omega \subset \mathbb{R}^2 \to \mathbb{R}^3$ where

$$S(\mathbf{x}) = \sum_{\mathbf{k} \in \mathbb{Z}^2} P_{\mathbf{k}} B^{\mathbf{n}}_{\mathbf{k},\mathbf{h}}(\mathbf{x}). \tag{3}$$

(see [6] and [7]) where $P_{\mathbf{k}}$ are the so called the *control points* and they are the elements that determine the B-spline surface.

3   Proposed Model

Let E the following energy functional: $E : \Phi(S) \to \mathbb{R}, \; S \mapsto E(S)$,

$$
E(S) = \int_{\Omega} \left(\omega_{10} \left| \frac{\partial S}{\partial u} \right|^2 + \omega_{01} \left| \frac{\partial S}{\partial v} \right|^2 + \omega_{11} \left| \frac{\partial S}{\partial u \partial v} \right|^2 \right.
$$

$$
\left. + \omega_{20} \left| \frac{\partial^2 S}{\partial u^2} \right|^2 + \omega_{02} \left| \frac{\partial^2 S}{\partial v^2} \right|^2 + \mathcal{P}(S(u,v)) \right) du\, dv,
$$

where $\Phi(S)$ is the set of all B-spline parametric surfaces, Ω is the domain of the surface S and $\mathcal{P}$ is a potential of the forces that works on the surface. ([12], [1], [10])

Our goal is to achieve the minimum of the previous functional using an evolution model. This minimum depends on the initial surface and the used evolution model.

Using the equations of Euler-Lagrange, it can be proved [1] that an energy local minimum must satisfy:

$$
-\omega_{10} \frac{\partial^2 S}{\partial u^2} - \omega_{01} \frac{\partial^2 S}{\partial v^2} + 2\omega_{11} \frac{\partial^4 S}{\partial u^2 \partial v^2} + \omega_{20} \frac{\partial^4 S}{\partial u^4} \tag{4}
$$

$$
+ \omega_{02} \frac{\partial^4 S}{\partial v^4} = -\nabla \mathcal{P}(S(u,v)) + \text{boundary conditions}
$$

The surface domain is $\Omega = [0,1]^2$. Let S_0 be the initial surface or the surface to be deformed. There are four boundary conditions that corresponds to the four "fixed" edges of our surface domain: $S(u,0) = S_0(u,0)$, $S(u,1) = S_0(u,1)$, $S(0,v) = S_0(0,v)$ and $S(1,v) = S_0(1,v)$. For example, if S_0 is a plane, the previous boundary conditions will be: $S(u,0) = (u,0,0)$, $S(u,1) = (u,1,0)$, $S(0,v) = (0,v,0)$, $S(1,v) = (1,v,0)$.

The next step is to develop the variational formulation of our problem and to discretize the equation to solve (see [5] for details).

At the end, the following differential equation has to be solved:

$$
M \frac{d^2 P_i}{dt^2} + C \frac{dP_i}{dt} + A P_i = L_i, \; i = 1, 2, 3. \tag{5}
$$

which corresponds to our dynamic evolution model. The matrix M is the mass matrix, C is the damping matrix, A is the stiffness matrix and L_i is the applied force on the surface.

The mass matrix M and the damping matrix C are diagonal and constant during all the time evolution.

The previous differential equation (5) can be solved analitically with a computational cost of order $O(\mathbf{N}^2)$, where $\mathbf{N} \times \mathbf{N}$ are the dimensions of matrix A. (see [5] for details).

4   Computation of the Control Points of the Initial Surface

In this section, we are going to find the control points associated to a initial surface F. That is, if the spatial components of F are $F(\mathbf{x}) = (X(\mathbf{x}), Y(\mathbf{x}), Z(\mathbf{x}))$, where $\mathbf{x} \in \Omega = [0,1]^2$, we want to find control points $P_\mathbf{k}$ such that:

$$S_0(\mathbf{x}) = \sum_{\mathbf{k} \in \mathbb{Z}^2} P_\mathbf{k} B_{\mathbf{k},\mathbf{h}}^\mathbf{n}(\mathbf{x}), \qquad (6)$$

and the difference between $F(\mathbf{x})$ and $S_0(\mathbf{x})$ has to be as small as possible.

The set of the previous sumation indexes is $\mathcal{M} = \{-n_x, \ldots, M_1\} \times \{-n_y, \ldots, M_2\}$. This set gives us the B-splines bases we use in order to find the control points.

These control points are found solving the linear system of equations $S_0(\mathbf{x_j}) = F(\mathbf{x_j})$, where the points $\mathbf{x}_j$ are chosen in Ω, $j = 1, 2, \ldots, (M_1 + n_x + 1) \cdot (M_2 + n_y + 1)$ and the unknowns are the control points. The previous linear system of equations takes the form $A \cdot P = b$, where $A = (B_{\mathbf{i},\mathbf{j}}^\mathbf{n}(\mathbf{x_j}))_{\mathbf{i},\mathbf{j} \in \mathcal{M}}$, P is the vector of control points and b is the vector of independent terms. For every component of the control points, we have a linear system of equation as the previous one where the matrix A is the same for all the components and the vector b is: $b = (X(\mathbf{x}_j))$,

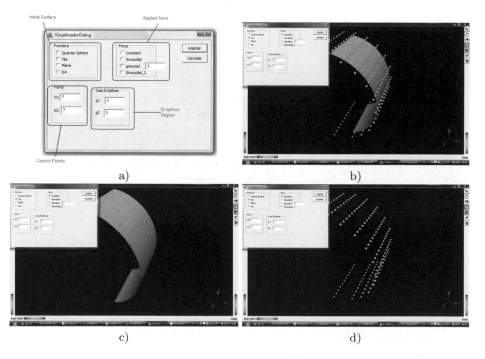

Fig. 1. General appearance of the application showing the Coin3D/OpenInventor window with different options enabled. The initial menu is also shown.

for the first component, $b = (Y(\mathbf{x}_j))$, for the second component and $b = (Z(\mathbf{x}_j))$, for the third component.

5   Surface and Deformations Representation

In order to simplify the user interaction, the surface representation and the application of a deformation, we need some graphic representation system. For this purpose a WYSIWYG environment has been developed.

The most extended API used to develop 2D and 3D graphics applications is OpenGL. With this environment, it is possible to implement interactive graphical applications in an easy way and it is developed strictly for graphics [8], being this a good reason to choose it. OpenInventor is an OpenGL based API, with it the representation of complex scenes and the development of complex visualization applications becomes more simple than using only OpenGL. In fact, it is the standard *de facto* 3D Computer Graphics API for complex visualization

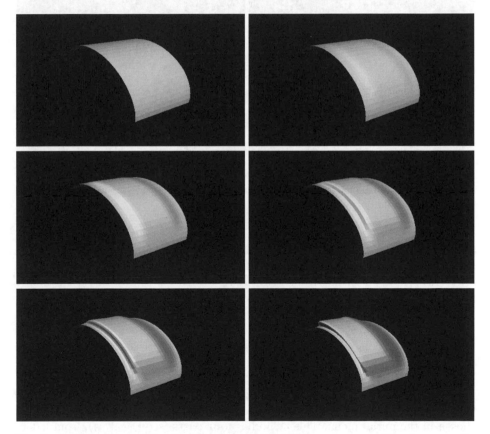

Fig. 2. Five iterations of a deformation of a half cylinder are shown. The figure on the upper left is the initial surface. The deformation was made using a constant force in the direction $(1, 4, 1)$ with all boundaries fixed.

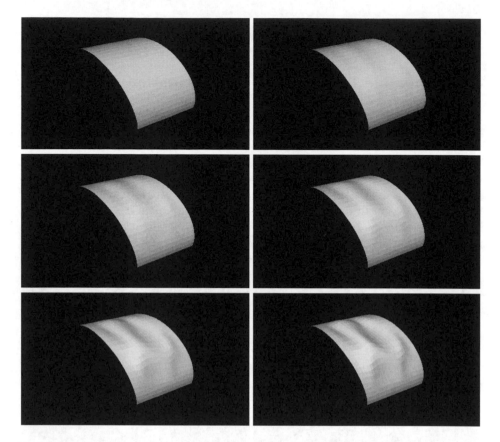

Fig. 3. Five iterations of a deformation of a half cylinder are shown. The figure on the upper left is the initial surface. The deformation was made using a constant sinusoidal force with all boundaries fixed.

applications [13], [14], unfortunately, the evolution of OpenInventor has been different from the evolution of OpenGL. The only way to have it available was under proprietary licensing from TGS (*Template Graphics Software*), but finally Silicon Graphics has released an open source specification.

In this work, we have used Coin3D an open source OpenInventor derived API, fully compatible with the original specification. Moreover, Coin3D brings the possibility to integrate a great powerful scene representation engine with a platform-independent interface which can be integrated in a broad range of windows environments (Windows, XWindow System, Aqua, and more).

In figure 1 several views of the developed application can be seen. The surface to be deformed and the force that defines the deformation to apply to it are chosen in the initial menu. This menu has four parts (see Fig. 1.a)), from left to right and from to top to bottom one can choose the initial surface, the force to apply, the number of control points of the surface and the B-splines degree. The default number of control points is 7 and the default degree of B-splines is 3.

Once the options are chosen, a window opens. This is the Coin3D examinator viewer. There are three keyboard buttons: the button s that enables or disables the display of the surface, the button p that enables or disables the display of the control points and, finally the button n that performs one step in the evolution model of the deformation. The three states that can be obtained with the buttons s and p in surface visualization can be seen in the figure 1. Our application allows to save the obtained images in such a way that a video of the deformation can be performed.

The data needed to implement the model involves the B-spline shape to be deformed but also requires the data describing the way in which the deformation has to be done. This can be supplied in two ways: requesting the information directly to the user via the graphical interface and accessing to files describing the data. There are two kinds of data files, one describing the B-Spline shape (the control points, the degree, and so on), and the other one describing the data

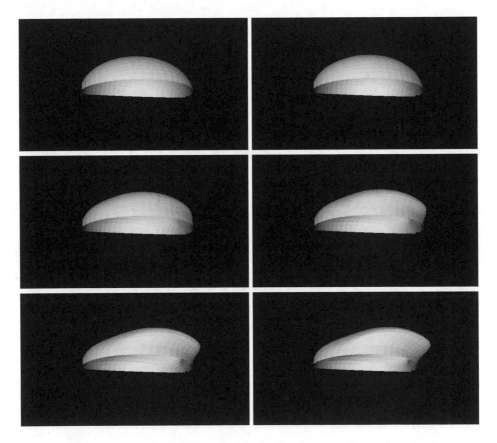

Fig. 4. Five iterations of a deformation of a half sphere are shown. The figure on the upper left is the initial surface. The deformation was made using a constant force in the direction $(1, 4, 1)$ with all boundaries fixed.

related with the deformation, that is the forces to be applied to the shape in order to deform it, the boundary conditions and the parameters ω_{ij}, $i, j = 0 \div 2$.

6   Numerical Examples

In this section, we show several examples of deformations using the model presented in the previous section. The applied forces are constant along time, because this condition is necessary for the analytical solution. If this is not the case we should use the numerical solution that can be found in previous work [7]. We have applied our model to three well-known surfaces: a tile, a half cylinder and a half sphere, all these surfaces parametrized on the square $[0, 1]^2$. Moreover we have considered different types of boundary conditions. On one hand we have considered all the boundaries fixed, and secondly, only a part of the boundary is

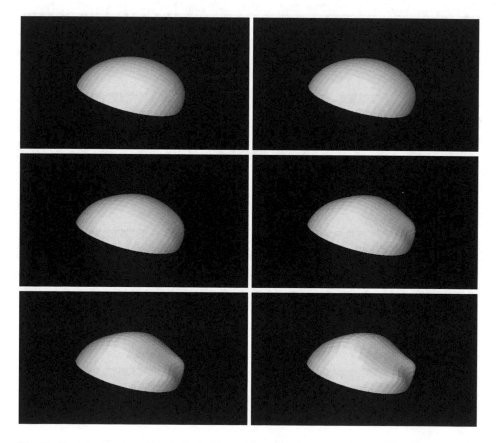

Fig. 5. Five iterations of a deformation of a half sphere are shown. The figure on the upper left is the initial surface. The deformation was made using a constant sinusoidal force with all boundaries fixed.

fixed. In previous works, in order to validate the proposed method, the deformed surface was a plane defined on the $[0, 1]^2$ domain with all the boundaries fixed.

The first step of our algorithm is to compute the control point of the considered surface as it is explained in section 4. Next, we have to set the energy functional parameters of our deformation. These are $\omega_{10} = \omega_{01} = 0.1$ and $\omega_{11} = \omega_{20} = \omega_{02} = 0.01$.

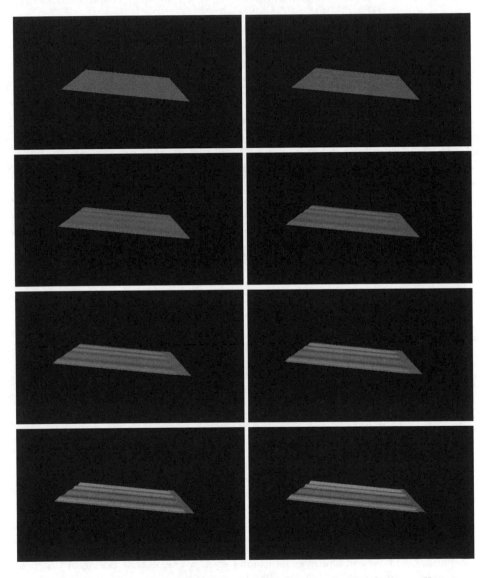

Fig. 6. Five iterations of a deformation of a plane are shown. The figure on the upper left is the initial surface. The deformation was made using the following sinusoidal force $(\sin(4\pi x), \cos(10\pi x)\cos(10\pi y), 2\sin(10\pi y))$ and only one part of boundary is fixed.

In the experiments of figures 2, 4, 3 and 5, $N_1 \times N_2 = 49$ control points are considered and bicubic B-splines are used.

In figures 2 and 4, the deformation of a half cylinder and a half sphere can be seen using a constant force in direction $(1, 4, 1)$ and module 42.42 and all fixed boundaries.

In figures 3 and 5, the deformation of the same kind of surfaces can also be seen using the following sinusoidal force $(\sin(4\pi x), \sin(4\pi y), \cos(4\pi x)\cos(4\pi y))$, $\mathbf{x} = (x, y) \in [0, 1]^2$ and all fixed boundaries.

Last experiment presented in this work is based on the change of the boundary conditions. Now, the plane has got free part of its boundary. The plane has $N_1 \times N_2 = 108$ control points that can be evolved. The applied force is $(\sin(4\pi x), \cos(10\pi x)\cos(10\pi y), 2\sin(10\pi y))$, $\mathbf{x} = (x, y) \in \Omega$.

7   Conclusions and Future Work

A model which allows deformations of B-splines parametric surfaces are introduced. This model includes the variational formulation, the analytical solution of the corresponding differential equation and the computational cost.

To check the model, different kind of surfaces have been tested with different kind of applied forces and different boundary conditions. The experimental results show that the model is efficient and gives good deformations. All the examples has been made using C++ and Coin3D libraries.

For the time being, a non constant forces in time are studied. Moreover, we are working on another kind of surfaces, as parabolloids, ellipsoids and closed surfaces in general. Also, more boundary conditions will be considered.

Acknowledgements

This work is supported by the projects TIN2007-67993, ITADA, and TIN2007-67896, PINes, of the Spanish Government, with FEDER support. The authors would like to thank to the Department of Mathematics and Computer Science of University of the Balearic Islands.

References

1. Cohen, I.: Modèles Déformables 2-D et 3-D: Application à la Segmentation d'Images Médicales. PhD thesis, Université Paris IX, Dauphine (1992)
2. Cox, M.G.: The numerical evaluation of B -splines. IMA Journal of Applied Mathematic 10(2), 134–149 (1972)
3. de Boor, C.: A practical guide to splines. Springer, New York (1978)
4. Farin, G.: Curves and Surfaces for Computer-Aided Geometric Desing: A Practical Guide. Academic Press, London (1997)
5. González-Hidalgo, M., Jaume Capó, A., Mir, A., Nicolau-Bestardo, G.: Analytical simulation of B -spline surfaces deformation. In: Perales, F.J., Fisher, R.B. (eds.) AMDO 2008. LNCS, vol. 5098, pp. 338–348. Springer, Heidelberg (2008)

6. González-Hidalgo, M., Mir, A., Nicolau, G.: An evolution model of parametric surface deformation using finite elements based on B -splines. In: Proceedings of CompImage 2006 Conference, Computational Modelling of Objects Represented in Images: Fundamentals, Methods and Applications, Coimbra, Portugal (2006)
7. González-Hidalgo, M., Mir, A., Nicolau, G.: Dynamic parametric surface deformation using finite elements based on B-splines. International Journal for Computational Vision and Biomechanics 1(2), 151–611 (2008)
8. Hawkins, K., Astle, D.: OpenGL game programming. Course Technology PTR, 1st edn. (May 1, 2002); Premier Press (2004)
9. Höllig, K.: Finite element methods with B-splines. Frontiers in Applied Mathematics. SIAM, Philadelphya (2003)
10. Montagnat, J., Delingette, H., Ayache, N.: A review of deformable surfaces: topology, geometry and deformation. Image and Vision Computing 19(14), 1023–1040 (2001)
11. Piegl, W., Tiller, L.: The NURBS book. Springer Verlag, Berlin (1997)
12. Terzopoulos, D.: Regularization of inverse visual problems involving discontinuities. IEEE PAMI 8(4), 413–424 (1986)
13. Wernecke, J.: The Inventor Toolmaker: Extending Open Inventor, release 2. Addison–Wesley, Reading (1994)
14. Wernecke, J.: The Inventor Mentor: Programming Object–oriented 3D graphics with Open Inventor release 2. Addison–Wesley, Reading (1995)

3D Head Pose Estimation and Tracking Using Particle Filtering and ICP Algorithm*

Mahdi Ben Ghorbel[1], Malek Baklouti[2], and Serge Couvet[2]

[1] Electrical Engineering Program
King Abdullah University of Sciences and Technology,
Thuwal, Makkah Province, Saudi Arabia
mahdi.benghobel@kaust.edu.sa
[2] Thales Research Departement
Division of Security and Services Solutions
Osny , Val-d'Oise Department, France
{malek.baklouti,serge.couvet}@thalesgroup.com

Abstract. This paper addresses the issue of 3D head pose estimation and tracking. Existing approaches generally need huge database, training procedure, manual initialization or use face feature extraction manually extracted.

We propose a framework for estimating the 3D head pose in its fine level and tracking it continuously across multiple Degrees of Freedom (DOF) based on ICP and particle filtering. We propose to approach the problem, using 3D computational techniques, by aligning a face model to the 3D dense estimation computed by a stereo vision method, and propose a particle filter algorithm to refine and track the posteriori estimate of the position of the face.

This work comes with two contributions: the first concerns the alignment part where we propose an extended ICP algorithm using an anisotropic scale transformation. The second contribution concerns the tracking part. We propose the use of the particle filtering algorithm and propose to constrain the search space using ICP algorithm in the propagation step.

The results show that the system is able to fit and track the head properly, and keeps accurate the results on new individuals without a manual adaptation or training.

1 Introduction

Estimating and tracking the pose of the head accurately for a wide range of motion is an ongoing research concern. Thus, extensive research has been carried out in order to tackle this issue [1, 2, 3, 4]. However, existing approaches generally need a huge database, training procedure, manual initialization or use face feature extraction manually extracted. A global and generic approach is, hence, not in the picture yet.

The growth of computational capabilities together with the emergence of stereoscopic vision have opened new opportunities for the development of new approaches based on 3D computational techniques.

---

* This work is sponsored by King Abdullah University of Science and Technology (KAUST).

F.J. Perales and R.B. Fisher (Eds.): AMDO 2010, LNCS 6169, pp. 224–237, 2010.

In this paper, we are presenting our approach to tackle the head pose estimation in its fine level (i.e., granular) and track the pose continuously across multiple Degrees of Freedom (DOF). We propose to approach the problem by aligning a Candide face model to the 3D dense estimation computed by a stereo vision method. We propose, then, a particle filter algorithm to refine the posteriori estimate of the position of the face.

Two main contributions are presented in this work:

- (1) The first contribution concerns the alignment part. To align two point sets in a same scale, Iterative Closest Point (ICP) algorithm is an accurate and fast approach; however, the transformation is usually isotropic and hence, does not handle the face variability between persons. We propose to extend the ICP algorithm and apply an anisotropic scale transformation by using a scale matrix. More over, we introduce a weighting Gaussian function to enhance the convergence by focusing more on the nose region, thereby avoiding local minima convergence.
- (2) The second contribution concerns the tracking part. Over the last few years, particle filters have proved to be powerful tools for object tracking. In our approach, we propose to constrain the search space using ICP algorithm in the propagation step to produce the potential set of particles. The weightening of the particles is computed relying on the alignment error.

The paper is organized into three sections. Section 2 reviews previous works related to 3D face pose estimation as well as a small comparative analysis. The overview of our approach is detailed in section 3. The two contributions are then detailed respectively in section 4 and 5 along with the main results.

2   Related Works

In the literature, many researches have focused on head pose estimation. Murphy-Chutorian and Trivedi [17] present a comprehensive survey comparing the different

Table 1. Properties of different head pose estimation methods

Approach	References	Tps^1	Acc^2	$Dim.^3$	$Cont.^4$	$Lear.^5$	Res^6
Statistical methods	[5, 18, 19]	+ +	-	2D	C	Yes	H/L
Models methods	[2, 3, 4, 6, 9, 8]	-	+ +	3D/2D	F	Yes	H/L
Geometrical methods	[7]	+ +	- -	2D	F	No	H
Depth based methods	[10, 11, 12, 13, 14, 15, 16]	+	+ +	3D	F	Yes/No	H/L

----

(1). Computation speed : (++) very fast, (- -) very slow ;

(2). Accuracy : (++) accurate, (- -) inaccurate ;

(3). Dimensions : (3D) able to estimate the 3D pose, (2D) 2D estimation only;

(4). Continuity : (C) coarse estimation, (F) fine estimation ;

(5). Learning : Need of a learning procedure (Yes/No) ;

(6). image resolution : (H) High image quality needed, (H/L) can be used with high and low image quality;

approaches by focusing on their ability to estimate coarse and fine head pose. The survey highlights also the approaches that are well suited for unconstrained environments.

The different works can be regrouped into 3 classes regarding their approach : (1) using statistical/classification methods, (2) using geometrical methods, (3) using depth information.

Statistical methods use generally a similarity operator to compute the resemblance between an image of the head and a set of templates in different poses. The problem is viewed as a pattern classification problem. Many statistical tools have been used such as non-linear regression [1], Support Vector Regressors [18], neuronous networks [19], etc. Although the classification techniques are interesting, they are not generic enough because of the very large variability between different users (skin color, luminosity, and facial expressions).

Geometrical methods use geometric information like the configuration of facial landmarks. [7] uses geometrical constraints provided by the location of a certain key points to determine the pose of human faces. The pose of the face can be deduced using symmetry of the face and geometric relations between these points. Manifold Embedded Methods [2, 3, 4] and Flexible Methods [6] have also been extensively applied for head pose estimation.

This kind of approach requires the ability to extract reliably the characteristic data point which can be hard or not feasible in low resolution, high variations (profile view) or with occlusions.

The exploitation of the **depth information** brings new perspectives to tackle the problem of accurate head pose estimation (in its granular scale). Many works were proposed in this context. They generally use specific head model [13, 14, 15] or deduce the pose from the nose pose [10, 11]. These methods are very accurate and very fast(In [10], the mean rotation error is 2 to $2.5°$ while the mean translation error is 1 to 2 mm, the computing time is 18 ms). However, their approach requires a pre-processing step to design the model and depends highly on the quality and the speed of the disparity computation.

Table 1 gives a brief summary of the literature review. Using the depth information seems an interesting approach to address the problem of head pose estimation without requiring a database or a learning procedure. The following of this paper presents our approach.

3   Proposed Approach

The overall framework of our head pose estimation system is described in figure 1. In our development, we assume the head being a globally rigid 3D object whose pose is described by a total of six parameters $R(R_x, R_y, R_z)$ and $T(T_x, T_y, T_z)$. The framework can be break down into two parts: The first part consists in estimating the 3D points set using stereoscopic acquisition and the second one deals with aligning a simplified Candide-1 model with the 3D points set. Under alignement, the transformation matrix of the Candide model corresponds to the head pose parameters. We propose finally to track this alignment using particle filtering.

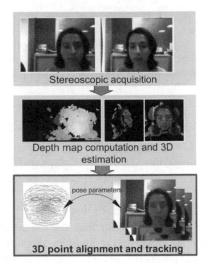

Fig. 1. Overview of the approach

The dense disparity map estimation is computed based on belief propagation inference algorithm. Previous work [20] shows good results regarding both accuracy and computational cost.

This paper details the second part of the framework. Let $M \in \mathbb{R}^{3 \times n}$ be the matrix containing the n point coordinates of the Candide model and $F \in \mathbb{R}^{3 \times n'}; n' > n$ the matrix containing the n' 3D head point set, where n' is usually bigger than n because of the 3d dense estimation. Estimating the head pose consists in finding the transformation f that aligns M to a subset of F. In the following, we will present and discuss:

- the initial pose estimation which consists in aligning at the initial step the 3D point set with the Candide model;
- the tracking of the pose initally estimated by adapting the particle filtering algorithm to our issue.

4   Initial Pose Estimation Using ICP

The initial pose estimation is computed by point-to-point mapping from the Candide model onto the 3D dense estimation of the face, where each point from the mask gets a correspondent point in the face.

The ICP (Iterative Closest Point) algorithm has widely been used for this issue. The mapping (or registration) is computed iteratively where in each step a new transformation is computed from a selection of the closest points as correspondences. ICP proved to be very effective as hence was used in many applications and many variants of ICP have been proposed [21, 22, 23, 24]. Usually, the modifications affect all phases of the algorithm from the selection and matching of points to the minimization strategy.

4.1   Classical Approach Using an Isotropic Transformation

Using ICP algorithm, the optimal transformation f that aligns M to a subset of F is iteratively estimated. Usually, to be scale independent, alignment approaches introduce a scale factor c and the transformation f is defined as in equation 1.

$$f: \quad \mathbb{R}^3 \quad \rightarrow \qquad \qquad \mathbb{R}^3$$
$$p \in M \mapsto \quad f(p) \in F \text{where} \qquad \qquad (1)$$
$$f(p) = c \times R \times p + T$$

Correspondence search: Algorithm 1 details the steps involved in ICP algorithm. The major steps in terms of complexity and performances are the correspondences search and error minimization.

In the literature, two criteria are generally used to determine the correspondences between points in two sets. The first criterion uses the euclidean distance as measure to map the closest points. The second criterion involves the surface particularities where each point is associated to the points whose tangent is the closest to the first one. We use the first criterion within a Kd-tree structure [25, 26] for an efficient computation cost.

Algorithm 1. Iterative Closest Point

Require: $M \in \mathbb{R}_{N*3}, F \in \mathbb{R}_{N'*3}$: two clouds to align;
    $R_{init}, T_{init}, c_{init}$: Initial transformation (by default no initial transformation);
Ensure: $R_{global}, T_{global}, c_{global}$ representing the global transformation;
1: $R_{global} \leftarrow R_{init}$, $T_{global} \leftarrow T_{init}, c_{global} \leftarrow c_{init}$
2: Build Kd-tree of the 3D points F : $Ftree \leftarrow Tree3D(F, 1)$
3: **while** $Error > threshold$ **do**
4:      Closest point search : $F^0 \leftarrow Closest\_Point(M, Ftree)$
5:      Error minimization : $(R, T, c) \leftarrow argmin\frac{1}{N}\sum_{i=1}^{N}||F_i^0 - (c \times R \times M_i + T)||^2$
6:      Error computation : $Error \leftarrow min\frac{1}{N}\sum_{i=1}^{N}||F0_i - (c \times R \times M_i + T)||^2$
7:      Update of the points set M : $M \leftarrow c \times R \times M + T$
8:      $R_{global} \leftarrow R \times R_{global}$
9:      $T_{global} \leftarrow c \times R \times T_{global} + T$
10:      $c_{global} \leftarrow c \times c_{global}$
11: **end while**
12: RETURN $(R_{global}, T_{global}, c_{global})$

Minimization procedure: In each iteration, the transformation is the error minimization argument. This minimization can be calculated using SVD [27], quaternions method [28,29] or orthonormal matrices [30]. [31] shows that these algorithms have similar performance and stability in presence of noise and outliers.

For isotropic transformation, the minimisation based on SVD decomposition works well [32]. The optimal transformation is obtained by equation 2.

$$\begin{cases} R = & U \times S \times V^T \\ c = & \frac{Trace(D \times S)}{\sigma_M^2} \\ T = \mu_F - c \times R \times \mu_M \end{cases} \qquad (2)$$

where

- μ_M and μ_F denote respectively the mean Vector of the model points in M and F;
- σ_M^2 and σ_F^2 denote respectively the model points and face points variance;
- Σ_{MF} the covariance between model points and face points;
- U and V are the Singular Value Decomposition (SVD) of the covariance matrix $\Sigma_{MF} = U \times D \times V^T$.

The results of this approach are shown in figure 3. We run this algorithm on synthetic data and a random transformation applied to a VRML head model that has been manually designed (figure 2(a)). The final transformation is then applied to the Candide mask (figure 2(b)). We obtained a mean alignment error of about 3.4 mm. We can conclude that while the algorithm globally converges, the alignment is not perfect in all directions. This is mainly due to the fact that a generic mask was used and the scale adaptation is done uniformly in all directions using the scale factor c. For instance, one can notice that the result is accurate in the horizontal direction but very bad in the vertical (forehead and chin zones) (figure 3(b)).

Here comes our first contribution in this work. We propose to extend the ICP algorithm and apply an anisotropic scale transformation. More over, we propose to introduce a weight matrix in the error computation step that enforces the contribution of the points in the nose region who detain more information about the head pose.

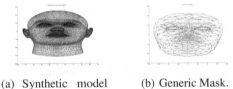

(a) Synthetic model representing the face.

(b) Generic Mask.

Fig. 2. Generic mask and synthetic model used in tests

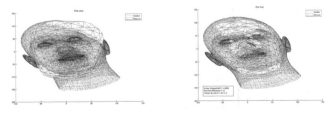

(a) Initial alignment between the model and the mask.

(b) Final alignment using ICP algorithm.

Fig. 3. Result of the ICP algorithm using synthetic data

4.2 Extended ICP Algorithm Using Anisotropic Transformation and Weighted Error Function

Obviously, when using a scalar for the scale adaptation as in equation 1, the scale transformation can only register two isotropic point sets. However, head shapes is highly variable and the scale transformation should be anisotropic to be generic. Our approach introduces a scale matrix C into the alignment problem to fit the head shape and thereby working on new individuals without a manual adaptation or training. The global transformation is given in equation 3.

$$f(p) = R \times C \times p + T \tag{3}$$

A similar approach was introduced in [33] but the mathematical developments shown here are easier and this approach will be included then in the tracking phase to construct a complete framework.

4.3 Mathematical Development

When introducing a scale matrix C, the solution provided earlier using SVD decomposition can not be used anymore. In this paper, we present one way to solve this optimization problem.

As mentionned before, the aim is to look for the optimal transformation minimizing the quadratic error function between the transformed 3D point of the Candide model and the 3D point set of the face (estimated by stereoscopic computation) $||f(p) - r||^2, r \in F$.

Equation 3 can be written as:

$$\widetilde{F} = X * \widetilde{M} + e \tag{4}$$

where e is a measure error and $\widetilde{F}$ and $\widetilde{M}$ defined as follow:

$$\begin{cases} X = \left(\begin{pmatrix} Bxx & Bxy & Bxz \\ Byx & Byy & Byz \\ Bzx & Bzy & Bzz \\ (0\ 0\ 0) \end{pmatrix} \begin{pmatrix} Tx \\ Ty \\ Tz \\ 1 \end{pmatrix} \right) \ ; \ B = R \times C \\[3em] \widetilde{F} = \begin{pmatrix} F_{1x} & F_{2x} & \dots & F_{Nx} \\ F_{1y} & F_{2y} & \dots & F_{Ny} \\ F_{1z} & F_{2z} & \dots & F_{Nz} \\ 1 & 1 & \dots & 1 \end{pmatrix} \\[3em] \widetilde{M} = \begin{pmatrix} M_{1x} & M_{2x} & \dots & M_{Nx} \\ M_{1y} & M_{2y} & \dots & M_{Ny} \\ M_{1z} & M_{2z} & \dots & M_{Nz} \\ 1 & 1 & \dots & 1 \end{pmatrix} \end{cases} \tag{5}$$

The optimal estimator using the mean square error criterion of the problem 4 is:

$$\widehat{X} = \widetilde{F} \times \widetilde{M}^T \times (\widetilde{M} \times \widetilde{M}^T)^{-1} \tag{6}$$

The estimator of X gives then the estimator $\widehat{B}$ as well as $\widehat{T}$. Using then the orthogonality constraints of R and the symetry of C, we can deduce the estimators of the matrix C and the Rotation R since:

$$B^T \times B = (R \times C)^T \times (R \times C) = C^T \times R^T \times R \times C = C^2 \tag{7}$$

Then:

$$\widehat{R} = \widehat{B} \times \widehat{C}^{-1} \tag{8}$$

Notice: The solution to equation 7 is not unique. Since R is a rotatin matrix then it satisfies $det(R) = 1$. This condition, injected in equation 7 implies that $det(C)$ and $det(B)$ have the same sign. The matrix C is computed, then, using the spectral decomposition of the matrix $B^T \times B$. Since $B^T \times B$ is a symmetric positive matrix, then, it exists an orthogonal matrix U and a diagonal matrix D verifying: The diagonal elements of D are the eigenvalues values of $B^T \times B$; they are positive. We order them in decreasing order $\lambda_1 \geq \lambda_2 \geq \lambda_3$. Taking into account the condition of same determinant sign, The estimator of C is deduced by the following formula:

$$\widehat{C} = \begin{cases} U * \begin{pmatrix} \sqrt{\lambda_1} & & \\ & \sqrt{\lambda_2} & \\ & & \sqrt{\lambda_3} \end{pmatrix} * U^T \; if \; det(B) > 0 \\[20pt] U * \begin{pmatrix} \sqrt{\lambda_1} & & \\ & \sqrt{\lambda_2} & \\ & & -\sqrt{\lambda_3} \end{pmatrix} * U^T \; if \; det(B) < 0 \end{cases} \tag{9}$$

To avoid local minima convergence, we have introduced a weightening function to emphasize the points that contain more information on the face orientation.

The weight matrix promotes pair points with high certitudes. For the case of the face, the nose region is the most distinguishable in depth computing. We used a Gaussian function centered on the nose as shown in figure 4.

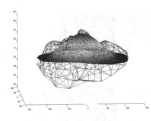

Fig. 4. Gaussian filter superposed to the generic mask

4.4   Results

Figure 5 shows the obtained results using this extended algorithm. We can notice that the alignment is more accurate in the different directions. The results of the weightening function are represented on figure 6. We tested this approach on real data using stereoscopic frames. The obtained results on different persons with different poses are shown on figure 7.

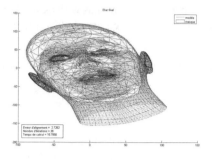

Fig. 5. Mask and model alignment using Extended ICP algorithm

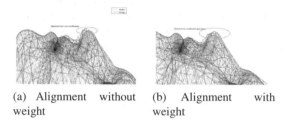

(a) Alignment without weight

(b) Alignment with weight

Fig. 6. Impact of the weights matrix on alignment results

Fig. 7. Alignment result using real data

5   Head Pose Tracking Using Particle Filtering

This part deals with the particle filtering algorithm. Once the initial pose estimation is computed, the aim is to track the face position in its fine level. In the literature, many approaches have been used but the most adapted for head pose are the probabilistic approaches based on Kalman filtering and Particle filtering. The Kalman filter is known by its efficiency in variant domains for dynamic systems tracking. It was demonstrated in [34] that it is the optimal tracker when the system verifies the Kalman hypothesis. In the case of vision tracking, these hypothesis are not verified because of the noise of registration. Thus, Kalman filter is not suitable. A new approach appeared which is Particle filtering [35, 36]. It is based on numerical simulations of the system evolution.

In tracking algorithms, the system is defined by two equations representing the dynamic evolution of the system state and the relation between the state and the observation. The following notations will be used in this paper:

– k the time step ;
– $X_{k;k=1..N}$ the system state (the unknown vector) ;
– $Z_{k;k=1..N}$ the observation vector (used to control the system by correcting the initial estimation).

Using these notations, the system can be defined using the Dynamic Evolution state and the Observation Equation as following:

– **Dynamic Evolution state**

$$X_{k+1} = f_k(X_k, u_k, W_k) \tag{10}$$

  f_k is a function that describes the dynamic model evolution (linear or non linear). u_k is a control term and W_k is a noise representing the errors of this model.
– **Observation Equation**

$$Z_k = g_k(X_k, V_k) \tag{11}$$

  g_k is the observation equation between state and measures. V_k is the measurements error.

The particle filtering approach consists in a stochastic simulation of the system evolution based on Monte Carlo simulations. It operates using three consecutive steps : (1) Propagation (2) Weighting (3) Re-sampling.

The propagation step consists in generating the particles that will represent the system's state based on equation 10. We propose in our approach to constrain the search space using ICP algorithm. Potential set of particles are then generated using ICP. This makes us avoiding random propagation and improve the overall alignment's precision. The total number of particles is also reduced making the system faster.

Regarding the weighting step of the particle filtering algorithm, the alignment error is used directly to estimate the weight. The weight represents the similarity of each particle to the real state of the system (which is inversely proportional to the alignment error). The state estimator can be then computed using a weighted sum of the particles or simply by affecting the particle which has the maximal weight ($X = \sum_{i=1}^{N} \omega^{(i)} * X_i$ or $X = X_{i_0}/\omega^{(i_0)} = \max_i(\omega^{(i)})$).

5.1   Results

Figure 8 shows the testing results on synthetic data. We applied a simulated transformation on the 3D point set and added numerical noise to these position to simulated the real conditions. We can notice that the system tracks the pose in the 3D transformations with an error which does not exceed 2° for rotations and 10 mm for translations. To ensure the validity of our approach, we tested our system on real data. Using stereoscopic acquisition, we track the position of the face; the results are shown in figure 9 at specific frames. These results show the effectiveness of our algorithm even using real noisy data. The 3D movements of the head were tracked accurately. Despite the errors that may exist in some frames, the system was able to adjust and catch up in the following frames.

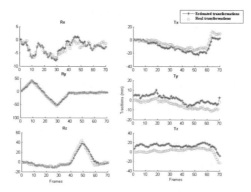

Fig. 8. Relative error between real and estimated transformation using Particle Filtering

Fig. 9. Results of head pose tracking using stereoscopic frames

6   Conclusion

Head pose estimation is a main research issue due to its important applications. Many limitations occur in the existent works such as the lack of genericity, the need of initialization and the dependence on training samples. In this paper, we propose an algorithm which estimates and tracks the head pose in 3D without pre-training or initialization.

The head pose estimation algorithm that we developed is based on aligning a generic Candide mask to the 3D point set reconstructed from stereoscopy computation. There are two main steps: In the first we proposed an extended version of the ICP algorithm to determine the initial pose. In the second, the particle filtering approach is adapted to track the head motion.

The principal contributions of our approach are the adaptation of the ICP Algorithm to use an anisotropic transformation by introducing a transformation matrix instead of a scalar scale adaptation. This generalization permits the use of the same generic mask with different faces and thereby fitting on new individuals without a manual adaptation or training.

The second contribution consists in including of the ICP algorithm in the Particle filtering, specifically, in the "Propagation" step to produce the potential set of particles. This approach leads to more efficient particles generation than the random propagation which permits the reduction of the number of particles.

We validated our approach using synthetic data as well as on real data. The obtained results show the performances of our algorithms: robustness to large variations, genericity regarding variability of persons and accuracy of alignment.

References

[1] Osadchy, M., Miller, M.L., Cun, Y.L.: Synergistic face detection and pose estimation with energy-based models. Machine Learning Research 1, 1197–1215 (2007)
[2] Balasubramanian, V., Ye, J., Panchanathan, S.: Biased manifold embedding: A framework for person-independent head pose estimation. In: IEEE Conf. Computer Vision and Pattern Recognition (2007)
[3] Fu, Y., Huang, T.: Graph embedded analysis for head pose estimation. In: IEEE Int'l. Conf. Automatic Face and Gesture Recognition, pp. 3–8 (2006)
[4] Yan, S., Zhang, Z., Fu, Y., Hu, Y., Tu, J., Huang, T.: Learning a person-independent representation for precise 3d pose estimation. In: Workshop Classification of Events Activities and Relationships (2007)
[5] Niyogi, S., Freeman, W.: Example-based head tracking. In: Automatic Face and Gesture Recognition, pp. 374–378 (1996)
[6] Kruger, N., Potzsch, M., von der Malsburg, C.: Determination of face position and pose with a learned representation based on labeled graphs. Machine Learning Research 1, 665–673 (1997)
[7] Wang, J.-G., Sung, E.: EM enhancement of 3D head pose estimated by point at infinity. Image and Vision Computing 1, 1864–1874 (2007)
[8] Raytchev, B., Yoda, I., Sakaue, K.: Head pose estimation by nonlinear manifold learning. Pattern Recognition 1, 462–466 (2004)
[9] Wu, J., Trivedi, M.M.: A two-stage head pose estimation framework and evaluation. Pattern Recognition 41, 1138–1158 (2008)

[10] Breitenstein, M.D., Kuettel, D., Weise, T., van Gool, L.: Real-time face pose estimation from single range images. In: CVPR (2008)

[11] Malassiotis, S., Strintzis, M.G.: Robust real-time 3D head pose estimation from range data. Pattern Recognition 38, 1153–1165 (2005)

[12] Morency, L.P., Rahimi, A., Darrell, T.: Adaptative view-based apperance models. In: Proceedings of IEEE Computer Society Conference on Computer Vision and Pattern Recognition, vol. 1, pp. 1803 – 1810 (2003)

[13] Breitenstein, M.D.: Pose estimation for face recognition using stereo cameras. Ph.D. dissertation, Swiss Federal Institute of Technology Zurich (2006)

[14] Chen, Q., Yao, J., Cham, W.K.: 3d model based pose invariant face recognition from multiple views. Computer Vision, IET 1, 25–34 (2007)

[15] Morency, L.P., Sundberg, P., Darrell, T.: Pose estimation using 3D view-based eigenspaces. In: IEEE International Workshop on Analysis and Modeling of Faces and Gestures. AMFG 2003, vol. 1, pp. 45 – 52 (2003)

[16] Terada, K., Oba, A., Ito, A.: 3D human head tracking using hypothesized polygon model. In: IEEE International Conference on ISystem, Man and Cybernetics, vol. 2, pp. 1396 – 1401 (2005)

[17] Murphy-Chutorian, E., Trivedi, M.M.: Head pose estimation in computer vision: A survey. IEEE Transactions on Pattern Analysis and Machine Intelligence 31, 607–626 (2009)

[18] Murphy-Chutorian, E., Doshi, A., Trivedi, M.M.: Head pose estimation for driver assistance systems: A robust algorithm and experimental evaluation. Intelligent Transportation Systems 1, 709–714 (2007)

[19] Stiefelhagen, R., Yang, J., Waibel, A.: Modeling focus of attention for meeting indexing based on multiple cues. IEEE Trans. Neural Networks 1, 928–938 (2002)

[20] Boufarguine, M., Baklouti, M., Guitteny, V., Couvet, S.: Real-time dense disparity estimation using cuda's api. In: Internation Conference on Computer Vision Theory and Application, VISAPP (2009)

[21] Zinsser, T., Schmidt,J., Niemann, H.: A refined ICP algorithm for robust 3-D correspondence estimation. Image Processing (ICIP 2003), vol. 2 (2003)

[22] Chavarria, M.A., Sommer, G.: Structural ICP algorithm for pose estimation based on local features

[23] Jost, T., Hugli, H.: A multi-resolution ICP with heuristic closest point search for fast and robust 3D registration of range images. In: 3-D Digital Imaging and Modeling (2003)

[24] Rusinkiewicz, S., Levoy, M.: Efficient variants of the ICP algorithm. In: Third International Conference on 3D Digital Imaging and Modeling (2001)

[25] Fleury, C.: Le KD-Tree: une methode de subdivision spatiale, Universite de Rennes 1, INSA (2008)

[26] Zhou, K., Hou, Q., Wang, R., Guo, B.: Real-time KD-tree construction on graphics hardware. In: International Conference on Computer Graphics and Interactive Techniques (ACM SIGGRAPH Asia 2008) (2008)

[27] Arun, K.S., Huang, T.S., Blostein, S.D.: Least square fitting of two 3-d point sets. IEEE Transactions on Pattern Analysis and Machine Intelligence 9(5), 698–700 (1987)

[28] Horn, B.K.P.: Closed-form solution of absolute orientation using unit quaternions. Journal of the Optical Society of America A 4, 629–642 (1987)

[29] Walker, M.W., Shao, L., Volz, R.A.: Estimating 3-d location parameters using dual number quaternions. In: CVGIP: Image Understanding, vol. 54, pp. 358–367 (1991)

[30] Horn, B.K.P., Hilden, H.M., Negahdaripour, S.: Closed-form solution of absolute orientation using orthonormal matrices. Journal of the Optical Society of America A 5(7), 1127–1135 (1988)

[31] Lorusso, A., Eggert, D., Fisher, R.: A comparison of four algorithms for estimating 3-d rigid transformations. In: 4th British Machine Vision Conference, BMVC '95 (1995)

[32] Umeyama, S.: Least-squares estimation of transformation parameters between two points. IEEE Transactions on Pattern Analysis and Machine Intelligence 13, 376–380 (1991)
[33] Shao-Yi, D., Nan-Ning, Z., Shi-Hui, Y., Qubo, Y.: An Extension of the ICP Algorithm Considering Scale Factor
[34] Brown, R.G., Hwang, P.Y.C.: Introduction to Random Signals and Applied Kalman Filtering, 2nd edn. John Wiley and Sons, Chichester (1996)
[35] Menezes, P., Lerasle, F., Dias, J., Chatila, R.: Suivi visuel de structures articules 3D par filtrage particulaire
[36] Paul, N.: Filtrage particulaire. Conservatoire National des Arts et Metiers, Tech. Rep. (2006)

Faking Dynamics of Cloth Animation for Animated Films

Fabian Di Fiore, Bram Gerits, and Frank Van Reeth

Hasselt University - tUL - IBBT
Expertise Centre for Digital Media
Wetenschapspark 2
BE-3590 Diepenbeek, Belgium
{fabian.difiore,frank.vanreeth}@uhasselt.be
http://www.edm.uhasselt.be

Abstract. In this paper we argue for the concept of *fake dynamics* to allow animators to interactively create visually pleasing animations of cloth models while keeping him/her in full control of the animation process. Existing animation and simulation techniques depend on real dynamics simulation and are often prohibitive in terms of computational cost and user control. Our approach allows the user to interactively model and animate cloth models over time using intuitive deformation tools and keyframe animation techniques. During modelling, the cloth's surface is first approximated by means of 3D catenaries between constraint points. An iterative relaxation process is then performed to arrive at the natural rest shape. Concerning the animation phase, the animator has disposal of many interactive fake dynamics control tools to perform gross modifications or wave-shaped deformations. Multiple instances of deformations can be layered allowing to create realistic as well as exaggerated types of animations. We believe our system is effective in terms of ease-of-use, visual appeal and dynamic behaviour, and offers a new fresh perspective on cloth animation for animated films.

Keywords: Fake Dynamics, Cloth Animation, Cloth Simulation, Computer Animation, Computer Assisted Animation.

1   Introduction

Motivation. Simulating and animating cloths is much in demand for many purposes ranging from the entertainment industry (movies and games) to the professional clothing industry (fashion and textile).

Existing cloth simulation and animation [1,2] involves a very expensive process in terms of computational cost due to the flexible nature of the cloth objects. However, when targeted for animated movies it also implicates a very expensive process in terms of user control. This is because animators particularly focus on movement and not necessarily on realism. They do not always desire realism, instead they demand for fake, yet very impressive or dramatic animation effects

F.J. Perales and R.B. Fisher (Eds.): AMDO 2010, LNCS 6169, pp. 238–249, 2010.
© Springer-Verlag Berlin Heidelberg 2010

such as squash and stretch, anticipation and surreal exaggerations, which are impracticable when depending on 'real' dynamics simulation [3,4].

High-end feature animation films nevertheless can achieve these subtle animation effects as their production counts with enough resources to enable dedicated programmers and animators working closely together in an elaborate process of trial and error [5].

In this article, however, we look for solutions to be used in smaller-scale productions where animators have to find their way more independently. More specifically, it is our objective to allow the user to interactively create visually pleasing animations of cloth models while keeping him/her in full control of the animation process.

Contribution. In this paper we present the concept of *fake dynamics* for cloth animation in animated films, in which a cloth is hanging from arbitrary constraint points. Our system allows the user to interactively create and control the animation by adjusting the shape of models over time using intuitive deformation tools and keyframe animation techniques. Primarily it features following characteristics:

- interactive modelling of a polygonal cloth mesh which can be suspended at arbitrary constraint points;
- the cloth's physical properties are directly configured by the animator (e.g., dimensions, elasticity, constraint points);
- real-time manipulation of the shape using fake dynamics (e.g., waving, swaying and bending deformations);
- multiple instances of all deformations can be used together (i.e. combining multiple waves, swaying etc.) allowing to create realistic as well as exaggerated types of animations;
- immediate and direct control over the animation using a keyframe animation system.

As the goal of this paper is on keeping the animator in full control of the animation process we do not explicitly consider collisions and interactions. However, the most common techniques should easily be integrated because of the underlying polygonal mesh.

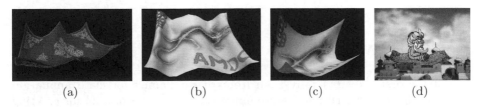

(a)   (b)   (c)   (d)

Fig. 1. Snapshots of animated cloths using fake dynamics. a) Table cloth being pulled up near the back. b) Undulating flag. c) Swinging with exaggerated elasticity. d) Magic carpet in action.

The pictures in the inset (Figure 1) show some snapshots of interactively animated cloths using fake dynamics. We emphasise that all animation results were obtained by a completely novice user and that at no time any common cloth modelling techniques nor dynamics simulation were employed to support the modelling and animation processes.

Approach. Technically the challenge is to achieve a stable and controllable cloth model that easily can be animated in a key framed manner. Whilst just turning to cutting edge simulation techniques [1,2] would seem obvious, this is often prohibitive in terms of user control. Especially for animation movies realistic behaviour is not always desired. Many dramatic animation effects (including squash and stretch, anticipation and surreal exaggerations) are almost unfeasible when the simulation is subject to real dynamics.

To tackle this challenge, we distinguish between a modelling phase and a separate animation phase. In the modelling phase a cloth is conceived starting from a rectangular grid structure on which arbitrary constraint points have to been chosen indicating the points from which the cloth will hang. Then the shape of the cloth, which is defined by the surface interior to the constraint points, is approximated by means of 3D catenaries. Next, a relaxation process is performed on all points on the surface to arrive at the natural rest shape. The result is a three dimensional cloth object which is hanging and supported by the constraint points. Concerning the animation phase, animators directly create motion by placing keyframes in time and indicating how to generate the in-betweens. Key frames are easily created by building new rest shapes through adding, removing or moving constraint points, or manipulating the relaxation process (e.g., making the cloth's fabric more or less stiff). Furthermore, the user has disposal of many interactive fake dynamics controls (e.g., to perform gross modification or wave-shaped deformation of the natural rest shapes).

This way animators interactively create and control visually pleasing animation of cloth models while staying in full control of the animation process.

Paper Organisation. This paper is structured as follows. Section 2 surveys work we consider related to our goals. Section 3 describes the important factors of our approach, starting from the cloth representation and the use of fake dynamics to the animation process. Section 4 elaborates on a system use case example. Finally, Section 5 is our concluding section in which we also set the context for future work.

2   Related Work

One of the first attempts to restrain from real dynamics for cloth animation was made in the 1992 Disney feature animation movie *Aladdin* [6] for creating the Magic Carpet. Initially, a CGI model was about to be employed to ease the animators' work, in particular for applying the detailed Persian texture. However, although texturally very pleasing, the cloth dynamics worked out bad for the animation itself as it looked too computerish [5]. As a solution, a hybrid (2D and 3D) approach was followed. That is, the magic carpet animation was entirely drawn on paper by a traditional animator after which a 3D model artist carefully laid out a computer model over the drawn carpet, frame after frame. Then, for each frame a texture map (depicting the Persian texture) was applied to the surface of the carpet model. Finally, the corner tassels were manually drawn on top of the textured carpet. Through this approach, a realistic appearance is achieved while preserving the artist's animation style but at the (labour intensive) cost of manually creating each frame twice.

Barzel's work on fake dynamics describes a simple method for modelling 1D flexible linear bodies such as ropes and springs without using dynamic simulation [7]. His approach has been used successfully in the Toy Story movies. The idea is to provide a default natural rest shape and provide controls that perform gross modification and wave-shaped deformation of the rest shape. Animators then create motion by adjusting the shape of models over time using traditional keyframe methods. Unfortunately, this approach is limited to the 1D case only and the author states that it is not trivially suited for modelling 2D bodies including cloth and clothing.

Other works on flexible objects in computer graphics include hair animation [8] and rope simulation [9], but their connection to cloth simulation is tenuous due to their relatively simple geometry.

3   Approach

In this section we describe the steps involved in modelling and animating cloths. The system we envisage is inspired by Barzel's idea of faking dynamics by adjusting the shape of models over time using intuitive deformation tools and keyframe animation. Figure 2 depicts a schematic overview of the main parts involved when modelling and animating a piece of cloth.

Starting from a grid structure the user first specifies some constraint points from which the cloth will hang, as well as some textile parameters such as the fabric's elasticity. An approximation of the cloth's surface is then made within the convex hull of the constraint points by tracing 3D catenaries between pairs of constraint points. After this, the user still can reshape the cloth by repositioning the constraint points. The next step involves an iterative relaxation process on all points on the surface to come to a final rest shape. The entire process can be repeated more than once where each rest shape can act as a key frame for the final animation. Dynamic motions can be superimposed by interactive controls that perform gross modifications or wave-shaped deformations of the cloth's surface. Convincing cloth animation is then achieved by layering these deformations (i.e. combining multiple dynamic motions together) and varying all parameters over time.

Parts of the approximation and relaxation step in the modelling phase are based on Weil's work on physically simulating the threads in a cloth [10]. We, however, diverged from it in the approximation step as we were not satisfied with the resulting shape. The following subsections describe all steps in detail.

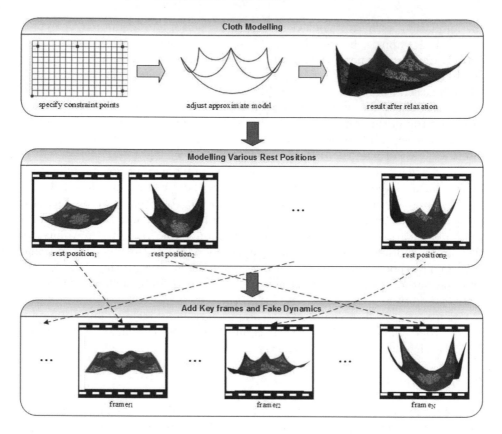

Fig. 2. Schematic overview of the main parts of the modelling and animation steps

3.1   Cloth Modelling

This section discusses how to represent and create a cloth model.

Representation. For reasons of simplicity the cloth's surface will be modelled using as a quadrilateral mesh. To this end, the cloth is initially represented by a 2D grid consisting of 3D coordinates (see Figure 3(a)). The density and dimensions of the grid are user specified, as well as the corner points and inner constraint points from which the cloth will hang (depicted by the red dots).

Surface Approximation. For determining the shape of the cloth only the interior and constraint points will be taken into account as the remaining exterior points do not contribute to the cloth model.

As at this point only the positions of the constraint points are known, the following logical step is to determine the internal points between each pair. This

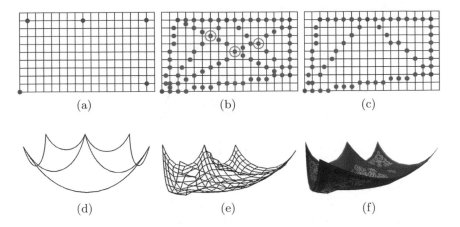

Fig. 3. Cloth modelling. a) Grid representation with constraint points (red dots). b-c) Conflicting catenaries (conflicting points in green). Before and after. d) Approximated cloth model. e-f) Cloth model after relaxation.

narrows down to calculating a catenary between each pair of constraint points taking into account the grid distance and the elasticity (Equation 1).

$$y = a \cosh(\frac{x}{a}) \tag{1}$$

Notice that when looking at the grid catenaries can cross each other (Figure 3(b)) at an internal point. This causes the internal point to be positioned differently in 3D depending on which catenary to use. We know by definition that catenaries are built as low as they naturally can fall. Thus, during the relaxation step they only can be lifted but never will fall any further. This means that we can remove the lowest catenary passing through a conflicting point. Once we have processed only the points for the highest located catenaries, we end up with a triangular structure as depicted in Figure 3(c).

At this point Weil suggests subdividing each triangle in two subtriangles using the highest of the three catenaries passing from the vertices through the triangle's centroid. This should be repeated recursively until all interior points have been positioned in 3D. Unfortunately, as Equation 1 only outputs the height coordinate y, the x en z coordinates have to be approximated using interpolation. We noticed, however, that due to the recursive process the approximation errors add up when calculating new catenaries and this is noticeable when positioning the remaining interior points.

To overcome this issue, our system also takes into account each point's position in the grid when positioning in 3D. So, after deriving the first triangular structure (Figure 3(c)) we immediately show the corresponding catenaries (Figure 3(d)). At this point the user still can reposition the constraint points (and, hence, the catenaries) in order to adjust the cloth's shape to his desire. Then, we process all remaining interior points at once, hence skipping the subdivision steps. For each point p we first lookup the triangle T it belongs to. Next, we draw straight

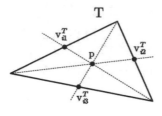

Fig. 4.

lines between the vertices of T and p; the intersections of these lines with the triangle's edges are called v_{i1}^T, v_{i2}^T and v_{i3}^T (see Figure 4). We compute the 3D positions for each v_i^T as follows: the x and z coordinates are derived directly by interpolating between the edge's end points (which are constraint points), for the y coordinate a catenary is constructed between the edge's end points after which an arc length function is employed to find its value. Lastly, we construct catenaries between the vertices of T and v_{i1}^T, v_{i2}^T and v_{i3}^T. The coordinates p_x and p_z are then calculated by interpolation while for p_y the highest located catenary is employed.

In the end, our method advances Weil's algorithm as all internal points are correctly positioned relying on the initial constraint points.

Relaxation. The relaxation process is intended for fine-tuning the cloth's surface. This is an iterative process and involves displacing the grid points until some constraints are obeyed. As we aim for visually compelling and controllable results, real physical constraints are not essential. So, in our case the following constraints suffice [10]: for each point, (i) its placement is at a certain distance d from its neighbours (d is influenced by the point's position on the catenary and the elasticity parameter), and (ii) the angle formed with consecutive neighbours is related to the stiffness parameter. The final result is depicted in Figure 3(e) and Figure 3(f).

3.2   Cloth Dynamics

In this section we elaborate on how to superimpose dynamic motion in a key framed manner. We show this by means of two cases: swaying and waving.

Sway Deformation. Cloths typically can swing back and forth or to and fro when an external force (e.g., the wind) is exerted on the entire model. To simulate a swaying deformation we calculate a displacement vector for each point p according to following equation:

$$\overrightarrow{d_{sway}^p} = \frac{d_{cp}^p}{d_{max}} \times m \times \overrightarrow{dir} \times v \qquad (2)$$

In this equation, d_{cp}^p stands for the distance between p and its closest constraint point, d_{max} is the maximal distance found between an internal point and a constraint point, while m, $\overrightarrow{dir}$ and v are adjustable parameters indicating the magnitude, direction and speed of swaying. This way the displacement of a point is in proportion to its distance to the closest constraint point. Now, if we choose to variate, for example, m over time in the interval $[-d_{max}, +d_{max}]$ we get a smooth swinging animation. Figure 5 shows some snapshots of a carpet swinging from side to side.

Fig. 5. Snapshots depicting a sway from left to right

Wave Deformation. A typical wave deformation is defined by the parameters *magnitude, frequency, phase* and *azimuth*. For our cloth animation, however, we leave out the azimuth as it will twist the cloth making it look less realistic. To create an undulating surface Equation 3 is employed in which the magnitude, frequency and startphase are denoted by m, $freq$ and *startphase* respectively. We also added a time (t) and speed (v) parameter to shift, and thus animate, the waves in time. In addition we multiply the whole by an attenuation coefficient a which causes a larger waving effect in the centre of the cloth and a fall off near the constraint points; d_{cp}^p stands for the distance between p and its closest constraint point while d_{max} is the maximal distance found between an internal point and a constraint point. Figure 6 illustrates the effect of the magnitude and frequency parameters for an undulating motion.

$$y = m \times \sin(x \times freq + startphase + t \times v) \times a \qquad (3)$$

$$a = \frac{d_{cp}^p}{d_{max}} \qquad (4)$$

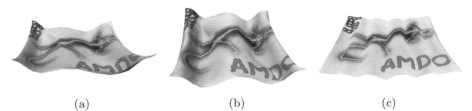

(a)   (b)   (c)

Fig. 6. Undulating flag. a) Default magnitude and frequency. b) Increased magnitude. c) Increased frequency.

3.3   Cloth Animation

For creating animations, a keyframe animation system is employed as it is essential in allowing animators to easily adjust and edit pose and timing with per-frame accuracy [3,4,7].

Key frames are easily created by building rest shapes as described in Section 3.1. That is, the user specifies the elasticity and the constraint points from which the cloth will hang, adjusts the rough shape of the cloth, and after relaxation use the rest shape as a key frame. The entire process can be repeated more than once and so different key frames can consist of different and a different number of constraint points. This is illustrated in Figure 7.

Fig. 7. Different rest shapes of the same cloth model

Dynamic motions as discussed in Section 3.2 are then incorporated in the timeline easily by superimposing them on the key and in-between frames. Moreover, multiple instances of all deformations can be used together. It is this layered approach and varying all parameters over time which leads to convincing animations.

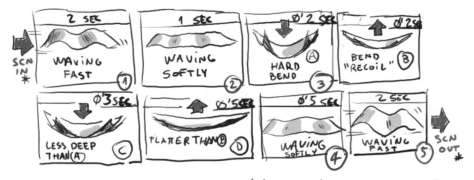

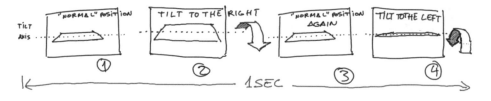

Fig. 8. Thumbnail storyboard for the magic carpet animation shown in Figure 9

Fig. 9. Snapshots of an animated magic carpet illustrating subtle animation effects (including a squash and stretch bend and an undulating motion) achieved by fake dynamics

4   Results

In this section we elaborate on a system use case example which was carried out to capture the system's effectiveness in terms of *ease-of-use, visual appeal* and *dynamic behaviour*. To this end an external animator was involved who was not acquainted with our system at all.

Figure 8 shows the animator's thumbnail storyboard which led to the magic carpet animation shown in Figure 9. The animation is guided by 5 key frames and several interpolation algorithms (including ease-in/ease-out and speed up/down) were used to generate the in-betweens. For the key frames four different rest shapes were created and in particular the elasticity coefficient was used to establish the bending effect. Dynamic motion was added by superimposing animated deformations. For example, the transition between the bending and moving carpet is established by slowly increasing the magnitude of the wave deformation. This cloth animation (not counting drawing the background and the character) took our animator less than 30 minutes to model all rest shapes and to establish the dynamics, clearly illustrating the effectiveness of our system.

All other results (shown in the figures throughout this article) were created by novice users, i.e. the authors, illustrating all the more the ease of use of our approach.

All examples run at an interactive frame rate on a commodity personal computer (Pentium Dual-Core 2.67 GHz, onboard graphics card).

5   Conclusion and Future Work

In this paper we presented the concept of *fake dynamics* for cloth animation in animated films, in which a cloth is hanging from arbitrary constraint points.

Existing animation and simulation techniques are often prohibitive in terms of user control. Especially for animation movies realistic behaviour is not always desired, instead they demand for fake, yet very impressive or dramatic animation effects (including squash and stretch, anticipation and surreal exaggerations) which are impracticable when real dynamics are involved.

Our system allows the user to interactively model and animate cloth models over time using intuitive deformation tools and keyframe animation techniques. We believe our system is effective in terms of ease-of-use, visual appeal and dynamic behaviour, and offers solutions to be used in smaller-scale productions where animators have to find their way more independently.

Future Work. In this paper, we did not explicitly consider collisions and interactions. However, we believe most common approaches should easily be integrated because of the underlying polygon mesh of the cloth objects.

Furthermore, it is possible that during relaxation displacements of grid points cause the cloth surface to intersect itself. Imposing extra constraints (i.e. predicting intersections before displacing grid points) can prevent this, although we did not experiment any problems in the cases we tested.

Acknowledgements

We gratefully express our gratitude to the European Fund for Regional Development (ERDF) and the Flemish Government, which are kindly funding part of the research at the Expertise Centre for Digital Media.

Many thanks goes also to Xemi Morales for his artistic contribution.

References

1. Hauth, M., Fedkiw, R., House, R.: Clothing simulation and animation. SIGGRAPH Course notes 29 (2003)
2. Bridson, R., Zhang, D.: Advanced topics on clothing simulation and animation. SIGGRAPH Course notes 6 (2005)
3. Whitaker, H., Halas, J.: Timing for Animation. Focal Press (1981) ISBN: 0-240-51714-8
4. Lasseter, J.: Principles of traditional animation applied to 3D computer animation. In: Proceedings of SIGGRAPH, vol. 21, pp. 35–44 (1987)
5. Walt Disney Home Video. Diamond in the Rough: The Making of Aladdin. Aladdin Platinum Edition, Disc 2. DVD (2004)
6. Walt Disney Feature Animation. Aladdin (1992)
7. Barzel, R.: Faking dynamics of ropes and springs. IEEE Computer Graphics and Applications 17, 31–39 (1997)
8. Hadap, S., Cani, M.-P., Lin, M., Kim, T.-Y., Bertails, F., Marschner, S., Ward, K., Kacic-Alesic, Z.: Realistic hair simulation: Animation and rendering. SIGGRAPH Classes (2008)
9. Brown, J., Latombe, J.-C., Montgomery, K.: Real-time knot-tying simulation. The Visual Computer 20(2), 165–179 (2004)
10. Weil, J.: The synthesis of cloth objects. SIGGRAPH 20(4), 49–54 (1986)

Data-Driven On-Line Generation of Interactive Gait Motion

Liang Zhang, Stephan Rusdorf, and Guido Brunnett

Faculty of Computer Science, GDV
Chemnitz University of Technology, Germany
{lizh,sru,brunnett}@cs.tu-chemnitz.de

Abstract. In this paper, we present a novel constraint-based method that is able to adapt captured gait motions to new paths while preserving the original gait style. Foot-plant constraints are ensured automatically and no post-processing for foot-skate removal is necessary. The main contribution of the paper is an analytical algorithm that is able to move the avatar without violating foot-plant constraints. The algorithm works with few dependencies, which allows other motion controllers to be easily integrated to fulfill other tasks.

Keywords: Locomotion Synthesis, Motion Editing, Motion Path.

1 Introduction

A convincing gait motion is one of the most essential factors in human motion synthesis. Motion capture techniques are able to create the most realistic gait motions with regard to physical correctness and natural motion patterns. Among active research on reusing the captured gait motions, adapting a gait motion to new paths is prominent. To avoid foot-skate artifacts introduced during path adaption, most of the proposed approaches work in the adapt-then-repair manner: The gait motion will be adapted to the new path and the foot-plant constraints are re-established in the post-processing [7][15][8]. In addition, a time window is often necessary for smoothing the resulting poses.

In this paper, we present a novel analytical method to modify captured gait motions such that the avatar can follow an interactively controllable path. Unlike most of the other approaches, foot-plant constraints are automatically ensured and thus no post-processing for foot-skate removal is necessary. Since no filtering or blending is involved in the adaption phase, the algorithm works fast and on-line. The contributions of our work are twofold: A closed-form expression for constraint-based root translation according to two adjacent poses, and a simple method to modify the avatar's walking direction while retaining much of the gait characteristics.

The remainder of this paper is organized as follows: After an overview of related work, the gait style is discussed in section 3. Then, the algorithm of the gait motion generation is provided in detail in section 4. In section 5, the experiment results are presented and we conclude the paper with an overview of future work in section 6.

F.J. Perales and R.B. Fisher (Eds.): AMDO 2010, LNCS 6169, pp. 250–259, 2010.

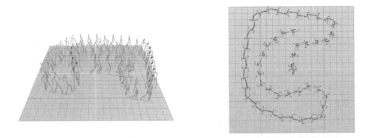

Fig. 1. A synthesized gait motion that follows a user defined target path

2   Related Work

In order to reuse motion capture data, many research groups have been focused on the modification of low-level data such as joint angles with kinematics and dynamics tools [5][6][10], or with the techniques from the signal processing domain [3][16]. Notice has also been given to the approaches that generate new motions by re-arranging motion capture data. Captured motions can either be preprocessed into short clips, which can be concatenated interactively [2][1], or, more generally, be preprocessed into motion graphs [9], which allow synthesis of higher variety.

The data-driven gait motion synthesis involves many above research efforts. Gleicher [7] adapted existing locomotion motions to new paths by aligning the root positions and orientations to the new path. Foot-plant constraints are re-established in the post-process with kinematics-based techniques proposed in [10]. Park et al. [15] employed motion blending to morph locomotion paths. To avoid foot-skating introduced by the blending, the foot currently touching the ground is fixed during the blending and relevant joints are modified accordingly. Kim et al. considered motion paths as a serie of general spatial constraints [8]. The foot-plants are reconstructed with general Inverse Kinematics solvers after these path constraints are satisfied.

In the above approaches the foot-plant constraints have a lower priority than the constraints given in the new gait path. Furthermore, motion blending is necessary to avoid the discontinuity introduced when geometrically re-enforcing the foot-plants. Such an approach implies an off-line method, which is not eligible for highly interactive situations such as games.

In this paper, we give a closed-form analysis for positioning the avatar based on foot-plants. From there, we present an on-line method for gait motion synthesis that can follow new paths. Foot-plant constraints are satisfied automatically and no blending during the synthesis is needed. The is a real-time method due to the absence of numerical solvers. Our method can be well deployed to generate gait motions with interactively changing paths. Since the input poses themselves are not constrained, motion retargeting and blending can be easily integrated without introducing foot-skates.

3   Gait Style

We distinguish the gait style in two levels: the high-level style embedded in the *path variation* and the low-level style described by the actual *joint configurations* (vector of joint orientations) and the root orientation in the *moving frame*. The moving frame at a point on the path is $\{x, y, z\}$, where x is the tangent at that point, y is the up-vector and $z = x \times y$.

A gait path is the trajectory of the avatar's root (at pelvis) in a motion sequence. With some loss of generality, only the gait motions on a planar terrain are considered, because such motions are better accessible and this simplification does not affect the core idea of our algorithm. Since the root's height is adjusted automatically based on the foot-plant (Sect. 4.3), a gait path can be represented by a 2D trajectory.

The path variation is the difference between the *target gait path*, which is the path the avatar should follow, and the *actual gait path*, which is the path the avatar actually travels. This variation exists, since the target path is normally a low-frequent curve for simplifying the user input, and in reality the actual gait path always has high-frequent noise. In comparison to the path variation, the *joint configurations* and the root orientation in the *moving frame* define the gait personality in a more obvious way. In the synthesis, both levels of the gait style embedded in the captured sequences are preserved as much as possible.

4   Gait Motion Generation

In this section, we firstly introduce the simple motion graph with existing motion sequences which models the human gait cycle. Then, the pose decomposition and a closed-form expression describing the relation between root translations and support positions are given in detail. Based on that, we present a method to modify the avatar's walking direction such that it can follow a new path without much loss of the original path variation.

4.1   Motion Sequences

Human biped gait is a cyclic movement that can be separated by foot strikes and take-offs [13]. Accordingly, we organize motion sequences representing each phase in the cycle as a simple motion graph with clustered nodes and predetermined edges [2](Fig. 2). The gait motion is then synthesized by interactively concatenating appropriate motion sequences. The advantages of such approaches are threefold: First, one is able to utilize the good pose coherence within the sequences. Second, the path variation can only be described with motion sequences. Third, the sequences can be directly segmented from a single motion clip with a full gait cycle to yield smooth sequence transitions.

4.2   Pose Decomposition

A pose consists of components that define the root position and orientation of the avatar as well as the *joint configurations*. With the knowledge, how each

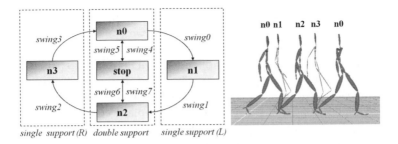

Fig. 2. Gait cycle and motion sequences. Left: A simple motion graph according to the gait cycle. Right: Motion sequences corresponding to the phases in the gait cycle.

component affects a pose, one is able to control the avatar by just modifying the desirable component without disturbing the other ones. Thereby, the characteristics of the original motion capture data can be preserved as much as possible while one still has the desired control over the avatar.

In a motion sequence, the i-th pose π_i describes the root transformation M_i together with the joint configurations θ_i defined in the root space. We call θ_i the *local pose*. Transformation M_i can be defined by a rotation R_i followed by a translation T_i in the global space. Applying R_i is equivalent to applying two unit rotations, $R_{\mathrm{n},i}$ and $R_{\mathrm{f},i}$ successively, where $R_{\mathrm{f},i}$ is a rotation around the axis perpendicular to the floor plane ($\boldsymbol{y}$-axis). Hence, the pose π_i can be uniquely determined by four components T_i, $R_{\mathrm{f},i}$, $R_{\mathrm{n},i}$ and θ_i.

According to these components, the pose π_i affects the avatar in a 4-step-process: First, the local pose θ_i is applied and the joint configurations are modified. In the second and third step, $R_{\mathrm{n},i}$ and $R_{\mathrm{f},i}$ are applied successively and the local pose θ_i is also rotated. We denote the resulted pose with $\theta_{\mathrm{r},i}$ and also name the transformed space with the *rotated root space*. The last step is the application of translation T_i, after which the root is moved to its final position in the global space. If $L_{j,i}$ transforms the coordinates from the local space of the j-th joint to the root space, then there is:

$$G_{j,i} = T_i \times R_{\mathrm{f},i} \times R_{\mathrm{n},i} \times L_{j,i}, \tag{1}$$

where $G, T, R_{\mathrm{f}}, R_{\mathrm{n}}$ and L are transformation matrices. Matrix $G_{j,i}$ transforms the coordinates from the local space of the j-th joint to the global space. The local space of the joint j is where the foot-ground collision is detected. Moreover, $L_{j,i}$ is fully embedded in θ_i and is calculated by tracing from the joint j backwards to the root.

4.3   Support Position

In this paper, we only consider the poses with at least one foot on the ground. This is always the case for relatively slow locomotion. In case when both feet are not on the ground (in a short "flying" phase), the avatar is actually controlled by the laws of dynamics instead of the foot-plant constraints. Since dynamics-based controllers can also work in an on-line manner, we consider the dynamics as a plug-in which can be integrated in our method later.

The matrices in (1) are functions of index i. The motion is then a series of applications of these matrices on the avatar. Every two neighboring poses share the same *support position* (the contact point between the feet and the ground), since their application must not violate the foot-plant constraint.

Let $sp_{\text{loc},i}$ be the support position of π_i in the local joint space, then this support position in the global space is $sp_{\text{g},i} = G_{j,i} \times sp_{\text{loc},i}$. The support position in the rotated root space is $sp_{\text{r},i} = R_{\text{f},i} \times R_{\text{n},i} \times L_{j,i} \times sp_{\text{loc},i}$.

4.4   Translating the Root

Given two poses π_i and π_{i+1} with the same single support situation (i.e. the support feet in both poses are the same) and their support positions in the global space is denoted as $sp_{\text{g},i}$ and $sp_{\text{g},i+1}$, respectively, then there must be $sp_{\text{g},i} = sp_{\text{g},i+1}$ due to the foot-plant. The global root positions of π_i and π_{i+1} are denoted as q_i and q_{i+1}, respectively, then the translation vector $v_{i+1} = q_{i+1} - q_i$ describes the root translation caused by applying the pose π_{i+1} (Fig. 3).

Since the difference between the global space and the rotated root space of π_i is the translation T_i, the difference between the rotated root spaces of π_i and π_{i+1} is exactly v_{i+1}. Hence, there is

$$v_{i+1} = sp_{\text{r},i} - sp_{\text{r},i+1} . \tag{2}$$

Equation (2) describes the relation between the root translation and the support positions in the rotated root spaces (Fig. 3). Upon applying π_{i+1}, the components of π_i including $sp_{\text{r},i}$ are already determined and cannot be changed. The translation v_{i+1} only depends on $sp_{\text{r},i+1}$, which is in turn determined by the quadruple $(R_{\text{f},i+1}, R_{\text{n},i+1}, L_{j,i+1}, sp_{loc,i+1})$ (see Sect. 4.3). Among all the components of π_{i+1}, we only modify $R_{\text{f},i+1}$ in order to control the walking direction.

Considering that the rotation matrix $R_{\text{f},i+1}$ can be denoted with a rotation angle φ_{i+1} around the y-axis, the root translation v_{i+1} is a function of φ_{i+1}, or $v_{i+1} = F(\varphi_{i+1})$. If we modify $R_{\text{f},i+1}$ by rotating the avatar around the y-axis by an incremental angle $\Delta\varphi$, then we have a new root translation v'_{i+1} with

$$v'_{i+1} = F(\varphi_{i+1} + \Delta\varphi) . \tag{3}$$

The new root position after applying π_{i+1} is then $p'_{i+1} = p_i + v'_{i+1}$, where p_i is root position afater applying π_i. This means that one can translate the root to a new position by overwriting the avatar's root orientation φ_{i+1} with $\varphi_{i+1} + \Delta\varphi$, as illustrated in Fig. 3.

4.5   Path Adaption

For a sequence with n poses, the root trajectory C_{a} is a polyline obtained by connecting the projected root positions of each pose $p_i (i \in [0, n))$ successively.

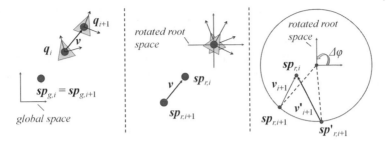

Fig. 3. Derive root translation from two support positions. Left: The situation upon applying π_{i+1} is shown in the global space. Middle: the same situation in the rotated root space. Right: The root translation is a function of a rotation angle $\Delta\varphi$. The circle indicates the possible positions of $\boldsymbol{sp}'_{r,i+1}$ when $\Delta\varphi$ changes.

This is the actual gait path if no change is applied. The tangents $\boldsymbol{u}_0$ and $\boldsymbol{u}_{n-1}$ at the start and end points of $\boldsymbol{C}_a$ are estimated with finite differences. We additionally define $\ell = \text{Len}\,(\text{H}\,(\boldsymbol{p}_0,\boldsymbol{u}_0,\boldsymbol{p}_{n-1},\boldsymbol{u}_{n-1}))$, where Function $\text{H}\,(\boldsymbol{s},\boldsymbol{u}_\text{s},\boldsymbol{e},\boldsymbol{u}_\text{e})$ interpolates a curve between $\boldsymbol{s}$ and $\boldsymbol{e}$ (with tangents $\boldsymbol{u}_\text{s}$ and $\boldsymbol{u}_\text{e}$, respectively) using *Hermite Interpolation* and function $\text{Len}\,(x)$ calculates the arc length of curve x. We call ℓ the *effective length* of this sequence, as this Hermite curve is a low-frequent approximation of the actual gait path, and ℓ estimates the distance the avatar effectively travels when this sequence is applied.

Since $\boldsymbol{C}_a$ is a polyline, we can morph it discretely by rotating each segment of $\boldsymbol{C}_a$ by an angle γ. The moving frame at each point $\boldsymbol{p}_i$ on $\boldsymbol{C}_a$ is therefore also rotated by the same angle. In addition, since the avatar is bound to the moving frame for retaining the root local orientation in the moving frame (see Sect. 3), the avatar is also rotated by γ at each frame. The new root position can then be obtained through (3).

The original gait path polyline $\boldsymbol{C}_a$ defines $n-1$ vectors $\boldsymbol{p}_i\boldsymbol{p}_{i+1}$. The $n-2$ angles $\Delta\alpha_i = \arccos\,(\langle\boldsymbol{p}_{i-1}\boldsymbol{p}_i,\boldsymbol{p}_i\boldsymbol{p}_{i+1}\rangle)$ describe the relative rotations between two adjacent vectors. Let $\boldsymbol{C}_t$ be the target path. Given a start position $\boldsymbol{s}$ on $\boldsymbol{C}_t$, we can find a point $\boldsymbol{e}$ on $\boldsymbol{C}_t$ upon a sequence transition, such that the arc length between $\boldsymbol{s}$ and $\boldsymbol{e}$ is the effective length of the sequence that is going to be applied. Let $\boldsymbol{w}_\text{s}$ and $\boldsymbol{w}_\text{e}$ be the tangents at $\boldsymbol{s}$ and $\boldsymbol{e}$ and we denote $\boldsymbol{u}_\text{s}$, $\boldsymbol{u}_\text{e}$, $\boldsymbol{w}_\text{s}$, $\boldsymbol{w}_\text{e}$ with their angles between the horizontal axis with α_s, α_e, β_s, β_e, respectively (Fig. 4).

The change of the walking direction after the avatar has walked over the *effective length* of $\boldsymbol{C}_a$ is $\alpha_\text{e} - \alpha_\text{s}$ (which is an approximation of the curvature of $\boldsymbol{C}_a$). Since a curve piece on $\boldsymbol{C}_t$ with the same *effective length* has been found, there should be $\alpha_\text{e} - \alpha_\text{s} = \beta_\text{e} - \beta_\text{s}$ in order to adapt $\boldsymbol{C}_a$ to $\boldsymbol{C}_t$. We firstly rotate $\boldsymbol{C}_a$ around $\boldsymbol{s}$ such that $\boldsymbol{u}_\text{s} = \boldsymbol{w}_\text{s}$, and then morph the curve $\boldsymbol{C}_a$ by replacing $\Delta\alpha_i$ with $\Delta\beta_i = \Delta\alpha_i + \gamma$, where

$$\gamma = (\beta_\text{e} - \beta_\text{s}) - (\alpha_\text{e} - \alpha_\text{s})\,/\,(n-2)\,. \tag{4}$$

Since the difference between $\beta_e - \beta_s$ and $\alpha_e - \alpha_s$ is evenly distributed to all $\Delta\alpha_i$, the change for each $\Delta\alpha_i$ is minimal, and hence the path variation which is embedded in $\Delta\alpha_i$ is retained as much as possible. After the morphing of C_a for the current sequence, the end point e becomes the new start point s upon next sequence transition. This process repeats until s the end point of C_t arrives and the avatar stops following the target path.

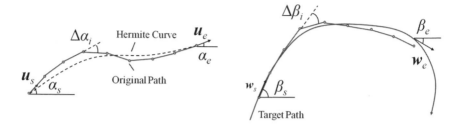

Fig. 4. Gait path adaption. Left: An Hermite curve is created for estimating the effective length of the original path. Right: A piece of target path with the same effective length is found. Each segment on the original path is rotated by the same angle. Note that the end point of the original path is not necessarily on the target path.

5   Results

The calculation of the effective length and the path morphing can be done in $O(n)$ with n poses. In a single threaded implementation on a computer with Q8800 and 4 GB RAM, it took less than 200 milliseconds for precessing the motion with about 10000 frames. The path following works in real-time: For 10 user-defined control points, the target path is interpolated within 10 milliseconds. Pose decomposition is done in 7 milliseconds.

To evaluate the algorithm that calculates the root translation, we took as the ground truth the root positions in an original locomotion with about 8000 frames. We applied our algorithm on the same motion and compared the calculated root positions to the ground truth at each frame. The result is shown in Fig. 5. The foot size (22 cm) of the avatar (height 158 cm) is shown for a more intuitive evaluation. The variation on the floor plane $\mathrm{VarXZ} = \sqrt{\Delta X^2 + \Delta Z^2}$ are mainly less than the foot size. However, the error accumulation is still to be noticed (Fig. 5 left). This originates from the error when calculating the support position using a simplified feet model which is inconsistent with the one used during producing the motion capture data.

To evaluate the path following ability, we compared the target path with the actual path that is yielded with our path adaption method. As shown in (Fig. 5 right), the avatar followed the target path well, although the avatar took more shortcuts with increasing path curvatures. This is due to the approximation of the path curvature and the effetive length of the original path during the path adaption.

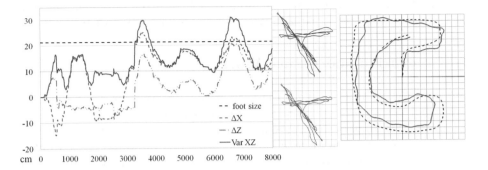

Fig. 5. Evaluation of the root translation and path adaption methods. Left: Variation at each frame. Middle: The ground truth (top) and the calculated trajectory.(bottom). Right: Target path (dashed) and actual path.

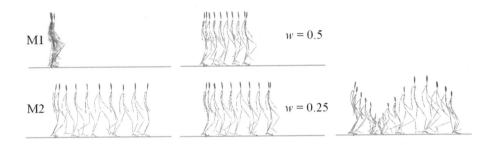

Fig. 6. Integration with motion retargeting and motion blending. Two original motions: in-place locomotion M1 and normal walking M2 (left column). Blended motions with different blending weights (middle column). Motion M2 is retargeted to an avatar with dynamically varying size (right column).

Our method does not constrain the poses, as long as the input poses are well connected and the support positions can be calculated. This feature allows us to apply our method on blended or retargeted poses, so that one can utilize the power of motion blending and retargeting without concerning foot-skates. For experiment, we applied our method after retargeting a motion to avatars of different sizes (but with the same skeleton structure). We morphed the avatar by scaling the bone lengths dynamically during a gait motion and used our method to calculate the root position. As shown in Fig. 6, our method is able to generate a gait motion with strict foot-plants despite a varying stride length. The root height is also adjusted automatically, since the foot-plants are constrained in the 3D space.

We further used our method on blended motions. We interpolated an in-place locomotion and a normal gait motion with $w \cdot M1 + (1-w) \cdot M2$, where M1 and M2 are the original motions and w is a blending weight between 0 and 1. The avatar was driven by the blended poses and the root positions were calculated with our method. As shown in Fig. 6, new motions that inherit both original gait styles are generated while the foot-plants are ensured without any post-processing.

6   Conclusion and Future Work

In this paper, we introduced a novel data-driven approach for gait motion synthesis that can follow new paths in real-time. Original motion sequences were organized in a simple motion graph according to the gait cycle. We then expressed the root translation as a closed-form function of a unit root rotation. Based on that, we derived an algorithm that is able to position the avatar without violating the foot-plant constraints. With a path adaption method, the avatar is able to follow new paths on-line.

The gait style of the original motion is preserved at two levels of details: The gait details are fully preserved based on the pose decomposition. and the gait path variation is largely retained with the path adaption method. Since the root translation only depends on the support positions of adjacent poses, our method can be applied to any motion in which support positions can be determined. Other motion controllers can be integrated to accomplish other tasks. We showed this possibility by synthesizing gait motions with retargeted and blended poses.

There are several limitations in our method. First, the synthesis is based on the gait motions captured on planar terrains and no joint configuration is modified in our method. It is not possible to synthesize gait motions on uneven terrains without altering the joint configurations. Second, we considered the foot-constraints only as point constraints. The orientation of the supporting foot is not constrained. Third, dynamic factors are not considered. Synthesizing highly dynamic locomotion using our method may produce unrealistic results. For improvement, the proposed method is to be extended in order to synthesize gait motions on uneven terrains. The authors are also working on the integration of dynamics-based controllers and minimizing the error during the path adaption.

Acknowledgment

The authors would like to acknowledge the anonymous reviewers for their constructive comments and many thanks to Christian Hörr and Tom Kühnert for their valuable suggestions. This work was supported by the SAB project No. 13282/2254. The data used in this project are obtained from HDM05 [14].

References

1. Arikan, O., Forsyth, D.A., O'Brien, J.F.: Motion synthesis from annotations. In: ACM SIGGRAPH 2003 Papers, pp. 402–408. ACM, San Diego (2003)
2. Arikan, O., Forsyth, D.A.: Interactive motion generation from examples. In: Proceedings of the 29th annual conference on Computer graphics and interactive techniques, pp. 483–490. ACM, San Antonio (2002)

3. Bruderlin, A., Williams, L.: Motion signal processing. In: Proceedings of the 22nd annual conference on Computer graphics and interactive techniques, pp. 97–104. ACM, New York (1995)
4. Cohen, M.F.: Interactive spacetime control for animation. SIGGRAPH Comput. Graph. 26, 293–302 (1992)
5. Gleicher, M.: Motion editing with spacetime constraints. In: Proceedings of the 1997 symposium on Interactive 3D graphics, pp. 139–148. ACM, Providence (1997)
6. Gleicher, M.: Retargetting motion to new characters. In: Proceedings of the 25th annual conference on Computer graphics and interactive techniques, pp. 33–42. ACM, New York (1998)
7. Gleicher, M.: Motion path editing. In: Proceedings of the 2001 symposium on Interactive 3D graphics, pp. 195–202. ACM, New York (2001)
8. Kim, M., Hyun, K., Kim, J., Lee, J.: Synchronized Multi-Character Motion Editing. ACM Trans. Graph. 28(3), 1–9 (2009)
9. Kovar, L., Gleicher, M., Pighin, F.: Motion graphs. ACM Trans. Graph. 21, 473–482 (2002)
10. Kovar, L., Schreiner, J., Gleicher, M.: Footskate cleanup for motion capture editing. In: Proceedings of the 2002 ACM SIGGRAPH/Eurographics symposium on Computer animation, pp. 97–104. ACM, San Antonio (2002)
11. Kwon, T., Shin, S.Y.: A steering model for on-line locomotion synthesis. Comput. Animat. Virtual Worlds 18, 463–472 (2007)
12. Lee, J., Chai, J., Reitsma, P.S.A., Hodgins, J.K., Pollard, N.S.: Interactive control of avatars animated with human motion data. ACM Trans. Graph. 21, 491–500 (2002)
13. Multon, F., France, L., Cani-Gascuel, M., Debunne, G.: Computer Animation of Human Walking: a Survey (1999)
14. Müller, M., Röder, T., Clausen, M., Eberhardt, B., Krüger, B., Weber, A.: Documentation Mocap Database HDM05. Technical report, No. CG-2007-2, ISSN 1610-8892, Universität Bonn (2007)
15. Park, S.I., Shin, H.J., Shin, S.Y.: On-line Locomotion Generation Based on Motion Blending. In: Proceedings of the 2002 ACM SIGGRAPH/Eurographics symposium on Computer animation, pp. 105–111. ACM, San Antonio (2002)
16. Witkin, A., Popovic, Z.: Motion warping. In: Proceedings of the 22nd annual conference on Computer graphics and interactive techniques, pp. 105–108. ACM, New York (1995)

Automatic 3D Facial Model and Texture Reconstruction from Range Scans

Guofu Xiang, Xiangyang Ju, and Patrik O'B. Holt

Cognitive Engineering Research Group, School of Computing,
The Robert Gordon University, Aberdeen, AB25 1HG, UK
{prs.xiang,x.ju,p.holt}@rgu.ac.uk

Abstract. This paper presents a fully automatic approach to fitting a generic facial model to detailed range scans of human faces to reconstruct 3D facial models and textures with no manual intervention (such as specifying landmarks). A Scaling Iterative Closest Points (SICP) algorithm is introduced to compute the optimal rigid registrations between the generic model and the range scans with different sizes. And then a new template-fitting method, formulated in an optmization framework of minimizing the physically based elastic energy derived from thin shells, faithfully reconstructs the surfaces and the textures from the range scans and yields dense point correspondences across the reconstructed facial models. Finally, we demonstrate a facial expression transfer method to clone facial expressions from the generic model onto the reconstructed facial models by using the deformation transfer technique.

Keywords: Surface reconstruction, texture reconstruction, range scans, scaling iterative closest points (SICP) algorithm, template fitting, expression transfer.

1 Introduction

Modeling and animating realistic facial models is a substantial challenge in computer graphics, especially for facial expressions, because we are so familiar with human faces and very sensitive to "unnatural" subtle changes in faces. Such a challenge has drawn intensive academic and industrial interest in this area [8,14]. However, creating a convincing synthetic character requires a tremendous amount of artistry and manual work. There is a clear need for more automatic techniques to reduce the painstaking work of artists and to make reuse of existing data.

One avenue for creating realistic facial models is 3D scanning technology. However, starting from a range scan, substantial effort is needed to process the noisy and incomplete surface into a model suitable for analysis and animation. Template-fitting methods are widely used for this purpose to fill holes, reduce the noise level, and capture characteristic features of range scans [1,21,22]. In addition, dense point correspondences, which are fundamental requirements in many applications such as morphing and shape analysis, can be also established

F.J. Perales and R.B. Fisher (Eds.): AMDO 2010, LNCS 6169, pp. 260–269, 2010.
© Springer-Verlag Berlin Heidelberg 2010

across various models. Generally, template-fitting methods require users to provide a small set of manually specified landmarks to initially align or warp a template with targets [1,21,22]. The process of positioning landmarks seems to be tedious and error-prone.

Besides Modeling facial expressions directly from range scans of human faces, it would be better to reuse existing facial expressions to generate new ones on desired targets instead of creating them from scratch, which is the idea of *expression cloning* [12]. One key problem for expression cloning is to build good dense correspondences between models.

In this paper, we present a fully *automatic* approach to reconstructing 3D facial models and textures from range scans without requiring manual intervention. This paper makes several specific technical contributions. First, we introduce a *Scaling Iterative Closest Points* (SICP) algorithm to compute the optimal rigid registrations between a generic template facial model and range scans with different sizes. Second, we propose a unified optimization framework to reconstruct facial surfaces and textures from the range scans. We also present a method to automatically generate new facial expressions on the reconstructed facial models from expressions on the generic model by using the deformation transfer technique.

In the following section, we review some topics related to our work. In Section 3, we present the details of SICP to rigidly register a template facial model to range scans with different scales and show an optimization framework to reconstruct facial models and textures from range scans. Results and conclusions are presented in Sections 5 and 6, respectively.

2 Related Work

Modeling and synthesizing faces is an active research field in computer graphics and computer vision. Here we review three topics most related to our current work: ICP-based registration, template fitting, and expression transfer. Other related work is discussed throughout the paper, as appropriate.

ICP-based Registration. Since the first paper of ICP [2], ICP has been widely used for geometric alignment of 3D models and many variants of ICP have been proposed [16]. Generally, the original ICP can only deal with models with the same scale. To account for the scale problem, Du *et al.* proposed an extension of the ICP algorithm, called the Iterative Closest Points with Bounded Scale (ICPBS) algorithm, which integrated a scale parameter with boundaries into the original one [6], but it's unclear how to determine the upper and lower boundaries of scales that contain the optimal scale.

Template Fitting. Due to its great challenge in many research fields, numerous research efforts are devoted to establishing correspondences between different meshes [9]. The template-fitting method [1,17] deforms a template to a target object to minimize the combining errors of smoothness and fitness between them. Recently, template fitting has become particular popular due to its simplicity and robustness to noisy range data [11,21]. Our reconstruction method shares the similar idea, but it is derived from physically based elastic deformations of thin shells by variational methods [4].

Expression Transfer. Noh and Neumann first proposed the concept of *expression cloning* that facial expressions of one 3D facial model were copied onto other facial models [12]. The dense point correspondences were established by volume morphing with Radial Basis Functions (RBFs) through dozens of initial corresponding points. Sumner *et. al.* [5,17] generalized the idea to transfer arbitrary nonlinear deformation exhibited by a source triangle mesh onto different target triangle meshes. To build triangle correspondences, they manually specified a small set of initial corresponding feature points and then fitted the source meshes to the target using the template-fitting method. Vlasic *et al.* proposed a method, which used multilinear models for mapping video-recorded performance of one individual to facial animations of another [20]. An example-based approach [15] proposed by Pyun *at al.* clones facial expressions of a source model to a target model while reflecting the characteristic feature of the target model.

3   Automatic Facial Model and Texture Reconstruction

In this paper, we assumed that the range scans to reconstruct were upright front faces, in which some other unwanted parts (such as hair, neck, shoulder) might also present. Given such a range scan, our goal is to build a new facial model with texture to reflect the shape and texture of the range scan from a template facial model. The missing data in the facial region of the range scan should be filled and the noise level should be reduced as well.

Our reconstruction method consists of two steps: the first step is to compute the initial rigid registration between a template and a range scan; the second step is to iteratively deform the template model toward the range scan to capture the shape of the range scan and the texture is obtained in the same way.

We prefer triangle meshes for the representation of our models and range scans for efficiency and simplicity. Before elaborating our method, let us introduce some notations used in this paper. A triangle mesh $\mathcal{M}$ consists of a geometrical and a topological component, i.e., $\mathcal{M} = (\mathcal{P}, \mathcal{K})$, where the latter can be represented by a simplicial complex with a set of vertices $\mathcal{V} = \{v_i, 1 \leq i \leq |\mathcal{V}|\}^1$, edges $\mathcal{E} = \{e_i \in \mathcal{V} \times \mathcal{V}, 1 \leq i \leq |\mathcal{E}|\}$ and triangles $\mathcal{F} = \{f_i \in \mathcal{V} \times \mathcal{V} \times \mathcal{V}, 1 \leq i \leq |\mathcal{F}|\}$. The geometric embedding of a triangle mesh into $\mathbb{R}^3$ is specified by associating a 3D position $\mathbf{p}_i$ for each vertex $v_i \in \mathcal{V}$: $\mathcal{P} = \{\mathbf{p}_i := \mathbf{p}(v_i) \in \mathbb{R}^3, 1 \leq i \leq |\mathcal{V}|\}$.

3.1   SICP Registration

In order to reconstruct the surface of a range scan using a template, we need first roughly place the template close to the range scan. Traditionally, this is

---

^{1} $| \cdot |$ denotes the number of elements in the set.

done by manually specifying a small set of landmarks [1,17,21,22]. Our method deals with this problem with no manual intervention.

[?] Since the template facial model and the range scans of human faces have much similarity in shape, it is intuitive to use the ICP algorithm to compute the initial rigid registrations between them. However, there is a challenge dealing with the scale problem, because the size of the facial region in the range scans is not known a priori and the range scans may also include some unwanted parts (see Figure 4).

To deal with the scale problem, we employed an extension version of the ICP algorithm, called the Scaling Iterative Closest Points (SICP) algorithm [7], which integrates a scale parameter s to the original ICP equation and iteratively refines the scale from an estimated initial scale until convergence.

Given a template mesh $\mathcal{M}_{\text{template}}$ and a range scan mesh $\mathcal{M}_{\text{scan}}$, the goal of SICP is to find the transformation (scale s, rotation $\mathbf{R} \in \mathbb{R}^{3\times3}$ and translation $\mathbf{t} \in \mathbb{R}^3$) so that the distance between the registered template mesh $\mathcal{M}'_{\text{template}}$ and $\mathcal{M}_{\text{scan}}$ is as close as possible. Obviously, we should avoid degenerate cases such as $s = 0$ by providing a good initial value for s.

As the original ICP algorithm, SICP is an iterative algorithm, which iteratively refines the registration based on previous registrations until it satisfies a certain termination condition. Let us denote a sequence of registrations by $\mathcal{T} = \{\mathbf{T}_k = (s_k, \mathbf{R}_k, \mathbf{t}_k), 0 \leq k \leq |\mathcal{T}|\}$. Then the registration process can be formulated mathematically as follows,

$$\mathcal{C}_{k+1} = \{\arg\min_{c\in\mathcal{M}_{\text{scan}}} d(s_k\mathbf{R}_k\mathbf{p}_i + \mathbf{t}_k, \mathbf{c})\}, \tag{1}$$

$$(s_{k+1}, \mathbf{R}_{k+1}, \mathbf{t}_{k+1}) = \arg\min_{s,\mathbf{R},\mathbf{t}} \sum_{i=1}^{|\mathcal{P}_{\text{template}}|} \|s\mathbf{R}\mathbf{p}_i + \mathbf{t} - \mathbf{c}_i\|^2, \mathbf{c}_i \in \mathcal{C}_k, \tag{2}$$

where $\mathbf{p}_i \in \mathcal{M}_{\text{template}}$, $d(\cdot)$ is a distance function. Equation 1 is to find the corresponding closest points on $\mathcal{M}_{\text{scan}}$ for the points of $\mathcal{M}_{\text{template}}$ and Equation 2 is the absolute orientation problem [10].

As mentioned above, the initial registration state, $s_0, \mathbf{R}_0, \mathbf{t}_0$, is important for the local convergence of SICP. In our examples, we set the initial values as following,

$$s_0 = \frac{\sum_{i=0}^{N} |\mathbf{q}_i - \bar{\mathbf{q}}|/N}{\sum_{i=0}^{M} |\mathbf{p}_i - \bar{\mathbf{p}}|/M}, \quad \mathbf{R}_0 = \mathbf{I}, \quad \mathbf{t}_0 = \bar{\mathbf{q}} - s_0\mathbf{R}_0\bar{\mathbf{p}}, \tag{3}$$

where $\bar{\mathbf{p}}$ and $\bar{\mathbf{q}}$ are the centroids of the template and the scan meshes, M and N the number of points of the two meshes, and $\mathbf{I}$ the 3×3 identity matrix. Although SICP has many degenerate cases and does not guarantee the global convergence, our tests show its capability to register the template to different range scans (see Figures 1 and 4).

3.2 Deformable Model

Due to the shape diversities between the template facial model and range scans, we need further deform the template after the initial rigid registration. There are two criteria that should be considered during the deformation process. One is the regularity that penalizes dramatic changes in mesh. Another criterion is the fitting error, which can be formulated as the total distance between corresponding points.

Since the template mesh is a two-manifold surface, the change of the surface can be measured by the change of the first and the second fundamental forms and therefore yields a measure of stretching and bending [18]. Given a two-manifold surface $\mathcal{S}$, after deformation, it becomes $\mathcal{S}'$, we can represent the deformed surface $\mathcal{S}'$ by $\mathbf{p}' = \mathbf{p} + \mathbf{d}$, where $\mathbf{p} \in \mathcal{S}$, $\mathbf{p}' \in \mathcal{S}'$, and $\mathbf{d}$ is the displacement. The minimization of the physically based elastic energies yields the so-called Euler-Lagrange partial differential equation (PDE) [4]:

$$-k_s \Delta \mathbf{d} + k_b \Delta^2 \mathbf{d} = 0, \qquad (4)$$

where k_s and k_b are coefficients, Δ and Δ^2 represent the Laplacian and the bi-Laplacian operator, respectively. The Laplacian operator can be extended to triangle meshes to obtain the discrete form of the Laplace-Beltrami operator $\Delta_{\mathcal{M}}$ (refer to [4]). Thus, we can formulate our deformable model as follows,

$$\min_{\mathbf{d}_i} \sum_{i=1}^{M} \| -k_s \Delta_{\mathcal{M}_{\text{template}}} \mathbf{d}_i + k_b \Delta^2_{\mathcal{M}_{\text{template}}} \mathbf{d}_i \|^2 + k_c \sum_{i=1}^{M} w_i \| \mathbf{d}_i - (\mathbf{c}_i - \mathbf{p}_i) \|^2, \quad (5)$$

where $\mathbf{p}_i \in \mathcal{P}_{\text{template}}$, $\mathbf{c}_i \in \mathcal{M}_{\text{scan}}$ is the corresponding closest point of $\mathbf{p}_i$, $\mathbf{d}_i$ is the unknown displacement, and k_s, k_b, k_c represent the contribution of stretching, bending and fitting in the total energy, respectively. $w_i = 1$ if the corresponding closest point satisfies a certain compatible conditions, otherwise 0. We employed the similar compatible conditions as [17,19] to reject pseudo point matching, such as, requiring the angle between two corresponding normals should be greater than 60 degrees, rejecting boundary vertices. The minimization problem can be reformulated as a sparse linear system in terms of least squares [4].

An annealing-like deformation scheme is employed in our experiments. At the initial stage, k_s and k_b are set to relatively large values compared to k_c (In our tests, k_s, k_b and k_c are initially set to 50, 20, 2, respectively). Because at the initial stage we cannot estimate good correspondences between the template and the range scan by the closest points due to the shape diversity and large values of k_s and k_b do not allow dramatic change of the mesh. Then we relax the stiffness of the template facial model by gradually decreasing the values of k_s and k_b toward 1.

3.3   Texture Reconstruction

Texture can improve the reality of facial models. Thus it is desirable to make the textures available for the reconstructed facial models. However, the original range scans usually have holes (missing data). We cannot find all the texture coordinates for the reconstructed facial models.

We solve the texture reconstruction problem in the similar way proposed in the previous section, but here we consider the texture coordinates $\mathbf{u}_i \in \mathbb{R}^2$ as the unknown variables and the equation becomes

$$\min_{\mathbf{u}_i} \sum_{i=1}^{M} \| -k_s \Delta_{\mathcal{M}_{\text{template}}} \mathbf{u}_i + k_u \Delta^2_{\mathcal{M}_{\text{template}}} \mathbf{u}_i \|^2 + k_c \sum_{i=1}^{M} w_i \| \mathbf{u}_i - \mathbf{u}'_i \|^2, \quad (6)$$

where $\mathbf{u}'_i$ is the texture coordinates of the corresponding closest point on the range scan for the point $\mathbf{p}_i$.

When reformulating Equations 5 and 6 in matrix form, we can see that the two equations have the same sparse matrix and only differ in the right hand side. Thus the texture reconstruction can be efficiently solved because the sparse matrix is only factorized once.

4   Facial Expression Transfer

After the facial model and texture reconstruction, all the reconstructed facial models have the same topology as the template one, i.e., the dense point correspondences are automatically established across models. These dense correspondences have numerous applications in many areas such as shape space analysis [1], linear facial model [3], morphing. In this paper, to demonstrate the reconstructed facial models, textures and the correspondences, we show the facial expression transfer from the generic facial model onto various reconstructed facial models by using the deformation transfer technique [17]. The results are shown in Figure 5.

5   Results

We reconstructed 3D facial models from six 3d range scans, which are from the Face Recognition Grand Challenge (FRGC ver2.0) data set [13]. The statistics for the results are shown in Table 1. All computations were performed on a 2.4 GHz Intel Core2 CPU machine with 3 GB RAM. Timings are measured in seconds and exclude I/O operations. The order of the IDs of range scans in

Table 1. Statistics for the results shown in Figure 4

ID	#Points	#Triangles	Registration Time	Reconstruction Time	Total Time
template	1880	3580	-	-	-
02463d550	104425	205176	38	51	89
04485d284	112154	221296	49	68	117
04202d438	60544	118766	28	48	76
04201d368	103061	202160	43	54	79
04213d280	120792	234534	34	53	87
04279d283	112497	219790	38	52	90

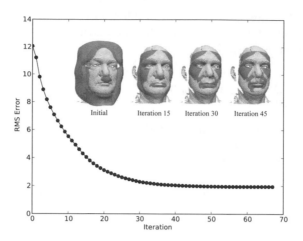

Fig. 1. The RMS error of SICP registration. The inset figures show the overlap between the template model and the range scan (02463d550) during the registration.

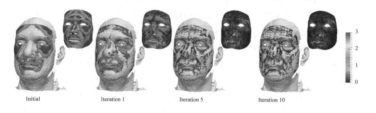

Fig. 2. Deformation process of the deformable model. The colour mapping shows the distances between the template and the range scan (02463d550).

Table 1, which are the unique numbers in FRGC, is the same as that in Figure 4 (a) and (b).

Figure 1 shows the curve of the root-mean-squared (RMS) error during the SICP registration of the template to the range scan (02463d550). The curve definitely indicates the convergence of SICP, which is also shown by the inset figures.

Figure 2 shows the deformation process during reconstruction of the range scan (02463d550). The distances from the template to the range scan are encoded

Fig. 3. The results of texture reconstruction

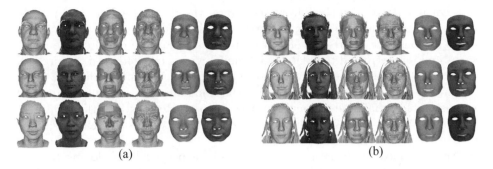

(a)   (b)

Fig. 4. The results of automatic 3D facial model and texture reconstruction. The six range scans, shown in shaded and texture-mapped renderings in the first and second columns, are from the Face Recognition Grand Challenge (FRGC ver2.0) data set [13]. The third (fourth) column in (a) and (b) shows the overlap between the range scans (gray) and the rigid (non-rigid) registered template model (blue). The final reconstructed facial models are shown in the last two columns in shaded and texture-mapped renderings. All these reconstructed models have the same mesh structures.

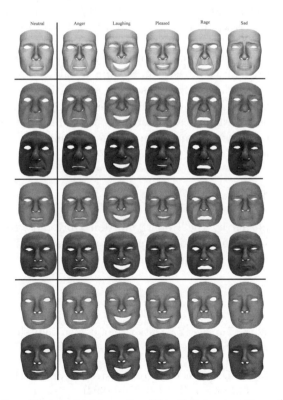

Fig. 5. The results of expression transfer. Five facial expressions (anger, laughing, pleased, rage, sad) of the template facial model, shown in the first row, are transferred onto three reconstructed facial models from range scans by the deformation transfer technique.

into colours. As we can show from the figure, the reconstruction error rapidly decreases across the face during the first several iterations.

To demonstrate the results of texture reconstruction, we rendered the range scans and reconstructed template facial model with a checkerboard texture and the original texture respectively as shown in Figure 3. We can see that the facial features are faithfully matched between the template and the range scan. The reconstructed facial model along with the reconstructed texture (the rightmost in Figure 3) is more realistic than the original range scan as the holes are filled and the noise level is reduced.

We performed the facial expression transfer experiments of cloning five expressions from the template facial model onto three reconstructed facial models. The results are presented in Figure 5.

6   Conclusions and Future Work

We have presented a robust algorithm for 3D facial model and texture reconstruction from range scans of human faces. One of the main benefits of our method is fully automatic. Our method requires no manual intervention and we do not require a small set of corresponding feature landmarks. Our system demonstrates that high quality results can be obtained for a variety of range scans, with a realistic reconstruction of shape and texture. Key to the success of our algorithm is the robust rigid registration based on Scaling Iterative Closest Points (SICP) algorithm and the template fitting based on an elastic deformable model. As future work, we plan to extend our method to 4D range scans. We want to track a temporal sequence of range scans, faithfully reproduce the motion sequences in reconstructed facial models, and then transfer the motion sequences onto any other facial models.

Acknowledgments

This work is supported by the Robert Gordon University Research Development Initiative (RDI) PhD Studentship. The authors would like to thank the FRGC[13] organizers for providing data.

References

1. Allen, B., Curless, B., Popović, Z.: The space of human body shapes: reconstruction and parameterization from range scans. In: Proc. SIGGRAPH '03 Papers, pp. 587–594. ACM, San Diego (2003)
2. Besl, P.J., McKay, N.D.: A method for registration of 3-D shapes. IEEE Trans. Pattern Anal. Mach. Intell. 14(2), 239–256 (1992)
3. Blanz, V., Vetter, T.: A morphable model for the synthesis of 3d faces. In: Proc. SIGGRAPH '99, pp. 187–194. ACM, Los Angeles (1999)
4. Botsch, M., Sorkine, O.: On linear variational surface deformation methods. IEEE Trans. Vis. Comput. Graph. 14(1), 213–230 (2008)

5. Botsch, M., Sumner, R.W., Pauly, M., Gross, M.: Deformation transfer for detail-preserving surface editing. In: Proc. VMV '06, Aachen, Germany, pp. 257–364 (2006)
6. Du, S., Zheng, N., Ying, S., Wei, J.: ICP with bounded scale for registration of m-D point sets. In: Proc. ICME '07, pp. 1291–1294. IEEE Computer Society, Beijing (2007)
7. Du, S., Zheng, N., Ying, S., You, Q., Wu, Y.: An extension of the ICP algorithm considering scale factor. In: Proc. ICIP '07, vol. 5, pp. 193–196. IEEE Computer Society, San Antonio (2007)
8. Haber, J., Terzopoulos, D.: Facial modeling and animation. In: Proc. SIGGRAPH '04 Courses, p. 6. ACM, Los Angeles (2004)
9. Hormann, K., Polthier, K., Sheffer, A.: Mesh parameterization: theory and practice. In: Proc. SIGGRAPH Asia '08 Courses, pp. 1–87. ACM, Singapore (2008)
10. Horn, B.K.P.: Closed-form solution of absolute orientation using unit quaternions. J. Opt. Soc. Am. A 4(4), 629–642 (1987)
11. Li, H., Adams, B., Guibas, L.J., Pauly, M.: Robust single-view geometry and motion reconstruction. In: Proc. SIGGRAPH Asia '09 Papers, p. 175, 1–10. ACM, New York (2009)
12. Noh, J.y., Neumann, U.: Expression cloning. In: Proc. SIGGRAPH '01, pp. 277–288. ACM, Los Angeles (2001)
13. Phillips, P.J., Flynn, P.J., Scruggs, W.T., Bowyer, K.W., Chang, J., Hoffman, K.J., Marques, J., Min, J., Worek, W.J.: Overview of the face recognition grand challenge. In: Proc. CVPR '05, pp. 947–954. IEEE Computer Society, San Diego (2005)
14. Pighin, F., Lewis, J.P.: Performance-driven facial animation. In: Proc. SIGGRAPH '06 Courses. ACM, San Diego (2006)
15. Pyun, H., Kim, Y., Chae, W., Kang, H.W., Shin, S.Y.: An example-based approach for facial expression cloning. In: Proc. SCA '03, pp. 167–176. Eurographics Association, San Diego (2003)
16. Rusinkiewicz, S., Levoy, M.: Efficient variants of the icp algorithm. In: Proc. 3DIM '01, pp. 145–152. IEEE Computer Society, Quebec City (2001)
17. Sumner, R.W., Popović, J.: Deformation transfer for triangle meshes. In: Proc. SIGGRAPH '04 Papers, pp. 399–405. ACM, Los Angeles (2004)
18. Terzopoulos, D., Platt, J., Barr, A., Fleischer, K.: Elastically deformable models. In: Proc. SIGGRAPH '87, pp. 205–214. ACM, Anaheim (1987)
19. Turk, G., Levoy, M.: Zippered polygon meshes from range images. In: Proc. SIGGRAPH '94, pp. 311–318. ACM, Orlando (1994)
20. Vlasic, D., Brand, M., Pfister, H., Popović, J.: Face transfer with multilinear models. In: Proc. SIGGRAPH '05 Papers, pp. 426–433. ACM, Los Angeles (2005)
21. Weise, T., Li, H., Van Gool, L., Pauly, M.: Face/off: live facial puppetry. In: Proc. SCA '09, pp. 7–16. ACM, New Orleans (2009)
22. Zhang, L., Snavely, N., Curless, B., Seitz, S.M.: Spacetime faces: high resolution capture for modeling and animation. In: Proc. SIGGRAPH '04 Papers, pp. 548–558. ACM, Los Angeles (2004)

A Reusable Model for Emotional Biped Walk-Cycle Animation with Implicit Retargeting

Marco Romeo, Marcelo Dematei, Julian Bonequi, Alun Evans, and Josep Blat

Grup de Tecnologies Interactives, Universitat Pompeu Fabra
Carrer Tanger 122-140, 08005 Barcelona, Spain
{marco.romeo,alun.evans,josep.blat}@upf.edu

Abstract. This paper presents a reusable model for rapid animation of the walk-cycle of virtual biped characters, with implicit retargeting of motion capture to any character, regardless of dimensions. Despite modern software continuously improving the quality of automatic assistance, the process of animating a biped character still requires substantial manual intervention. Our research contributes to this field by creating a theoretical model for emotional character walking, defining a series of proportional variables which can be changed to create different emotional walk cycles. We used motion capture data to assign real-world values to these variables, which are then used to procedurally create 'emotional' walk cycles. Due to the fact that we avoid fixed values and work solely with proportions, the system implicitly retargets the data to any biped body shape, regardless of the size and structure of the skeleton.

Keywords: Animation, retargeting, virtual characters.

1 Introduction

Since the idea of technological convergence arose in the early 1990s, the media industry has consistently looked at systems that share resources and interact with each other, cooperating in order to create content in a more efficient and cost-effective manner. This search for more efficient systems is caused, in part, by the nature of digital media production, which remains a very labour intensive, high-risk and high-cost industry. One of the reasons for this is that productions are crafted, almost without exception, at very low levels, in order to better satisfy artistic needs. Indeed, in many applications, the existence of more sophisticated digital tools has actually pushed up costs, as more time is spent on complex off-line processes in the quest for quality.

An excellent example of this can be seen in the design and animation of virtual characters or avatars. These are used in many fields of the audiovisual industry, such as television, video games, internet, and mobile phones. Believable animation (both for bodies and facial expressions) is crucial so that such characters can properly express emotions, improving their ability to communicate. While this issue has been solved in the film industry and, increasingly, in the high-end video games industry, the same techniques cannot be applied to lower-budget productions, due to strong time and hardware resources constraints. Typically, time consumption could be due to

F.J. Perales and R.B. Fisher (Eds.): AMDO 2010, LNCS 6169, pp. 270–279, 2010.
© Springer-Verlag Berlin Heidelberg 2010

the difficulties in creating a good animation rig for preparing handcrafted deformations that express a character's current emotional state. Those difficulties directly affect the hardware resources as complex animation rigs or a high number of different deformations make real-time animations hard to be replayed while maintaining the desired frame rate. In that sense there is the need for an animation methodology that can rapidly (and in real-time) animate a character by using fewer hardware resources and being sufficiently straightforward for animators to setup.

This paper presents one aspect of our research towards this goal, focusing particularly on the typical human walk-cycle animation. Our approach has been to view the problem from the traditional animator's point of view, attempting to apply well-established philosophies of hand-drawn animation within a modern computing framework. Thus, by studying the relationship between a character's apparent centre of gravity and the curvature of it's spine, we present a new model for walk-cycle animation which classifies the possible walk-cycles into one of four separate gaits.

By studying this model, we define a series of proportional variables of body movement (e.g length of stride in proportion to length of leg). Motion capture data was used to provide real values for the defined variables. As the all the data is stored as proportions, this leads to the creation of an algorithm that allows the implicit retargeting of 'emotional' walk-cycle data to any biped with the correct skeletal structure. The result is real-time modification of a basic walk-cycle animation to allow the character to express a wide variety of emotions while walking. Crucially, our system modifies the walk-cycle while *maintains the underlying animation*, thus if a character is limping, the limp is maintained even though the system may tweak aspects of the animation to change the characters expressed emotion.

We demonstrate the system working both as a plugin for Autodesk 3DS Max (for use by animators) and as a self-contained C++ API, for use in custom real-time graphics engines.

2   Related Work

Early efforts to control the animation of walk cycles were made by both Badler et al.[1] and Hodgins et al.[2], who use similar parameter and goal based techniques that are solved by the animation system. This idea of scripting character animation was extended by Perlin and Goldberg[3], who parameterized human 'actions' and blend the motion data to achieve combinations of movement based on different classes (gestures, stances etc.). A logic system prevents clashes between classes such that a character will not sit and stand at the same time.

The major achievement of these studies was to introduce the idea of abstract descriptions of motions, yet they made little effort to generate those motions (either via motion data or manually created animation). This problem was tackled from a more mathematical point of view by several studies[4][5] that attempted to generate movement based on interpreting the movement curves of the joints of the body. These concepts were further extended by the use of multiresolution filters to modify the 'signals' of the movement curves[6].

Grunvogel et al.[7] introduced the concept of *Dynamic Motion Models,* where the combination of abstraction of movement and procedural generation allows complex animations sequences to be rapidly created. A more general version of this is used by

Abadia et al. [8] who use a dynamic timeline to cue animation clips, and provide the framework for automatic creation of such clips based on an overall emotional theme.

The issue of retargeting of motion captured data was tackled by Meredith and Maddock[9], who use weighted inverse kinematics to adapt motion capture data. This results in individual walk-cycle animation for each character, and enables rapid application of unique characteristics, such as a limp.

Research into procedural walk-cycle animation has differed notably from equivalent work into facial animation, in the sense that it has focused less on the use of emotions. In the facial animation field, perhaps the most cited work is that of Ekman[10], who specified the six basic emotions that can be deduced from facial expressions, independent from cultural background. Densley[11] et al did introduce emotion to the characters appearance, by constraining joint angles based on the emotional state of the character.

In a sense, of all the previous research in this field, it is the work of both Densley et al[11] and Meredith and Maddock[9] that bears the most similarity to the work in this paper. In a sense, our approach combines their philosophies but underpins it with a more formal and focused theoretical background.

As mentioned above, our approach has been to tackle this issue using traditional character animation techniques, applied within a modern computing and mathematical framework. For an introduction to animation techniques and their evolution over the years, both Williams[12], and Johnston and Thomas[13] present the subject in detail.

3   Overview of Approach

Figure 1 is intended as an overview of our approach. A Conceptual Model (introduced in Section 4), based on traditional theory of animation, was used to guide and direct motion capture sessions involving male and female actors (see Section 5). The motion data from these sessions was processed (as described in Section 6) and used as an input for our novel retargeting algorithm. We have created two implementations of this algorithm, one as a plugin for the popular modeling and animation software, Autodesk 3D Studio Max, and the other as separate C++ API than can be used to retarget animation in custom 3D animation or games engine.

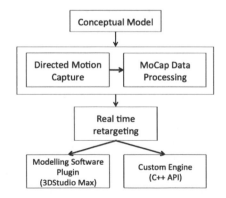

Fig. 1. Diagrammatical overview of the system architecture

4   Conceptual Model

In this section we present our conceptual model that describes how a character's walk cycle may express the character's emotion. Extending some of the principals of the basic walk cycle animation Williams[12], our model is focused on modeling how a character's general posture changes according to the current emotional state. The typical distribution of body mass situates the character's centre of gravity in the lower abdomen. Yet we base our model on the characters *apparent* centre of gravity – the area of the body that, in effect, guides the remainder of the body according to the principals of 'follow-through' animation and 'overlapping action' that are described by Johnston[13]. We use the phrase 'apparent' centre of gravity because we are not physically modeling any changes in the character's actual centre of gravity. In contrast, we are following the traditional animation route of abstracting the concept to a different level in order to allow the animation to better convey the required message.

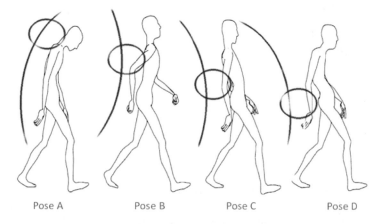

Fig. 2. The four poses of our model. The circle represents the *apparent centre of gravity* – the area of the body that is leading the character while walking. The associated curve shows how the spine is curved in each pose.

Table 1. The four poses of the model, and examples of associated emotions

Pose	Characteristics	Associated emotions
A	Apparent COG is head or neck.	Sadness, Depression Concentration/Worry
	Spine curved into a 'C' shape.	Anger, Hurry Fear
B	Apparent COG at chest height	Happiness, Joy,
	Spine opposite to Pose A	Pride
C	Apparent COG at abdomen	Satisfaction
	Spine curved as B	Relaxation, Serenity
D	Apparent COG dropped to Pelvis	Sensuality, Arrogance Fear
	Spine curved back further than C#	Hurry

Figure 2 shows the four basic poses (or gaits) that we define in our model, based on the location of the characters centre of gravity (COG). Each of these poses associates a particular curve of the spine with a centre of gravity position, which accordingly represents a different manner of walking. The model structures the poses to show the apparent COG dropping in height, from its highest point in the head, to its lowest point in the hips.

So that we could use this model practically in a computer animation system, we translated it into a **series of equations** that describe the movement of the body at each key-frame of the walk cycle[12]. Crucially, all the parameters of these equations are expressed as proportions relating joint position and rotation to the individual dimensions of each skeleton. The list of equations is as follows:

Wrist relative position:
$\mathbf{wrist}.x = \mathbf{wt}.x - (\mathbf{ht}.x + \mathbf{hw}/2)/sw$
$\mathbf{wrist}.y = (\mathbf{wt}.y - \mathbf{ht}.y)/al$
$\mathbf{wrist}.z = (\mathbf{wt}.z - \mathbf{ht}.z)/ll$

Ankle relative position:
$\mathbf{ankle}.x = (\mathbf{at}.x - (\mathbf{ht}.x + hw/2))/hw$
$\mathbf{ankle}.y = \mathbf{at}.y/al$
$\mathbf{ankle}.z = (\mathbf{at}.z - \mathbf{ht}.z)/ll$

Hip relative position:
$\mathbf{hip}.x = \mathbf{ht}.x/hw$
$\mathbf{hip}.y = \mathbf{ht}.y/ll$
$\mathbf{hip}.z = \mathbf{ht}.z$

where **wrist, ankle** and **hip** are location vectors;
wt = wrist translation vector; **at** = ankle translation vector; **ht** = hip translation vector;
sw = Shoulder width (Euclidean distance between left and right shoulder);
hw = Hip width (Euclidean distance between left and right joints);
ll = Leg length (Euclidean distance between leg hip joint and ankle);
al = Arm length (Euclidean distance between the shoulder and the wrist).

For joint **rotations**, wrist, spine, pelvis and neck are taken into account. Neck and spine rotations are considered as a concatenation of local rotations.

These equations then form the core of the model, as by assigning different values to the parameters of the equations we can procedurally generate a variety of different animated walk-cycles.

5   Focused Motion Capture and Extraction of Data

While it is possible to fill the equations of Section 4 with randomly selected values, in order to generate meaningful procedural animation, it is necessary to base the values on some form of real data. To achieve this, we carried out a series of motion capture sessions, where male and female professional actors were carefully directed to walk in a manner that expressed the emotions identified from the different poses of the model (see Table 1). However, the motion capture director was careful not to actually instruct the actors the change their performance based on the model. At the time of recording the motion data, the actors were completely unaware of the model, and were merely told to attempt to express the requested emotion through their gait alone. Figure 3 shows example of the emotions recorded during the capture sessions.

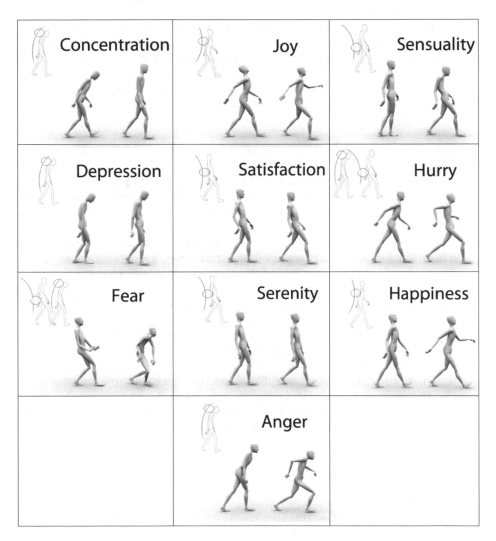

Fig. 3. Still images of real motion capture data, grouped by emotion. Of the two shaded characters in each cell of the table, the one on the right is representing data from the female actor, the character on the left is the male actor. In the upper left corner of each cell is the equivalent pose from the conceptual model (see Figure 2).

6 Implicit Retargeting of Data

Following the motion capture sessions, the recorded data was analysed and the values for the proportional variables for the different emotions were extracted for the five key-frame poses of the typical walk-cycle animation, identified by Williams[12] ("Contact", "Down", "Pass", "Up", "Second Contact"), using the set of equations presented in Section 4.

This resulted in a matrix of proportional values that enable us to mathematically describe the emotions expressed by the actor during the motion capture i.e. a set of values for each emotion. By blending these proportional values into an existing virtual character walk-animation, we are able to transfer the aspects that make the motion captured data "emotional" to the virtual character. It is possible to proportionally blend the data, such that a character can be made to be "a little bit" sad, by blending in only a small percentage of the *Sad* emotion variable set.

Furthermore, there are two very important aspects that separate our system from anything that has been previously produced:

1. **The existing underlying animation of the character is maintained.** The system does not *create* the walk-cycle animation, but modifies the existing animation. This ensures that characters maintain their personality, and any individual quirks added by the animator are not removed.
2. **The dimensions of the character are unimportant.** Because the system is based on the relationship between the proportions of the body, it works on a wide variety of body shapes, so long as the basic skeletal structure is that of a biped.

The equations presented in Section 4 allow values to be *extracted* from the motion capture data. To take those values and apply them to another character (thus carrying out the retargeting) we merely need to inverse the equations to calculate the offsets to the existing animation. As our system only directly controls ankles, hips and wrists, standard inverse kinematics are used to ensure the remainder of the bones of the skeleton move in a believable manner. The side-advantage of this (other than convenience) is that retargeting is *independent of joint-chain length*.

Finally, the system implements time stretching to ensure that the resulting animation matches the average speed of the target emotions (i.e. a sad character should walk slower than a happy one).

6.1 3D Studio Max Plugin

We have created two software implementations for the system, a plugin for 3D Studio Max, and an independent C+ API. Screenshots of our plugin for 3D Studio Max are shown in Figure 4. The plugin allows an animator to easily incorporate the system into an existing walk cycle, using a slider-based GUI to proportionally add or remove aspects of each of the emotions. 10 emotions are explicitly mapped to sliders (those in Figure 3, derived from studying the conceptual model and from studying the literature[10][11][12][13]), by combining the sliders in different proportions, the animator can experiment until the walk-cycle is modified to their satisfaction.

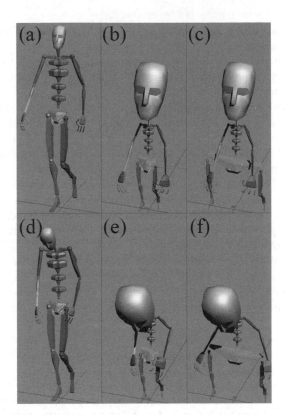

Fig. 4. Screenshots of the results of the plugin developed for Autodesk 3D Studio Max. (a), (b) and (b) show a standard walk animation applied to characters of different dimensions. (d), (e) and (f) show the same characters with the 'Sad' emotion blended in. In (c) and (f), the characters hip joint has been scaled artificially to three times the width, yet the retargeting still works perfectly.

6.2 Independent API

We have also extended the plugin into an independent C++ API that can be used to modify walk-cycles in real time. The API is designed to be used to be used with a variety of graphics and game engines, and we have tested it successfully with two such engines[8][14]. The API gives the developer the option to build in real-time changes to a character's walk-cycle, thus allowing the character to respond directly to actions occurring within the specific application (be they from user input, or from internal factors that may affect the character).

Both the 3D Studio Max plugin and the C++ API are currently being used by our industrial partners in the creation of real-time animated productions.

7   Discussion and Future Work

The contributions of this paper are twofold. First, we present a conceptual model that has enabled us to define a series of proportional variables that describe the biped walk-cycle. Motion capture data was used to creating a matrix of these values for a series of different emotions.

Second, this matrix enabled us to programmatically retarget the emotion-based capture data to any suitable biped walk-cycle, irrespective of character size or shape, and maintaining the underlying animation.

This approach of this system is different to those taken by previous authors. We are not attempting to adapt motion capture mathematically, such as Meredith and Maddick[9]. Neither are we attempting to create a global dynamic motion model such as Grünvogel et al.[7] Rather, we have approached the problem from the practical position of the traditional animator/artist, created a conceptual model, and then used applied modern mathematical and programming solutions to create the final system. This said, the manner in which it has been developed means that it could be easily combined with the weighted inverse kinematic approach of Meredith and Maddock, given that both approaches produce results that *extend* (or tweak) the existing animation, rather than completely replace it.

There are two typical applications of the work, reflected in the two implementations that we have developed. The first is in computer animation for film or television, where our system allows the animator to rapidly add, remove or combine specific emotions to a character, while maintaining the personality that they have created for the that character.

The second, and possibly more powerful, application is for real time situations such as in video games, or 'serious' games for developed for training or educational purposes. Currently in such applications, character emotional state is frequently heavily pre-scripted. Our system opens the door for dynamic linking of emotional walk-cycle animation to non-scripted factors that may affect the 'emotional state' of the character. This enables the character to behave in a more believable way, and reduces the amount of scripted animation work required for the application.

Our future work lies in integrating the system into with other methods in which a character can express emotion, such as static posture, gestures, and facial animation. While systems for both static postures and gestures can be generated using a very similar system that has been presented in this paper, facial animation requires a different approach, and this is the focus of current research.

Acknowledgements

These authors would like to acknowledge the support of the i3Media project and Activa Multimedia Digital, Barcelona, Spain.

References

1. Badler, N., Phillips, C., Lynn, B.: Simulating Humans: Computer Graphics and control. Oxford University Press, Oxford (1993)
2. Hodgins, J., Wooten, W., Brogan, D., O'Brian, J.: Animating human Athletics. Computer Graphics 29, 71–78 (1995)
3. Perlin, K., Goldberg, G.: Improv: A system for scripting interactive actors in virtual worlds. Computer Graphics 30, 205–218 (1996)

4. Witkin, A., Popovic, Z.: Motion Warping. Computer Graphics 29, 105–108 (1995)
5. Unama, M., Takeuchi: Fourier Principals for Emotion-based Human Figure Animation. In: International Conference on Computer Graphics and Interactive Techniques, pp. 91–96. ACM Press, New York (1995)
6. Bruderlin, A., Williams, L.: Motion Signal Processing. Computer Graphics 29, 97–104 (1995)
7. Grünvogel, S., Lange, T., Piesk, J.: Dynamic Motion Models. In: Eurographics (2002)
8. Abadia, J., Evans, A., Ganzales, E., Gonzales, S., Soto, D., Fort, S., Romeo, M., Blat, J.: Assisted Animated Production Creation and Programme Generation. In: ACM Advances in Computer Entertainment Technology, pp. 207–214. ACM Press, New York (2009)
9. Meredith, M., Maddock, S.: Adapting Motion Capture Data Using Weighted Real-Time Inverse Kinematics. ACM Computer in Entertainment 3(1) (2005)
10. Ekman, P., Friesen, W., Ellsworth, P.: What emotion categories or dimensions can observers judge from facial behaviour? In: Ekman, P. (ed.) Emotion in the Human Face (1982)
11. Densley, D., Willis, P.: Emotional Posturing: A Method Towards Achieving Emotional Figure Animation. In: IEEE Computer Animation 1997, pp. 8–14. IEEE Computer Society, Washington (1997)
12. Williams, R.: The Animator's Survival Toolkit. Faber and Faber, London (2001)
13. Johnston, O., Thomas, F.: The Illusion of Life: Disney Animation. Disney Editions (1995)
14. OGRE – Open Source 3D Graphics Engine, http://www.ogre3d.org

CageIK: Dual-Laplacian Cage-Based Inverse Kinematics

Yann Savoye and Jean-Sébastien Franco

LaBRI-INRIA Sud-Ouest, University of Bordeaux
{yann.savoye,jean-sebastien.franco}@inria.fr

Abstract. Cage-based deformation techniques are widely used to control the deformation of an enclosed fine-detail mesh. Achieving deformation based on vertex constraints has been extensively studied for the case of pure meshes, but few works specifically examine how such vertex constraints can be used to efficiently deform the template and estimate the corresponding cage pose. In this paper, we show that this can be achieved very efficiently with two contributions: (1) we provide a linear estimation framework for cage vertex coordinates; (2) the regularization of the deformation is expressed on the cage vertices rather than the enclosed mesh, yielding a computationally efficient solution which fully benefits from cage-based parameterizations. We demonstrate the practical use of this scheme for two applications: animation edition from sparse screen-space user-specified constraints, and automatic cage extraction from a sequence of meshes, for animation re-edition.

1 Introduction

Nowadays, mesh editing and animation techniques play an important role in Computer Graphics. This research domain has been intensively studied over the years. Nevertheless, the relentless increase in demand of industry has inspired researchers to exhibit new coordinate systems as well as new optimization frameworks. Building simple pipelines able to provide more flexible output for animation re-use is a challenging issue. Deformation techniques can be seen as an energy minimization process (defined locally or globally) that measures how much the object has been deformed from its initial pose given a support domain (for instance surface or volume). Approximating the global shape characteristics of the surface aims to produce specific surface resistance properties (like rigidity, flexibility or elasticity). One major challenge is to find a fast framework to achieve plausible boneless inverse kinematics that produce pleasing deformations and preserve the global appearance of the surface.

In this paper, we combine surface and volume deformation techniques. We focus on the estimation of desired enclosed models in a linear framework, which will allows artists to drag sparse surfel displacement constraints over the enclosed mesh surface itself or to fit a given cage across a mesh sequence. We explore a new approach, using a least-square cage as an intermediate and transparent tool, not directly edited by the user for the minimization process. The

F.J. Perales and R.B. Fisher (Eds.): AMDO 2010, LNCS 6169, pp. 280–289, 2010.

model is embedded in an adapted volumetric bounding cage using generalized barycentric coordinates having local properties. We take advantage of optimal reduced parameters offered by the given coarse cage surrounding the surface. To avoid artefacts induced by the large number of degrees of freedom, the cage layer is enhanced with laplacian regularization. The laplacian cage maintains a volumetric deformation of mesh vertices coordinates, more powerfully than applying separately surface-based or cage-based techniques.

The rest of the paper is organized as follows. After briefly reviewing some relevant works concerning surface and volume deformation and discussing in section 2, we give an overview of our system in section 3 and we present the key components of our method in section 4. Section 5 incorporates our novel deformation technique into our novel minimization framework to achieve cage estimation and extraction. We show the effectiveness of our method by both efficient applications in section 6. This paper is concluded and limitations are discussed in section 7.

2   Previous Work

In this section, we briefly overview the large body of relevant work on current techniques addressing the problem of interactive mesh deformation in recent years.

Intrinsic Surface Deformation. Many efforts have been expanded on surface-based deformation. There are several types of approaches exploiting a differential descriptor of the edited surface in terms of laplacian and differential coordinates for mesh editing [1,2]. Differential information as local intrinsic feature descriptors has been massively used for mesh editing in various frameworks over the decade. For instance, the proposed method in [3] allows the reconstruction of the edited surface by solving a linear system that satisfies the reconstruction of the local details in a least-squares sense.

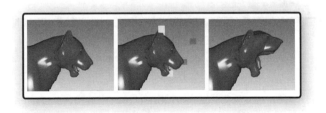

Fig. 1. Laplacian-based Deformation

Early approaches such as [4] motivated the use of Dual Laplacian system to reduce distortion in parametrization and geometry. Another mesh editing method working in the dual domain for regions of interest can be found in [5]. Dual laplacian are a class of approach where the laplacian is not directly expressed on mesh vertices. Unfortunately, laplacians cannot satisfy all natural properties and the differential coordinates are not invariant under rotation. Observing the local behavior of the surface has been proposed recently in [6], where as-rigid-as-possible surface modeling is performed by the minimization of the deformed surface under local rigidity transformation constraints.

Volumetric Space Deformation. There has been a great deal of work done in the past on developing techniques for deforming a mesh with generalized barycentric coordinates. Inspired from the pioneering work presented in [7], caged-based methods are ideal for coherently deforming a surface by improving space deformation techniques. The cage parametrization allows model vertices to be expressed as a combinaition of cage vertices to generate realistic deformation. This family of methods has important properties: quasi-conformal mappings, shape preservation and smoothness. To animate the model, cage vertices are displaced and the vertices of the model move accordingly through a linear weighted combination of cage geometry parameters. An approach to generalize mean value coordinates is introduced in [8]. The problem of designing and controlling volume deformations used to articulated characters are treated in [9], where the introduction of harmonic coordinates significantly improves the deformation stability thanks to a volumetric heat diffusion process respecting the connectivity of mesh volume. This work has been extended in [10,11] to realize spatial deformation transfer. A non linear coordinates system proposed in [12] called Green Coordinates leads space deformations with a shape-preserving property. However such approaches require to obtain automatically a fairly coarse control mesh approximating enough a given surface [13,14].

Fig. 2. Cage-Based Deformation

Boneless Inverse Kinematics. Furthermore, there has been a great deal of work made feasible thanks to the work presented in [15,16,17], where the authors use an analogy to the traditional use of skeleton-based inverse kinematics. A volumetric laplacian approach to preserve the volumetric properties for large deformations has been studied in [18]. Volume preservation is addressed in [19] with a non-linear framework that projected the deformation energy onto the control mesh vertices.

3   Overview

The idea of combining space deformation techniques with surface based techniques proposed in [20] and the lack of reusable surface parameterization for non-rigid surface invited us to abandon the idea of requiring an underlying skeleton and to propose a novel approach called Indirect Cage-Based Dual-Laplacian Deformation. We aim to estimate a sequence of cage parameters expressing the mesh at each animation frame. To realize this cage-based inverse kinematics process we cast the problem as a minimization problem for cage retrieval. The main challenge is to deal with the high number of degree of freedom provided by the coarse cage. We express constraints directly over the enclosed surface and we transfer them to cage using its indirection. In our system, we employ laplacian on the cage to perform a volume deformation surfacically that allows us to obtain a coherent cage estimation.

Even if our work shares similarites with [21] on the idea of producing an hybrid mesh deformation and with [22,10] on the idea of integrating the cage into a minimization framework, our work is novel for the presented optimization problem. However, the key contribution is to solve a sparse linear system to estimate the best cage parameters reproducing the desired deformation of the enclosed model. Besides, such constraints are expressed on the enclosed model and transfered to the subspace domain using the indirection of the bounding cage.

4   Energy Formulation

This section presents the laplacian-based regularization applied on the cage structure only instead of the traditional used on the enclosed mesh. We introduce the association of harmonic subspace deformation with cage-based dual laplacian. In the rest of the paper, we use the following terminology. The coarse bounding mesh $\mathcal{C}$ and the enclosed mesh $\mathcal{M}$ are respectively called *the cage* and *the model*. We assume that both entities are 2-manifold triangular mesh fully-connected. The set of n cage vertices is denoted with $\mathcal{V}_{\mathcal{C}} = \{c_1, \cdots, c_n\}$ where c_i is the location of ith cage vertex, and the set of m model vertices with $\mathcal{V}_{\mathcal{M}} = \{v_1, \cdots, v_m\}$ where v_i is the location of ith model vertex. Vertex location are represented using absolute three dimensional cartesian coordinates.

4.1   Harmonic Subspace Deformation

A cage is a coarse closed bounding polyhedral volume. This flexible low polygon-count polytope, topologically similar to the enclosed object, can efficiently control the deformation of enclosed object and produce realistic looking deformations. Model vertices are expressed as a linear combination of cage vertices. The weights are given by a set of generalized barycentric coordinates stored in a $m \times n$ deformation weights matrix denoted by $\mathcal{H}$. We also denote by $g_k(l)$ the normalized blend weights representing the deforming influence of the kth cage vertex on the lth model vertex. Furthermore it is also possible to deform an arbitrary point on the enclosed mesh written as a linear combination of the coarse mesh vertex position via a constant weight deformation. The forward kinematic a-like function is:

$$v'_i = \sum_{k=1}^{n} g_k(i) \cdot c'_k \qquad (1)$$

where v'_i is the deformed cartesian coordinates according to a vector of cage geometry $\{c'_1, \cdots, c'_n\}$. In order to produce as-local-as possible topological changes on the enclosed surface, the model is rigged to the cage using harmonic coordinates. The harmonic rigging is the pre-computed solution of Laplace's equation with Dirichlet boundary condition obtained by a volumetric heat diffusion in the cage interior. The resulting matrix corresponds to the matrix $\mathcal{H}$. A more efficient technique is to compute harmonic coordinates in a closed-form manner using the BEM formulation, proposed in [23].

4.2   Cage-Based Dual Laplacian

Given the fact that a fairly coarse cage preserves the mesh model structure, we prefer to define the Laplacian on the cage instead of the model to improve the computation process and to keep model detail properties good enough. Therefore expressing the Laplacian on the cage can be seen as expressing a model dual laplacian. Thus, this Dual Laplacian provides an external parameterization of the enclosed mesh ensuring its internal global characteristic thanks to an over determined linear system of equation. Let's denote the Dual Laplacian operator defined at each cage vertex domain by $\mathcal{L}_C(\cdot)$ by the weighted sum of the difference vectors between the vertex and its adjacent neighbors. We also denote the differential coordinates of the cage by $\hat{\delta}$. Encoding each control vertex relatively to its neighborhood preserves the local geometry using differential coordinates. Differential coordinates are obtained by computing the original difference between its absolute cartesian coordinates and the center of mass of its immediate neighbors in the mesh. We determine the internal energy functional $E_{int}(c')$ that measure how smooth the cage is and how similar the deformed cage c' is to the original shape in term of local detail as follows:

$$E_{int}(c') = \left\| \mathcal{L}_C(c') - \hat{\delta}' \right\|_2^2 \qquad (2)$$

This functional guarantees smoothness on large deformation in order to preserve the subspace boundary intrisinc properties without rigidity assumption. Ensuring such a property leads to guarantee global characteristic of the model linearly.

4.3   Surface Constraints

Contrary to existing frameworks where positional constraints enforce vertices to move to a specific target 3D position, we prefer to enforce surface features that are not limited to the set of enclosed mesh vertices. In other to deform the bounding cage, positional constraints are defined on the model using barycentric anchor points. A barycentric anchor a on a piecewise linear surface can be evaluated and described using a linear combination of the barycentric coordinates $\{\gamma_1, \gamma_2, \gamma_3\}$ associated to three vertices $\{v_1, v_2, v_3\}$ of the surrounding triangle T that contains this anchor point as follows:

$$a = \sum_{v_i \in T} \gamma_i \cdot v_i \qquad (3)$$

In the scenario where the user directly specifies source and target positions over the enclosed mesh surface in screen space, dragged-and-dropped barycentric anchors always offer suitable and precise sparse positionnal deformation constraints. To estimate the target point in world space coordinates, we compute the intersection point between the ray passing through the target screen point and the parallel plane to the screen plane defined by the source point. Barycentric informations are collected in a map computed on GPU.

Mixing Equation 2 with Equation 3 leads to a new formulation expression of the cartesian coordinates of a point q_α over the model in term of the cage parameters only:

$$q_\alpha = \sum_{v_i \in T^\alpha} \sum_{k=1}^{n} \gamma_i \cdot c_k \cdot g_k(i) \qquad (4)$$

We denote by q'_α the cartesian coordinates position of the target point associated to q_α to form a positional constraint. The last equation is key component of the proposed method for the handling interaction. The transfer of surfacic contraints into the volumetric domain exploiting the cage indirection is expressed by this function. In other words, the last formulation permits to express surface constraints directly in terms of cage parameters linearly using a inverse quasi-conformal harmonic mapping, motivating the idea of boneless inverse kinematics.

We determine the external energy functional $E_{ext}(c')$ that measure how smooth the cage enforces l positional constraints as follows:

$$E_{ext}(c') = \sum_{j=1}^{l} \left\| q'_j - q_j \right\|_2^2. \qquad (5)$$

5   Indirect Dual-Laplacian Cage-Based Fitting

After having presented the key component of our method, we propose to develop in this section the core of our approach including the linear minimization process.

During the minimization process the cage is seen as a connectivity mesh and feature constraints are seen as external deformation. The surface-and-space based deformation technique preserves the mesh spatial coherence. The geometry of the cage can be reconstructed efficiently from their harmonic indirect coordinates and relative coordinates by solving a system of linear equations. We cast the problem of deformation as least-square laplacian cage reconstruction process using a consistent minimization approach of an objective function requiring linear constraints such as the positional edited constraints. Following the idea presented in [24], the cage parameters recover the sparse pose feature by minimizing an objective function in a least square sense in order to fit a continuous volume. Then the geometry of the desired model is simply obtained by generating its position vertex according to the reconstructed cage parameters obtained on the concept of Least-Square Cage.

Given the differential coordinates and laplacian operator of the default cage, and the harmonic weights $g_k(i)$ according the cage and the model at the default pose, and a several 2D sparse surface constraints the absolute coordinates of the model geometry can be reconstructed by estimating the absolute coordinates of the cage geometry. The combination of the differential coordinates and harmonic coordinates allows the reconstruction the edited surface by solving a linear system that satisfies the reconstruction of the local detail in least squares sense.

Since no exact solution generally exist, our linear least square system reconstructs the geometry of the coarse mesh that allows us to reconstruct the enclosed mesh using a linear caged-based deformation process. The key component of our inverse deformation algorithm is a least-squares minimization. We can formulate overall energy to lead an overdetermined linear system to extract the cage parameters as follows:

$$\min_{c'_i} \left(\alpha \sum_{i=1}^{n} \left\| \mathcal{L}_C (c'_i) - \hat{\delta}'_i \right\|_2^2 + \beta \sum_{j=1}^{l} \left\| q'_j - q_j \right\|_2^2 \right) \tag{6}$$

This least-squares minimization problem can be expressed exclusively in term of cage geometry from Equation 6 as follows:

$$\min_{c'_k} \left(\alpha \sum_{k=1}^{n} \left\| \mathcal{L}_C (c'_k) - \hat{\delta}'_k \right\|_2^2 + \beta \sum_{j=1}^{l} \left\| q'_j - \sum_{v_i \in T^j} \sum_{k=1}^{n} \gamma_i \cdot c'_k \cdot g_k (i) \right\|_2^2 \right)$$

Note that the first term of the energy preserves the global detail of the cage and ensure a pleasant deformation under sparse constraints. The second term of the energy enforces the position of vertices to fit the desired model defined by positional constraints. The system can be weighted by α and β to penalize or advantage both objectives. To our best knowledge, the simple global optimization component of our framework with such formulated constraints to minimize, do not already exist in the litterature. Overall energy performed by our technique reproduce harmonic space deformation recovery under indirected dual laplacian mesh editing. After the cage retrieval process, the geometry of the desired enclosed model is reconstructed in linear combination fonction of cage geometry parameters related to the new estimation, preserving the fix connectivity of the cage using Equation 1.

6   Results

This section describes our experiments using this system. Our framework proposes a robust mechanism to extract a cage for various applications. We demonstrate the feasibility and validity in practice with two experimental applications.

Cage-based Modeling. For the user-driven approach, we apply our algorithm by specifing sparse screen-space positional constraints over the enclosed surface. We have developed an intuitive user interface that allows the user to modelize specific constraints by sketching them. The indirect cage estimation improves the computation of the modeling because of the small system size envoling the cage indirection. The example shown in Figure 3 was generated in 78 microseconds.

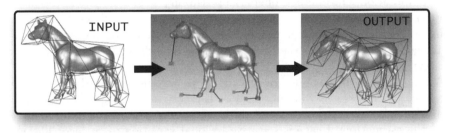

Fig. 3. surface-regularized volume-based deformation under sparse constraints

Cage Recovery. Our framework can also extracts a sequence of cages from a sequence of meshes. For the data-driven approach, we give a sequence of meshes sharing the same connectivity and a default cage. As a result, the system retrieves the corresponding sequence of cage expressing the given animation as output. The system generated automatically the positional constraints using a dense per-vertex mesh displacement mapping from one frame to another to ensure the volume preservation itself. We have processed more than 2000 frames with

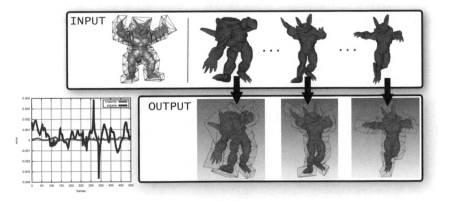

Fig. 4. Cage extraction from mesh sequence

success. The RMS error is shown in green and the volume change in blue in Figure 4. Outputs are reusable to reedit the animation and to re-skin the model.

7   Conclusion

In this paper, we have presented a unified deformation framework based on a new hybrid surfacially-constrained volume deformation system. A mix of generalized barycentric coordinates and laplacian coordinates are used inside a linear minimization framework, to reconstruct an enclosed mesh. This indirect dual-laplacian caged-based mesh editing technique allows users to produce visually pleasing deformations. The linearity of the underlying objective functional makes the processing very efficient and improves the effectiveness of deformable surface computation. Our method offers the possibility to encode global topological changes of the shape with respect of local influence and allows animators to re-use the estimation paraterization. Our framework is not restricted to harmonic coordinates as far as the cage-based coordinate system is linear and local preserving.

A limitation is the cage design, because it is very tedious to define a default cage able to express every animation pose correctly according to a binding process. Last but not least, because of the reduction of parameter induced by the cage, the estimation of cage is sensitive to local variation of surface. The main benefit of our method is that the minimization framework is fully independent of the model resolution. We also observe that the connectivity and positional information of the default cage encode non-trivial soft kinemantic constraints as well as motion signal. We believe this novel approach will offer promising new directions because of the strong interest in hybrid deformation and boneless inverse kinematics.

Acknowledgments

We thanks Scott Schaefer and Qian-Yi Zhou for providing useful datasets. This work was partially supported by ANR-06-MDCA-003-01 DALIA project. In addition, authors thank member of the Iparla project-team for helpful discussions.

References

1. Lipman, Y., Sorkine, O., Cohen-Or, D., Levin, D., Rössl, C., Seidel, H.P.: Differential coordinates for interactive mesh editing. In: Proceedings of Shape Modeling International, pp. 181–190. IEEE Computer Society Press, Los Alamitos (2004)
2. Sorkine, O.: Differential representations for mesh processing. Computer Graphics Forum 25, 789–807 (2006)
3. Lipman, Y., Sorkine, O., Alexa, M., Cohen-Or, D., Levin, D., Rössl, C., Seidel, H.P.: Laplacian framework for interactive mesh editing. International Journal of Shape Modeling (IJSM) 11, 43–61 (2005)
4. Au, O.K.C., Tai, C.L., Liu, L., Fu, H.: Dual laplacian editing for meshes. IEEE Transactions on Visualization and Computer Graphics 12, 386–395 (2006)

5. Luo, Q., Liu, B., Ma, Z.g., Zhang, H.b.: Mesh editing in roi with dual laplacian. In: CGIV '07: Proceedings of the Computer Graphics, Imaging and Visualisation, pp. 195–199. IEEE Computer Society Press, Los Alamitos (2007)
6. Sorkine, O., Alexa, M.: As-rigid-as-possible surface modeling. In: Proceedings of Eurographics/ACM SIGGRAPH Symposium on Geometry Processing, pp. 109–116 (2007)
7. Meyer, M., Lee, H., Barr, A., Desbrun, M.: Generalized barycentric coordinates on irregular polygons. Journal of Graphics Tools 7, 13–22 (2002)
8. Ju, T., Schaefer, S., Warren, J.: Mean value coordinates for closed triangular meshes. In: SIGGRAPH '05: ACM SIGGRAPH 2005 Papers, pp. 561–566. ACM Press, New York (2005)
9. Joshi, P., Meyer, M., DeRose, T., Green, B., Sanocki, T.: Harmonic coordinates for character articulation. ACM Trans. Graph. 26, 71 (2007)
10. Ben-Chen, M., Weber, O., Gotsman, C.: Variational harmonic maps for space deformation. In: SIGGRAPH '09: ACM SIGGRAPH 2009 papers, pp. 1–11. ACM, New York (2009)
11. Ben-Chen, M., Weber, O., Gotsman, C.: Spatial deformation transfer. In: SCA '09: Proceedings of the 2009 ACM SIGGRAPH/Eurographics Symposium on Computer Animation, pp. 67–74. ACM, New York (2009)
12. Lipman, Y., Levin, D., Cohen-Or, D.: Green coordinates. In: ACM SIGGRAPH 2008 papers, pp. 78:1–78:10. ACM, New York (2008), doi:10.1145/1399504.1360677
13. Ju, T., Zhou, Q.Y., van de Panne, M., Cohen-Or, D., Neumann, U.: Reusable skinning templates using cage-based deformations. ACM Trans. Graph. 27, 1–10 (2008)
14. Xian, C., Hongwei Lin, S.G.: Automatic generation of coarse bounding cages from dense meshes. In: IEEE International Conference on Shape Modeling and Applications (Shape Modeling International 2009) (2009)
15. Sumner, R.W., Zwicker, M., Gotsman, C., Popović, J.: Mesh-based inverse kinematics. ACM Trans. Graph. 24, 488–495 (2005)
16. Der, K.G., Sumner, R.W., Popović, J.: Inverse kinematics for reduced deformable models. In: SIGGRAPH '06: ACM SIGGRAPH 2006 Papers, pp. 1174–1179. ACM, New York (2006)
17. Shi, X., Zhou, K., Tong, Y., Desbrun, M., Bao, H., Guo, B.: Mesh puppetry: cascading optimization of mesh deformation with inverse kinematics. ACM Trans. Graph. 26, 81 (2007)
18. Zhou, K., Huang, J., Snyder, J., Liu, X., Bao, H., Guo, B., Shum, H.Y.: Large mesh deformation using the volumetric graph laplacian. ACM Trans. Graph. 24, 496–503 (2005)
19. Huang, J., Shi, X., Liu, X., Zhou, K., Wei, L.-Y., Teng, S.H., Bao, H., Guo, B., Shum, H.Y.: Subspace gradient domain mesh deformation. ACM Trans. Graph. 25(3), 1126–1134 (2006)
20. Cohen-Or, D.: Space deformations, surface deformations and the opportunities in-between. J. Comput. Sci. Technol. 24, 2–5 (2009)
21. Borosan, P., Howard, R., Zhang, S., Nealen, A.: Hybrid mesh editing. to appear in Proc. of Eurographics 2010 (short papers), Norrkoping, Sweden (2010)
22. Chen, L., Huang, J., Sun, H., Bao, H.: Cage-based deformation transfer. Computers & Graphics (2010)
23. Rustamov, R.M.: Boundary element formulation of harmonic coordinates. Technical report (2008)
24. Sorkine, O., Cohen-Or, D.: Least-squares meshes. In: Proceedings of Shape Modeling International, pp. 191–199. IEEE Computer Society Press, Los Alamitos (2004)

Automatic Key Pose Selection for 3D Human Action Recognition

Wenjuan Gong, Andrew D. Bagdanov, F. Xavier Roca, and Jordi Gonzàlez

Universitat Autònoma de Barcelona, Computer Vision Center
Campus UAB Edifici O, 08193 Bellaterra, Spain

Abstract. This article describes a novel approach to the modeling of human actions in 3D. The method we propose is based on a "bag of poses" model that represents human actions as histograms of key-pose occurrences over the course of a video sequence. Actions are first represented as 3D poses using a sequence of 36 direction cosines corresponding to the angles 12 joints form with the world coordinate frame in an articulated human body model. These pose representations are then projected to three-dimensional, action-specific principal eigenspaces which we refer to as *aSpaces*. We introduce a method for key-pose selection based on a local-motion energy optimization criterion and we show that this method is more stable and more resistant to noisy data than other key-poses selection criteria for action recognition.

Keywords: Human action recognition, direction cosine, key poses, bag of words.

1   Introduction

Human action recognition is an important problem in computer vision. Applications include video surveillance, automatic video indexing and human computer interaction. In surveillance systems installed in places requiring high security, such as banks, human action recognition can be applied to detect abnormal human actions and potentially dangerous situations before they become truly dangerous. Human action characterization is also making inroads in the area of security and safety monitoring. Behavior analysis systems are being built to monitor the safety of children and the elderly, and in such scenarios, abnormal action detection can be used to detect dangerous situations like falling down. Automatic video indexing for video and image libraries can be enhanced using human action recognition and by allowing semantics-based access to multimedia content. Human action recognition can also be applied in human computer interaction, where recognition results can be used to understand human behaviors so computers can react accordingly.

Despite increased interest in recent years, human action recognition remains a challenging problem. The flexibility of the human body and the variability of human actions produce high-dimensional motion data. How to represent these

F.J. Perales and R.B. Fisher (Eds.): AMDO 2010, LNCS 6169, pp. 290–299, 2010.
© Springer-Verlag Berlin Heidelberg 2010

data in a compact and effective way is the first challenge. Also, as a classification problem, the extreme variability of pose and body articulation occurring in instances of the same action type make class characterization very difficult. Conversely, similarities of pose and cadence across different action types, for example running and jogging, make identifiable action classes difficult to discriminate. How to model human actions to be generic enough for one action and specific enough to distinguish different actions is another challenge.

Some researchers utilize 3D motion data in the original dimensional space, for example [7], [8] and [12], while others explore polar angles [3] or direction cosines [14]. Our representation to human action recognition is as follows. We use a 3D stick figure of twelve limbs to model the human body. The orientation of each limb is represented by three direction cosines of the angles made by the limb and the world coordinate system. Direction cosines posses a number of useful invariants, and in particular by using them we eliminate the influence of different limb lengths. Another advantage of using direction cosines compared to Euler angles is that they do not lead to discontinuities in motion sequences. Also, compared to quaternion, they have a direct geometric interpretation [17]. Motion sequences are then represented as a sequence of static human postures, each represented as a vector of direction cosines. Since the natural constraints of the human body motion lead to highly correlated data in the original space [16], we derive a compact, non-redundant representation of human pose by applying Principle Component Analysis (PCA) to these pose sequences. This space (*aSpace*) then becomes the basis for vocabulary selection. Considering the impressive performance of recent applications of bag of words architecture in classification [6,5,2], we introduce this architecture to solve the action recognition problem. In the bag of words model, the target is represented as an unordered collection of representative features (vocabulary). In our approach, we modify the bag of words architecture by computing the vocabulary as the most representative poses, or *key poses*, resulting in a *bag of poses* model for human action recognition.

The main contributions of this work are:

- We calculate the most representative poses, or *key poses*, as the vocabulary. By doing this, we pick the most representative features and the vocabulary is very concise.
- We extend the human walking model in [14] to include 'jump', 'box' and, 'run' actions. And we utilize all these action models as priors in action recognition.
- We compare our method of extracting key poses with other methods: poses corresponding to randomly spaced frames [1], equally spaced frames [10], local maximum distances [3] and centers of clusters calculated using k-means clustering. Our method has a comparatively stable performance and is more resistant to noisy data.

In the next section we introduce our representation of human posture and human motion. Section 3 explains our classification method, and we give experimental

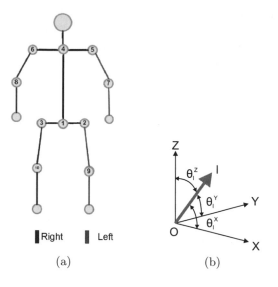

Fig. 1. (a) The 3D stick figure model used for representing human pose. Ten principal joints corresponding to the markers used in motion capture are used [15]. (b) Angles $(\theta_l^x, \theta_l^y, \theta_l^z)$ between the limb l and the axes [14].

results in Section 4. We conclude in section 5 with a discussion of our results and future work.

2   Human Posture and Human Motion Models

We use the same representations for human posture and human motion as in [14]. In this section, we give a brief introduction to how we represent a static human posture using direction cosines derived from a human body model. Then, we explain our extensions to the human motion models of [14].

2.1   Representing Human Posture and Motion

In our method, a human body is modeled as twelve rigid body parts: hip, torso, shoulder, neck, two thighs, two legs, two arms and two forearms. These parts are connected by a total of ten inner joints, as shown in figure 1(a). Body segments are structured in a hierarchical manner, constituting a kinematic tree rooted at the hip, which determines the global rotation of the whole body.

A static human posture is represented as a vector of limb orientations. Limb orientation is modeled using three parameters, without modeling self rotation of limbs around its axes, as shown in figure 1(b). The posture of the subject in each frame is represented using a vector of direction cosines measured on twelve limbs. This results in a 36-dimensional representation:

$$\psi = [\cos(\theta_1^x), \cos(\theta_1^y), \cos(\theta_1^z), \ldots, \cos(\theta_{12}^x), \cos(\theta_{12}^y), \cos(\theta_{12}^z)], \tag{1}$$

where θ_l^x, θ_l^y and θ_l^z are the angles between the limb l and the axes as shown in figure 1(b).

After representing static human postures using direction cosines, we represent a motion sequence of one performer as a sequence of static postures:

$$\Psi = [\psi_1, \psi_2, \dots, \psi_n], \tag{2}$$

where n is number of postures (frames) in this motion performance.

2.2   The Projected Parameter Space: *aSpace*

Using the representations mentioned above, a human motion sequence with n postures will have a $36 \times n$ dimensional representation. Since the natural constraints of the human body motion lead to highly correlated data in the original space [16], we apply PCA to decrease dimensions of the representation (refer to [14] for more details). Figure 2 are visualizations of variations in *aSpaces* re-projected to the original parameter space. From figure 2, we can see what pose variations each eigenvector accounts for in the eigenspace decomposition. For example, we can see that the most significant eigenvectors in the walking and running spaces correspond to their characteristic, vigorous, and simultaneous motion of the arms and legs. The most significant eigenvector for 'box', on the other hand, accounts for the boxer's characteristic footwork and torso rotation. And the first three eigenvectors represent most of the energies from all the actions.

2.3   Human Motion Model

The authors of [14] propose a method of modeling human walking. First, they synchronize the data (the same method as in [13]) to find corresponding postures from different motion performances with different frame numbers and map all performances to the same length. Second, they calculate mean performance from synchronized data and model human walking using this mean performance, the standard deviation, the mean direction of motion and the covariance matrix of the error. This model achieved high performance in tracking walking humans. Considering the capability of extracting common characteristics of walking action, we introduce this model into action recognition problem.

We consider four actions: 'walk', 'run', 'box' and 'jump'. Figure 3 shows the mean performances for all actions in their respective *aSpaces*. We observe that mean performances from different actions are distinguishable enough and based on these models, we propose "bag of poses" architecture for action recognition.

3   Bag of Poses

The bag of words architecture (sometimes called bag of features) was first proposed for text document analysis and further adopted for computer vision applications. The main steps in the bag of words model are as follows: compute

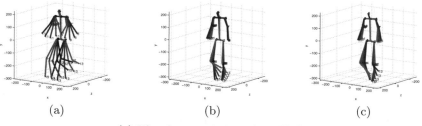

(a) The three variations for *aWalk*.

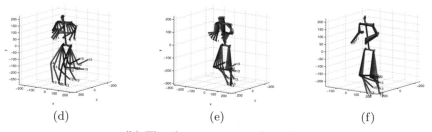

(b) The three variations for *aRun*.

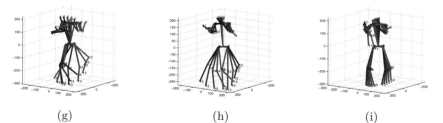

(c) The three variations for *aBox*.

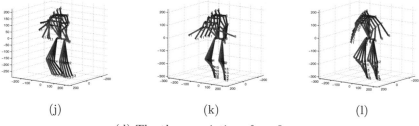

(d) The three variations for *aJump*.

Fig. 2. Visualizations of variations in *aSpace*s re-projected to the original parameter space. Figures in the first, second and third columns correspond to eigenvectors with the largest, the second largest and the third largest eigenvalues separately. Figures in different rows are from different actions. Variations of postures in one figure are re-projections of −3 to 3 times its corresponding eigenvector in *aSpace*s.

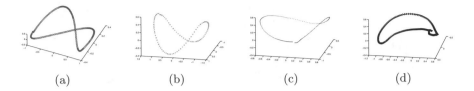

(a)   (b)   (c)   (d)

Fig. 3. Mean performances for (a) 'walk', (b) 'run', (c) 'box' and (d) 'Jump'

descriptors for input data; compute representative words using k-means cluster-ing over feature descriptors to form vocabulary; quantize descriptors into words and represent input data as histograms over the vocabulary, of a *bag of words*. We modify the architecture by calculating the vocabulary using energy opti-mization over human motion sequences instead of k-means clustering. Since we represent motion sequences as occurrences of poses, we name our model the "bag of poses".

3.1   Vocabulary

In bag of words architecture, k-means is the most frequently used method for vocabulary computation. Instead of k-means, we calculate words as poses with local maximum and local minimum energy differences. Given the mean perfor-mance of an action, the motion energy at the i-th frame is defined as [9]:

$$E_i = |\overline{\psi}_{a_k}^i - \overline{\psi}_{a_k}^{i-1}|^2, \tag{3}$$

where $|.|$ denotes Euclidean distance. We calculate frame numbers with local maximum and local minimum motion energies.

After obtaining the frame numbers with local maximum and local minimum energies in *aSpace*, we reconstruct them to get human poses in the original space:

$$\psi' = \mathbf{E}_b \widetilde{\psi} + \overline{\psi}, \tag{4}$$

where $\mathbf{E}_b$ is the matrix of principal eigenvectors constituting basis for this par-ticular *aSpace*. This step is important, as each *aSpace* represents an independent and action-specific sub-manifold of the original space, and as such two *aSpace* representations from different actions are not directly comparable. Re-projecting to the original space, however, makes this comparison possible.

Using the above method, we calculate key poses for each action separately and then concatenate them to compose the vocabulary. Figure 4 shows key poses extracted for all actions. These key poses are now the vocabulary of poses used in our model. For each human motion sequence, each human pose is assigned to a single key pose by computing the Euclidean distance between it and each key pose in the vocabulary. The result is a the histogram of occurrence of these key poses for each motion sequence.

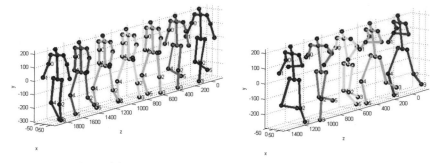

(a)   (b)

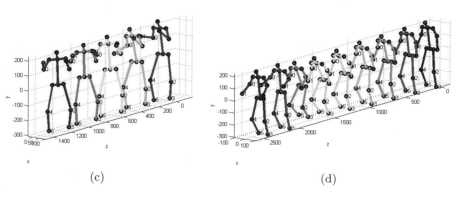

(c)   (d)

Fig. 4. Key poses extracted using energy measurement for (a) 'walk', (b) 'run', (c) 'box', and (d) 'jump'

3.2   Classification

A support vector machine is trained using training motion sequences. We use a linear kernel in all experiments. We tried voting for classification: given a test motion sequence, we calculate the nearest key poses for all postures and label them with the action type of the nearest key poses, finally the test sequence is labeled as the action type with the maximum occurrences. The performance of voting is not as good as histogram and support vector machine, due to the fact that for action recognition, the occurrences of key poses are also important characteristics. We will show classification results in the next section.

4   Experimental Results

We test our method on CMU Graphics Lab Motion Capture Database[1]. This database includes 23 motion categories (run, walk, jump, varied and so on). The data are joint positions in world coordinates captured using a marker set. In our experiments, we consider four actions: 'walk', 'run', 'box' and 'jump'. We split

---

[1] http://mocap.cs.cmu.edu/

Table 1. The composition of the dataset for all experiments. Each action type consists of a number of performances, which in turn contain a number of cycles of that action and finally the postures comprising these cycles.

Action	Performances #	Motion Cycles #	Body Postures #
Walk	67	126	16,891
Run	23	23	2,032
Box	1	37	6,865
Jump	18	24	3,504

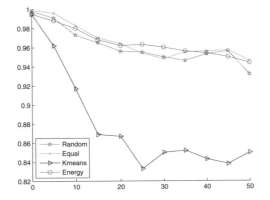

Fig. 5. Classification accuracy of different methods with different scale of noises

the motion cycles for each recorded motion sequence and then synchronize the motion cycles using methods in [13]. Thus, a motion *cycle* becomes the basic unit of classification in our experiments. The composition of the data is shown in Table 1.

We add zero-mean Gaussian noise to the performance data with covariance equals $\kappa \cdot \sigma$, where σ is the covariance between the mean performance $\overline{\Psi}$ and all the training performance in an action, and κ is a scale factor controlling the noisy degree. Noise from reconstructions of human poses from videos or images are not necessarily the same distribution as those from capturing motion data. We choose to add noise of the same distribution instead of adding some random unknown noise to check the trend of performances and the stability of the methods. After adding noise to the test data, we perform leave-one-out cross validation over the entire dataset.

To compare with our method, we implemented four additional methods for computing the vocabulary of key poses:

1. Poses corresponding to randomly spaced frames: $\Psi^r = \{\psi_1, \psi_2, ..., \psi_k\}$, where each ψ_j is randomly selected.
2. Poses corresponding to equally spaced frames [10]: $\Psi^e = \{\psi_1, \psi_2, ..., \psi_k\}$, where each ψ_j and ψ_{j+1} are equally spaced in time.

3. Poses with local maximum Mahalanobis distances [3]: Key poses are defined from a probabilistic point of view where characteristic postures are the least likely body postures of each mean performance.
4. The center poses of the clusters: $\Psi^r = \{\psi_1, \psi_2, ..., \psi_k\}$, where ψ_j is the center of the cluster C_j calculated using the k-means methods.

We test the four methods with step size as 5 and noise κ ranging from 0 to 50. N equals 210, the number of all the performances. We set the number of key poses in the first and the second methods 26, the same as the vocabulary size in our method. Also, we set the number of the clusters in the fourth method as 26.

The experiment results are shown in figure 5. The horizontal axis represents the added noises, the vertical axis represents the classification accuracy and we compare our method with other three methods. From the figure, we can see that methods based on 'randomly spaced key poses', 'equally spaced key poses' and 'key poses from energy optimization' outperform method based on 'k-means clustering'. Method based on 'distance' is not shown in the figure, since the rest four methods outperform this one. The reason that method based on 'distance' does not give good performance might be different ways of comparison with the vocabulary: in our architecture, we compute the distance using Euclidean distance while in method based on 'distance', they use Mahalanobis distance. Methods based on 'equally spaced key poses' and 'randomly spaced key pose' outperform our 'energy optimization' method with small noises, but their performances sometimes increase while increasing noise scales. We conclude that our selected key poses are more representative, so our method is more stable than the others and more resistant to noisy data.

5   Conclusions and Future Work

We propose a "bag of poses" model for action recognition and report on experiments with the CMU Graphics Lab Motion Capture Database. We show that our method is effective and more stable than other implemented methods. By using a statistical method to model human actions, we extend the work of [14] to include more actions. Our resulting model is able to represent all actions using a very compact representation consisting of histograms of key pose occurrences. Experiments show that our approach is also robust over a wide range of noise intensities in the underlying pose representation.

We should note that there is a body of work in computer graphics on action characterization in 3D motion capture databases [4,11]. Although the goals of these approaches are different from us, and they focus mostly on retrieval, an eventual comparison with these techniques in the future could be fruitful.

Acknowledgements

This work has been supported by the Spanish Research Program Consolider-Ingenio 2010: MIPRCV (CSD200700018) and by the Spanish projects TIN2009-14501-C02-01 and TIN2009-14501-C02-02.

References

1. Arie, B.J., Wang, Z., Pandit, P., Rajaram, S.: Human Activity Recognition Using Multidimensional Indexing. IEEE Trans. Pattern Anal. Mach. Intell. 24(8), 1091–1104 (2002)
2. Bosch, A., Zisserman, A., Munoz, X.: Representing shape with a spatial pyramid kernel. In: CIVR '07, pp. 401–408. ACM, Amsterdam (2007)
3. Gonzàlez, J., Varona, J., Roca, F.X., Villanueva, J.J.: Analysis of Human Walking Based on a Spaces. In: Perales, F.J., Draper, B.A. (eds.) AMDO 2004. LNCS, vol. 3179, pp. 177–188. Springer, Heidelberg (2004)
4. Kovar, L.: Automated Extraction and Parameterization of Motions in Large Data Sets. ACM Transactions on Graphics 23, 559–568 (2004)
5. Lazebnik, S., Schmid, C., Ponce, J.: Beyond Bags of Features: Spatial Pyramid Matching for Recognizing Natural Scene Categories. In: CVPR '06, Anchorage, Alaska, pp. 2169–2178 (2006)
6. Li, F., Perona, P.: A Bayesian Hierarchical Model for Learning Natural Scene Categories. In: CVPR '05, Washington, DC, USA, pp. 524–531 (2005)
7. Lv, F., Nevatia, R., Lee, M.: 3D Human Action Recognition Using Spatio-temporal Motion Templates. In: CVHCI '05, p. 120
8. Lv, F., Nevatia, R.: Recognition and Segmentation of 3D Human Action Using HMM and Multi-Class AdaBoost. In: Leonardis, A., Bischof, H., Pinz, A. (eds.) ECCV 2006. LNCS, vol. 3954, pp. 359–372. Springer, Heidelberg (2006)
9. Lv, F., Nevatia, R.: Single View Human Action Recognition using Key Pose Matching and Viterbi Path Searching. In: CVPR'07, Minneapolis, Minnesota, USA , pp. 1–8 (2007)
10. Masoud, O., Papanikolopoulos, N.: A Method for Human Action Recognition. Image and Vision Computing 21(8), 729–743 (2003)
11. Müller, M., Röder, T., Clausen, M.: Efficient content-based retrieval of motion capture data. ACM Transactions on Graphics 24(3), 677–685 (2005)
12. Raptis, M., Wnu, K., Soatt, S.: Flexible Dictionaries for Action Classification. In: Proceedings of the Workshop on Machine Learning for Visual Motion Analysis (2008)
13. Rius, I., Gonzàlez, J., Mozerov, M., Roca, F.X.: Automatic learning of 3D pose variability in walking performances for gait analysis. International journal for computational vision and biomechanics 1, 33–43 (2007)
14. Rius, I., Gonzàlez, J., Varona, J., Roca, F.X.: Action-specific motion prior for efficient Bayesian 3D human body tracking. Pattern Recognition 42(11), 2907–2921 (2009)
15. Sigal, L., Black, J.M.: HumanEva: Synchronized video and Motion Capture Dataset for Evaluation of Articulated Human Motion. Brown University (2006)
16. Zatsiorsky, M.V.: Kinematics of Human Motion. Human Kinetics Publishers (1998)
17. Zatsiorsky, M.V.: Kinetics of Human Motion. Human Kinetics Publishers (2002)

Adjusting Animation Rigs to Human-Like 3D Models

Jorge E. Ramirez, Antonio Susin, and Xavier Lligadas

Universitat Politècnica de Catalunya
Barcelona, Spain
jramirez@lsi.upc.edu, toni.susin@upc.edu, xavi@lsi.upc.edu
http://www.lsi.upc.edu/~moving/

Abstract. In the animation process of a human-like 3D model, a skeleton must be specified to define the model's surface deformation of its limbs. Nowadays the skeleton specification is hand made and very time consuming task. In this paper we propose a novel semi-automatic method for rigging a 3D model in an arbitrary pose using a skeleton defined in an animation datafile with no specific initial pose. First a skeleton is extracted from the voxelized model, this skeleton is refined and transformed into a tree-data structure. Because the 3D model can be in an arbitrary pose, user interaction is required to select the five limbs correspondence (head, hands and feet), and finally a skeleton taken from an animation data file or a external source is adjusted to the geometric skeleton.

Keywords: Skeleton driven animation, rig adjustment, skeletonization, thinning, voxelization,skinning,animation.

1 Introduction

In skeleton driven animation one of the most time consuming tasks is the rig process. The rig process places a set of controls (joints) that interconnected by artificial bones (links) specify which parts of the 3D model must be rotated and translated to produce the desired motion (skeleton binding). Nowadays, the rig process is done manually, and it is created by placing the joints in the character's medial axis where an articulation should be. The number of joints that a skeleton will have depends directly on the animator and the chosen animation technique. If it concerns to a hand-made animation the number of joints used in a skeleton will be defined entirely by the animator. If the technique used is motion capture the number of joints used in a skeleton will depend on the number of captured joints.

The rigging process is tedious and time consuming, to reduce this time we have developed a human assisted method that allows an easy reuse of predefined skeletons that can be taken from motion captured files or previous character animations and adjust it to an arbitrary 3D model. Our method extracts a skeleton using a thinning process over a previously voxelized 3D model. In this

F.J. Perales and R.B. Fisher (Eds.): AMDO 2010, LNCS 6169, pp. 300–309, 2010.
© Springer-Verlag Berlin Heidelberg 2010

paper we define a **geometric skeleton** as the obtained skeleton after finishing the thinning process, and a **logic skeleton** as the one created by an animator or taken from a motion capture file. A logic skeleton could be used in different 3D models if joints parameters were properly adjusted, this adjustment can be done manually or automatically. In this paper we present a method to adjust a logic skeleton to a geometric skeleton. While other approaches are constrained to an initial pose (T-pose or anthropometric pose), which makes the adjustment easier, our method is not pose constrained and we deal with models without a specific initial pose. Nowadays, these kind of models are becoming popular because they can be obtained from scanners or vision systems.

1.1 Related Work

Our work is initially based on the skeleton extraction, in 2D this problem was solved using hexagonal sampling [11] as an alternative to the classic square sampling.

In the 3D case we can find several thinning algorithms ([2],[1],[8],[7]) based on removing voxels from the surface of the voxelized model until only a skeleton remains. In [10] the Euclidean distance and the Discrete medial surface is used to extract a 3D skeleton. A penalized algorithm [9] based in a modified dijkstra method is used for skeleton extraction, and a hybrid method [3] use a modified version of the thinning algorithm mixed with force fields to refine the process. For the automatic rigging [4] and [12] propose two different approaches. In [4] a predefined skeleton is embedded into the model's medial surface. A new method to extract the skeleton is proposed in [12], where using two 3D silhouettes and the mid points of the internal edges of a Delaunay triangulation, a skeleton is estimated.

1.2 Method Overview

The main idea of our method is to use an existing logic skeleton, and adjust it to an arbitrary human-like model. The geometric skeleton creation process is based on the method described in [5]. A geometric skeleton is the mapping to a tree data structure of the skeleton obtained after the thinning process is applied over the voxelized closed mesh.

There are two main advantages of representing a geometric skeleton as a tree data structure:

1. **Fast and easy traversal over all the skeleton:** When the thinning procedure has been applied to the model, we define a node for each obtained voxel. All the operations (coordinate transforms, neighborhood and classification of the nodes) done over the voxelized space are applied and stored in a data structure.
2. **Allow us to perform operations over nodes:** Modify or delete a node or an entire set of nodes (loops).

The chosen data structure to represent our geometric skeleton is a n-ary tree.

2   Creation Process

To create a geometrical skeleton we use a modification of the traversal algorithm described in [5]. Basically we create a node of the tree each time the algorithm is traversing a new voxel. As starting point we choose a random voxel from the thinned model.

Node classification. In [5] the voxels or points of the skeleton where classified by their neighborhood, in this paper we are going to use this classification for the nodes of the geometric skeleton. The nodes are classified as:

- **Flow nodes:** Nodes with two neighbors, these nodes represent tubular segments of the skeleton, usually limbs (legs, arms, neck, etc.). In our tree data structure this kind of nodes will have one child and one parent.
- **Connection nodes:** These nodes will have a number of neighbors greater than two. They usually represent a solid-rigid part of the model, like the hips or the chest. In our tree data structure this can be a node with or without parent and more than one child.
- **End nodes:** Nodes with only one neighbor. These nodes will represent the final section of a limb, like the hands, feet, or the head. In our data structure this will be a node with only one neighbor, its parent.

2.1   Geometric Skeleton Post-processing

Once the geometric skeleton is created, we apply a post-process to refine it. This post-process will have the following steps:

1. **Deletion of loops and redundant nodes:** The result of the thinning process over a voxelized model is a set of voxels that represents a skeleton. Usually, this set has voxels which could be noisy or redundant nodes (voxels which can not be removed because of their topology condition [2]). We must have in mind that the size of the voxel in our space can change the number of details and noise in the geometric skeleton. If the voxel size is small, the thinning algorithm tends to introduce more voxels as end nodes, this will generate more branches in the geometric skeleton (fig. 1) .

2. **Root node adjust:** Because we use a random voxel as starting point in the creation of a geometric skeleton, the root node must be adjusted. Only connection nodes can be root nodes. The main reason for this is that in practically all the animation formats, the hips are taken as the center of mass for translations and rotations, and it can be considered as a solid-rigid. If the root node in the geometric skeleton is not a connection node, the nearest connection node is assigned as the root, and the geometric skeleton tree is balanced to the new root node.The assigned connection node is the first approximation to the model's hip, the appropriate assignment will be done in a posterior step.

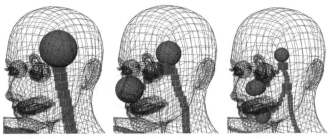

(a) Voxel size at 1% **(b)** Voxel size at **(c)** Voxel size at
of height.   0.65% of height.   0.4% of height.

Fig. 1. Extracted skeleton at different voxel sizes

3. **Skeleton smoothing:** A smoothing step is mandatory because in a vox-
   elizated space, changes of position between nodes of the skeleton in the
   same neighborhood are mainly produced in the edges of the voxel. This lead
   to undesirable artifacts if this data is used to calculate direction changes
   between two voxels. By changing the position of the voxels from edge to
   face neighborhood a smooth transition is granted. We use a window based
   method as our smoothing process.

3   Segments

Segments are the core elements in the adjustment of a logic skeleton (rig) to a
geometric skeleton. We define a segment as:

Segment: *A set of nodes traversing the skeleton from a connection node to an
end node.(fig.2. b.).*
   Using our definition of segment, a skeleton(geometric or logic) can be defined as:

Skeleton: *A set of segments with the same connection node as starting point
(fig.2. a).*

In full body animation only five end nodes are needed (head,hands and feet) [4],
furthermore the great majority of full body motion capture data is produced with
five end nodes [13]. Therefore we have restricted our method to logic skeletons
with five end nodes.

4   Node Selection and Root Assignment

The main problem of adjusting a logic skeleton to a geometric skeleton is finding
the correspondence between their body segments (head,hands and feet). Logic
skeleton's limbs are specified by a tag, this tag can be obtained from a file, a user

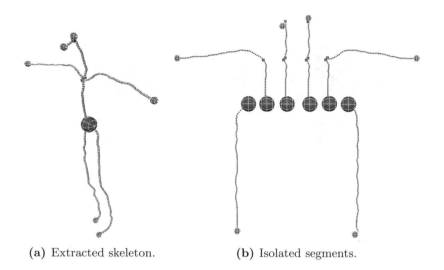

(a) Extracted skeleton.   (b) Isolated segments.

Fig. 2. Extracted skeletons and its segments, the third segment (root to nose) will be deleted

interface or if the model was in a specific pose it could be tagged automatically by its segments positions in the space.

4.1   End Node Selection

Geometric skeleton's limbs are not specified. The used 3D models are in an arbitrary pose, therefore there is no simple method capable of automatically tagging the limbs of a 3D model. Moreover, there are models with human like forms but with an extra limb (for instance the tail of an armadillo model). Limbs detection is a very challenging task and its out of the scope of this paper, to solve this problem we have implemented an interface that allows the user to select which are the end nodes that correspond to their appropriate limbs.

In our interface the end nodes are marked with a sphere and the flow nodes are represented by cubes. The user must decide which end node corresponds to its logic limb selecting the appropriate sphere (fig. 1 b and c).

4.2   Root Assignment

Once the limbs are assigned, we delete all the nodes that are not part of an assigned segment.(fig.2 b.).

When the segments are assigned, the number of connection nodes will decrease, and only connection nodes that represents non-articulated parts of the model(hips and chest) will be preserved.

It is customary to set the hip as the root node. In our case the hip will be one of the connection nodes but depending on the number of connection nodes the next situations can arise:

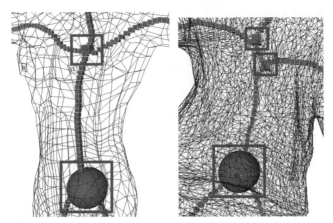

(a) Skeleton with two connec-(b) Skeleton with three con-
tion nodes.   nection nodes.

Fig. 3. Root assignment cases

- **Two connection nodes:** In this case the difference between the chest and
  the hip comes from the fact that the chest will have three segments without
  connection nodes(the hands and the head, fig. 3 a.) and the hip will have
  two (the feet). To apply this rule we are going to build two sets of segments
  (one per connection node), each set of segments will have its starting node in
  one of the connection nodes. Finally we assign the set with the least number
  of segments as the hip (root) of our skeleton.
- **Three connection nodes:** In this case we calculate the summation of the
  euclidian distances between flow nodes from one connection node to the
  other. The two nearer connection nodes will represent the chest and the other
  one the hip. Therefore to find the hip we create three set of segments, one
  per connection node. For each set we select the segment with the minimum
  number of flow nodes between the segment's starting node and its nearest
  connection node, an from these three segments we choose the one with the
  maximum number of flow nodes. The starting node of the selected segment
  will be assigned as the hip (root) of the skeleton.

5   Skeleton Adjustment

A logic skeleton can also be viewed as set of segments, if we have followed the
previous steps correctly, we must have the same number of segments in the geometric and logic skeletons but in the logic skeleton we will have additional tagged
nodes (elbow,neck,ankle...) that are not tagged in the geometrical one. Adjusting a logic skeleton to a geometric one is reduced to find the correspondence
between logic tagged nodes and geometric untagged nodes.

5.1   Scaling Segments

As is mentioned in the section 3, our skeletons will be represented by a set of five segments. Because a segment in the logic skeleton has its equivalent in the geometric skeleton we can define a normalized distance in our skeletons segments, being *zero* the starting node position and *one* the end node position, with this distance we can find the position of the logic skeleton tagged nodes and map it to our geometric skeleton untagged nodes.

The distance of the logic skeleton segments its defined as the sum of the distance between two neighbor nodes(joints) in a segment from the root node to the end node. We have defined the distance of the geometrical skeleton segment as the sum of the distances between the center of two neighbors nodes(voxels) in a segment from the root node to the end node. Basically adjusting a logic skeleton to a geometric skeleton is finding a partition of the node graph formed by the logic skeleton segment, and map its internal nodes to its correspondent arc curve formed by the geometric skeleton segment. The union of all this mapped nodes(with its hierarchy implicit) will be the adjusted skeleton.

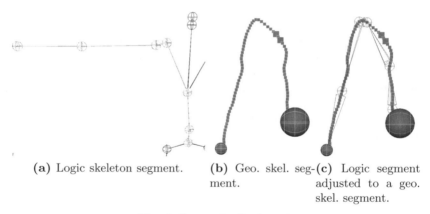

(a) Logic skeleton segment.   (b) Geo. skel. seg-(c) Logic segment
                                  ment.   adjusted to a geo.
                                                     skel. segment.

Fig. 4. Segment adjustment

6   Results

We have implemented our method as an *Autodesk Maya* plug-in with a 2.1 GHz Intel Core 2 Duo with 4 Gb RAM memory and Windows Xp 64 O.S. In the fig.5 we show the results obtained aplying our method to arbitrary models in different positions.The voxelization and skeletization time will depend on the model's pose and its number of triangles, the chosen voxel size is 0.65% of the model's height with processing times in the range of 2 and 3 seconds.The geometric skeleton creation and the logic segment adjustment processing time will be increased if more connection nodes and segments are obtained, our times are in the range of 2 to 3 seconds for models with a density of 20K and 28K triangles. (see table 1) The skin attachment of the skeleton has been done with Maya's mesh binding, the mesh deformation method used by Maya is SSD but we have modified these weights with a mesh segmentation algorithm(fig.5 last column).

Table 1. Processing times

Model	Triangles	Voxelizat.+Thin.(sec.)	Assign+adjust.(sec.)
Woman.	28820	1.9543	1.0874
Man jumping.	20000	3.0031	3.1689
Man marching.	20000	2.5508	2.4632
Man hand standing.	20000	2.0604	1.4756

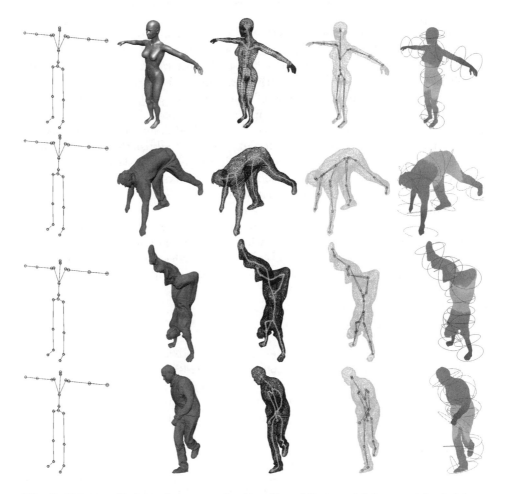

Fig. 5. Columns:Skeleton from an animation file, arbitrary model, geometric skeleton, adjusted logic skeleton, binded model

7   Conclusions and Future Work

Our method can be used as part of any animation pipeline to improve or saving time in the development of an animation rig, because it can be applied to any human-like model in any pose. Our method can be combined with any SSD technique, but due to animations files are usually in an initial pose, a transformation between the animation file's initial pose and our adjusted rig pose must be done. This transformation can be easily implemented with any matrix or quaternion library.

We have proposed an easy and practical way to adjust logic skeletons to human-like models (or at least to skeletons with five or more end points) in an arbitrary pose.

The main contribution of our method is that instead of creating a new logic skeleton [12] or taking a predefined skeleton [4] we adjust an arbitrary skeleton(and its hierarchy) with its related motion data to an extracted skeleton, which is a new approach to the existing automatic skeleton rig methods. The logic skeleton can be taken from any motion data base [13], produced by a motion simulation software or a motion capture file, the only restriction is that the logic skeleton must have five end nodes. Our method is human like models oriented, but is not restricted to them. It can be used to adjust the rig of a human to a any model with at least five end nodes in its geometric skeleton.

The main limitation of our method is that it can not deal with any pose automatically, to produce the adjusted skeleton the user must select the limbs (end nodes).

As future work we want to use a skinning procedure different than SSD, we believe that our method can be used with a cage based deformation technique such as [6]. The cage base deformation needs an effective mesh segmentation based in the links of a rig, we are currently working in an algorithm to achieve this goal.

Acknowledgments

Authors are supported by grants from the "Consejo Nacional del Ciencia y Tecnologia " (CONACYT) MEX, TIN2007-67982-C02-01 ESP, "El comissionat per a universitats i recerca del departament d'innovació d'universitats i empreses de la Generalitat de Catalunya" and the European Social Fund, and we thank to our fellows of the LABSID for their valuable discussions.

References

1. Brunner, D., Brunnett, G.: An extended concept of voxel neighborhoods for correct thinning in mesh segmentation. In: SCCG '05: Proceedings of the 21st spring conference on Computer graphics, pp. 119–125. ACM Press, New York (2005)
2. Palágyi, K., Sorantin, E., Balogh, E., Kuba, A., Halmai, C., Erdohelyi, B., Hausegger, K.: A Sequential 3D Thinning Algorithm and Its Medical Applications. In: Insana, M.F., Leahy, R.M. (eds.) IPMI 2001. LNCS, vol. 2082, pp. 409–415. Springer, Heidelberg (2001)

3. Liu, P.-C., Wu, F.-C., Ma, W.-C., Liang, R.-H., Ouhyoung, M.: Automatic Animation Skeleton Construction Using Repulsive Force Field. In: PG '03: Proceedings of the 11th Pacific Conference on Computer Graphics and Applications, p. 409. IEEE Computer Society, Los Alamitos (2003)
4. Baran, I., Popović, J.: Automatic rigging and animation of 3D characters. In: SIGGRAPH '07: ACM SIGGRAPH 2007 papers. ACM, San Diego (2007)
5. Ramirez, J.E., Lligadas, X., Susin, A.: Automatic Adjustment of Rigs to Extracted Skeletons. In: Perales, F.J., Fisher, R.B. (eds.) AMDO 2008. LNCS, vol. 5098, pp. 409–418. Springer, Heidelberg (2008)
6. Tao, J., Qian-Yi, Z., van de Michiel, P., Daniel, C.-O., Ulrich, N.: Reusable skinning templates using cage-based deformations. In: SIGGRAPH Asia '08: ACM SIGGRAPH Asia 2008 papers, Singapore, ACM, NY (2008)
7. Lohou, C., Bertrand, G.: A 3D 12-subiteration thinning algorithm based on P-simple points. Discrete Appl. Math. 139(1-3), 171–195 (2004)
8. Palágyi, K., Kuba, A.: A 3D 6-subiteration thinning algorithm for extracting medial lines. Pattern Recogn. Lett. 19(7), 613–627 (1998)
9. Bitter, I., Kaufman, A.E., Sato, M.: Penalized-Distance Volumetric Skeleton Algorithm. IEEE Transactions on Visualization and Computer Graphics 7(3), 195–206 (2001)
10. Wade, L., Parent, R.E.: Automated generation of control skeletons for use in animation. The Visual Computer 18(2), 97–110 (2002)
11. Staunton, R.C.: An analysis of hexagonal thinning algorithms and skeletal shape representation. Pattern Recognition 29(7), 1131–1146 (1996)
12. Pan, J.J., Yang, X., Xie, X., Willis, P., Zhang, J.J.: Automatic rigging for animation characters with 3D silhouette. Comput. Animat. Virtual Worlds 20(2-3), 121–131 (2009)
13. ACCAD - Motion Capture Lab, http://accad.osu.edu/research/mocap/mocap_data.htm

Author Index

Printing: Mercedes-Druck, Berlin
Binding: Stein + Lehmann, Berlin